LESSONS FROM ISLAM

SAYYID MUHAMMAD SUHUFI

Published by
Cultural and Guidance Section
AL-KHOEI FOUNDATION

LESSONS FROM ISLAM

Original Title: *Ta`alim-i Asmani Islam*
Author: Sayyid Muhammad Suhufi
Translator: Muhammad Fazal Haq

First Published in Pakistan in 1985 by
ISLAMIC SEMINARY PUBLICATIONS
A Publishing Division of
ISLAMIC SEMINARY PAKISTAN
P. O. Box 5425 KARACHI-74000

This Impression 1999
Printed at Prima Printers, Karachi.
Copyright © Islamic Seminary

ISBN 0-941724-44-1

Mailing Address
The General Secretary
Al-Khoei Foundation
Chevening Road,
London NW 6,
ENGLAND.

This book or any part thereof is sold subject to the condition that it shall not be way of any trade or otherwise be lent or resold, hired out or otherwise circulated in any form of binding or cover other than what it is published in, without a similar condition including this condition being imposed on the subsequent purchaser or donee, except with prior written permission of the copyright owner.

ISLAM

"Have you fully realized what Islam is?
It is indeed a religion founded on truth.
It is such a fountain-head of learning
that several streams of wisdom
and knowledge flow from it.
It is such a lamp
that several lamps will be lighted from it.
It is a lofty beacon
illuminating the path of Allah.
It is such a set of principles and beliefs
that will satisfy every seeker of truth and reality.
Know you all!
that Allah has made Islam the most sublime path
for the attainment of His supreme pleasure
and the highest standard of His obedience.
He has favoured it with
noble precepts
exalted principles
undeniable wisdom
undoubtable arguments
and unchallengeable supremacy.
It is upto you to maintain the eminence
and dignity granted to it by the Lord,
to follow it sincerely,
to do justice to its articles of faith and belief,
to obey implicitly its tenets and orders
and to give it the proper place in your lives".

Nahjul Balagha By:
Imam Ali (Peace be on him)

بِسْمِ اللهِ الرَّحْمٰنِ الرَّحِيْمِ

اَلْحَمْدُ لِلّٰهِ الَّذِىْ عَلَّمَ بِالْقَلَمِ
عَلَّمَ الْاِنْسَانَ مَا لَمْ يَعْلَمْ
وَصَلَّى اللهُ عَلٰى مُحَمَّدٍ وَّآلِهٖ وَسَلَّمْ

CONTENTS

FOREWORD 11

WORK AND EFFORT 16
Good Deed 17
Work is Worship 17
Work is Jihād 18
Campaign Against Unemployment 18
Conduct of the Leaders of Islam 20
Efforts on Two Fronts 22
Work, But not Every Work 24
Different Aspects of Good Deed 25
Quotations 26

KNOWLEDGE 29
A Misunderstanding 35
Merits of the Scholars 37
Campaign Against Knowledge 37
Quotations 39

MOTHER 40
Mother's Influence on Her Child 44
Kindness to Mother is an Atonement for One's Sins 48
Mother's Displeasure 49

Recommendations in Favour of Mother 50
Mothers' Day 51
After Mother's Death 52
Quotations 53

BENEFICENCE 54
Kindness to the Orphans 56
Meeting the Needs of Others 60
Quotations 65

LIQUOR 67
Quotations 79

GAMBLING 80
A Basic Campaign Against Gambling 90
Quotations 93

FALSEHOOD 94
Falsehood is Justified by its Motive 105
Explanation 107
Quotations 108

SOCIAL RELATIONSHIP 109
Creating Happiness 116
Meeting the Needs of the People 116
Back-biting 116
Offending People 117
Fault-finding 117
Mockery 118

Quotations 120
SOCIAL ETIQUETTE...........................121
Showing Respect to the People 123
Treating the People with Courtesy 127
Being Gentle and Modest......................130
Keeping One's Promises.......................133
Quotations 136

FRATERNITY AND BROTHERHOOD................137
Fraternity (Muwāsāt) 139

FRIENDSHIP 149
Quotations 159

CLEANLINESS.................................161
Quotations 173

CODE OF INSTRUCTION 174

TRAINING OF CHILDREN 188

GOOD LOAN 203
Usury is Prohibited 205
Giving Gift to the Lender 209
House of the Debtor should not be Occupied ...213

CAMPAIGN AGAINST CORRUPTION 215
Propagating One's Sins 223
National Supervision.........................223
Punishment for the Sinners in the Hereafter ..225
Punishment for the Sinners in this World 225

THE RIGHTS OF SPOUSES 227

THE STATUS OF TEACHER 239
Rights of Teacher 242
The Role of Teacher 247
We all should be Teachers 248

RESTORATION OF TRUST IN ISLAM 250
Breach of Trust 254
Restoration of Trust is a Human Obligation 256
Misappropriation is a Sign of Faithlessness 257
Kinds of Trust 258

MORAL CODE 262
A Few Note-worthy Points 271

SCIENTIFIC REALITIES IN ISLAM 272
Teaching of Medical Science 273
Earth and Air are not Simple Elements 274
Oxygen 276
Rotation of Earth on its Axis 277
The Genesis 279
Parts of Human Body 280
Oxygen and Hydrogen in Water 283
Pollution of the Atmosphere 284
Keeping the Infant on the Left Side of Mother ...286
Light, a Means of Transmission of Disease 292
Sciences of Other Worlds 295

KEEPING ONE'S PROMISE 300

MODERATION..................................313
Moderation in Worship 316
Moderation in Expenditure......................318
Moderation in Food 319
Moderation in Friendship and Enmity............322
Moderation Recommended Once Again 323

RESPONSIBILITIES OF THE RICH 324
The Rich are the Pillars of the Society 325
Warning to the Rich 326
Two Brothers in Two Different Poles 328
Right of Wealth................................329
Spending in the Path of Allah 331
Rendering Help to the Needy 332
The Effects of Alms 333
Guardianship of Orphans........................334
According Respect to the Indigent 335

STEADFASTNESS..............................337
Perseverance of the holy Prophet 343
Steadfastness in Good Behaviour..................345
Steadfastness in Adversity.......................347
Conclusion 353

FOREWORD

Islam gives due attention to the total needs of mankind. Its guidance is for all times and for all places.

From a deep study of the Islamic teachings it becomes abundantly clear that as and when one becomes enlightened with knowledge and insight one submits himself to the greatness of Islam. Hence, an enlightened person endowed with knowledge and wisdom is in a better position to comprehend the teachings of Islam. Islam is a viable religion. It is such a source of sustenance as ensures viability and provides ways and means for man's prosperity and salvation.

Islamic laws and principles are not the product of human mind so that its usefulness should remain confined only to one particular time or place. On the contrary its laws and regulations have been fashioned by that All-Powerful Allah who by His Will has created man and who knows all the problems of his existence. Therefore, it is only Allah who knows better as to which thing is beneficial for his prosperity and happiness and which things will lead him to misfortunes and destruction.

The advent of Islam has established this fact without any shadow of doubt that if Almighty Allah wills He can turn a downtrodden, foolish and miserable community into a civilized and enlightened nation in so short a span of time that it could assume the pioneering role of guiding the humanity to a cultured society as well as to the acme of knowledge and wisdom.

If one looks back to history and shuffles its pages which give an account of the events before the advent of Islam, he will notice the pitiable and miserable condition in which the people were passing their lives. If one makes a careful study of the history of the rise of Islam one will find how those very people of the Dark Age made a leap forward towards progress and prosperity and established a really benevolent society full of knowledge, wisdom and virtue and furthermore in what a magnificent manner the Islamic principles and teachings transformed their entire existence into a well-disciplined nation.

But it is regrettable to say that the enemies of Islam have sown the seed of discord between the Divine code and the Muslims and have set the Muslim ummah to disunity, discord and corruption with the result that they have become deprived of their past glory and power.

The holy Prophet declared during his lifetime that the holy Qur'an and his *Ahlul Bayt* (the chosen descendants of the holy Prophet) will never get separated and for the right guidance, prosperity and salvation of the Muslims both of them are of paramount importance. Hence, any Muslim who is desirous of attaining prosperity and salvation must obtain the Qur'anic teachings from the real successors and vicegerents of the holy Prophet i.e. Imam Ali and his eleven accredited sons, appointed by the Prophet and faithfully follow those teachings.

It has been endeavoured to present in this book the Islamic teachings in the language of the holy Qur'an and of the holy Prophet and his holy Progeny and to discuss them in various aspects of human life in a simple and lucid manner so as to make them comprehensible.

An important point that has to be taken into consideration is that during our discussions on various topics the views of various scholars have also been noted so that it may show that they have after several years of efforts have acknowledged the viability and the utility of the teachings and principles of Islam that were offered to the mankind by its leaders over 1400 years ago. And furthermore it should be brought home to the readers that the Muslims have under their possession a valuable treasure but they are completely oblivious of it. Would that the doors of wisdom had opened before us and awakened us from a long slumber and taken us back to Allah and the Divine teachings so that our past errors and omissions might be recompensed.

Another important point that cannot be lost sight of is that in the modern times the young generation as well as the educated people are showing such an exceptionally keen interest in knowing and understanding the real message of Islam that its example cannot be found in preceding times and era.

Only those books and treatises that are written on religion from the stand-point of logical reasoning and are free from unnecessary interpretations and commentaries are in good demand these days as compared to other books.

The learned like to grasp religious teachings from the view-point of knowledge and wisdom and Islam also approves of such an approach of thinking and in fact its principles and teachings are based on this aspect.

Islam has on all occasions exhorted its followers and all others to apply their intellect and reason. It never advises the people to accept its principles blindly.

In Islam there is no such thing as does not stand to reason. This is one of the reasons why Islam has been successful in making a forward march in the light of scientific advancement and has maintained its glory and honour.

The present-day generation is well aware of the viewpoints of various schools of thought originating from the oriental and occidental sources and it is also in touch with various philosophical concepts and notions. Therefore, man wishes that in line with the higher education that he has received, his faith too should be at a higher pattern from the stand-point of spiritual values. But the religion which cannot fulfil the demands of the time will succumb to the influence of science and reason.

When the British philosopher, Bertrand Russell raises a question as to why he is not a Christian and dissociates himself from his religion, the main reason behind it is that in reality Christianity does not provide any solution for his contentment and salvation. Besides, he is unable to visualize the very existence of Allah which Christianity potrays because neither the very concept of God nor the religion itself come to the standard of knowledge and reason. Even some great Christian scholars and thinkers usually do have such an opinion about Christianity because they do not consider it to be a religion based on intellect and logical reasoning. Their opinion and views about their own religion are being published from time to time and there are also certain categories of people who have supperficial knowledge of their religion because such a knowledge only comes to them from the Church and as such they have become morbidly pessimistic and without trying to scrutinize they harbour animosity and rancour against Islam too and consider them unreliable and unacceptable.

Hence, all those who study such books should bear in mind that since the authors of such publications happen to be Christians they consider and portray Islam with grudge and prejudice and from the view-point of Christianity they are nothing more than a pack of superstitious ideas and absurdities. The opinion of such authors can be right for Christianity but it cannot be applied to Islam.

When a Christian scholar who has deeply studied other religions, becomes acquainted with the role and merits of the teachings of Islam, he without hesitation submits himself to the greatness of the Divine religion of Islam and acknowledges its Divine impact with commendation.

In the present age, our educated younger generation and scholars have an unflinching faith in the abiding principles of Islam because it has often been observed that our enlightened youths make a research in the pursuit of acquiring knowledge about their religious teachings so that with the application of intellect and reason they could attain peace, prosperity and salvation.

Islamic Seminary which keeps a close contact with the various classes of people within and outside the country and particularly with the new generation and which daily receives hundreds of letters enquiring about religious information, is fully alive to the intense interest and attachment of the Muslims towards their religion.

The research-orientated books and other authentic publications which have been written by great scholars, professors and other renowned personalities on religious teachings, knowledge and learning, stand testimony to the fact that these enlightened writers have so much devotion towards this Divine religion and it is heartening to note that this sphere of activity is expanding day by day.

Islamic Seminary hopes that the book in hand will enlighten the minds of our conscientious young men and women, and will serve as an introduction to a wider study of Islam. It will induce them to recognize Islam as a great and creative school of thought, help them in shaping out their lives and preparing them for great sacrifices. It will most certainly inspire the young people to form a much better, healthier and happier society.

Publishers

* * * * * *

WORK AND EFFORT

In Islam much importance has been attached to work and effort and it is reckoned to be one of the main factors for the prosperity of man in this world as well as in the Hereafter.

In more than eighty verses, the Holy Qur'an has treated faith and noble deeds to be the pre-requisites for the prosperity and good fortune of man and his deserving of Paradise.

The scholars have given various definitions of work. However, in common parlance, "work means devoting time and toil to achieve an object".

Hence every act performed by man to achieve an object is commonly called 'work'. An electrician who toils to repair an electric motor he actually works. An engineer who draws lines on a piece of paper to prepare a plan for the construction of a building also works. A painter who paints a natural scenery on a tableau by spending time and taxing his brain also performs a work. A watchman who stands on the path opposite a building and watches and looks after it also remains busy in a work.

The society does not consider such persons to be without any work and treats all these acts to be 'work'. However, it considers a person who walks on the footpath or draws lines on a paper without any aim or object to be without any work and the strolling or drawing lines on a paper for the sake of fun cannot be called 'work'.

Keeping the above examples in view it is realized that the society does not consider 'work' to be limited to physical actions and material efforts. For example when a person in a court of law makes an admission of a fact which is detrimental to his own interests but by which another person becomes entitled of his due right, the society considers that he has done a great work. A teacher who teaches the students or an orator or a preacher who delivers a lecture for the guidance of the people only speaks but the society does not consider him to be without doing any work. On the other hand it reckons his teaching and lecturing to be a valuable work.

Good Deed

The phrase 'good deed' used in the holy Qur'an which carries a general sense of a decent work, is accomplished with a good purpose and to achieve a reasonable objective. For example, a mother's awakening at night to suckle and nourish her child is a decent work but remaining awake to drink wine and to create an uproar is an indecent work.

To make efforts to earn lawful livelihood is a good deed and a decent work but to become a parasite and to beg from others is an indecent work.

In Islam the occupasions which are useful for an individual and the society and are beneficial for the people in both the worlds are treated to be decent deeds.

Work is Worship

Lawful efforts and activities to which one resorts to meet his needs are treated by Islam to be 'worship'.

A well-built person who possessed a stature, strong arms, muscular and healthy body passed by the holy Prophet and his companions. The holy Prophet's companions looked at that man with admiration and said to one another: "What a good thing it would have been if this man had employed his bewildering strength in the path of Allah and to seek His pleasure". The holy Prophet said to them: "If this man works to provide the means of subsistence to his parents or endeavours to meet the needs of his young daughters or works to provide the expenses of his wife by lawful means or works to earn his own livelihood so that he may not have to beg from others he works in the path of Allah".

According to another tradition the holy Prophet says: "If a person takes a cord and goes to the mountains, collects firewood and carries it on his shoulder and earns his livelihood by these means is better than begging". (Sahih Bukhari)

Work is Jihād

In the words of the dignified leaders of Islam, work and effort have been recommended in such a way that it is not possible to recommend them in stronger terms.

Imam Riza, the eighth Imam, considers work to be superior to jihād (holy war) in the path of Allah and says: "The reward and recompense of a person who toils to earn his own livelihood as well as that of the members of his family and seeks his sustenance with the blessings of Allah and by means of his work and effort is greater than the reward of one who performs jihād in the path of Allah". (Wasā'ilush Shi'ah)

Campaign Against Unemployment

Islam has campaigned earnestly against idleness and unemployment and it considers idleness to be the source of affliction and bad luck.

Imam Sadiq, the sixth Imam, enquired about the condition of Umar bin Muslim. He was informed that he (Umar) had resolved upon engaging himself in worship. He had abandoned work and his trade and had remained busy in worship all the time. The holy Imam was not pleased to learn this and he said "Pity on him! Does he not know that the supplications of one who does not work are not accepted by Allah?" Then he further continued his remarks thus: "When some companions of the holy Prophet heard this verse: 'And whosoever fears (obeys) Allah, He will provide him a way out (of his difficulty) And will grant him wealth and sustenance from a source that he never imagined (Surah Talaq, 65 :2 — 3), they abandoned their work and effort, closed the door before themselves and resorted to worship and imagined that it was no longer necessary for them to engage themselves in work or trade. When the holy Prophet became aware of their activities he summoned them and asked: 'Why have you abandoned work and contented yourselves with worship only?' They replied: "The Almighty

Allah has guaranteed our sustenance. We have, therefore, given up work and resorted to worship". The holy Prophet reprimanded them and said: "The supplications of one who adopts this course and abandons work will not be granted. It is necessary for you to work and earn your livelihood by seeking assistance of Allah".

The holy Prophet says: "The purest food which one eats is that which he earns by hard work".

Although Islam considers directing one's attention to Allah and offering of prayers to be obligatory act but it strictly opposes to devote one's entire time in prayers without doing any work.

'Alā bin Ziyād Harthi, one of the well-to-do companions of Imam Ali was unwell. One day Imam Ali went to enquire about his health. His house was magnificent and spacious. Imam Ali said to him: "What a good thing it would have been if you had such a house in the other world which you would have occupied permanently. Even now, if you invite the needy and helpless people in this house as guests and receive and honour your kinsmen and convey to their owners the rights which have been made obligatory by Allah, He will grant you a similar house in the Hereafter".

Notwithstanding the fact that 'Alā bin Ziyād while submitting himself in obedience to the holy Imam said: "O Commander of the Faithful! I have complain to you against the attitude of my brother 'Āsim. The Imam asked: "What has he done?" 'Alā replied· "He has put on worn-out and shabby garments, abandoned work and his affairs of life and resorted to worship". The Imam said: "Bring him before me".

'Āsim bin Ziyad came, Imam Ali said to him: "O enemy of your ownself! Satan has pulled you to perplexity and distress. Why did you not take pity on your wife and children and why have you adopted this wrong course? Do you think that while Allah has made His bounties lawful for you He does not like that you should make use of them?"

'Āsim said: "O Commander of the Faithful! I have followed you in wearing rough dress and eating coarse food".

The holy Imam said: "Pity on you! I am not like you and your obligation is not the same as mine. Almighty Allah has made it incumbent upon the true religious leaders and Imams that they should lead such a life as led by the poor and helpless persons so that poverty of the poor may not make them suffer from distress and sense of deprivation".

When we keep the above event in view it becomes clear to us that none of the Muslims, in whatever conditions he may be and even if he be self-sufficient from his needs, is entitled to give up work and make himself ineffective in the society.

Conduct of the Leaders of Islam

The way and conduct of the distinguished leaders of Islam and their participation in useful activities is a clear proof of the fact that Islam is a progressive and benevolent religion which, besides strengthening the spirit and guaranteeing the happiness in the other world, encourages its followers to strive in different fields of activity so that they may become an ideal, prosperous and active nation.

Christianity teaches and invites people to seclusion and monastic life and ask them to abandon the world and disregard it. It also says: "The world is like a bridge; cross it but do not stay on it". But Islam is a living religion which gives vitality. It keeps in view the body, the soul and the welfare of the people in both the worlds.

The Prophet of Islam remained engaged in tending flocks and in trade for many years. Imam Ali resorted to farming and planting the trees. Other leaders of Islam worked and enjoyed performing useful works.

Muhammad bin Munkadir, who was one of the so-called anchorite suffis, says: "One day I went to one of the small villages situated outside Madina. I saw Imam Muhammad Baqir who was leaning on the shoulders of two servants and perspiring and was going to look after matters relating to cultivation of his farm. I said to myself: 'Allah be praised! One of the elders of Quraysh is going in this extremly hot weather to seek worldly gain. I must contact him and counsel him'. With this idea in my mind I went near the holy Imam and said to him after salutation· 'Are you seeking worldly gain in this hot weather? If death overtakes you at this moment what will be your position?' The holy Imam stopped and replied to me in explicit and decisive words which were indicative of the greatness of the teachings of

Islam: "If I die at this moment I shall be dying exactly at the time when I shall be busy in the worship of Allah. I am busy in doing work so that I may not depend on you and others like you and may provide means of subsistence to my family and if my death occurs in this condition I have nothing to fear because I am worshipping Allah".

Muhammad bin Munkadir felt ashamed. Apologizing for his childish and baseless objection said: "I wanted to advise you but on the other hand you have given me a piece of advice and delivered me from a great misunderstanding".

Imam Ali during his well-dignified life taught the people a lesson of useful activity by practically doing things himself.

Abu Nizār, the custodian of the farm of Imam Ali says: "One day the holy Imam came to inspect the condition of the farm. As it was breakfast time he asked me whether I had anything to eat. I said: 'I do have some food but it is not fit for the Commander of the Faithful. I have cooked some pumkins after plucking them up from this very farm'. The holy Imam said: 'Go and bring them'. Then he got up and went to the bank of a small canal which was flowing nearby and washed his hands. Thereafter he ate something out of those cooked pumpkins, washed his hands and said, 'Cursed be he whom his belly pulls towards the Fire of Hell'. Then he held a pick in his hands, entered the subterranean canal and began digging it. He worked for an hour, got tired and sweat began to flow down from his face. Then he came out of the subterranean canal, wiped out the sweat from his face, held the pick once again and entered the canal. He continued digging till the water began gushing out. He then came out of the canal quickly and said: 'I call Allah to witness that I have resolved to give this subterranean canal in charity so that its income may be spent for the benefit of the needy'.

Then he said to me: 'Bring a pen and paper'. I complied and brought pen and paper for him. He wrote in his own hand:

In the Name of Allah, the Beneficent, the Merciful.
According to this deed the Commander of the Faithful Ali has declared two farms named *Qanat Abi Nizar* and *Baghibghah* to be alms for the benefit of the poor and indigent persons of

Madina and those persons who become penniless while journeying. I have performed this act so that I may earn Divine pleasure and remain safe from torture on the Day of Judgement.

These two farms cannot be sold or given in gift but should be utilized for the welfare of the needy till the Almighty Allah inherits them and He is the best Inheritor".

The holy Prophet says: "One who is sluggish and languid with regard to his worldly affairs will be more sluggish with regard to affairs related to the Hereafter".

In another tradition the holy Prophet says: "The best person amongst the Muslims is not he who forsakes the Hereafter for the world or abandons the world for the Hereafter. On the other hand the best Muslim is he who benefits from the world as well as from the Hereafter". (Hayātul Haiwān)

The holy Qur'an in connection with the recommendations of the wise men of his time to Qārūn says: *Seek through your wealth the gains of the life to come without ignoring your share of this life. Do favours to others just as Allah has done favour to you.* (Surah Al-Qasas, 28:77)

It is the distinction of Islam that in its commandments people have been invited to combine the world and the Hereafter and to achieve happiness of both the worlds by performing decent deeds and making all-sided efforts.

Efforts on Two Fronts

Many persons pose the question that if Islam really supports work and effort and has recommended to its followers to be active and hard-working how is it possible to explain and interpret the traditions which have come down in condemning the world? The answer to this question is that the world has not been condemned absolutely in the Islamic traditions and narrations. On the other hand in a series of traditions that world has been condemned which is tainted with selfish motives and the object whereof is acquisition of base desires, injustice to others and obliteration of sentiments and realities.

In some traditions love for the world has been condemned because if love for the world penetrates in the heart of a person it leads him to errors, sins and condemnation and ultimately fall a prey to misfortune.

Islam exhorts that people should look at the world in a realistic manner, assess its real worth, make efforts wisely to benefit from it, become active in a correct and lawful manner and in the meantime should not ignore the life Hereafter so that they may also achieve eternal happiness and prosperity.

A study of the lives of past and present nations indicates clearly that a group of persons committed crimes, bloodshed, theft and oppression for the sake of their love for the world and became indelible shame on the fair name of human dignity.

Islam says: "Do not adopt inhuman methods to acquire worldly gains and do not cross the limits of piety and excellence".

Hence, there is no doubt about the fact that Islam has attached great importance to the life in this world and enacted detailed rules and regulations for it because the entire discussions about transaction, all of which relate to the social problems and are connected with the worldly life of human beings, deal with the most extensive and most important civil rights of mankind. And notwithstanding the fact that the jurists of the world have made extensive studies about civil rights and carried them to a high level, they have not yet achieved the standard of rights which Islam has enjoined on mankind.

The regulation which have a legal standing and which are being acted upon in the Islamic countries these days are not even one hundredth part of the discourses composed by the Islamic scholars and jurists in this regard.

It may be said that the material which has been deduced from the Islamic jurisprudence is lesser than a primary book of the first year as compared with the syllabi of a university spread over a number of years.

If Islam had not attached importance to the social problems and the various worldly affairs of the people and the regulations thereof and had treated life to be something fictitious and absurd it would have not enacted so many regulations and laws. And incase if it had, like Christianity considered the world to be like a carcass which should be hated and discarded there would have been no necessity of enacting any law.

Besides the discourses on transaction, all of which relate to the worldly affairs of the people, many material and mundane aspects have also been taken into account while discussing acts of worship.

Besides the fact that people should pay attention and have contact with the Almighty Allah there are other aims of worship also most of which are related with the worldly life of man. Even in prayers and fasting, which are considered by many people to be mere worship and only a means of contact with Allah, so many advantages and benefits for the worldly life of people are hidden that if we start discussing them we shall be digressing from our main subject.

On the basis of what has been said above it may be concluded that Islam has paid special attention to the worldly affairs of the people and has enacted minute regulations for the welfare of individuals and society.

In short it should not be forgotten that Islam invites people to struggle on two fronts and, keeping in view the needs of their body and mind should protect themselves from pollutions and should have means for a prosperous life in both the worlds.

Islam says: "Make efforts and be prosperous and happy in both the worlds with rational and reasonable activities".

Work, but not Every Work

In Islam a number of occupations have been declared to be unlawful because corruptions and evils crop up by performing them. For example, making of tools for gambling is an occupation, but it is an occupation which brings great evils in its wake.

Manufacturing and selling wine is an occupation. However, it is an occupation which has been declared unlawful in Islam due to its injurious and detrimental effects.

The holy Qur'an says: *Believers, wine, gambling, idols and arrows used for divination are all acts of Satan; so keep away from them to achieve prosperity. Satan only wishes to create among you enmity and hatred through wine and gambling, and to divert you from the remembrance of Allah and prayers. Will you therefore not desist?* (Surah al-Maidah, 5:90 — 91)

Innumerable differences crop up among friends while gambling and irreconcilable animosity is created on account of gambling. Large amounts of wealth slip out of the hands of their owners and many rich men are reduced to penury as a result of gambling. As a consequence of gambling numerous crimes are committed by men.

Wine and alcoholic beverages are disastrous things. The scholars and researchers of the world have conducted detailed research and have written numerous articles for the information of the public regarding the harmful effects liquor on the human body, the crimes which are committed by drunkard and the dangerous implications with which the society is threatened.

On account of such maleficent effects which gambling and drinking have on human beings, Islam has considered them to be inauspicious and have prohibited their manufacturing and sale and declared their use to be unlawful.

Keeping the above facts in view we conclude that work and effort has been considered in Islam to be praiseworthy and it carries the spiritual reward like acts of worship provided the work in question is reasonable and useful for the people.

Different Aspects of Good Deed

It should be remembered that the phrase 'good deed' referred to earlier carries numerous senses:

(i) It is used in the various acts which the individuals perform for the betterment of their lives and get wages for the hours of work.

(ii) It is used in various steps which individuals should take for the betterment of their social relations and for achieving their spiritual accomplishments.

(iii) Kindness and goodness towards people, social activities, efforts to ensure welfare of fellow-beings etc. are the best and most decent deeds.

The holy Qur'an says: *Allah commands (you) to maintain justice, kindness and proper relations with the relatives. He forbids to commit indecency, sin and oppression. He warns you so that you may take heed.* (Surah al-Nahl, 16:90)

The holy Prophet says: "The person liked most by Allah is the one who is more useful to others".

What work can be better than that a person whose being should be the source of goodness and service for the society and the people benefit from him.

In every society there are numerous aged, sick and feeble persons and in every nation there are children who are orphans and there is no one to look after them.

What work can be better than that a person should increase his hours of work by one hour and allocate the wages of that hour to the provision of the sustenance of a child without a guardian or an ailing or indigent person.

These decent deeds and services become the cause of a person being liked by Allah and his conscience remains satisfied. Almighty Allah recompenses his deeds in both the worlds.

Imam Ja'far Sadiq says: "Do good to those who are worthy of it and those who are not. If they are not worthy of goodness you should be worthy of it".

Imam Baqir says: "If I look after the members of a Muslim family and make provisions for their food and clothing and protect their honour in the society I like it more than performing seventy recommended Hajj". (al-Kāfi, Tarā'iful Hikam)

Hours of leisure and unemployment occur in the life of every person and people choose different ways to spend these hours. Unfortunately most of the people waste these valuable hours in absurd activities although they can take useful steps in various fields and make maximum use of their free time.

In the hospitals there are hundreds of our fellow-beings who are confined to bed with weak and ailing bodies and dejected and depressed souls. They stand in need of consolation and sympathy. Some of them also need financial help.

If as a sign of thankfulness for our good health we enquire about the health of the sick during our free time, lend our ears to their grievances, sympathize with them and render them such help as is within our competence it will be a source of our prosperity in both the worlds.

Quotations
1. Whoever strives, strives for himself. Allah is independent of the inhabitants of the world. (The holy Qur'an)
2. Effort closes the path of poverty.
3. Allah dislikes an idle person.
4. Whoever is a burden on others is accursed.

(The holy Prophet)

5. Avoid impatience and sluggishness because if you are impatient you will not be contented with any right and if you are sluggish you will not be able to pay any right. (Imam Sadiq)

6. Sluggishness in doing work leads to failure in achieving one's objective.

7. A wise man depends on his own efforts and a fool depends on his forlorn hopes.

8. Make efforts and be assured of success. (Imam Ali)

9. If you are not sure that what you have done is useful for the society you cannot say that you have done something honourable. (Tolstoy)

10. The purpose of life lies in three things — determination, work and success. (Pasteur)

11. Happiness is for that person who works for the happiness of others. (Ashtur Gatha)

12. None is fortunate save those who do good deeds. (Ciceron)

13. Ninety nine per cent of 'genius' is the sweat of the forehead and one per cent thereof is the inspiration of the soul.
(Edison)

14. Work is the capital of prosperity. (Socrates)

15. Work is the best friend of one's body and soul. (Galileo)

16. Great men do not depend on anything save their own work and do not seek help from anyone else. (Confucius)

17. The Earth is the property of the perseverant.
(German proverb)

18. Work and effort is the means and the straight path for achieving the goals. (Dr Garlank)

19. Work and effort not only makes life good and easy for us but it also makes man worthy and great. (Schiller)

20. We have been brought into being so that we may be useful for others. (Akambas)

21. Victory is for those who are more perseverant than others.
(Napoleon)

22. The secret of my advancement and progress lies in two words — work and faith. (Edison)

23. The more a man works the more competent he will be to do more work. (William James)

24. One of the good things about work is that it makes the day short and the life long. (Diedro)

25. The more a person occupies himself in work the nearer he comes to the goal of happiness. . (Ciceron)

26. Work and activity of one hour satisfies the heart and fills the pocket with money more than slandering and back-biting for one mouth. (Benjamin Franklin)

27. I am obliged to work, for otherwise my morals will be polluted. (Tolstoy)

28. Fools can be trained by means of excessive work and toil. (Buzar Jumhayr)

29. Just as men acquire personality amongst the masses and in the society the women can also acquire position in the environments of the house by bringing up children and performing duties with regard to them. (Balzac)

30. If you desire that others should act according to what you say. You yourself should act according to what you say. (Anushirwan)

* * * * * *

KNOWLEDGE

One of the matters to which Islam has attached the greatest importance and has made very strong recommendations in connection therewith is that of knowledge and wisdom.

Acquisition of knowledge has been reckoned to be one of the Islamic duties.

In this treatise we do not propse to preach Islam under the title of 'knowledge and wisdom' and to quote from the Qur'an and the Islamic traditions and history and to say that Islam has supported knowledge in such and such a way and encouraged people to acquire it. No. It is not believed that this matter is hidden from any one and so much has been written and said on this topic that it does not appear necessary to repeat it.

Furthermore, writing and speaking about these matters does not serve the purpose because after speaking and writing for centuries the condition of the Muslims is as we see it.

The late Sharfuddin 'Āmili, the great Shi'ah leader of Lebanon toiled for years and wrote and published valuable and useful books for the benefit of the Muslim scholars. However, after all this hard work he cast a glance on the deplorable condition of the Shi'ah of Lebanon and most sorrowfully found them to be at a very low level.

He saw that the most indigent, the most afflicted and the most backward people among the various classes in Lebanon were the Shi'ah. There were no physicians, engineers, professors or dignified personalities among them and even if there were any such persons they were so few that they were not worth consideration. However, the Shi'ah were engaged in running public bath houses, barber's shops and in doing such menial jobs as that of porters and scavengers.

On observing these conditions that great man began to think as to what effect would his books have when the Shi'ah were leading such a backward and pitiable life and the people who would read my books and see the conditions of the Shi'ah would say that if the Shi'ah school had been viable and a redeemer faith, the Shi'ah, who are the followers of this school, would have been in a better and more honourable condition!

As a consequence of this thinking he girded up his loins and decided to improve the conditions of the Shi'ah and to bring about a basic and fundamental change. He established many welfare associations and schools and was able, with the full support of his followers, to elevate the Shi'ah of Lebanon and release them from ignorance and backwardness.

Truly speaking it is very surprising that we Muslims have contented ourselves with words only and have lagged behind in traversing the path of knowledge and wisdom.

In his last will Imam Ali, warned the Muslims of the world lest the non-Muslims should steal a march over them in enforceing the sublime teachings of the Holy Qur'an and they themselves might lag behind. (Nahjul Balaghah)

The French writer, Dr. Gustav Leabon says: "At the time when Islamic culture had reached its zenith in spain our centres of learning consisted of castles in which our landlords and nobles led semi-barbaric lives and prided themselves in the fact that they were not able to read and write. Amongst we, Christians, the most learned were the ignorant monks who spent their entire lives in bringing out books of Greece and Rome from the churches and the nonastries, erased their writings and wrote unintelligible religious words and recitals on the parchment papers".

Will Durant writes: "In the Middle Ages, the Muslims enjoyed unravelled supremacy in the field of science and appreciable advancement took place in Āzarbaijān and Morocco in the field of Mathematics which manifested once again the maturity of Islamic civilization. The science of Botany which had gone into oblivion after Theophrastus was revived by the Muslims. Idrisi wrote a book about plants and described the properties as many as 360 of them. His attention was not confined to medicine only. On the other hand he discussed subjects relating to science and botany as well.

During this period also, as during other periods the great physicians of Asia, Africa and Europe rose from amongst the Muslims. Islam was the leader of the world in the matter of the establishment of well-equipped hospitals. The hospital which was established by Nuruddin in 556 A.H. (1160 A.D.) provided free treatment to the patients for three centuries and also gave them gratis the medicines needed by them. Lunatic asylums also existed in all big Islamic cities for looking after the lunatics". (History of Civilization, Vol. XI, pp. 297 — 301)

At a time when Europe and Christianity were burning in the fire of ignorance, the Muslims possessed a civilization, only a short account whereof has been given by the historians.

Undoubtedly the civilization which the Muslims had secured was acquired by them under the auspices of the teachings of Islam because before Islam they too were immersed, like other nations, in ignorance and perverision and history tells us clearly in what horrible conditions they were leading their lives.

Islam came with a comprehensive system and with vital and redeeming teachigs it gradually led that polluted and perverted society towards prosperity. It transformed those backward people into a learned and progressive nation.

Islam does not specify any condition for the acquisition of knowledge and has made it compulsory for the Muslims during all stages of life, at every place and through any teacher.

The above statement is confirmed by the following four instructions given by the holy Prophet of Islam :

(i) Acquisition of Knowledge is Compulsory for Every Muslim

In this statement no condition or exception, like those which exist in most of the Islamic commandments, can be observed and in this matter there is no difference between man and woman because the word 'Muslim' covers both the sexes. In this tradition the holy Prophet has told mankind that the acquisition of knowledge is an obligatory and general duty and is not confined to a particular class or sex.

(ii) Seek Knowledge From the Cradle to the Grave

In this tradition the condition of time and age has been done away with and it has been said that there is no special time or period of age during which knowledge and wisdom should be acquired. On the other hand it should begin with one's birth and should continue till one's death.

(iii) Wisdom is the Lost Property of a Believer

Wisdom consists of firm, rational and correct words. In this tradition the Muslims have been advised not to bother about the source from which knowledge and wisdom is obtained so much so that they should acquire knowledge even if it is available from the polytheists and the hypocrites.

It must, however, be pointed out here that the word used in this tradition 'wisdom' *(hikmat)*. It means that true and rational words should be accepted from whomsoever they may be available. This is, however, subject to the condition that there should be no doubt about the correctness of those words. Hence, those persons who do not possess the power of judgement and cannot distinguish between true and false remarks, should not lend ears to the words of everyone and be influenced by the propagands of misleading persons.

(iv) Seek Knowledge, Even Though it may be Available in China

In this tradition the condition of place has been dispensed with and it has been stated explicitly that knowledge should be acquired even though it may be available at far-off places and its acquisition may involve hardships and financial expenditure.

The gist of the above-quoted four instructions is that it is necessary for all the Muslims during all stages of their lives to acquire knowledge and wisdom from wherever and whomsoever it may be available and it is a religious duty.

What has been mentioned above is a specimen of the recommendations made by Islam with regard to the acquisition of knowledge and wisdom and as stated in the beginning it is not our aim to mention the directions prescribed by Islam in this regard. Muslims of the early days of Islam acted on these sublime teachings for some centuries and were then the most exalted nation of the world.

As already hinted, great physicians, renowned chemists, geographers, astronomers and scholars well-versed in other fields of science and industry rose from amongst the Muslims. The readers who are desirous of detailed information in this behalf are advised to refer to History of Civilization by Jurji Zaidān, History of Civilization by Will Durant, Civilization of Islam and the Arabs by Gustav Leo Bon and Fehrist Ibn Nadim.

Keeping in view what has been stated above, is it not a matter of great regret that inspite of their possessing such redeeming religious teachings, such brilliant historical past and such learned personalities, the Muslims should go in deep slumber and, not to speak of their possessing various degrees of knowledge, their majority could not be able even to read and write and their hand should always be extended for assistance towards the enemies of Islam?

The basic factor for all this affliction and misfortune is the carelessness of the Muslims during the Middle Ages and the sabotage by the colonialist Christians.

Will Durant says: "The high towers of the Christian churches and the belfries are indebted to the minarets of the masjids. The revival of artistic pottery in Italy and France was the result of the migration of Muslim craftsmen to these two countries which took place in the 12th century and was also the result of the journeys of these Italian potters to Islamic Spain. The ironsmiths, the glass-blowers and the book-binders of Italy and the manufacturers of chain mails and armours of Spain all learnt their arts from the Muslim artisans.

In almost all the regions of Europe, the weavers looked towards the Islamic States to obtain specimens and samples from there so much so that even the gardens were laid on the pattern of the Iranian gardens.

This penetration of Islam and Muslims in European countries took place by means of trade, crusades, translation of thousands of books from Arabic into Latin and journeys by scholars like Gerbert, Michelscot and Adelaid Bath to Islamic Spain and also by Christian young men whose Spaniard fathers sent them to the courts of Muslim princes to get trained and learn horsemanship because some Muslim nobles were considered to be expert riders and well-refined.

Christians and Muslims in Syria, Egypt, Sicily and Spain maintained permanent mutual contact. As and when the Christians made an advancement in the Islamic Spanish territories the impact of the literature, science, philosophy and art of the Muslims was carried in its wake to Christian territories.

As an example it may be said that the domination of the Christians over Talitala in 478 A.H. (1080 A.D.) helped to increase the standard of knowledge of the Christians in the field of astronomy and it confirmed their belief about the spherical nature of the earth.

However, these borrowings did not extinguish the fire of grudge. This was due to the fact that after food man loves nothing more than his religious beliefs. Man cannot live only on food and in order to live he needs faith also which inspires hope in his life. For this very reason man flares up by a thing which endangers one's food or faith.

For three complete centuries the Christians had witnessed the invasions of the Muslims who continuously captured Christian territories one after the other and successively took the Christians to the territories in which they had penetrated. The strong hands of the Muslims had captured Christian trade and it was heard everywhere that the Muslims considered the Christians to be infidels.

At last the clash which was expected took place and the two civilizations grappled with each other in the crusades and the best part of the people from the East and the West were put to death.

This interchangeable enmity was an influencing factor in the history of the Middle Ages. The third religion i.e. Judaism had to suffer blows from both the conflicting parties. The West lost the crusades but it became victorious in religious bickerings. All the war-mongering Christians were turned out of the holy Land but the Muslims whose delayed victory had sucked their blood and whose countries had been devastated by the Mongols, were confronted with the dark age and ignorance and indigence prevailed over them. On the other hand the defeated West which had gained experience from continuous efforts forgot the defeats, quenched the thirst for knowledge and love for advancement from the enemies, constructed lofty churches and began traversing the path of knoweldge.

In fact an ordinary reader wonders at this long discourse

about Islamic civilization whereas a research scholar regrets its inopportune brevity. Only during the golden periods of history a society had been able to produce in quite a short span of time, great men in the fields of politics, education, literature, geography, history, mathematics, astronomy, chemistry, philosophy and medicine who appeared during the four Islamic centuries extending from Harunal Rashid to Ibn Rushd". (Will Durant, History of Civilization, Vol. XI, pp. 320 — 322).

This is the past history of the Muslims and this is their civilization. This is the decline and the fall of the Muslims and these too are its causes and factors.

Here it should be understood that only writing and saying: *Allah will raise, the believers and those who have knowledge, in position.* (Surah al-Mujādilah, 58:11) and reading: *Can those who know, and those who do not know be equal?* (Surah al-Zumar, 39:9) and traditions on the subject do not solve the problem and these sacred slogans should be brought into effect and a practical movement should appear amongst the Muslim masses for the acquisition of knowledge and perfection. It should be just as the civilized nations have achieved honour and success by means of the indefatigable efforts of their scholars.

Edison always continued his scientific activities and experiments with surprising perseverance and at times worked for twenty hours a day. He usually said: "I have much work to do and the life is short. I must, therefore, hurry up". While making experiments he had to suffer from injuries. Once the acid of the battery spilted and burnt his new dress and scalded his skin. A number of times he suffered by receiving electric shocks. He used to work very hard during the day and his rest at night consisted of only a brief nap on one of the benches in the factory.

The entire life of Edison covering a span of half a century passed in this manner. He did not give up work and investigations till the last day of his life.

A Misunderstanding

Some persons think that by 'knowledge' Islam means only the knowledge of theology — the Resurrection, the individual and social duties, the articles of worship and other things like them, although on most occasions the word 'knowledge' has been used in general sense and without any condition attached to it. Furthermore, keeping in view the object which Islam has with regard to the Muslim ummah we realized that 'knowledge' is not confined to only one branch of learning.

Islam desires that the Muslim ummah should be honourable, free and independent.

Islam desires that Muslims should have economic and social freedom.

Islam desires that the Muslims should not stretch out their hands before others.

Islam desires that in all material and spiritual fields the Muslims should be the most superior among the nations. For achieving these objects the Muslims society should possess outstanding scholars well-versed in various branches of science and arts and distinguished specialiist and experts should perform their duties in various fields.

If we do not have experts in the fields of economics, agriculture, medicine, industry and other modern arts and science we shall certainly have to depend on others and this is something which is absolutely opposed to the object of Islam.

Hence, our religious duty demands that everyone of us, whatever his status and situation may be, should perform his part for the promotion of knowledge and wisdom. He should teach others what he knows himself. He should impart his knowledge to others by writing articles and books and arranging meetings and conferences. He should translate into his own language the useful books written in other languages. He should encourage the young men to acquire knowledge and excellence and persuade them to continue their studies and attain various degrees of advancement. He should prevent young men from wasting their time and with a view to achieve this end he should set up libraries and centres of learning. He should purchase useful books and provide the same to the students and seekers of knowledge.

This responsibility — promotion and expansion of knowledge — should be associated and linked with another more sacred duty of strengthening the faith and implementation of good manners and discipline in the society.

It is necessary that with the scientific advancements the

spiritual and moral principles should also be strengthened so that the results achieved may be brilliant and useful and knowledge should ensure the prosprerity of the society. Otherwise, knowledge without spirituality will be something very dangerous.

Merits of the Scholars

Two groups of the Muslims were sitting in two different corners of the masjid at Madina. The holy Prophet entered from the gate, cast a glance at each of those groups and asked: "What are they doing?" He was informed that one group was busy in recitals and supplications whereas the other was engaged in scholarly discussions.

The holy Prophet said: "Both the groups are pursuing the path of goodness and prosperity. However, I shall join the group which is discussing scholarly matters, because I have been appointed to the prophetic mission to lead the people to knowledge and perfection". Then he joined that group and sat in their company. (Munyatul Murīd)

In a meeting in which his senior and aged companions were also present Imam Ja'far Sadiq exalted Hishām bin Hakam, who was the youngest of all. (Bihārul Anwār, Vol. IV). As Hishām was a learned man, a forceful orator and a true and sincere servant of Islam, Imam Sadiq exalted his rank.

Honouring and exalting the scholars and seekers of knowledge is one of the best methods of attracting others to the acquisition of knowledge and wisdom and this method has always been practised by the honourable leaders of Islam.

Campaign Against Knowledge

The Christian colonialists, through their supporters and agents, have started the propaganda among the enlightened Muslim young men that the reason for the backwardness of the Islamic countries is their religion. Hence, if they want to get rid of this backwardness they must free themselves from the bond of religion so that they may achieve the development enjoyed by the civilized nations, just as the Christians freed themselves from the chains of Christianity and consequently succeeded in making all this wonderful progress.

They have created this misunderstanding and confusion on

the intentional level so that by misleading the young Muslims they may exploit the Muslim countries to a larger extent and keep the Muslims backward.

It is true that the Christians made progress and proceeded on the path of advancement by freeing themselves from the bonds of the church and discarding the so-called religious regulations of the priests. However, placing the superstitions of the church at par with the eternal laws of Islam will be a great sophistry and an inhuman injustice.

By means of the childish laws forged by the Christian priests the church blocked the passage of scientific advancement and industrial progress and persecuted and tortured the scholars and researchers.

The church had imposed some so-called scientific views and ideas on the European society with the name of sacred Divine laws and when science proved the thinking of the Church to be incorrect and absurd there was no alternative left except that the people should get disgusted with the church and its regulations, free themselves from the yoke of the priests and believe in knowledge and wisdom. In the meantime the thing which helped the overthrow of the church and its religion most was the persistence of the leaders of the church for the preservation of their prestige and their lost position.

This persistence reached such limits that in order to enforce its notions the church resorted to despotism and it cast its shadow on all walks of life of the people like a dreadful ghost and deprived them of peace and tranquillity.

As ordered by the leaders of the church the dangerous and horrible organization called 'Inquisition' came into existence which severely persecuted the opponents of the ideas of the Church and tortured the learned men and scholars. It burnt the scholars in furnaces for the only offence that they believed in the rotation and spherical shape of the earth which was constant and had thus revealed a reality.

This persecution assumed such proportions that every enlightened person considered it his duty to co-operate with others to destroy this oppressive devil and to suppress it with full force so that the church might be ousted from all spheres of activity for ever and its authority should be abolished.

This was the attitude of the church towards the enlightened persons, the researchers, the scholars and all other progressive and broad-minded people.

It is evident that the secret of the success and advancement of Europe lay in getting rid of such an organization which had obstructed progress and scientific advancement under the name of religion and Divine laws. However, such dreadful events have not been seen amongst the Muslims, even by way of specimen, and as we have noticed in earlier pages that Islam is not only compatible with knowledge and wisdom but it is also the greatest supporter of the seekers of knowledge.

Hence, the view that religion obstructs the advancement of the nation is correct as regards Christianity but so far as Islam is concerned it is not true. It is our enemy who is trying to make us believe in it and thus make us careless and irresponsible in order to achieve their colonial targets.

In the circumstances, it is the great responsibility of the Muslims in general to strive against this propaganda and to promote the luminous realities of Islam in the society which nourish the spirit of humanity, excellence and advancement and thus fulfil their obligations towards Islam and the Muslims.

Quotations
1. Allah will make the learned believers honoured and dignified by raising their ranks. (The holy Qur'an)
2. Strive to acquire knowledge from the cradle up to the grave.
3. Learned persons are the heirs of the Prophets.
4. Knowledge is a strong support for faith.
5. The most valuable among the human beings is he who possesses more knowledge and the most worthless among them is he who is more ignorant. (The holy Prophet)
6. Learned are alive even though they may be resting in the graves and the ignorant are dead even though they may be alive.
7. One who teaches me even a word makes me his slave.
(Imam Ali)
8. Teach others what you know so that the foundation of your knowledge may become strong and also seek knowledge from others so that the level of your information may rise.
(Imam Hasan)

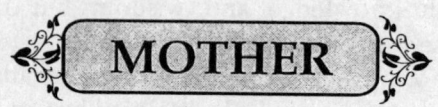

MOTHER

What a beautiful and sacred word 'mother' is. It is a word from which one smells the fragrance of love and sentiment and feels warmth and sincerity.

The western world has realized the worth and importance of 'mother' only recently whereas the Muslims have acknowledged her high status for centuries under the auspices of the Divine teachings of Islam.

Islam has attached great importance to mother and has drawn the attention of the people to her value and worth by various remarks.

Islam considers mother's pleasure to be a pre-requisite for the attainment of the highest degree of perfection viz. Paradise and says: "The Paradise is under the feet of mothers".

The above tradition which has been quoted from the holy Prophet is the medal of honour which has been given to the mothers and if all the discourses, expressions and words of the people about the rank of 'mother' are placed in one pan of a scale and the sentence 'The Paradise is under the feet of mothers' is placed in the other pan, the pan containing the statement of the holy Prophet will certainly be heavier.

In order to glorify 'mother', Islam has not contented itself with only recommendations and a series of remarks. On the other hand at the stage of enacting laws, it has declared obedience to the positive and negative commands of mother, in some cases, to be obligatory. For instance, when Divine act is confronted with prohibition by a mother the children are under obligation to obey the order of their mother and not to enforce the 'recommended' Divine order. If a son or a daughter wishes to undertake a 'recommended' fast to earn spiritual reward and excellence or to go on a 'recommended' journey and their mother prohibits them from doing so it is obligatory upon them to obey their mother. If they defy her order they will not only be deprived of Divine reward but will also be punished for it.

Another occasion when the order of a mother is given precedence to a Divine command is that when an obligatory Divine command is faced with prohibition by a mother, provided that act in question is not an irreplaceable duty (like daily prayers and fast of the month of Ramazan), obdience to one's mother enjoys precedence over Divine command; for instance an occasion for jihād (holy war) arises for those who are fit to fight against the enemies and who should participate in the war. However, if a man fulfills all the conditions for participating in jihād, but his mother does not permit him to participate (and his non-participation in the jihād is not detrimental for the Muslims) that man can, in compliance with the orders of his mother, refrain from participating in jihād and can stay with his mother.

A man who had the honour of visiting the holy Prophet said to him: "O Prophet of Allah! I am healthy, fit and desirous of participating in jihād for the advancement of Islam. However, my mother does not like that I should be separated from her and participate in the battle".

The holy Prophet said: "Go and stay with your mother. I swear by Him who has appointed me to the prophetic mission that the Divine reward for your spending one night in the service of your mother and her being happy to see you is greater than your performing jihād for one year". (al-Kāfi, Vol. II)

Islam considers respect to one's parents and observance of their rights to be the most important duty of the people after observing the rights of Allah. The holy Qur'an says thus in this behalf: *Be grateful to Me and to your parents.* (Surah Luqman, 31:14) Here, after mentioning His own right, Allah immediately gives a command about the right of one's parents.

A man came before the holy Prophet and said: "O Prophet

of Allah! Guide me as to whom I should do good so that I should get full reward for my goodness".

The holy Prophet replied: "Do good to your mother". He asked: "And after her?" The holy Prophet replied. "Do good to your mother". The man asked: "To whom should I do good after her?" The holy Prophet replied: "Do good to your mother". The man asked: "To which other person should I do good?" The holy Prophet replied: "To your father". (Bihārul Anwār, Vol. LXXIV)

A man asked Imam Ja'far Sadiq: "What is the meant by goodness to one's parents about which Allah has given orders in the holy Qur'an?"

The Imam replied: 'The goodness' is that while associating with them you should behave in a decent manner and should not permit that while they are in need they should ask you to satisfy their needs (on the other hand you should satisfy their needs before they approach you in that behalf). Almighty Allah says: *You will not attain piety until you spend of that which you love.* (Surah Ale Imran, 3:92) If your parents displease you, you should not displease them. On the other hand you should pray for them and should not look at them save with love and kindness and should not raise your voice above theirs and should not walk ahead of them". (al-Kāfi, Vol. II)

Imam Sajjad says: "The right of your mother is that you should know that she sustained and carried you in her womb for a number of months and nourished you with the fruit of her heart and the syrup of her soul. She commissioned her entire being for your protection and sustenance. She did not mind that she should be hungry while you should be satiated or that she should be thirsty while you should quench your thirst, or that she should not be dressed while you should be dressed or that she should be in the sun whereas you should be under the shade. She forsook her sweet sleep for your sake and bore the trouble of sleeplessness. She protected you from the heat of summer and the cold of winter. She bore all these troubles so that she might possess you and you might belong to her.

You should know that you are not competent enough to thank your mother, except that Allah may help you and grant you strength to pay her right". (Makārimul Akhlāq)

The rights which have been fixed for a mother in Islam and specimens whereof have been quoted above are on account of the hardships which she bears in bringing up her child, nourishes a human being and delivers him to the society.

Evidently only that mother is entitled to these rights who performs the duties of a mother in their true sense and brings up a useful and able person by her all-out efforts.

A mother who shirks tending her child on account of self-indulgence or to attend dance parties and centres of corruption or evening parties and hands him over to a nursery or a kindergarten commits an unpardonable crime with regard to her child and is not entitled to enjoy the status and rights of a mother.

The life of children in a kindergarten is apparently very good and agreeable. Their clothes are clean and tidy, their heads are combed and their hair are well-set. A kindergarten is fully equipped with hygienic conditions and its rooms are constructed according to technical specifications. The bedsteads are covered with bedsheets and the food for the children is prepared properly. The children play according to the time table and sleep at the proper time. In short an important part of the physical and psychological desires of the children is satisfied.

However, a child possesses some other feelings and sentiments also which cannot be satisfied in the collective atmosphere of the kindergarten. The particular caressing which creates joy and mirth in a child can become available only in the lap of the mother and not in the kindergarten.

A child who lives with a hundred children and does not lead an independent life cannot become aware of his true personality and individual freedom which are important human characteristics.

In family environments all the activities of a child like laughing and playing are the object of great love peculiar to parents and the child learns lessons from such attention and enjoys it. However, the activities of a child amidst a hundred other children in the kindergarten are like an invisible and broken up wave amidst hundreds of other different waves.

The education and training of a child needs permanent care which cannot be provided by anyone except by the parents because from the very beginning of the life of the child it is only they, and especially the mother, who recognizes his physical and mental characteristics and aptitudes, the development whereof should be the object of his training and education.

The great aberration from which the modern society suffers is that it has substituted, from the very early age of the child, the nursery and the kindergarten for the family and the lap of the mother. Mothers who hand over their children to the kindergarten so that they may engage themselves in official assignments or to indulge in passions and desires or literary and artistic pursuits or only to waste their time in playing bridge or seeing films make their homes and family atmosphere dull. It is the family surrounding where children can acquire good many things. The development of the children who live in their families is much more than that of the children who live in boarding houses.

A child very soon lays the foundation of his mental, physical and sentimental characteristics on the model provided by his environments and for this reason learns lesser than his coevals. And when he lags behind in the school as an obscure individual he does not make good progress.

Such mothers not only mar the future of their children but they also deal a severe blow to the society and furthermore they themselves do not derive nay advantage from their children.

If a child does not receive love and kindness from his mother and has not felt her emotional attachment, it cannot also be expected from him when he grows up.

Mother's Influence on Her Child

The great men of the world are mostly indebted for their achievements to their mothers who performed their onerous duty and played a pivotal role in moulding their character.

The late Hāj Shaykh Murtaza Ansari, the great scholar of Islam, wept bitterly on the death of his mother. He sat by the side of her dead body and shed tears. One of his scholarly pupils said to him by way of condolence and cosolation: "It is not proper that inspite of your enjoying such a high position as a scholar you should shed tears and feel so much agony on the death of an old woman".

That great man raised his head and said: "It appears that

you are not yet aware of the high status enjoyed by a mother. The proper training given by this mother of mine to me and the numerous hardships borne by her for my sake elevated me to this position and the initial training given by her to me paved the way for my making all this progress and acquiring this high status in the world of knowledge".

This was one example of the influence of a mother on her child and there are many scholars the greatest factor of whose advancement has been the effort and training of their mothers.

During his boyhood Edison not only did not show any talent, but appeared to be very dull. As his head was very big his associates thought that he was mentally abnormal. This view of theirs was also supported by the strange questions when he asked his teacher and he was given the title of 'idiot' (He did not attend school for more than three months). For this very reason he returned hom one day from the school weeping and informed his mother about the matter. His mother caught his hand and went to his school. She said to the teacher: "You do not understand what you say. My son possesses more intelligence than you do and herein lies the trouble. I am taking him home and shall teach him myself and shall then show you what talent is hidden in him".

This was the strange prediction of Edison's mother. Thereafter, as she had told his teacher, she began teaching him herself. A friend of Edison family writes in this regard: "When at times I passed by the house of Edison I saw Mrs. Edison sitting in front of the vestibule and teaching her son. That vestibule was the class room and Edison was the only student. The ways and manners of this child resembled those of his mother. He loved his mother very much. When his mother said something he was all attentive. It might be said that his mother was an ocean of knowledge".

As a result of the efforts of his mother Edison studied weighty books of writers like Gilbon, Hume, Plato and Shakespeare before he was nine years of age. Besides these his wise and sagacious mother also taught him geography, history, mathematics and ethics. Edison did not go to school for more than three months and whatever he learnt during his boyhood was that which he was taught by his mother. Edison's mother was his educator in all respects because she did not only teach him but also took care to find out the naural talents of her son and to promote them. Later, when Edison reached the zenith of greatness, he said: "I realized from my very boyhood what a good thing mother is. When my teacher called me 'idiot' she defended me. I determined seriously to prove that she had not formed a wrong idea about me". He has also said: "I shall never forget the good impressions of the education and training provided to me by my mother. If she had not encouraged me I would not have become an inventor. My mother believed that as regards most of the persons who become bad after coming of age they would not have become useless members of the society if more attention had been paid to their training and education during their childhood. The experiences which my mother had gained as a teacher revealed most of the secrets of human nature to her. I was always careless. If my mother had not paid attention to me I would have gone astray. However, her perseverance and goodness were effective forces which prevented me from deviating and being misled".

Smiles says: "An example and a specimen is the most important factor for the moral training of a child. If a person wishes that his children should possess good manners and merits he should certainly provide best examples for them. And the effective specimen which permanently remains before the eyes of a child is his mother.

Intelligent and kind mothers take pains to lay the foundation of the prosperous life of their children and prepare them for their future life whereas stupid and selfish mothers drive their children to misfortune by their wrong actions.

While discussing the deep impression which the parents make on their children Will Durant says: "The best house, the best school and the best of everything else is that in which commands are fewer. It can very well be observed as to how the children can be made to behave properly without admonition or order. If in some cases this liberal attitude does not prove to be effective it is mostly on account of the fact that we parents do not practise what we preach to our children.

We advise moderateness but indulge in extravagance in the matter of eating and drinking. We recommend kindness but ourselves quarrel before the people. We warn a child against eating sweets or seeing films which are based throughout on fighting, but consider these things permissible for ourselves and one day the child becomes aware of our activities.

We teach leniency with coarseness and good manners with rudeness. We expect humility from the child but display ourselves like an invincible god. However, the children keep in mind our character and not our words and their uneasiness and agitation of mind is mostly due to the fact that they imitate our past acts. Show me your children so that I may tell what you yourself are worth. If you want your child to be polite be polite yourself and if you desire piety from him be pious yourself. Nothing else is necessary.

Even if you are severe and say harsh words at the time of intense anger you will keep the harsh and biting words alive in his mind by way of imitation. Good behaviour can be taught only by setting an example and that too by means of continued perseverance. This is a difficult task and makes it necessary to some extent that we should train ourselves de novo. In this way we are trained by the children".

Islam considers the presence of deviated parents to be one of the main reasons for the deviation of the individuals. The holy Prophet has said in clear terms: "Every child comes in the world with a nature which is pure and fit for believing in the Unity of Allah and possessing moral virtues. It is the parents who, by their bad training, make him deviated and corrupt and at times drive him to infidelity and polytheism". (Safinatul Bihār, Vol. II, p. 373)

It is on account of the deep influence of the parents on the minds of their children that the honourable leaders of Islam have made numerous recommendations to the parents and have attached great value to the pains taken by them.

The holy Prophet says· "Respect your children and teach them correct manners so that you may be blessed by Allah". On another occasion he says: "It is better to bring your children with good manners and morals than spending a part of your property in the path of Allah". (Makārimul Akhlāq, p. 255)

In another tradition he has been quoted to have said: When a person dies his deed-sheet is closed and his connection

with the world ends except as regards the following three things:
(i) The good deeds done by him during his life, the benefit whereof accrues to the people permanently.
(ii) Knowledge left behind by him for the benefit of the people.
(iii) A pious son left behind by him who prays for him".

When the parents have performed their duty towards their children in the matter of their proper training they will enjoy perfect parental rights and the blessings of having pious children and it is at this stage when Islam addresses the children and makes recommendations to them regarding their parents.

Imam Ja'far Sadiq says: "Kindness towards parents is the proof of one's having recognized Allah because no worship pleases Allah as much as showing respect to one's parents". (Misbahush Shari'ah, p. 48)

The holy Prophet says: When a person looks at his father or his mother with affection and kindness this act of his is treated to be 'worship'. (Kashful Ghumma, p. 243)

Imam Riza says: "If you wish that Allah may grant you long life make your parents happy".

The holy Prophet says: "Allah's pleasure is the pleasure of one's parents and His anger is their anger".

Imam Baqir says. "There are four such things that if they are possessed by anyone the Almighty Allah grants him a house in Paradise: (i) Protecting the orphans and providing them asylum. (ii) To take pity on the helpless and the distressed. (iii) To be kind and well-behaved to one's parents. (iv) To be moderate and lenient with one's subordinates and servants. (Khisāl Sadūq)

Kindness to Mother is an Atonement for One's Sins

Islam considers goodness to mother as a means of atonement for one's sins and a source of Divine pleasure and pardon.

A man came before the holy Prophet and said: "O Prophet of Allah! I have committed innumerable sins during my life. Is the door of repentance open for me and will Almighty Allah accept my penitence?"

The holy Prophet asked: "Is anyone of your parents alive?" He replied: "Yes. My father is alive". The holy Prophet said: "Go and do good to him" (so that your sins may be pardoned).

When that man took leave and left, the holy Prophet said:

"I wish that his mother were alive!" (Bihārul Anwār) By this he meant that if his mother had been alive and he had served her, his sins would have been forgiven sooner.

It has been stated in another tradition that a man said to the holy Prophet: "O Prophet of Allah! The Almighty Allah granted me a daughter and I brought her up till she grew up and reached the age of maturity. One day I adorned her and made her wear good dress. Then I took her to the brink of a well and pushed her down into it. The last words which I heard from the mouth of the innocent girl from within the well were: "O my dear father!" Now I regret the sin committed by me. What is the atonement for my sin and what should I do so that it may be forgiven?"

The holy Prophet asked: "Is your mother alive?" He replied in the negative. Then the holy Prophet asked: "Is your maternal aunt alive?" He replied: "Yes". The holy Prophet said to him: "She enjoys the position of your mother. Go and do good to her and your being good to her will be the means of your sin being forgiven". (Safinatul Bihār, Vol. II, p. 687)

Mother's Displeasure

In Islam mother's anger and displeasure has been reckoned to be the cause of her child's annihilation and adversity.

In some traditions it has been stated that a person who misbehaves with his parents will not smell the fragrance of Paradise and will not see the face of prosperity.

One of the companions of the holy Prophet fell ill and became bed-ridden. The holy Prophet went to enquire about his health. His condition was critical and he was at death's door.

The holy Prophet said to him: "Acknowledge the Unity of Allah and say: *There is no god but Allah*". The man began to stammer and could not pronounce the recital. The holy Prophet then asked a woman who was present there: 'Is the mother of this man alive?' She said: "Yes. I am his mother". The holy Prophet asked her: "Are you annoyed with him?" She replied: "Yes. And it is for six years that I have not even spoken a word with him". The holy Prophet advised her to overlook the mistakes of her son and forgive him. She said: "O Prophet of Allah! I forgive him for your sake and am now pleased with him".

Then the holy Prophet turned to the man and said: *"There is no god but Allah"*. His tongue then began to speak and he was able to pronounce it easily". (Amāli Tusi, Vol. I, p. 62)

Imam Ja'far Sadiq says: "A person who desires that the pangs of death may become easy for him should do good to his kinsfolk and behave well with his parents. Death will become easy for a person who acts in this manner and will not suffer from poverty and indigence". (Amāli Sadūq, p. 234)

A man enquired from the holy Prophet about kindness to one's parents. The holy Prophet recommended to him thrice to do good to his mother and made a similar recommendation once in favour of his father. He also gave precedence to the recommendation made for his mother to that made for his father. (al-Kāfi, Vol. II, p. 162)

Recommendation in Favour of Mother

Zakariya bin Ibrahim narrates: "I was a Christian and then embraced Islam and had the honour of performing pilgrimage to the House of Allah. During the journey I had the honour of presenting myself before Imam Ja'far Sadiq. I told him that I was a Christian and had professed Islam".

Imam Sadiq asked me: "What is the reason for your professing Islam?" I replied: "It was this verse of the holy Qur'an which made me embrace Islam: *Before, you did not even know what a Book or Faith was, but We have made the Qur'an as a light by which We guide whichever of Our servants We want"*. (Surah Ash-Shūra, 42:52)

Imam Sadiq says: "Allah has guided you to Islam and illuminated your heart with its light". Then he prayed for me and requested the Almighty for providing me more guidance. I said to him: "My parents and kinsfolk are still Christians and my mother is blind. Is it permissible for me to live with them?

Imam Sadiq asked: "Do they eat pork?" I replied in negative. Imam Sadiq said: "Your association with them is not prohibited". Then he added: "Take care of your mother. Be good and kind to her and as and when she breathes her last assume the responsibility of her funeral rites.

When I returned from pilgrimage and reached Kufa I showed much kindness and affection for my mother as ordered by

Imam Sadiq. I myself served her food, arranged her dress, combed her hair and performed other services for her.

When my mother observed all these changes in my behaviour she said: "Son! When you followed my religion you did not behave with me like this. What is the reason for your loving me so much after professing Islam?"

I replied: "One of the descendants of the holy Prophet of Islam has ordered me that I should behave with you kindly".

She asked: "Is he the Prophet?" I said: "No. None is going to be appointed to the prophetic mission after our holy Prophet. He is the son (descendant) of our Prophet. She said: "These orders are the orders of the Prophets and your religion is better than mine. Guide me so that I may become a Muslim".

I taught her the fundamentals of Islam and she professed Islam. She offered noon and afternoon prayers and evening and early night prayers and become indisposed at midnight.

I was by the side of her bed and was nursing her. She said to me: "Dear son! Repeat the Islamic beliefs for me". I repeated them and she acknowledged all of them. During the same night she passed away.

Morning came. Her funeral was escorted according to Islamic ceremonies. I offered prayers for her dead body and buried her with my own hands".

Many such incidents have been quoted in the traditions which have come down from the chosen descendants of the holy Prophet. In all of them the importance of the position of mother has been stressed upon and the children have been advised to endeavour to pay the rights of their mothers.

Mothers' Day

The point which must be mentioned here is that every year the 10th of May is celebrated as Mothers' day and some ceremonies are performed in connection therewith. The newspapers publish articles suited to the occasion, the poets recite laudatory poems and people present gifts to their mothers.

Of course, this is something good, but only the performance of certain ceremonies and presenting gifts is not sufficient to pay the rights of the mothers. On the other hand it is necessary that efforts should be made that the mothers should become aware of their momentous responsibility and should know that administration of household affairs and bringing up the children is one of the greatest and most valuable occupations and there is no work which should be more important and more dignified than the bringing up of noble children.

Napoleon has said · "The mother rocks the cradle with one hand and the world with the other". Hence, it is possible that by wisdom and tireless efforts a mother may rear a child who may bring about a revolution in the world of mankind.

Mothers should endeavour to hand over trained and faithful children to the society and should be especially very particular about their faith and beliefs because experience has shown that a faithless child is not only useless for the parents, but at times becomes dangerous as well.

We often see and read in the newpapers that a young man struck his mother or father and even besmeared his hands with their blood. Why it is so? Experience tells that the reason for the commission of such crimes is nothing other than faithlessness and lack of spiritual support. And if the parents wish to get a good result from their children in this world and in the Hereafter they should pay full attention to the matters relating to their religion and faith in the same way in which they look after their health and education.

Furthermore, the children should be fully aware of the duty which they owe to their parents and should know that the real welfare of the children is linked with the heartfelt satisfaction of the parents.

If the writers, the orators and the poets utilize the Mothers' Day in this manner and acquaint the mothers and the children with their basic responsibilities it may be said that they have rendered a service and performed a duty.

After Mother's death

The death of one's mother is an irreparable loss, but according to Divine wisdom the system of creation is based on this principle that living being has to breathe his last one day. Man must submit before this Divine Decree, but after the death of one's mother or father certain duties devolve upon the children the performance whereof is the means of their own prosperity. In other words the rights of the parents do not cease to exist after their death and the children must pay their rights even after their death.

Imam Muhammad Baqir, says: "It is possible that a child may be kind and good to his parents during their lifetime, but after their death he may not pay their debts and may not seek Divine forgiveness for them (and may forget them). Consequently, Almighty Allah treats him as one who has misbehaved with his parents". (al-Kāfi, Vol. II, p. 130)

Therefore it becomes necessary that if one's parents are indebted to someone, the children should endeavour to repay the debt and should also seek Divine forgiveness for them. He should give alms for their sake and should feed a needy person or support and protect an orphan or do other good acts for comforting their souls. The benefit and spiritual reward for these acts accrue to the parents of the person concerned as well as to himself and Allah favours him with excessive blessings for this goodness. (al-Kāfi, Vol. II, p. 127)

Quotations

1. We have instructed man about his parents. His mother carries him in her womb in weakness and delibility, wearing him in two years. So he should be grateful to Me and his parents. To me is the return of all things. If they try to force you to associate with Me that of which you have no knowledge then do not obey them. Live with them respectfully in this world.
2. Your Lord has ordained that you must not worship anything other than Him and that you must be kind to your parents. (The holy Qur'an)
3. Paradise lies under the feet of mother.
4. To look at the parents with love and kindness is 'worship'.
5. Allah's pleasure lies in the pleasure of one's parents and His anger lies in their anger. (The holy Prophet)
6. If you wish that Allah may grant you long life, make your parents happy.

(Imam Ja'far Sadiq)

* * * * * *

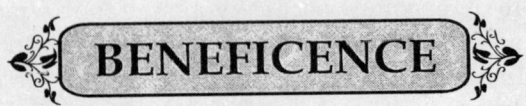

BENEFICENCE

Life of man is pleasant only when it has a human tinge and his relations with the society are founded on good deeds.

Only those persons are entitled to assume the glorious name of 'man' whose objective in life is goodness to human beings and whose happiness lies in kindness to the people.

In Islam special attention has been paid to the question of virtuous deeds and it has been strongly recommended to the Muslims to be good and kind.

The holy Qur'an says: *Allah commands (men) to maintain justice, kindness and proper relations with their relatives. He forbids them to commit indecency, sin and oppression, Allah exhorts you so that you may take heed.* (Surah an-Nahl, 16:90)

In this verse the Almighty Allah has recommended the establishment of justice and kindness togather because the society needs justice as well as kindness. If a society is devoid of justice its foundation will become shaky and if it lacks kindness it will be a dry and spiritless society.

Kindness and beneficence which springs from human sentiments give life to the society and warms up the mutual relations of human beings.

It is friendship and companionship, love and cordiality, fidelity and sympathy, the visiting of the sick, kindness and affability towards the oppressed and depressed, love and affections to orphans and other human traits which create generosity and energy in human life and stops monotony and boredom.

Man is not a machine and the members of a society are not lifeless wheels of a machine so that they may revolve without mutual understanding and without paying heed to one another so as to lead their individual lives.

The Almighty Allah has endowed man with certain sentiments which are reckoned to be great and valuable assets like other natural resources and if they are developed in a favourable atmosphere and in proper conditions they render much help to man in connection with his progress and prosperity.

In the sublime teachings of Islam such orders have been given the enforcement of which carries a sentimental value and which produce fruitful results in human life and all these orders depend upon virtuous deeds.

There are verses in the holy Qur'an and statements in the traditions narrated by the chosen descendants of the holy Prophet, encourage and invite people to the principle of virtuous deeds. Some of them are mentioned below:

The holy Qur'an says: *For a single good deed, one will be reward tenfold. But the recompense for a bad deed will be equal to that of the deed and no injustice will be done to anyone.* (Surah al-An'am, 6:161)

In another verse it has been said: *If you do good it will be for your own benefit but if you do bad you will do it for your own loss.* (Surah Bani Isra'il, 17:7)

Imam Ali says: "Do good deeds and do not consider a good deed to be insignificant because a noble deed is great, howmuchsoever small it may be". (Nahjul Balaghah)

The holy Prophet says: "Do not stretch out your hand except to do a good deed and do not say anything except good".

Imam Ali says: "Whomsoever Allah gives wealth is duty-bound that with that wealth he should help his kinsfolk, invite the hungry to take meals with him, arrange for the freedom of the prisoners and captives, render financial assistance to the poor and the indigent, assist those who are indebted to repay their debts and engage himself in paying the rights of others and doing good deeds so that he may acquire Divine recompense and spiritual reward, because a person who develops such habits and spends his wealth in the said manner attains greatness and dignity in this world and prosperity in the Hereafter". (Nahjul Balaghah, Vol. I)

Imam Baqir says: "Doing good deeds protects the virtuous person from becoming involved in adversity and the persons who do good deeds in this world will be prosperous in the Hereafter". (Amāli Sadūq, p. 153)

Imam Riza says: "Do good to all the people whether they be worthy of it or not. Even if they do not deserve it you should be worthy of doing good". ('Uyūnul Akhbār, Vol. II, p. 35)

The holy Prophet says: "The greatest wise deed after accepting the religion is to treat the mankind with love and kindness and to do good to all individuals". ('Uyūnul Akhbār, Vol. II)

In another tradition the holy Prophet says: "The best deed in this world and in the Hereafter is that you should forgive one who has oppressed you; establish relations with one who has dissociated himself from you; do good to one who has done harm to you; and give gifts to one who has deprived you of your rights". (al-Kāfi)

What has been quoted above from the holy Qur'an and the traditions of the holy Prophet and his chosen descendants, relate to the principle of beneficence and encouraging and guiding the people to do good deeds.

When we cross over from this general discussion we find that Islam has ordered the performance of all acts, whether big or small which fall under the category of noble deeds and has promised reward for performing them in both the worlds.

The point which should not be lost sight of is that by concentrating a little on the Islamic instructions, it is learnt that the good acts recommendd by Islam are not performed only for spiritual reward in the Hereafter. On the other hand, in addition to ensuring such reward, they also have a miraculous effects on the happiness and prosperity of the persons concerned in this world. We give below a few examples to make the point clear:

Kindness to the Orphans

Islam has made numerous recommendations about the orphans wherein it has stressed that their property should be protected, they may be guarded and consoled and kindness may be shown to them.

The holy Qur'an says: *Do not handle the property of the orphans except with good reason until they become mature.* (Surah an-An'am, 6:152)

In another verse it says: *Those who devour the property of the orphans unjustly, in fact, devour only fire, and will surely burn in Hell.* (Surah Nisa, 4:10)

Other verses occurring in Surah al-Baqarah, an-Nisa, Bani Isra'il, Fajar and Ma'ūn revealed about the orphans elaborate the importance of the question of orphans.

Imam Ja'far Sadiq says: "Whoever wishes that Allah may favour him with His blessings and accommodate him in Paradise should refine his morals, behave justly with the people, take pity on orphans, help the weak and the helpless and be humble before Allah who has created him". (Amāli Sadūq, p. 234; Amāli Tūsi, p. 46)

The holy Prophet says: "Whoever assumes guardianship of an orphan and meets his expenses shall be in Paradise with me". (Qurbul Asnād, p. 45)

Imam Ali said thus in his bequest while recommending the most important matters to his sons and followers. "Keep Allah in mind regarding the orphans lest they should remain hungry at one time or another and take care that they do not grow up as spoiled and useless persons". (Nahjul Balaghah)

Now that we have become acquainted with some of the recommendations of Islam regarding the orphans, we would like to study this matter from the psychological point of view so that the philosophy of all this emphatic recommendations may become clear to a great extent.

"Orphanhood, whether due to the death of the child's father or mother carries grave consequences for the individuals as well as for the society.

Usually, while conducting investigation in this matter, the psychologists and educationists have always found that vagrancy, backwardness in the school and the society and acts of misdemeanours, felony and crime are related to orphans.

One of the German psychologists who has made investigations on the studies of the children has noted that out of the students who failed in the examinations 44% were those who had lot their fathers and 33% were those had lost their mothers that is on an average 77% of those students were orphans.

In connection with another similar investigation carried out in America regarding difficulties in the matter of education one of the schools in New York showed that 25% of those, who had educational problem regarding the children, were orphans.

Similarly another research carried out in Germany regarding the children and young men who were guilty of misdemeanours has shown that out of 2704 young men who committed felonies 1171, that is more than 43% were orphans.

Another similar research which has taken place in America about the prisoners has shown that on an average 60% of the prisoners subjected to test belonged to afflicted families because either they had lost their mothers or fathers during childhood.

Another German scholar who has conducted research about the causes of vagrancy and criminal conducts of children and youngsters who have not yet come of age legally has arrived at this conclusion as a result of his studies that more than 38% of the girls who committed theft and more than 40% of those persons who were guilty of establishing illicit sexual relations or committing acts of aggression were orphans. And finally we observe from a social and psychological investigation conducted in America that 70% of the girls who are spending their days in asylum for female delinquents had either lost their one parent or both.

Besides being a personal misfortune orphanhood is a great problem for the society as well. Large number of adversities, vagrancies, failures, backwardness, murders, suicides, obscene acts and psychological abnormalities originate from the state of becoming orphans". (Dr Sahibuz Zamāni, Rūh-i Bashar)

In order that the orphans may not become paralysed and decayed limbs of the society and may not be driven to vagrancy, crime and corruption and may not endanger the society and also in order that decent and able persons may be produced from amongst these very orphans, Islam has given emphatic orders and useful guidance, the enforcement whereof eliminates all risks and prevents psychic problems.

It is possible that steps are being taken in developed countries for the welfare of the orphans. However, these steps may be concerned with the physical needs of the orphans but it may not have been possible for taking care of spiritual side of the orphans' life.

It is possible that orphanages equipped with the facilities

of modern life like trained nurses, neat and clean clothes, proper and sufficient food, physical training, education etc. However, all these facilities cannot constitute a sufficient substitute for the feelings and sentiments of a child who finds himself to be an orphan and fatherless and feels an inferiority complex as compared with other children.

This is a great tragedy. It is from here that the danger originates and what is important is that a basic remedy for this misfortune should be found out.

In order to remove this difficulty Allah, the Creator of man who is aware of all his problems has, besides securing the material needs of the orphans, also taken into account their mental and sentimental feelings and enacted all-pervasive laws accordingly.

Besides the fact that in Islam, the Muslims have been asked to look after the orphans and meet their needs they have also been advised emphatically to show affection to them.

Islam says: "Whoever places his hand over the head of an orphan with love and affection is rewarded by Allah equivalent to the number of the hair on his head and whoever takes his meal with him purifies his heart from evil and becomes noble". (Safinatul Bihār, Vol. II)

The bahaviour of the pioneering leaders of Islam with the orphans is the best lesson which should become the object of attention for the Muslims in general.

During his lifetime Imam Ali was always kind to the orphans. He took them to his house, granted them freedom to play like his own children and eat whatever was available in the house. The people called him 'the father of the orphans'.

This compassion and kindness to the orphans which is a part of the luminous programme of Islam is of the paramount importance for the welfare of the society and it prevents evils and corruption with which the non-Islamic societies are faced.

The point which must be mentioned in the end of this discussion is that what has been stated above should not depress the orphans and become the cause of their distress because they become involved in the hardships of orphanhood when the society does not treat them according to the commandments of Islam. If, however, they are brought up according to the instructions of Islam, it is possible that they may be trained up to be the ablest persons of their time. Furthermore, Islam does not view orphanhood to be a disadvantage because as the holy Qur'an clearly says the holy Prophet of Islam was himself an orphan and besides him some other distinguished personalities of Islam have also been orphans.

Meeting the Needs of Others

Making efforts to meet the needs of the servants of Allah is one of those noble acts which have been emphasised much in the commandments of Islam.

Imam Ja'far Sadiq has been quoted to have said that Allah sent revelation to Prophet Daūd and told him: "When one of my servants performs a good act, I award him Paradise in lieu thereof. Prophet Daūd asked: O Lord! "What is that good act?" The revelation came: "It is making one of My faithful servants happy even if it may be only a palm-date".

Prophet Daūd said: "O Lord! Whoever has recognized You and perceived the greatness of Your kindness and generosity should not feel despair of Your blessings".

Imam Muhammad Baqir says. "The best deed in the eyes of Allah is making his servants happy, whether it be by feeding him or paying off his debt, if he is indebted".

Imam Musa Kazim says: "Allah has some of His servants who endeavour to meet the needs of the people. Such servants will be safe from inconvenience on the Day of Judgement. And if one makes a believer happy Allah will fill his heart with mirth on the Day of Judgement". (al-Kāfi, Vol. II)

Imam Ja'far Sadiq has been quoted to have said that Almighty Allah says: "All persons eat the crumbs of the tablecloth of My kindness and the one liked by Me most from amongst them is he who is more kind to my servants and endeavours more to meet their needs". (al-Kāfi, Vol. II)

A man named Sadqa-i Halwani says: "One of my friends asked me in Masjidul Harām to lend him two dinars. I told him that I would do the needful after having performed the *tawāf* (circumambulation). My *tawāf* had not yet come to an end when Imam Ja'far Sadiq also arrived for *tawāf*. He placed his hand on my shoulder and both of us began performing *tawāf*.

My *tawāf* came to an end, but I continued it for the sake of the company of the Imam.

That man was sitting in a corner. He did not know the holy Imam and gained the impression that I was neglecting his request. Every time, therefore, I passed by him he made a sign to me and reminded me of the matter.

The Imam asked me: "Why is this man making signs to you?" I replied: "May I be your ransom! He is waiting for me so that after completing the *tawāf*, I can arrange some loan for him. As, however, you have placed your hand on my shoulder I did not wish to leave you".

The Imam removed his hand from my shoulder immediately and said: "Leave me alone. Go and meet his need". I went and acted as I had promised that man.

Next day I visited the Imam. He was conversing with his companions. On seeing me he stopped conversing with them and said: "If I endeavour to meet the need of a brother-in-faith, it is more dear to me than freeing 1000 slaves and equipping 1000 persons for participating in jihād in the path of Allah". (Safinatul Bihār, Vol. I)

Imam Ja'far Sadiq says: "When someone requests me to meet his need I make haste to meet his request lest the thing which he has asked me to provide should reach him so late that it may cease to be of use to him". ('Uyūnul Akhbār)

Imam Muhammad Baqir says: "When a person smiles lovingly upon his brother-in-faith (and the smile is indicative of his heartfelt attachment) this action of his is reckoned to be virtuous deed". (al-Kāfi, Vol. II)

Imam Ja'far Sadiq says: "If a brother-in-faith of a person requests him for assistance and he, inspite of being in a position to assist him, does not accede to his request, Allah will raise him on the Day of Judgement with tied hands. (Bihārul Anwār)

Imam Sajjad says: "Endeavour to acquire high position in Paradise and remember, that person will be given higher rank and more magnificent places who is more useful for his brethren-in-faith and more helpful to the needy. And at times the uttering of only one sentence becomes the source of a man's proximity to Allah and his deliverance. Never consider kindness to your brethren-in-faith to be insignificant because these good acts will be useful for you on a day when nothing will be of any use". (Bihārul Anwār, Tafsir-i Imam)

In these commands which have been quoted as a specimen out of thousands of religious instructions an effort has been made that various decent deeds should become current among the Muslims and the Muslim society should become a human society in all respects.

The late Professor Shaltut, who was the head of the al-Azhar University in Cairo has written a chapter about virtuous deeds in Islam in his book entitled *Min Tawjihātil Islam,* a part of which is reproduce here: "The holy Prophet of Islam was very sympathetic and kind to the believers. He maintained contact with his kinsfolk, took the burden of the difficulties of others on his own shoulders and helped the weak. His limitless benevolence was not confined to human beings only but he also behaved sympathetically with the animals. So much so that he kept a pot filled with water before a cat for a long time so that it might quench its thirst".

The holy Prophet has been reported to have said: "Allah subjected a woman to the torture of Hell as a punishment because she tortured a cat and kept it confined for so long a time without providing it water and food that it died".

One day the holy Prophet narrated the following story to his companion: A man became thirsty in a scorching desert and quenched his thirst with the water of a well. When he came out of the well he saw a dog which was rubbing its snout on the earth on account of excessive thirst. The man thought within himself that the dog too was uneasy like him due to severe thirst. He, therefore, descended into the well once again, filled his shoes with water and placed them before the dog. The Almighty Allah forgave his sins for this very good act.

The companions of the holy Prophet said: "Are we rewarded by Allah for being kind to the animals also?"

The holy Prophet replied: "Yes, you will be rewarded for every suffering animal that you serve".

One day a man came before the holy Prophet and said that he was extremely hungry. The holy Prophet sent someone to his own house at once to bring food for the man. His wife, however, regretted that no food was available in the house. Upon this the holy Prophet turned to his companions and said: "Is anyone of you prepared to receive this man as a guest?"

One of the companions undertook to entertain that man. On reaching his house along with the guest however, he found that nothing was available there except food for the children. When the dinner-sheet was spread, he extinguished the lamp on some pretext. The guest was eating the food in darkness and was uder the impression that the host too was partaking in the meals whereas in fact the later was only extending his hand to the dinner-sheet and then pulling it back empty".

With how many persons are you acquainted in the modern society who may be possessing such sublime human qualities?

Some persons relax on soft beds with tranquil hearts and observe Divine blessings on all sides around themselves. The faces of their children and spouses are fresh and rose-coloured due to the comforts of life. O brother Muslim! If your circumstances, too, be similar to these, may they be wholesome for you! You should not, however, forget that among your fellow-beings who have, in the darkness of indigence and adversity, made the earth thir mattress and the sky their quilt. Again, when your eyes fall on your tidy and gleeful children you should not forget that there are parents who have passed their night in darkness by the side of their children with withered faces and empty bellies.

You play and laugh with your children with pleasure but you must also remember that there are some young children who at one time lived under the protection of their parents but now the dust of orphanhood has settled on their heads and faces and they weep helplessly on acocount of lack of food and dress. There is no one who may comfort them and wipe out the tears flowing from their eyes and satisfy their hunger. You should fear the day on which the powerful wheel of time may deal with your children in the same way.

O the happy and lucky lady who enjoys the shelter of her kind husband! Do not forget that there was a time when your sister and country-woman, who is now a widow, was also happy and prosperous like you. However, her husband was suddenly devoured by death and she became mournful and distressed.

O you self-indulgent and cheerful persons! Thank Allah

for His blessings, for He says: *Remember when your Lord said to you: 'If you be grateful, I shall bestow on you greater favours'.* (Surah Ibrahim, 14:7)

However, being grateful does not mean that you should utter a few words or sign and express feigned sympathy for the helpless. Which problems do these things solve? Which hungry and poor person can they help?

Expression of regret and sympathy should have a positive aspect. You should do something which may revive the spirit of generosity, forgiveness, bravery and justice in your nature. You should support your parents, children and all other members of the family in this manner. Are you doing so?

There are persons who sit at the round coloured tables and lose their wealth in gambling. There are others who are absorbed in game of chess, idle talk and hundreds of other sinful pastimes.

The ignorant persons have plunged themselves in games and lust. The society is threatened by indigence, disease, death, perplexity and thousands of other calamities; populated houses are becoming ruins, pious hearts are inclining towards impiety, the families are breaking the ties of kinship and unity and shelterless persons are sitting in the nooks and corners of the roads, whereas you are living in pleasure and luxury and you have engaged yourselves in revelries which are opposed to human dignity and status. Then what should be the duty of those who do not have a place to live and cannot provide a shelter to their dear and near ones?

Therefore, hurry up and vacate these houses of sin. Make haste and help the afflicted people even though it may be for a moment only. Gladden a heart, make a helpless person happy and caress an orphan at least once. And if you do these things you will continuously feel the real taste of faith and will acquire a tranquil conscience and a sweet life. In that case you will have pleased Allah, saved the society from the ruination and would have performed your human duty.

It is not only for the sake of religion and humanity that I invite you for compassion, forgiveness and goodness to the needy, as the welfare of the country as well as your own interest lie in these virtues.

By performing virtuous deeds, helping the needy and

preparing welfare schemes, it is possible to form a strong army from amongst the vagrants and to use all this strength for the progress and prosperity for the country and consequently prevent the corruption which threatens the society.

It is possible to rub off the rust of grudge from the hearts by means of noble deeds and to gain the good will, confidence and love of others and eventually to bring about co-operation and mutual trust among the members of the society.

As and when you do good to an afflicted person he considers himself to be your slave and shows meekness and humility before you.

Very often it is possible that with a little sacrifice a person can preserve a handsome quantity of wealth, and the good deeds of a man can also save him from perils.

Come forward and become real benefector of unfortunate people by reviving the human values and taking appropriate steps to consolidate the objectives of religion and the society.

Come and take pity on the dwellers of the earth so that the Lord of the earth and the skies may take pity on you.

What has been quoted so far regarding virtuous deeds is a very brief specimen of the teachings of Islam. The essential point in the matter is that Islam has endeavoured to inculcate the spirit of benevolence and beneficence in the individuals from their very childhood so that when they grow up they may sincerely perform good deeds. Furthermore, they should not feel disgusted while performing good deeds and the hours during which they render service to others should be the most pleasant hours of their lives.

The lives of the great leaders of Islam and the persons trained by them is the best witness of this claim. The same should be studied by the Muslims so that they may become acquainted with their morals and follow them in order to achieve peace, progress and prosperity.

Quotations
1. Do good. Allah loves the people who do good deeds.
2. For single good deed, one will be rewarded tenfold.
3. If you do good, it will be for your own benefit but if you do bad it will be for your own loss. (The holy Qur'an)

4. The best persons are those who do good to the people without taking into consideration whether they are good or bad.
(The holy Prophet)

5. Man is the slave of goodness and kindness. (Imam Ali)

6. The result of alms and good deeds is more pleasant than their beginning. (Imam Hasan Mujtaba)

7. The good act, which is nearer to spiritual reward than any other act, is virtue and justice. (Imam Baqir)

8. When a brother-in-faith of a believer approaches him for assistance it is a Divine blessing which has been sent to him.
(Imam Musa Kazim)

9. Allah has slaves who endeavour to meet the needs of others. They will be safe on the Day of Judgement.
(Imam Ali Riza)

10. Whoever is virtuous enjoys the status of the real king of the people and rules over the kingdom of hearts.
(George Herbert)

11. Whoever seeks the welfare and prosperity of others eventually acquires prosperity himself. (Plato)

12. Your reward lies in performing good deeds. (Ciceron)

13. If we do not attract the hearts of careless people with kindness in what other way is it possible to attract the hearts?
(Behrām Ghor)

14. There are two pleasant things the consequence whereof is never unwholesome and does not entail regret. One of them is doing good to the people and the other is the performance of one's duty. (Jean Jacques Rousseau)

15. Goodness defeats everything but it never gets defeated itself. (Tolstoy)

16. One who does good to others is rewarded by Allah in both the worlds. (Shaykh Sa'di)

17. As good proves to be useful everywhere, do good and be ashamed of doing evil. (Firdosi)

* * * * * *

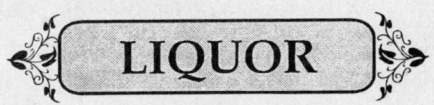

LIQUOR

Although a large number of books and articles about liquor have already been published and the matter has been studied and analyzed from various angles still in view of the importance of the subject and the dangers emanating from the use of liquor it has been considered expedient to conduct an allround and at the same time a brief and concise study in this behalf. It is hoped that by this means a service may be rendered to the society and the people may not be tempted by this dangerous liquid.

It is interesting to note that there is no difference of opinion among the learned persons about liquor and its harmful effects and we have enough convincing arguments in support of our claim.

It is possible that till a few years earlier some ignorant persons might have thought that liquor, if used in a small quantity was not only not injurious for health but was beneficial. However, as a consequence of research conducted recently by some American and European physicians and scholars this baseless view was rejected and it was proved that howmuchsoever small the quantity of the strong drinks may be they are harmful in the same proportion.

Here we direct your attention to the following report which has been obtained from official sources:

Some time ago when medical specialists from all the four corners of the world gathered once again in Washington to participate in the world congress to campaign against liquor and they once again gave a warning signal saying: 'Liquor is the enemy number one of the brain'.

Dr Melvin Kingsley who has spent many years in research in the field of liquor said in the first meeting of the Congress: "Even a small quantity of liquor causes much damage to the brain. When a person feels pleasure and joy by drinking a small quantity of liquor he does not know that he has helped the destruction of the cells of his brain".

Dr Kingsley who is the Head of the Research Institute of the College of Physicians of south Carolina is of the view that excessive use of liquor causes changes in the blood and the vains in such a manner that the brain cells are faced with shortage of oxygen and are thus destroyed or they are so much damaged that the person concerned becomes subjected to mental derangement. At times the effect of liquor in blood severly hampers the circulation of blood in the body and it has been seen that in some cases it leads to coagulation and blood clots.

Dr Kingsley said in this Congress at the very outset: "Unfortunately our efforts for campaigning against liquor which is claiming more and more victims day by day have proved fruitless so far and the number of people using liquor is continuously on the increase. As matters stand at present, millions of persons in the world have become addicted to liquor and there is no way out for them now.

The point under discussion is that unfortunately all people think that the use of a small quantity of liquor is not only not injurious but possibly appears to be necessary. Some persons hold the view that if, so to say, they only take a small sip in the parties they will not become addicted to liquor or it will not damage their brains, although the extensive research conducted in this behalf shows that liquor, even if used in a small quantity, causes disorder in the system of the cells of the brain".

Dr Raymond Penignon who presented a four-page report to the congress also believes that liquor is undoubtedly one of the most dangerous enemies of man and even those who, according to their own thinking, drink a small quantity thereof at one time or the other are in danger on account of this enemy.

According to Dr Penignon the first result of becoming addicted to liquor is forgetfulness and losing one's employment. He says: "By means of the research which I have conducted, I have come to know that the persons addicted to liquor are faced with forgetfulness after some time and cease to make any progress. They lose interest in their work and eventually lose their jobs and for this very reason take more refuge in liquor".

This physician further says: "It is a matter of great regret that drinking of liquor has become very much current among the young men and they treat liquor a means of escaping from their responsibilities of life. From the research conducted by us we have come to the conclusion that about 70% of young men have shown interest in liquor and from 20% to 30% of them have become addicted to it. Continuous increase in general crimes is one of the signs of daily increase in the use of liquor and the records available in the security organizations show that most of the persons who commit general crimes are those who are addicted to liquor".

Dr Herbert Miskoff, another physician who participated in the said Congress says: "Liquor weakens the cells of the brain and destroys the ability of a person to perceive matters. However, the more important problem is its hereditary effects. The child of a person addicted to liquor is weak, sluggish and stupid. He does not possess the capability of acquiring education and is always nervous. Besides this it has been observed at times that some children of such persons are born abnormal.

The result which may be obtained from this congress and the research of the specialists may be effective in the case of some persons but undoubtedly it is not the method of definite remedy. Liquor has spread its roots in the life of man and if an all-out campaign is not conducted against it its roots will become stronger and it will entangle many others in its trap".

It is the study of this scientific research which makes us bow our heads subconsciously in respect for Allah and his Prophet who declared liquor unlawful fourteen centuries before the coming into existence of the laboratories and the establishment of colleges and universities and prohibited the use of even one drop of it.

During the lifetime of the great Shi'ah reformist, the late Ayatullah Burujardi, Dr Arshah Tong, the General Secretary of the International Organization for Campaign against liquor visited Iran. During this visit he requested that he might be allowed to present himself before the great leader of the Shi'ah world and ask some questions.

This meeting was arranged through one of the professors of Tehran University and the Secretary of Iranian Society for Campaign against opium and liquor. A gist of the conversation which took place in the meeting is given below in the words of the said Professor and the Secretary of the Society:

At the time fixed in advance myself accompanied by Dr Arshah Tong reached in the presence of His holiness, Āyatullah Burujardi. Both of us took off our shoes outside the room and went together to kiss the hands of the Āyatullah. His simple and sincere manner was extraordinarily attractive. With enchanting countenance and an air of cordiality he expressed pleasure on having met us and inquired after our health. After thanking the Āyatullah for having agreed to meet us I said to him: "Dr Arshah Tong comes form Switzerland and is the Secretary General of the International Organization for Campaign against liquor. After having visited to Indonesia and Tehran for the advancement of his object viz. campaign against liquor he developed extraordinary interest in seeing your holiness and now requests that you may kindly give replies to some of his questions".

The Āyatullah permitted him to ask the questions. Thereupon Dr Arshah Tong said: "Your holiness! Why has the use of liquor and intoxicants been prohibited in Islam?"

The Āyatullah replied: "Man has been recognized to be the noblest of the creations on account of his possessing intellect and the purpose of his creation is indeed to traverse the path of gradual perfection for the recognition of Allah. The Almighty Allah, while granting us the invaluable gift of intellect and reason, has also given orders for safeguarding it. It is on this account, therefore, that the holy Prophet has prohibited the use of intoxicants which cause sluggishness and derangement of reason and the necessity of this prohibition appeals to good sense of a man of ordinary intelligence".

Dr Arshah Tong asked again: "If the use of liquor reaches the stage of intoxication it deranges intellect and reason. However, what do you say if it is taken in such a small quantity that it does not create dullness of mind?"

The Āyatullah said in reply: "When it becomes known that the superiority of man vis-a-vis animals is on account of his intellect and reason and when it is established that man is duty-bound to endeavour to safeguard the Divine gifts of intellect, reason and perception, everything which slackens these faculties will not be permissible and it is an established fact that liquor, in whatever quantity it may be taken, affects the senses. Besides this, there is another point which is important and it is that the Almighty Allah is fully aware of the disposition of human beings and knows that they naturally desire more than what they get. In case, therefore, had He permitted the use of liquor in a small quantity, it would have been difficult to fix the limit. Hence, in order that man may remain safe from the state of being intoxicated is incompatible with his very nature, He has totally banned the use of alcoholic drinks".

On hearing the second reply of the Āyatullah, Dr Arshah Tong said: "It is now more than ten years since I am incharge of the Organization of Campaign against liquor and during this period I have had detailed discussions with the great religious, political and social personalities of different countries. I, however, admit that so far none has expressed such comprehensive and convincing views as expressed by your holiness. Your remarks will be the greatest authority for us to fight against the use of alcoholic drinks in the world and in fact the greatest means for achieving our end will be to follow the commands of the great leaders of Islam. I thank your holiness on my own behalf as well as on behalf of the International Organization of Campaign against liquor and hope that under your guidance we shall emerge victorious in this holy war". (Symposium on liquor in the Medical college, Isfahan)

The British philosopher Bentham says: "One of the greatest teachings of the religion of Muhammad is that it has declared all intoxicants to be unlawful".

The great French writer and traveller Pierre Loti says: "Nothing more remains to be done so that I may consider myself to be a Muslim because I have never touched wine and other intoxicants".

A group of persons belonging to the tribe of Quraysh were sitting in Masjidul Harām. In the meantime Imam Baqir arrived. One of those persons pointed to the holy Imam and said to others: "He is the leader of the people of Iraq". They then decided to send someone to him to enquire about some religious problem.

A man got up, approached Imam Muhammad Baqir and asked him: "Which amongst the major sins is the biggest sin?" The Imam replied: "Drinking of wine".

The man returned and informed his companions about what the Imam had said. They, however, asked him to go to the Imam once again and to repeat the question. The man went and repeated the question. The Imam said to him cheerfully: "I have told you that drinking of wine is the biggest sin". The man returned to his friends and informed them about the matter. They, however, insisted upon him to go and ask the same question for the third time. He did so. The Imam told him cheerfully for the third time: "Drinking wine is the greatest sin, because wine leads one to adultery, theft, murder and polytheism and the sins which are based on wine are the greatest sins". (Wasā'ilush Shi'ah, Vol, XVII; Furū'al Kāfi, Vol. VI)

A man came to Imam Ja'far Sadiq and asked: "Why has Allah forbidden wine when it gives more pleasurable sensation then anything else?" The holy Imam replied: "Allah has forbidden wine because it is the mother of all evils. The drunkard loses his senses, does not recognize Allah, commits every crime, violates the honour of others, severs relationship and gets involved in uncleanliness and lewdness. The drunkard is controlled by Satan. If Satan orders him to prostrate before an idol he obeys him and goes wherever he leads him". (Wasā'ilush Shi'ah)

Before the advent of Islam and even during the early days of the holy Prophet, the preparation and transaction of wine was considered to be the most important business of the Arabs so much so that the word *'Tijārat'* (trade) was used exclusively for transaction pertaining to wine and the persons whose profession was to deal in wine was called a *Tājir* (trader).

When the sun of Islam rose and its sublime teachings were communicated to the people, the manufacturing of wine, which entailed many calamities and losses, was prohibited. The prohibition of liquor in Islam was so strong and decisive that this curse was eradicated from the Muslim society in a very short time.

Islam has not only prohibited drinking of wine but it has also declared manufacting of wine and all other acts connected with it to be unlawful.

The holy Prophet has cursed the following persons who are connected with the business of liquor:
(i) One who grows grapes in vineyard to prepare wine.
(ii) One who crushes grapes to distil wine.
(iii) One who sells wine.
(iv) One who purchases wine.
(v) One who drinks wine.
(vi) One who passes a glass of wine to someone else.
(vii) One who makes profits in any manner from a transaction of wine. (Wasā'ilush Shi'ah, Vol. XVII: Khasā'il, 'Iqābul A'māl)

Imam Ja'far Sadiq says: "Do not associate with the drunkards because as and when a calamity befalls them it will also engulf their associates". (Wasā'ilush Shi'ah, Vol. XVII)

Allah, who is aware of all the evil effects of liquor on the people and their children and the society has, besides prohibiting the drinking, preparation, distribution, purchase and sale of such drinks, also prohibited marriage with the drunkards on the ground that liquor also affects their sperms and makes their offsprings invalid, corrupt and abnormal.

Imam Sadiq says: "Whoever gives his daughter in marriage to a drunkard severs his connections with her".

The holy Prophet says: "If a person drinks wine after almighty Allah having declared it unlawful through me, he should not be given a girl in marriage if he asks for her hand and if anyone intercede for him his intercession should not be accepted and if he quotes a news it should not be acknowledged and no one should consider him to be honest or entrust anything to him. And if a person deposits something with another knowing him to be a drunkard, Allah is not responsible for that deposit and if that deposit is lost he will neither be rewarded nor compensated for it by Allah". (Li'āli'ul Akhbār)

Numerous traditions in this regard have come down from the holy Prophet and the holy Imams and special attention has been paid to pregnancy taking place under the influence of liquor because this is something very dangerous.

Imam Ja'far Sadiq says: "A woman who submits to sexual intercourse with her husband while he is drunk commits errors and sins equal in number to the stars in the sky and the child born of that man is unclean and filthy. Allah does not accept any repentance or atonement from her except that her husband may die or she may extricate herself from the bond of marriage". (Li'āli'ul Akhbār, p. 267)

The contemporary scholars do not entertain any doubt about the evil effects of liquor on the sperms and the scientific research has fully proved this claim, because the children born in such conditions usually suffer from mental ailments.

Besides the scientific research conducted by the scholars of the East and the West, experience has also proved that the children of persons addicted to strong drinks are weak and backward as compared with other children.

There is no doubt about the fact that insanity, stupidity and addiction to strong drinks has a great effect on the development and growth of the children and the children born of parents suffering from these abnormalities are abnormal and pitiable. For this very reason Islam has made strong recommendations to its followers on this subject and warned them of bad and impure matrimonial alliances.

The contemporary scholars have also paid much attention to this subject and strongly recommended that such matrimonial alliances should be avoided so much so that in some American countries special laws have been enacted for the purity of race. According to these laws the boys and girls who are chronically addicted to drinking are sterilized and are thus practically prevented from producing children.

Another harm which strong drinks do to the people is that their brain cells and nerve fibres are severly damaged to give rise to mental diseases.

One of the professors of Tehran University says: "Liquor is one of the anaesthetising agents and it depresses the central nervous system with the result that brain cells are damaged and which in turn causes insanity and mental derangement".

While commenting on the Qur'anic verse: *(O Prophet!) They question you about strong drink......* (Surah al-Baqarah, 2:219) an Egyptian exegetist in *Tafsir al-Manār*, quotes a German physician having said to his Government, "You should close down half of the taverns and bars so that the country's hospitals, lunatic asylum and prisons will be reduced to half their number".

In the Islamic traditions the damage done by liquor to

man's intellect and soul have been hinted at and it has been mentioned under the subject of prohibition.

Imam Riza says: "Allah has prohibited liquor on account of the evils resulting from it and because it renders reason and intellect null and destroys modesty". (Mustadrak, Vol. III)

Imam Sajjad says: "The sin which eliminates the strength of resisting other sins, that is that sin which paralyses the sense and breaks up man's moral fibres of defence is drinking and gambling". (Bihārul Anwār, Vol. XVI)

A psychologist says: "Liquor destroys modesty, tears the veil of chastity and freeing the man from all social, religious and moral obligations, suppresses his voice of conscience and converts the angel into a demon. Usually the first step which deviates a person from the path of chastity is the one taken in the state of intoxication, because when intoxication enters, reason and conscience quit the field and chastity does not carry any meaning in the absence of reason and conscience. The boys, girls and women who have gone astray are the persons who have been deviated from the path of life in the first instance by the daughter of grapevine (wine). Necessarily, therefore, they have wandered in the dreadful desert of life and eventually drowned themselves in the whirlpool of adversity and misfortunes".

Tolstoy says: "People are very well aware of consequences of liquor that it suppresses the voice of conscience and it is for this reason that it is being used".

There are many persons who are not prepared in ordinary circumstances to do something bad or say something unbecoming or take some unmanly step but do not desist from any indecent act or crime while they are intoxicated.

Dr Alexis Carrel says: "General decrease in intelligence and soundness of judgement results from the effects of liquor and all sorts of excesses and eventually modification in behaviour occurs. No doubt a relationship exists between the quantity of liquor used and the intellectual weakness of a society. From amongst all the nations which are engaged in scientific work more wine is consumed in France and that country secures lesser Nobel prizes than other countries".

The following statistics enlighten us to a large extent about the evil effects of liquor: "Adnre Minu, Secretary of the International Congress for Campaign against liquor announced that: "The ailment of 80% of the insane and 40% of the persons suffering from venereal diseases has been due to the use of liquor. Amongst the children 60% of the idots and 40% of the criminals were born in families which were addicted to liquor".

The losses which occur in human societies due to liquor is greater than all other losses and its casualties exceed the casualties of most dangerous diseases.

According to the statements of competent scholars, liquor causes cancer of digestive system, liver and stomach, chest and flanks and tuberculosis, mental diseases, neurasthenia, amnesia and over and above the congenital deformities of the newborns.

One of the other great social losses caused by wine are the road accidents. As a result of medical discussions and numerous observations it has been established that drinking modifies the driving faculty of habitual drunkards which leads to traffic hazards.

As acknowledged by the Security Council one-fourth of the deaths which take place as a consequence of traffic accidents are connected with the intoxication of the drivers.

Leograin says: "Out of 761 persons born of parents addicted to liquor 322 are depraved, 155 are insane and 131 are susceptible to apoplexy.

30% to 40% of psychic patients in mental hospitals are those who are addicted to liquor.

During the year 1344 A.H., 1875 persons in Iran died of poisoning due to liquor.

Liquor is the main cause of crimes. It has been responsible for 75% of murders, 38% of physical assaults and 82% of arson.

Taking into account all these sufferings and afflictions, Islam has carefully nipped the root of this evil in the bud.

Islam says: "Do not sit at a table where others are drinking wine. Do not participate in wine parties even if you do not drink. Do not associate yourself with the drunkards lest you should be tempted to fall into the ditch of evil".

One of the army officers of Mansur, the Abbasid Caliph, arranged a feast in Hayra in connection with the circumcision of his son and invited some dignitaries and persons of rank. Imam Ja'far Sadiq, the sixth Imam, was also one of the invitees.

When the guests were busy taking their meals one of them asked for water. Instead of water a servant brought a glass of wine. As soon as wine was brought on the dinner table Imam Ja'far Sadiq left the dinner table.

The host ran after him and enquired about the reason for his having left the party.

The Imam replied: "The holy Prophet has said that one who sits at a table on which others are drinking wine is accursed". (Bihārul Anwār, Vol. XI)

Besides what has been stated above a glance at the pages of history shows that it has often happened that wine has been the cause of annihilation of a nation or the extinction of a family.

History says: "With all their dignity and authority the Barmecids succumed to alcoholic addiction. If the Barmecid Ja'far had not been intoxicated and has not lost the sense of discernment of account of drinking wine the question of Abbasa, sister of Harun Rashid would certainly not have arisen and the Barmecids would not have been massacred on large scale.

Although bad luck overtook the Barmecids on account of a number of crimes committed by them one among them leading to the martyrdom of Imam Musa Kazim yet their misfortunes started due to Ja'far being intoxicated".

History says that the Kingship of Sultan Jalaluddin Khawarazm Shah came to an end on account of his drinking and leading lustful life and as a result he lost his head and his crown for the sake of wine. That strong and warlike king who fought with the savage Mongol army for years and perplexed Chenghizkhan and his soldiers eventually fell a prey to the vice of wine drinking.

During the nights when the Sultan was busy in merry-making and was passing his time under the state of intoxication his trusted courtier, Nuruddin Zaydri recited the following quatrain for him :

"O King! What will be the result of this deep drinking.

And what will be the result of the maddening intoxication?

The King is intoxicated, the country is desolate and the enemies are hovering all around.

The result which this state of affairs will produce is evident".

However, neither the king nor his associates paid any heed

to these words. All of them were intoxicated. At midnight, the Mongols conducted a surprise attack and besieged the Sultan's army and his tent. One of the Sultan's associates who had become aware of the attack reached by the side of his bed, awakened him of keep slumber with much difficulty and informed him of the position.

Being very much intoxicated, the Sultan was not able to mount the horse. He poured some water on his head to get rid of intoxication. However, it was now too late and no alternative was left for him except to flee. He fled in the same condition, but was killed by a stranger in the hills of Kurdistan who wanted to rob him of his horse and other belongings". (Tārikh Kāmil-i Iran, p. 316)

History says that the Safawid rule declined due to Shah Tehmāsib having become addicted to wine.

Whatever has been said so far pertain to the losses which accrue from wine the harm which it does to the body and the souls, the individuals and the society besides the financial losses. However, for us who are the firm believers in monotheism, the genesis and the resurrection, liquor has another aspect also and that is its everlasting horrible effects on the life in the Hereafter.

This aspect should also be given full attention because it is possible that one may be prepared to bear all losses and every harm accruing from wine in this world but a Muslim cannot at any cost give up his eternal happiness in the Hereafter.

Imam Baqir says: "A drunkard will appear in the Divine Court of Justice like an idolater". (Wasā'ilush Shi'ah, Vol. XVII)

Imam Ja'far Sadiq says: "The Almighty Allah has made Paradise unlawful for persons falling under three categories one of them is the drunkards".

The Holy Prophet says: "I swear by Allah that one who considers prayers to be insignificant and the one who drinks wine will not be benefited by my intercession". (al-Kāfi, Vol. II)

Hakim Sinā'i, a famous Persian poet, has mentioned the evils of liquor in the poetic verses as translated below.

"A wise man does not drink wine and does not become intoxicated. An intelligent person does not stoop so lowly.

Why do you drink a thing which, when drunk, shows you a reed to be a cypress tree and a cypress tree to be a reed.

If (in such a condition) you give a gift to someone it is said that it is wine, and not you, who has given it; and if you raise an uproar it is said that it is you and not wine who have raised it".

Quotations
1.   Muhammad, they ask you about wine and gambling tell them that there is great sin in them. Although they have benefits for men but the sin therein is far greater than the benefit.
2.   Believers, wine, gambling, the stone altars and arrows (that the pages associate with certain divine characters) are all abominable acts associated with satanic activities. Avoid them so that you may have everlasting happiness.
3.   Satan wants to induce hostility and hatred among you through wine and gambling and to prevent you from remembering god and prayer. Will you then avoid such things.
(The holy Qur'an)

* * * * * *

GAMBLING

Gambling is one of the harmful pastimes and dangerous amusements which has been prevalent among the people for centuries and has done immense harm.

In the modern world also gambling is a source of amusement for the people at an extensive level and with modern means the human societies have suffered heavily from the evils of this ruinous pastime.

For some countries gambling is important from the economic point of view. The production and sale of gambling implements and the collection of heavy taxes from this trade are the sources of government revenues. And not only that many people earn their livelihood from gambling institutions.

In some countries of Europe and America big centres of gambling have been established to attract the wealthy people. The owners of these centres earn fabulous income and a large sum of it goes to government treasury by way of taxes.

The economic aspect of gambling received attention of the law-giver of Islam fourteen centuries ago and the holy Qur'an has mentioned it explicitly. However, as its losses are greater than the benefits accruing from it, it has been made unlawful so that in order to gain material benefits, the Muslims may not suffer from a still greater material and spiritual harm.

The holy Qur'an says: *Muhammad they ask you about wine and gambling. Tell them that there is great sin in them. Although they have benefits for men, the sin therein is far greater than the benefit.* (Surah al-Baqarah, 2:219)

Although the countries of the world are aware of the dangers arising from gambling they do not ban it in earnest for the sake of financial benefits which accrue to them from it.

Gambling was made unlawful in England in 1853. However, after enactment of the relevant law 18 gambling houses were set up for the nobles and the dignitaries. Gambling was made unlawful in America in 1855, in Prussia in 1854 and in Germany in 1882 and Islam prohibited it several centuries earlier than these civilized countries.

At present big gambling centres exist in America and Europe. Thousands of gamblers assemble there every day from far and near with boxes full of sterlings and dollars and engage themselves madly in gambling.

A newspaper wrote thus about the city of Las Vagas which is the centre of gambling in America: "The exact number of the gamblers gambling there is not known, but it exceeds 40,000 persons during twenty four hours. In this gambling house not only one but hundreds of persons lose their stakes".

Hotel Sahara which is one of the big hotels of this city is the special gambling house for the millionaires and during every twenty four hours more than 10 million dollars are staked at this place alone. Hundreds of persons stand by the side of electric installations called slots. They throw coins regularly into the installation hoping to gain a few hundred or a few thousand dollars, they pull the handle of the installation with full force. However, as the pouring of dollars does not bring about any result, this task is continued and the dollars continue to be poured into the installation". (YearlyReview, 1962)

It is evident that the enormous profits which accrue to the owners of these centres and the governments concerned prevent them from shutting down these centres of corruption.

The reason for our calling these centres 'the centres of corruption' is that various evils are practised and heinous crimes are committed in these centres.

The news agencies and newspapers provide us with some glimpses of the atrocities committed in the gambling houses:

"In the city of Monte Carlo in Italy an Argentinian lost a sum of four million dollars in the space of nineteen hours. And when the doors of the gambling house were closed he went straight to the jungle, shattered his head and thus put an end to his life". (The Magazine, Roshan Fikr, 1962)

"The Statistical Organization named 'Gallop' has declared while publishing statistics that the number of suicides on account of gambling is on the increase. The statistics of the said organization showed that as compared with previous years more suicides were committed by gamblers during the year 1961". (Weekly Ittilā'āt, Issue No. 1060)

One of the Statistical Organizations of America concludes that gambling is responsible for 30% of the crimes.

"An American physician, after his having conducted research for many years came to the conclusion that only in America more than 2000 persons die every year on account of gambling. This physician has proved that while gambling the beatings of the hearts of the gamblers become very rapid and the heart of an expert player of poker usually beats more than 100 times per minute. As a result of this unusual palpitation of heart the gamblers either die of heart failure at the gambling table or become older by ten or fifteen years than the normal time and ultimately die". (The Magazine, Roshan Fikr 1964)

One of the other great evils of gambling which is very important from the social and psychological point of view is the enmity which it creates between the persons concerned. Gambling arouses the feeling of pessimism and vengeance in the individuals, severs friendship, love and sincerity and prepares the ground for revenge and awakens the instinct of wrath.

Allah says: *Satan wants to induce hostility and hatred among you through wine and gambling and to prevent you from remembering Allah and prayers.* (Surah al-Maidah, 5 -91)

A famous psychologist says: "In the game of poker it is not necessary that the destructive motives should change the pattern. Poker itself is based on combat. In this game, up to the limits which the regulations permit, every player endeavours to dominate over the other. It is possible that he may delude the other party or, as is commonly said, 'bluff' him, becuse the target of the game is either to delude the other party about one's own real strength or to demonstrate that strength.

The game of chess is also a demonstration of the inclination of man to refine his destructive instincts. The difference is that in this game there is a pattern of war between two countries.

While conducting a psychological study of chess, Earnest Johnson points out thus: "It is an admitted fact that the stimulant for those playing chess is not only the aspect of challenge of the game of chess which is the speciality of all games involving combat but they have a worse and more indecent motive which is the very aspect of 'patricide' of this game, because the target of this game is to captivate and check-mate.

John Hess regretted having played chess while he was in the prison because he believed that by doing so he had divulged his undesirable sentiments".

What has been stated by the aforesaid psychologist is one aspect of the matter and the other point is that gambling creates problems and animosity due to the material losses which the gamblers have to suffer.

It is evident that when the wealth and savings of one of the two parties are poured into the pocket of the other and the winner takes possession of that wealth with a victorious smile the seed of enmity is sown in the heart of the loser and eventually this enmity makes its inauspicious signs appear on a favourable and proper occasion.

This is something natural. Why should the rival not foster enmity in his heart when he sees that the wealth which he earned after undergoing great hardships is in the hands of another? Thus he feels no pity for him.

Another aspect of the matter which is more important than all other aspects is the question of defeat. As a result of defeat in the game the gambler is faced with serious psychological tension and in order to make amends for the defeat he forsakes sleep and rest, abandons his work and business and continues to play, hoping that he may secure victory over his rival and thus soothe his mental tension.

A newspaper with a wide circulation wrote thus: "In one of the cities a gambler attacked his rival with knife and killed him. During cross-examination he said: "The victim won a large sum of money from me and was not prepared to play again. Inspite of all my insistence he declined to continue the game and fled. I also pursued him and. . . . . .".

Even if the game is continued and the gambler, who has

already lost, loses again he does not give up gambling and, hoping to win, stakes not only his material capital but his personal honour as well.

Before the advent of Islam the people in the Dark Age of Ignorance also partook in different kinds of gambling. At first the players staked their savings and wealth and thereafter their houses and other belongings. And when a player lost all his wealth and property he staked his wife even and if he lost her also he handed her over to his rival with shameless abandon.

Imam Ja'far Sadiq says: "Quraysh used to bet their property and wives and gambled them away. Allah prohibited this obscene practice and warned the people against gambling". (Bihārul Anwār, Vol. XI)

Many persons may possibly wonder as to whether is it possible that a man may be so mean that he may gamble away his honour! However, when we keep in view the events which take place in the modern civilized world every now and then we realize that it is possible that as a result of being habituated to gambling any person may have to face such a situation.

Here we direct the attention of the readers to the following report: "Ricardo Lamos, one of the members of the Jazz orchestra of the Mexican television, who was very fond of poker arranged a gambling party in his house last night. After having lost everything in the game he decided to stake the only thing which was left with him and to continue the game. That thing was his wife. Unfortunately, he at last lost his wife as well. She refused to surrender herself. But inspite of his insistence, she did not agree to surrender herself to the winner. He beat her so much that she fainted. At present the unfortunate woman is confined to bed in a hospital and there is no hope of her recovery". (Mexico, French News Agency, 25th November)

An act which pulls down a man to such indeency and which becomes the cause of his disaster will surely be prohibited from the point of view of logical reasoning.

Islam, which is the religion based on reason and logic, declared according to the explicit contents of the holy Qur'an and the traditions of *Ahlul Bayt* (the chosen descendants of the holy Prophet) all sorts of gambling unlawuful for the Muslims 1400 years ago and besides this, prohibited the manufacture, purchase and sale of gambling implements. It also declared the income from gambling to be unlawful and warned the Muslims against the use of such property.

Imam Riza says: "Allah has made all kinds of gambling unlawful and ordered the people to refrain from it. Allah has called gambling as filth and the act of Satan and warned the people against getting involved in it like the games of chess, backgammons and other kinds of gambling. And the game of backgammons is worse than the game of chess". (Mustadrakul Wasā'il, Vol. II)

Imam Baqir says: "When the verse: Believers, wine gambling, the stone altars and arrows (that the pagans associate with certain divine characters) are all unlawful acts associated with satanic activities was revealed, the people asked the holy Prophet: What is *'Maisir'* (which has been declared by Allah to be unclean and an infamy of Satan's handiwork)? He replied: "Anything with which one gambles, it also includes bone-dices and walnuts". (Tafsiral Mizān, Vol. VI, p. 144)

The famous psychologist K. Platonev says: "In the rest houses of the Soviet Union gambling and card playing which involves winning or losing are strictly prohibited. . . . . . Card-playing was introduced in Russia in 1646 and a campaign started against it in the same year".

The greed and inclination of a gambler to win prompts him to continue the game and consequently weakens his intellect and reason. Examples of such excitement and tension can be seen in other kinds of gamblings. As for example in Russia there is a special game which children usually play. In this game children slap the hands of one another with the result that the back of their hands becomes sore and swollen with hitting and they become so much engrossed in it that they become unaware of the injury they are sustaining by this type of game. Similarly a gambler who becomes a victim to his inclinations and desires, does not care as to how much worth and strength of his has decreased and to what extent he has lost control over his nerves". (K. Platonev, Psychology, p. 227)

Imam Baqir says: "Prohibition of gambling covers chess, back-gammons and other games of chance". (Tafsir Majma'ul Bayān, Vol. III)

Under the protection of the sublime teachings of Islam, the Islamic society refrained from this dreadful curse. But unfortunately, the colonialists and the enemies of Islam introduced it to some extent among the ignorant persons and the means of gambling have found their way into some houses.

Gambling became current especially in the so-called modern society and people have become involved in this abominable and unlawful business only to imitate the West and to be recognized by their associates as civilized and modern, notwithstanding the fact that they can observe the misfortunes from which the gamblers in Europe and America suffer an and the felonies, stabbings, thefts, suicides and other evils which originate from gambling.

Some years ago a news was published in the newspapers which should serve as a lesson to those who are habitual gamblers. The text of that news which was published under the heading 'The King of Gamblers commits suicide': "The well-known multi-millionaire of Germany and the king of the gamblers of that country killed himself during this week when he became indebted to the Casinos for ten million German marks. This multi-millionaire whose name was Ralph Lodar had said years ago when he was not so wealthy: 'Rest assured. As and when my income falls below ten thousand marks per month I shall kill myself'. And recently a situation arose for him on account of which he did kill himself.

Ralph Lodar did not possess any wealth in Germany till after the War. However, after the war he entered business and acquired wealth in a short time as a result of his extraordinary competence and made a profit of as much as ten million marks in one transaction. He invested this money in stock exchange and added large sums to it.

Lodar was crazy about gambling and especially the game of roulette and every night he resorted to the famous Casinos of the world. Strangely enough he won regularly in roulette and according to one of his associates he acquired a large part of his wealth from gambling and especially from the game of roulette. He also won large amounts which always exceeded 100,000 marks. For this very reason he was given the name of 'King of Gamblers' in the Casinos. Whichever table in the Casinos he approached, the owner of the Casino counted his chips as he knew that he would lose a large amount.

Till two years ago he lost only four times during the entire period of his gambling and the total amount lost by him did not exceed five million marks. During the last two years, however, his luck had a turn for the worse and he lost regularly.

Lodar earned large amount of money from his transactions in the stock exchange but at night lost twice or thrice as much in gambling. Imagining that in the Casinos in Germany chance had turned its face from him he went to Monte Carlo. However, at that place also he lost about eight million marks.

Gradually Lodar lost his joy and energy and as he was unhappy and nervous on account of what he lost at night he could not also work properly in the stock exchange during day time. Consequently his income decreased and he continued to lose gradually his enormous wealth.

Till a month earlier only a few personal villas had been left with him out of his wealth. He sold these villas also and converted them into cash and said to his friends: "With this money I will again acquire the wealth lost by me".

Lodar first went to a famous casino which was situated near Hamburg and then to Monte Carlo. However, he lost at both the places and ceased to possess anything. Besides this, he became indebted for ten million marks. It was in these circumstances that a week earlier he went to his small apartment in Cologne and devoured a tube of sleeping pills with the intention of committing suicide. His body was recovered from his apartment when twenty four hours had passed after his death". (Weekly Ittilā'āt, Issue No. 1521, Bahman, 1349)

It was reported in an Iranian newspaper: "After losing 4,60,000 Tumans in a Casino a young man committed suicide". (Firdosi Magazine, Issue No. 998 5th Bahman 1349)

These are some examples of the tragic end of the gamblers who after toiling throughout their lives and possessing wealth in millions lose their health and peace of mind become indigent and perplexed and finding no way out of the calamities brought by them upon themselves put an end to their lives by committing suicide.

It is possible that some persons may think that the crimes

resulting from gambling are confined to the West and to the multi-millionaires. However, our own newspapers which report the tragic events arising out of gambling tell us that wherever gambling finds its way it carries adversity along with it and whoever resorts to gambling must await its disastrous end.

The following report was published in an Iranian newspaper some years ago: "A person who had shot his rival dead as a consequence of gambling was sentenced to life imprisonment. The Supreme court also rejected his application for fresh trial and decided that he deserved the punishment.

The person against whom the said sentence was passed is forty nine years old who committed this crime last year.

In the afternoon of that day on which this event took place he and the other person drank wine together in a tavern. Then they left that place and sat down on the way to gamble. At about 9.00 p.m. they began to quarrel during gambling. The murderer shot the other person in his chest and killed him.

On the basis of the investigation conducted in the case the court found him guilty of murder and the public prosecutor demanded the sentence of death. The file was referred to the High Court of Justice in Tehran and the Judges, reducing the sentence by one degree, sentenced the accused to life imprisonment. (Kayhān Daily Newspaper, Issue No. 8266)

Reflect carefully about the above event. Two families were deprived of their guardians. One person was killed and the other was imprisoned for life. And why did all this happen? For the sake of wine and gambling! Is it not proper that we should bow our heads with humility and devotion before the law-giver of Islam who said fourteen centuries ago: *Satan wants to induce hostility and hatred among you through wine and gambling and to prevent you from remembering Allah and prayers.* (Surah al-Maidah, 5:91)

Imam Riza says: "Desist from gambling with *'Khawatīm'* and *'Arba'h Ashar'* (tools for gambling in those times) and other tools of gambling and even from gambling with walnuts, almonds and bone-dices with which the children play games of chance". (Mustadrakul Wasā'il, Vol. II, p. 59)

It is necessary that we should explain here the Islamic injunctions with regard to different types of gambling in a concise manner so that there should remain no ambiguity:

The holy Qur'an has declared gambling to be unlawful in an explicit statement supported by reasoning. It alludes to the benefits and evils accruing from gambling and support its prohibition by pointing out that its evils are greater than its benefits.

As most of the people indulge in gambling by way of recreation and amusement or to earn money, the holy Qur'an reminds in connection with its small benefit but declares that the evils accruing from it are much greater. Then in the end of the statement it calls upon our intellect to arbitrate in the matter.

It is admittedly unwise that one should take the risk of big losses for probable and small benefits. And those who gamble for the sake of profit should remember that the financial, social, mental and moral losses entailed by gambling are much greater than the benefits which may possibly accrue from it.

In some verses of the holy Qur'an, gambling has been mentioned as Satan's handiwork and the means of perversion and the Muslims have been asked to refrain from it. In some other verses gambling has been recognized as a factor which creates enmity and hatred between the people, inspires their sense of revenge, involves them in loose morals and prevents them from attaining spiritual excellence and from maintaining contact with Allah. (Vide, Surah al-Maidah, 5:90 — 91)

In Islamic jurisprudence gambling (games of chance) means those games in which special facilities are used with the object of winning or losing in this manner that it is agreed that one who loses should pay an amount of money or some other commodity to the winner.

This type of gambling has been declared to be unlawful in Islam and all the jurists have recognized its illegality to be an essential part of Islamic beliefs. (Misbāhul Faqāhā)

Another kind of gambling is that a game of chance may be played with special tools (e.g. playing cards or chess) for the sake of recreation and without there being any condition for payment of anything in the event of winning or losing. According to the verdicts of Shi'ah jurists in general, games of this type are also unlawful. (Jame'ul Maqāsid; Tazkira-i Allama)

The third kind of gambling is that the same may not be played with special tools but the condition of payment in the event of winning or losing should be present. According to the well-known verdicts of Shi'ah jurists, such games are also unlawful.

Another point which should be kept in view is that gambling has been prohibited in Islam on two accounts. Firstly, because gambling in itself is unlawful and a sin in Islam. Secondly, because the money acquired by means of gambling is also unlawful. In other words the gambler who wins does not become its owner legally. He has, therefore, no right to possess it and must refund it to its owner.

A Basic Campaign Against Gambling

In order to uproot this grave calamity Islam has contented itself with declaring gambling to be unlawful, but has also prohibited the manufacture of the tools of gambling and their stocking, purchase and sale.

It is possible that some persons may ask as to why chess and similar other games should be unlawful if there is no condition of staking money in the event of winning or losing, when these games are played nowadays as a mental relaxation and have also found their place in the educational institutions?

The reply to such arguments is that it has not been proved that these games are not innocuous and harmless. On the other hand the remarks of the psychologists quoted in the foregoing pages go to show that these games do possess bad effects.

Besides, in order to conduct a basic campaign against gambling and to uproot it, Islam has declared all kinds of gambling unlawful even though winning and losing may not be involved in them and has also prohibited the production, purchase, sale and keeping of the tools of gambling so that people may have absolutely no concern with it.

No doubt an all-out campaign of this type is needed to eradicate such an evil because if the facilities and tools for gambling are manufactured and purchased and sold freely and their keeping is also permissible the people will make a beginning by way of recreation and amusement and this very act will prepare the ground for the outbreak of this evil.

In this way Islam has uprooted mischief and corruption decisively by declaring all kinds of gambling and its tools to be unlawful and those persons who believe sincerely in Islam do not at all involve themselves in this act which is one of the major sins.

Imam Ja'far Sadiq says: "It is a sin to greet a gambler and one who sits by a gambling carpet as an onlooker and one who looks at the face of the gambler are as much sinners as he who welcomes the gambler, and an assembly arranged for gambling is one of those assemblies which deserves Divine wrath and torture and which should expect it to come at any moment". (Jawāhir, chapter of Transaction)

Imam Musa Kazim, spoke eloquently against gambling and chess. A man belonging to Basra said to him: "I participate in an assembly in which people play chess. However, I myself do not play but am only a spectator".

The holy Imam replied: "What have you to do with an assembly which stands deprived of Divine blessing?"

Imam Ja'far Sadiq says: "It is unlawful to sell chess implements and to utilize its sale proceeds is faithlessness, to keep it is polytheism, to play with it and to greet a gambler is a sin, and to teach another person to play chess is a major sin. (Wasā'ilush Shi'ah)

The traditions quoted above are specimens of those numerous traditions about gambling wich have come down to us from the chosen descendants of the holy Prophet.

Persons who have conducted research studies and assess the matters correctly are very well aware of other evils of gambling and the adversities in which the gamblers are involved. Poets of different languages have also alluded to the evils of gambling in their works.

At times the curse of imitation becomes the cause of the appearance of evils like gambling and as we see in these days some persons have fallen a prey to this calamity only to imitate the West whereas the wise men of the West are very much disturbed on account of the conditions prevailigng in their society. These unlucky persons have resorted to gambling so that they may not lag behind the caravan of civilization by following in the footsteps of the gamblers of the West.

These are the persons who are not prepared and are also not competent to imitate the West in the matter of industry, science and technology and thus they do not take any step in the direction of prosperity but only wish to look like the Westerners by blindly following their vices!

Previously only men suffered from this destructive ailment and spent their nights in gambling in a state of apprehension and anxiety and returned home in the morning, absolutely tired. However, this evil has now entrapped the modern and civilized women of today also. It might be said that this too is a manifestation of the advancement of women and in order to prove their claim of superiority and equality with men they wish to become their equals even on the gambling table and they are no doubt treading on the wrong path.

Here, we briefly mention the curses of gambling

- Gambling is the cause of nervous and digestive ailments and mental problems.
- Gambling becomes the cause of strained relations of the individuals and severing of friendship and ends in animosity.
- Gambling becomes the cause of loss of wealth and results in poverty and indigence.
- Gambling becomes the cause of the break-down of families and the adversity in the private life of individuals. It prevents them from looking after private affairs, education and training of the children and other connected matters.
- Gambling pulls the individuals to the point of annihilation and makes them commit suicide.
- Gambling tarnishes the honour and reputation of the individuals and endangers their social status.
- Gambling makes the body of an individuals feeble and sick.
- Gambling destroys the faith and confidence of the individuals and becomes the cause of Divine wrath.

In short gambling destroys the prospects of this world and the Hereafter, the body and the soul, the honour and wealth and everything else belonging to the persons concerned.

Now it is the duty of every individual to prevent himself and his family from this curse and to abstain from associating with the gamblers and from attending gambling parties and everything else which may possibly become the cause of his becoming involved in this dirty business.

Truly speaking the demon of gambling should be treated like a contagious disease and an all-out campaign (which should, of course, be sound and wise) should be started against it.

When a dangerous disease (like cholera or plague) is likely to spread in a country, the health organizations, in order to combat with it, inform all the people about its danger, recommend preventive measures and provide the facilities for vaccination. If necessary they also resort to compulsory quarantine and inoccultation and prevent people from associating with those who are suffering from the disease. At times the dress of the patient is burnt. At times the area affected by the disease is burnt after evacuation of patients. The patients are secluded from their families. They are not permitted to meet the people (especially children and youngsters) and a number of free facilities are provided to them.

It is necessary, therefore, that similar but more minute and basic steps should be taken in the matter of gambling. People should be informed of the curses and dangers of gambling and its evils should be explained to them. The gambling centres should be closed. The gamblers should be employed on useful jobs. Constructive work should be provided for young men for their vacant hours. Association of the gamblers with the people (and especially with youngsters) should be prohibited and necessary steps should be taken for the reforming of the persons who are crazy about gambling by psychiatrists and religious leaders so that by the blessings of Allah, this dangerous evil may be eradicated from the Muslim society.

Quotations
1. Satan wants to induce hostility and hatred amongst you through wine and gambling and to prevent you from remembering Allah and prayers. (The holy Qur'an)
2. It is a sin to greet a gambler and one who watches gambling as an onlooker or one who wishes him good luck are equally sinful. An assembly formed for the purposes of gambling is one of those assemblies which are the object of Divine wrath which may be expected at any time. (Imam Ja'far Sadiq)
3. Allah has made all kinds of gambling unlawful and has ordered the people to avoid them. Allah has declared gambling to be uncleanness and the act of Satan and warned people of getting involved in it. (Imam Ali Riza)

FALSEHOOD

Human nature has been endowed by Allah with honesty and truth. If man retains his inherent nature and the external influence and factors do not make him deviate from the path of nature he will always be inclined towards piety and excellence and will be free from evils and obscenity.

By nature, man is truthful, honest, bold and noble. However, different factors like training, environments etc. prevent the appearance of these characteristics and even replace them by base qualities. One of the most essential responsibilities of the Prophets is to assist human naure against external factors in this sense that with their sublime teachings they strengthen the natural faculties and prepare the ground for the adoption of excellent human qualities.

Falsehood is opposed to the nature of man and it pulls him from truth and honesty to evils and destruction and it is even transmitted like a contagious disease from father to son, from teacher to pupil and from the customer to the seller and makes their nature deviate from their inherent nature.

Possibly most of the people consider falsehood to be something insignificant although the losses which accrue from falsehood are too great to be compared with losses resulting from other sins and the disaster to which the society is exposed on account of falsehood is beyond our imagination.

It has often happened that an impostor, in order to achieve his base ends, has made a false claim to prophethood and has, with one lie, pulled thousands of persons from the right path to perversion and absolute adversity or some other swindler has claimed to be *'Bāb'* or *'qutb'* etc. and a large number of persons have been misled on account of their false Divine claim.

With which other sins can such grave sins be compared and with the losses of which sins can the losses accruing therefrom be judged? It is for this reason that Islam has considered falsehood to be the characteristic of faithless persons and the holy Qur'an says explicitly: *Those who do not believe in the miracles of Allah invent lies and they are liars.* (Surah an-Nahl, 16 :105)

Imam Ali has considered falsehood to be the worst curse and says: "Falsehood is the most indecent act". (Amāli Sadūq)

Imam Muhammad Baqir has considered falsehood to be the destroyer of the root of faith and says: "Falsehood is the source of ruination of faith". (al-Kāfi, Vol. II)

Imam Ali considers the perception of the reality of faith as connected with the abandonment of various kinds of falsehood and says: "In no circumstances can anyone understand the reality of faith unless he forsakes falsehood, whether it is told seriously or in jest". (Mahāsin Barqi)

The holy Prophet was asked: "Is it possible that a true believer may be a coward?" He replied: "Yes".

Then he was asked: "Can he be a miser?" He replied: "Yes".

Then he was asked: "Is it possible that he may be a liar?" He replied: "No". (Wasā'ilush Shi'ah)

In another tradition the holy Prophet has been reported to have said: "The worst and the most indecent statement is a false statement". (Bihārul Anwār, Vol. LXXII, p. 659)

Imam Ali says: "The habit of telling lies is the source of indigence and perplexity". (Khisal Sadūq)

The holy Prophet says: "Let me tell you about the biggest of the major sins. They consist of: Associating anyone else with Allah and displeasing and misbehaving with one's parents and telling lies". (Makāsib, Shaykh Ansani, p. 50)

A famous psychologist says: "From amongst all the base characteristics and abominable qualities, falsehood is the most indecent and detestable thing. This miserable habit either takes its root from moral degradation or corruption or it is the result of loose morals and cowardice. It is very surprising that most of the people look at it unconcernedly and heedlessly and often instruct their servants and agents to tell lies. Of course, if they later find that their servants also tell them lies they should not be surprised and should not be annoyed with them". (Morals, Samuel Smiles, p. 281)

Imam Hasan Askari has considered falsehood to be the key of all evils and wickedness. He says: "When all evils and sins invade a house the root cause is falsehood". (Mustadrak, Vol. II) That is to say falsehood prepares a ground for all evils.

In Islam the Muslims, besides being prohibited strictly to tell lies, have been ordered not to associate themselves with liars.

Imam Ali made the following recommendations to his son Imam Hasan: "My son! Refrain from befriending a foolish person because even though he wishes to do good to you yet as he is unable to discern between good and bad thing, he does you harm. Refrain from befriending a miserly person because on account of his stinginess he withholds from you the thing which you need most. Do not befriend a debauche and a wicked person because he will not hesitate to sell you at the lowest price. And refrain from befriending a man who is an incorrigible liar because he is like a mirage which shows you the things which are at a distance to be near and those which are near to be at a distance. With his false statements he makes the easy tasks to look difficult and the difficult ones to look easy and thus prevents you from achieving your object". (Nahjul Balaghah)

Just as falsehood makes one indulge in other sins also, similarly, avoiding the habit of telling lies or feeling repentance for past falsehood will ensure him freedom from many other sins.

A man came before the holy Prophet and said: "O Prophet of Allah! I offer prayers but also commit adultery and tell lies. I now wish to repent for one of these sins and to give it up. Kindly advise me as to which of them I should give up".

The holy Prophet replied: "Abstain from telling lies".

The man accepted the holy Prophet's instruction and decided not to tell lies in any circumstances. He only gave up telling lies and consequently remained safe from other sins because when he thought of committing adultery he thought within himself: "If the holy Prophet asks me whether I have committed adultery since the day on which I repented for my lies what will be my reply? If I reply in the negative I will have told a lie and acted against the promise made by me. And if I reply in the affirmative I will be admitting having committed adultery and will be punished for it. The same will be the case as regards other sins. Thus his abstaining from falsehood became the cause of his immunity from many other sins". (Mustadrakul Wasā'il, Vol. II)

It is necessary here to allude to a point that since falsehood takes it root from the soul it is necessary for reforming the liars, the cause for this habit should be detected and thereafter the requisite remedy may be undertaken because so long as the cause is not detected, proper measure of eradicating this curse could not be adopted.

The holy Prophet says: "A liar does not tell a lie except when he feels himself inferior and small within himself". (Mustadrakul Wasā'il, Vol. II)

For this very reason, by undertaking a brief study of the condition of a liar it becomes known that the cause for one's telling lies is weakness of character, fear, helplessness and a sense of inferiority or any other similar mental illness.

The holy Prophet has been reported to have said: "The person most devoid of human instincts is the one who tells lies". (Ikhtisās, p. 232)

A person who possesses moral courage can never tell a lie. Only that person tells lies who feels weakness and humiliation within himself. In fact it may be said that characterless, timid and weak persons take refuge in telling lies.

Imam Ali says: "If various qualities are classified according to similarities, truth will be with bravery and falsehood will be with fear and cowardice". (Ghurarul Hikam)

A psychologist says: "Falsehood is the best weapon of weak persons and the quickest means for averting temporary danger. For this reason the habit of telling lies is current among the members of the coloured races who have been faced continuously with the sense of slavery and heavy pressures under the yoke of the white races and feel the authority which the white men exercises on them.

In some cases falsehood is nothing but the reflection of weakness. When we say to a child: 'Have you touched these sweets? or 'Have you broken this glass?' and the child knows that if he admits havng done these things he will be punished, his instinct of defence makes him reply: 'I have not done it'. (Raymond Peach)

At times this habit is observed in the children and if it is not amended properly by correct education and training it entails great dangers and sometimes becomes a helpless case.

The first and the most important duty of the parents and the tutors in general is that they should not tell lies to the children and should not make false promises to them.

The holy Prophet says: "May Allah bless the father who assists his child to do good". The narrator asked: "How should he assist his son?" The holy Prophet gave him the following four instructions in this behalf:

(i) He should assess the strength and the ability of his child and should accept from him the work which he does according to his capacity.

(ii) He should not impose on his child anything which exceeds his capacity.

(iii) He should not force him to commit sin and rebellion.

(iv) He should not lie to him and should not do foolish things before him". (al-Kāfi)

One of the reasons for the children telling lies is the imposition of heavy duties on them and expectig them to do things beyond their capacity. Severity of the guardians of the children and their wrong expectations from them which are beyond their capacity make the children take refuge in telling lies and create indecent habit in them.

Bertrand Russell says: "The possibility of telling a lie does not occur to the mind of a small child in the first instance. Later this possibility is revealed to him relatively i.e. he observes the possibility of telling a lie from his elders. Fear also obliges him to resort to it. The child discovers that the grown up persons tell him lies and if he tells them the truth it would be dangerous for him. He begins telling lies under the influence of these conditions and circumstances. If you yourself avoid telling lies the idea of telling a lie will not occur in the mind of a child".

Reymond Peach says: "I know a grown up girl who is now an incorrigible liar. When she was seven years old she attended a class in which twenty five children received education. A female attendant took her to the school every day and also followed her when the classes were over. This attendant was responsible for looking after the girl so that she carried out her duties and learnt her lessons. In short this woman was responsible for the education of child.

According to the educational system prevalent in those days, which has since been totally discarded and is considered to be fruitless, the children were awarded grades every day on the basis of written tests and it was determined as to which of them had acquired first, second, third positions etc. Every day, as soon as the girl came out of the classroom with satchel in hand her attendant asked her with great eagerness, "What position have you acquired?" And if she could reply that she had stood first or second it was all right.

However, once it so happened that on three consecutive days the girl got the third position and it may be said that standing third among as many as twenty five children is quite commendable. However, her attendant was not one of those persons who might perceive this reality. She tolerated the girl's standing third twice but could not bear it on the third day and while the child was very much frightened on account of perplexity she cried: "So there is no end to your standing third? Tomorrow you must stand first. Do you hear me? You must stand first".

The girl was absorbed in thoughts about this harsh and decisive order throughout the day and in the morning of the following day also she was scared on this account. On that day she made her best efforts to do well in the test. All her subtractions were correct. Answers to all the questions relating to additions were correct. She recited all her lessons well. Till about noon, therefore, when the turn of dictation came, her entire work was satisfactory. However, four mistakes occurred in the dictation and eventually on that day also she secured the third position. And this time also her standing third was to be a great affliction for her.

When the last bell rang the attendant was standing by the door of the classroom waiting for the girl to come out. Immediately on seeing her she asked: 'What news?' The girl could no not pick up courage to speak the truth and replied: 'I have stood first'. And this was the starting point of her habit of telling lies.

There are many parents who behave like this and thus take on their shoulders the heavy burden of sinfulness and responsibility for the lies told by their children".

Bertrand Russell says: "If a child begins telling lies it is for the parent to feel themselves responsible. They should remove the causes and tell him calmly and by adducing arguments as to why it is better not to tell lies. In order to correct the fault of the child they should not at all resort to beating and punishment, because doing so only increases fear which is the stimulant for telling lies".

Of course, if it is desired that the children may not tell lies there is no alternative except that the elders should strictly observe truthfulness before the children. When the parents teach their children not to tell lies but at the same time the children observe that they themselves tell lies, such parents naturally lose all authority and moral influence on them.

Another kind of falsehood which is very harmful for the children is that they are threatened with a punishment which it is not intended to put into practice.

Dr Ballard in emphatic words says: "Do not threaten, but if you do threaten do not allow anythig to prevent that threat being put into practice".

The vigilance of the parents and the tutors can protect the children from falling a prey to the curse of telling lies.

If the child is not belittled and his personality is not crushed; if the elders do not make him learn lying by telling lies themselves, if the factors of betaking oneself to lying (like fear, punishment etc.) are eliminated; if the parents are not harsh with him unnecessarily and do not behave in a despotic manner and in short if they adopt a wise step with kindness he will certainly not be forced to the bad habit of telling lies.

The parents are extremely annoyed on account of their children telling lies, especially when the lie is an unbelievable lie and the liar is unexperienced.

Why does a child tell a lie? At times the children tell lies because they are not permitted to speak the truth. If a child tells his mother that he hates his brother, his mother may at once give him a slap on his face, but if, after a few moments he tells her falsely that he has now begun loving his brother she may possibly kiss him warmly and also give him a fine gift. What does a child learn from such a behaviour? He may possibly conclude that speaking of the truth is the cause of trouble and telling lies on the other hand brings happiness and it also ends in receiving gifts from the mother.

Hence if we wish to teach truthfulness to a child it is necessary that we should lend ears to his bitter truths with the same ease and calmness with which we hear his sweet truths.

When a child is punished for telling the truth, naturally he will resort to telling lies in his self defence.

The parents should not ask their children questions which will compel them to tell lies in order to defend themselves. The children are reluctant to be interrogated by their parents unnecessarily, especially when they know that the replies to the questions are already known.

Our only aim should be to make the child understand that it is not necessary for him to tell lies.

The most important matter in this behalf is reminding the children about their religious duty viz. that it is a great sin to tell lies and Allah is displeased with a liar.

If the children are brought up according to the principles of Islam and their morals are compatible with the Divine teachings no abnormality will appear in them because no principle guarantees the enforcement of laws like Divine faith.

It is this very principle which holds the believers back from being involved in telling lies and committing other sins and provides them a sort of spiritual immunity.

The late Allama Narāqi says: "The best means of eradicating the bad habit of telling lies is that one should attend to the Qur'anic verses and traditions which have condemned the habit of telling lies in order that he may come to know that the telling of lies leads to eternal ruination. Besides, one should be made to realize apart from this ruination in the Hereafter, will also be deprived of social status and respect in the eyes of the people". (Jāmi'us Sādāt, Vol. II, p. 256)

Dr Alexis Carrel says: "The most injurious habits for the

elevation of one's soul are telling lies, instigating, slandering, committing theft, misappropriation and desiring everything for one's personal interest. Human sould can never prosper amidst pollution and falsehood".

Imam Ali says: "Speak the truth, because Allah is with the truthful. Keep away from falsehood because it destroys the faith. A truthful person is on the path of prosperity and salvation while a liar is at the brink of disgrace and disaster. (Biharul Anwār, Vol. LXXII, p. 260)

The famous Persian poet, Shaykh Sa'di says:

"Man should be truthful even though calamities rain on him like hail-stones.

Speak the truth and do not fear, because truth neither takes away one's sustenance nor brings about one's death.

The various losses entailed by falsehood become manifest when a little study of the conditions of the liars is conducted".

From the social point of view falsehood entails irreparable loss to the society. The reputation of a liar in the society is at stake and he is always looked down with disgrace. What disgrace could be greater than this that his lies should become known to the people and his self-respect is ruined.

Wise persons always endeavour to enjoy respect in the society and are prepared to spend their wealth to acquire social honour. The asset of self-respect is the most valuable of all assets. However, a liar loses this valuable asset with his own hands and by his own indecent act.

One of the leaders of Shaykhiya sect was speaking in Tabriz, from the pulpit. During his speech he mentioned the names of the kings of the genii and stated as to which of them ruled earlier and which came to the throne later. He said something like this: "The first king of this dynasty was Tehtamshah. He was followed by Qehqamshah and he by Jehjamshah and so on". The speaker continued his speech till he reached the name of the tenth or the eleventh king whose name too was similar to those of the earlier kings. In the meantime a witty person who was sitting by the pulpit got up and said: "Sir, will you kindly repeat the name of the fifth king?" The speaker could not give a reply because he did not remember as to which name he had given to the fifth fictitious king.

Now the learned readers can very well imagine the disgrace which this foolish speaker met on account of telling blatant lies.

George Herbert says: "In whatever guise and cover falsehood may be it will eventually appear in its true shape".

Besides the fact that a liar loses his respect in the society he also loses people's trust which is one of the most important basis of one's social life. No one accepts his words so much so that even if at one time he happens to speak the truth, people are not prepared to believe him.

Aristotle says: "Those who tell lies are punished in the way that even when they speak the truth nobody believes them".

Sa'di says: "If a person, who is truthful by habit makes a mistake people ignore it. However, if he is notorious for telling lies nobody believes him even if he happens to speak the truth".

The holy Prophet says: "Refrain from telling lies because falsehood brings disgrace to the liar".

Falsehood is also very harmful from the economic point of view, because acquisition of wealth usually necessitates transaction with the people and as we usually see the transaction, especially big transaction take place on credit and the support for such transaction is the mutual trust of the people. Falsehood destroys trust and this affects the business of the liar which results in loss.

Another loss consequent upon falsehood is arousing of the agitation of mind from which the liars suffer on many occasions and which involve them in serious mental cases.

One of the famous authors writes in his book: "I uttered one lie due to carelessness and as a consequence thereof suffered from mental pain for thirty years. The incident was like this: One night some friends and colleagues of mine were present in a party. Conversation started about travelling in foreign countries. Those present spoke about the jouneys which they had undertaken to Europe, America, the Middle East and the Far East. Being keen not to lag behind the caravan I also joined the conversation and spoke about my journey to France, notwithstanding the fact that I had not been to that country. However, it occurred to me suddenly that one of the persons present in the party who had visited France might ask me questions about it and this would be a matter of disgrace for me. I remained very much worried till eventually the party came to an end. From that night onwards, however, I perpetually saw the phantom of disgrace before my eyes and I was always worried lest one of the members of that party should be present at some place and I might carelessly say something opposed to my claim (i.e. visit to France) and be disgraced.

This mental pain tortured me so much that I decided to get rid of it by paying a visit to France. Unfortunately sufficient means did not become available to me to undertake this journey and my efforts in this behalf proved fruitless till after thirty years I did visit France and got rid of my mental agony.

Of course, I uttered one lie and suffered for thirty years. The result, however, was that I decided that very night that I would not tell a lie till the end of my life".

The historians have written thus: "Very cordial relations existed between Sultan Husayn Baiqara, the king of Khorasan and Zābulistan (Iran) and Sultan Ya'qūb, the King of Iraq and Āzarbaijān and they corresponded with each other regularly.

The King of Iran decided to send valuable presents for Sultan Ya'qūb. When the gifts were ready he ordered that a copy of the book entitled *'Kulliyāt-i Jāmi'* (Works of Jāmi), which carried much value in those days, might be brought from the royal library and be added to the gifts.

Mulla Abdul Karim, the chief librarian made a mistake while picking up the book and, instead of *'Kulliyāt-i Jāmi'*, added *'Futūhāt-i Makki'* to the gifts. The mistake was due to the fact that the two books resembled each other very much in the matter of size and cover.

Amir Husayn Abiwardi, who was a distinguished personality of the royal court, was deputed to take the gifts, including *'Kulliyāt-i Jāmi'* to the court of Sultan Ya'qūb and present the same to him. He also took the book without looking into it and proceeded to the place of his assignment.

When Amir Husayn reached Tabriz and was granted audience by Sultan Ya'qūb, the Sultan accorded a warm welcome to him and said: "You must have been troubled and got tired during this long journey". However, as Amir Husayn was aware of the Sultan's keen interest in Jāmi's book he submitted: "During the journey I had a close companion with me and

I, therefore, did not at all feel the rigours of the journey".

The Sultan asked: "Who was your co-traveller?" Amir Husayn replied: "The works of Jāmi.

The Sultan was immensely pleased to hear this and ordered that the book might be brought to him.

Amir Husayn sent someone and the book was brought. However, when it was opened it turned out to be *'Futūhāt-i Makki'* and not *'Kulliyāt-i Jāmi'*.

Amir Husayn was dumb-founded on account of the lie which he had told. Unfortunately, however, the die had been cast and no amends could be made for the incident".

The reputation of that politician and diplomat was ruined and he lost his esteem not only in the eyes of the two monarchs but in both the countries as well.

Numerous historical events have been recorded in the books of history which tell about the great losses which people suffered on account of telling lies.

Study of the lives of our contemporaries can also throw ample light on the evils of telling lies.

It is on account of these very losses that Islam has launched an intensive campaign against falsehood and considered it to be one of the curses of faithless and characterless persons and treated the liar to be cursed and condemned person.

The holy Prophet says: "The angels curse a person who tells a lie without sufficient excuse. (Jami'us Sādāt, Vol. II)

Imam Ja'far Sadiq says: "A liar is devoid of manliness". (Khisāl, Saduq, Vol. I)

Imam Riza considers truthfulness and repayment of deposits as the criterion of faith and worth of the people, and says: "Test the people with two things: One of them is truthfulness at the time of speaking and the other is being honest in the matter of holding the property of the people in trust". (Ghurarul Hikam)

Falshood is Justified by its Motive

In the foregoing pages it has been stated that falsehood is one of the major sins. We now propose to discuss falsehood which is justified by its motive.

As a matter of principle the sins which have been treated as unlawful and unpermissible in Islam are of two kinds:

(i) Those sins in which indecency is inherent and which are automatically treated to be a part of obscene acts, for example murder, oppression, violation of the rights of others, theft etc.

(ii) Those sins which are preliminaries to corruption and prepare the ground for other crimes as quoted in the foregoing narratives is the key to all sins and evils.

Hence, if an occasion arises when falsehood becomes the means of prevention of sin or the key to an oppressed person getting rid of oppression its inadmissibility is eliminated and it is excluded fundamentally from the category of sin. This is so because its indecency is not inherent and its accidental indecency is also eliminated for some good purpose. In such cases falsehood is not only not unlawful, but it is obligatory also if it ensures the safety and the honour of a Muslim.

Imam Ja'far Sadiq says: "If a Muslim is asked to give a trace of some other Muslim and he speaks the truth and as a result of his speaking the truth the other Muslim meets harm the name of that person who told truth will be recorded under the category of liars. And if a Muslim is inquired about some other Muslim and he tells a lie and as a result of his lying the other Muslim benefits, he (i.e. the person who told a lie) will be considered to be one of the truthful persons in the eyes of Allah.

Sa'di the renowned poet of Iran says in Gulistan:

"It is said that a king ordered the execution of a prisoner. The helpless person began abusing the king in a state of despair. For it has been said that one who loses hope of life speaks out whatever he has in his heart".

The king asked: "What is he saying?"

A good-natured minister replied: "Your Majesty! He says: "The king has taken pity on me and has condoned the death sentence". The king took pity and refrained from putting him to death.

Another minister who was opposed to the first one said: "We people should not speak before the kings except the truth. This man has abused the king".

The king got annoyed on hearing these words and said: "I have liked his lying more than your truth because that was directed to a good purpose and this is based on malice and the wise men have said: A lie directed to a good purpose is better than a truth which causes mischief".

The holy Prophet says: "There are three occasions on which falsehood is justified:
(i) Practising deception during war. (ii) A husband's promise to his wife, and (iii) Reconciliation between the people.

Explanation
(i) As regards deception during war the learned readers must note that Islam considers war for the purpose of conquest to be unpermissible. Islamic wars are a combat between truth and falsehood and deception in such wars is desirable because it becomes the means of strengthening the truth and weakening the falsehood.
(ii) As regards a promise made by a husband with his wife, it may be stated that Islam is keen for the prosperity and happiness of the spouses and wishes that they should lead their conjugal life with deep love and affection. It is for this reason that it has permitted the husband to make a false promise and the intention is that if he can meet the demand of his wife and keep his promise well and good, but even if he cannot meet her request or does not consider it expedient to accept it, he keeps his wife happy by making such a promise and does not injure her sentiments.
(iii) As regards reconciliation between the people it may be said that Islam wishes that friendly relations should exist between Muslims and if differences arise between two persons or two groups, efforts should be made to remove them. Removal of the mutual differences of Muslims is undoubtedly in the interest of the two parties concerned and the society and it is for this reason that telling lies to bring about reconciliation between the people has been reckoned to be commendable.

The holy Prophet says: "One who plans to bring about reconciliation between the people does not lie".

Imam Ja'far Sadiq says: "Lying is indecent and undesirable except in two cases: To repel the mischief of the oppressors and to bring about reconciliation between the people". (al-Kāfi)

Generally speaking as and when one who tells lies and his object is to protect a Muslim from mischief and harm or to bring about a reconciliation between the people, his lie is good and desirable. This is so because in this case falsehood is no longer a key to sins, but it is a key to beneficence and kindness to the people. Of course, such falsehood is also permissible and desirable only when it is not possible to speak the truth and it is only in such circumstances that falsehood becomes permissible or obligatory and speaking the truth becomes prohibited or unpermissible.

In the end it should also be noted that falsehood for good purpose is also permissible only in those circumstances in which it has been declared permissible by Islam and when its abandonment becomes the cause of dangers and losses. However, falsehood with the object of material benefits or personal gains does not fall under the category of 'falsehood for good purpose'. Such falsehood is absolutely unlawful and falls withing the purview of the Qur'anic verses and traditions prohibiting falsehood and is a source of humiliation and adversity in this world and in the Hereafter.

Quotations

1. Those who tell lies are not believers. (The holy Qur'an)
2. The most timid person is he who tells lies.
(The holy Prophet)
3. The habit of telling lies is the worst of all the evils.
4. It is proper that a Muslim may not establish friendship and brotherhood with a liar. (Imam Ali)
5. Falsehood destroys the foundation of faith. (Imam Baqir)
6. A wise man does not tell lies, even though by doing so it may be possible for him to achieve his carnal desires.
(Imam Musa Kazim)

* * * * * *

SOCIAL RELATIONSHIP

There is no doubt about the fact that man by nature is social and he must lead a social and collective life, because his needs make it necessary that he should meet them with the co-operation of other human beings. Every person should be responsible for some work and every group should solve a problem so that life should be happy and pleasant and prosperous for all.

There is also no doubt about it that living collectively can ensure prosperity and happiness only when the individuals are aware of their duties and respect the rights of one another.

Furthermore, the mutual relations of the individuals should be based on human relations mingled with sentiments and noble behaviour. If philanthropy, goodness towards subordinates, patience, benevolence, kindness, public service, co-operation etc. do not exist in a society, such a society cannot at all be called civilized and prosperous.

Islam, which is a Divine religion, has attached much importance to social relations and has given thorough and comprehensive orders for strengthening the ties of brotherhood and friendship of the individuals with one another.

If we wish to say sometihing absolutely correct in this regard we should say. "Islam has ordered the people to do things which are desirable and useful for the betterment and strengthening of social relations and has asked them to avoid things which do the least harm to these relations and become the cause of their being hampered.

Those who are well acquainted with the tenets of Islam do not stand in need of any reasoning to prove the correctness of what has been stated above. As regards others they can also realize this undeniable reality if they glance at the comprehensive rules enacted by the law-giver of Islam for the preservation, betterment and strengthening of social relations.

It is interesting to note that in the social programme of Islam those matters have been looked after which are not taken care of by most of the people and to which they do not attach much importance, whereas these are the very petty and insignificant matters which produce great results.

For example the simplest relations of the people with one another are their encounters and meetings on the roads and in the streets, the bus, the masjid, the school etc. These contacts are considered by most of the people to be quite unimportant, although from the view-point of Islam they should take place in special conditions so that they may promote mutual friendship, love and kindness.

Islam recommends that these simple contacts should take place with open heart and salutation and, if possible, with the shaking of hands with feelings of warmth. The holy Prophet says: "The person most worthy before Allah and His Prophet is he who makes the beginning with salutation".

Imam Muhammad Baqir says: "Allah likes those of His slaves who salute one another explicitly and openly".

Imam Ali says: "Do not be annoyed and do not annoy others. Salute one another openly and offer night prayers so that you may attain Paradise and eternal bliss". (al-Kāfi, IV)

The holy Prophet says: "I swear by the Lord in whose hands my life is that you cannot attain Paradise and eternal bliss unless you become true believers and you cannot become true believers unless you love one another". Then he asked the people: "May I guide you towards an act as a result whereof you will develop mutual friendship and love?" The people replied in the affirmative. Thereupon he said: "Salute one another open-heartedly". (Huqūq-i Islami, p. 341)

Though salutation is treated to be something petty and unimportant it plays a significant role in creating mutual friendship and love among the people which cannot be described.

Dale Carnegie carried out the study of a well-know person who enjoyed considerable popularity among the people and has said about him: "One of the reasons for his unusual popularity was that he used to wish everyone". (How to win friends and influence people, Dale Carnegie)

It is possible that everyone may have experienced during his life that many valuable friendships starts by means of a salutation or its repetitions and many enmities are also eliminated as a consequence of salutation.

Besides recommending salutation and insisting upon it so that this desirable practice may not be discontinued by the people, Islam has ordered that if a person begins talking without saluting in the first instance a reply should not be given to him.

The holy Prophet says: "Do not reply to a person who begins talking without having saluted". (al-Kāfi)

Furthermore the great leader of Islam has described those who abandon salutation to be the most miserly persons.

The holy Prophet says: "The most miserly person is he who is miserly in the matter of salutation".

Another duty which the Muslims must perform is that they should meet one another with cheerful and smiling faces.

Imam Muhammad Baqir says: "One's act of smiling while meeting a brother Muslim is reckoned to be a generous and noble act". (Makārimul Akhlāq, p. 314)

Imam Riza says: "Allah will give a good reward to a person who smiles when he meets his brethren-in-faith". (Safinatul Bihār, Vol. I, p. 613)

The contemporary psychologists consider this Islamic rule to be the secret of success in one's life.

Albert Hubbard says: "When you leave your house keep your head raised and breathe deeply and absorb the rays of the sun in your body and meet your friends and acquaintances with a smile and when you shake hands breathe your spirit in them".

Dale Carnegie says: "Action speaks louder than words and a smile says: 'I love you. You make me happy. I am glad to meet you". (How to win friends and influence people)

A Chinese proverb says: "One who does not have a smile on his face should not open his shop".

Another important matter which is the subject of emphatic

recommendation by the leaders of Islam in connection with the Muslims meeting one another is the shaking of hands and pressing them warmly.

The holy Prophet says: "As and when anyone of you meets a brother Muslim he should salute him and shake hands with him". Furthermore he is reported to have said: "Salutation at the time of your contact with one another will become complete only when it is accompanied by a handshake". (Huqūq-i Islami)

This is the first step towards creating good relations in the Muslim society so that they may meet one another in their daily contacts in a friendly and cordial manner and may establish their relations on the basis of cordiality and sincerity.

After attaining this stage we arrive at other instructions given by Islam to the Muslims to the effect that they should love their brethren-in-faith from the core of their hearts.

Loving others is one of the distinguished inclinations of man. It is this very spiritual inclination which makes man take notice of others and makes individuals kind to one another and creates the sense of responsibility to share in the weal and woe of one another.

Like other sublime human inclinations, the inclination of love for others is weak and lifeless and it does not become strong without training and guidance. If the parents and the educators pay attention to the children from their young age and perform their duties properly they can gradually develop this human attribute in their nature and bring them up as philanthropic and sympathetic persons.

If self-love is supported and strengthened it is aggravated and transgresses the limits of propriety. Consequently it is transformed into egotism and selfishness and creates great evils. It involves man in moral sins and violation of the rights of others and inclines him towards inhuman activities.

If love for others is supported and strengthened it prevails upon animal instinct, weakens the instinct of destruction, suppresses brutality and fierceness and endows man with one of the most sublime human qualities.

It must also be pointed out that what is meant by love for others is love and kindness for the human beings from the standpoint of moral excellence and human qualities. It does not mean that the object of love should be the satisfaction of material desires.

An ailing person expresses attachment for the doctor who treats him and the nurse who attends him. However, the psychological origin of this attachment is not love for others and sublime human inclination. On the other hand this attachment springs from the instinct of love for one's self and life. The regard of a patient for the doctor and the nurse is on this account that they treat him and restore his health and thus satisfy his instinct of self-love. Such love is found even among the animals and is not particular to human beings.

A real lover of others is one who loves human beings on account of their being human and whose love is inspired by pure human sentiments and which is free from the taint of selfishness and personal interest. Such love is indicative of the sublimity and purity of one's soul and is one of the specialities of man. Attachment and love of this kind distinguishes the life of human beings from the life of animals, maintans cordial relation of human societies with one another, joins the hearts of the people with the ties of human love and revives the spirit of brotherhood and co-operation. Such love keeps the people away from animal and brutal nature, provides them security and safety, creates an atmosphere of peace and sincerity and makes life sweet and pleasant.

In the Divine religion of Islam the question of love for other human beings has been paid much attention and the religious leaders have deemed this desirable trait to be one of the main factors of man's progress and prosperity and one of the means of attaining the Divine blessings.

Imam Musa Kazim says: "So long as the inhabitants of the earth love one another and return the things held in trust and behave in accordance with truth and reality they lead their lives under the blessings and kindness". (Majmū'ā Warrām, Vol. I)

Imam Ali says: "The most effective thing by means of which you can attain the Divine blessings is that you should have a kind heart for all human beings". (Ghurarul Hikam, p. 212)

He further says: "Allah likes that people should be the well-wishers of one another". (Ghurarul Hikam, p. 271)

Philanthropy and benevolence have been the outstanding

attributes of the Prophets of Allah and spiritual leaders. They were fond of the prosperity and happiness of human beings and were grieved on account of their perversion and ignorance.

The point which should be hinted at here is that whereas Islam recommends emphatically benevolence and goodness towards all human beings irrespective of their race and country it also believes that in order to create an unbreakable and durable tie it is necessary that there should be a strong and firm foundation which should never shake and should unite and join all human beings with one another.

Islam does not consider the proposition of common language, country, race etc. to be genuine and reliable because although it is possible that these things may become the cause of mutual realtions to some extent but if stronger factors like material frictions and conflicts crop up these connections break and yield their place to animosity and rebellion.

Islam believes that if all the human beings follow one law and religion the spirit of brotherhood will take its root and their mutual relations will be brotherly and sincere even though they may belong to different races and countries and may speak different languages. In that event no factor will be able to weaken their mutual relations or to make their behaviour inimical.

A glance at the history of the early days of Islam confirms this view. The day on which the holy Prophet was appointed to the prophetic mission with the sublime teachings of Islam for the salvation of mankind, the Arabian Peninsula, notwithstanding the fact that its inhabitants spoke one language and belonged to one race and one country, was burning in the fire of war, enmity and transgression and the thing which could not be seen in that region was security, peace and human relation between the people.

The holy Prophet undertook the guidance of that nation and within a short span of time the same people who had been inimical towards one another for centuries and had developed the habit of crime and bloodshed became the brothers of one another, under the auspices of the teachings of Islam in such a way that no trace of that malevolence, hatred, transgression and bloodshed remained any longer, and virtue, purity, benevolence and other noble human qualities took the place of those savage and undesirable attributes.

The holy Qur'an gives this relationship the name of 'the rope of Allah' and says: *All of you as one unit, seek the protection of Allah and recall how He favoured you when your hostility to each other had torn you apart. He united your hearts in one faith and through His Grace you became brothers. You were on the verge of falling headlong into the abyss of Fire, but Allah saved you.* (Surah Ale Imran, 3:103)

The religious relationship and unity is so strong and deep-rooted that every Muslim, to whichever race he may belong and in whichever region of the world he may be residing, does not consider himself to be separate from his brethren-in-faith. He shares their happiness and sorrow.

The holy Prophet has explained this reality in these words: "In the matter of their love, friendship and sentiments the faithful are like one body. When one of its limbs becomes uneasy other limbs sympathize with it in the form of uneasiness". (Islam wa Huqūq-i Bashar)

The holy Qur'an considers this unbreakable and genuine relationship to be the relationship of brotherhood and says: *Believers are each other's brothers. Restore peace among your brothers. Have fear of Allah so that perhaps you receive mercy.* (Surah al-Hujurāt, 49:10)

In relation to this tie it becomes necessary to establish relations and mutual love so that the Muslims should love one another for the sake of Allah.

It has been quoted from Imam Ja'far Sadiq that the holy Prophet said: "Allah has slaves who will find place, on the Day of Judgement, under the shadow of His Kindness and Blessings. Their faces will be very white and bright like the sun. They are the persons who have loved one another for the sake of Allah and have been kind to one another". (Huqūq-i Islami, p. 304)

In order that this tie of brotherhood may not be broken, Islam has encouraged the factors and directions which strengthen it and strictly instructed to observe them such as salutation, shaking hands, visiting the relations, friends and the sick, beneficence and charitable acts, public service, entertainment and hospitality and making efforts to meet the needs of others and has disapproved the acts which are the cause of severing the spirit of brotherhood and warned the Mulims against their commitment, for example, lack of regard for the people, back-biting and finding faults with others, teasing and hurting others, gossip-mongering, prying into the affairs of others, contempt and reproach, lack of co-operation, derision etc.

Here we mention very briefly some acts recommended and forbidden by Islam which have a great bearing on social relations and also quote a few specimens of the sayings of the illustrious leaders of Islam.

Creating Happiness

The holy Prophet says: "Whoever makes a believer happy makes me happy".

The holy Prophet further says: "The act most liked by Allah is making the believers happy". (Jāmi'us Sa'ādāt, Vol. II)

Meeting the Needs of the People

The holy Prophet says: "The spiritual reward of a person who meets the need of a brother believer is as much as if he had worshipped Allah for a lifetime". (Wasā'ilush Shi'ah)

Imam Musa Kazim says: "Allah has some slaves on the face of the earth who make efforts to meet the needs of the people. Those slaves of Allah will be safe from harships and afflictions on the Day of Judgement": (al-Kāfi)

Solving the problem and meeting the needs of others has a deep effect in creating love and strengthening the relations of the individuals and at times it so happens that such behaviour ends in forming a close and mutual friendship.

Back-biting

One of the curses which deals a serious blow to social relations and has been strongly opposed in Islam is back-biting.

The holy Qur'an says: *Do not spy on one another and back-bite.* (Surah al-Hujurāt, 49:12)

In one of his sermons the holy Prophet reproached the back-biters and said: "O you people who have expressed belief with your tongues but whose hearts are unaware of it! Do not open your mouths to slander the Muslims and do not seek to discover their faults because when a person peeps at the faults of his brother-in-faith Allah tears his veil, divulges his faults and disgraces him". (Jāmi'us Sa'ādāt)

The holy Prophet says: "Any assembly which flourishes and becomes lively with back-biting and vilification will be desolate from the view-point of religion. O Muslims! Keep your ears away from hearing because one who vilifies and one who hears vilification are partners in sin". (Ihyā'ul Ulūm, Vol. III)

A psychoanalyst says: "One who vilifies others eventually meets disgrace and trouble one day in this sense that his words somehow reach the ears of the other party and as a result thereof he loses a friend. One who hears him gets tired of his ill-speaking and criticism. It is possible that back-biting may become a habit so that a person may begin slandering others unintentionally in every gathering and assembly. Vilification of others goes to show, in fact, that the slanderer is jealous of them and endeavours to show himself superior to others and to introduce others as inferior to him. Furthermore, when a person does not possess self-confidence and is doubtful about his worth and position he resorts to speaking ill of others".

Offending People

Offending people tarnishes the relations between the individuals, destroys mutual love and cordiality, creates hatred and drives the individuals to grudge and revenge.

In the Islamic rules the Muslims have been strictly prohibited from annoying and hurting the feelings of others.

The holy Prophet says: "A Muslim is he from whose hands and tongue other Muslims remain safe". (Huqūq-i Islami) That is to say a Muslim should not harm others with his hands and should not also vex them with his tongue.

On another occasion he says: "A Muslim is not entitled to glance at his brother Muslim in a manner which may be annoying to him". (Jāmi'us Sa'ādāt, Vol. II)

It means that a Muslim must not vex and annoy another Muslim by looking at him with anger, derision, contempt etc.

He is also reported to have said: "If a person treats a believer with contempt Allah remains annoyed with him till he makes amends for his indecent deed". (Ihyā'ul Ulūm, Vol. II)

Fault-finding

There is an undesirable inclination in the nature of some

persons which makes them pry into the private affairs and secret matters of others. This inclination brings about inauspicious events which in the first instance affect those who have it and leads them to misfortune.

The factor which makes a person to find fault with others is a sort of inferiority complex and the person concerned resorts to divulging the defects of others so that he may create peace within himself. He is however, oblivious of the fact that such an action rouses contempt and aversion of the people for him. He loses his friends and strains his relations with others. If such persons who waste their energy in finding faults of others utilize that faculty for recognizing and curing their own defects, they are likely to achieve brilliant results.

In order to secure the social relations, Islam has prohibited finding faults which is the cause of separation and dissension and has warned the Muslims against indulging in it.

Imam Muhammad Baqir says: "In order to prove the defect of a man it is sufficient that he only observes a defect in others but may not detect the same defect which exists within himself or that he reproaches others for an act which he himself is not able to avoid or that he troubles his friend with matters with which he is not concerned". (al-Kāfi, Vol. II)

Imam Ali says· "Whoever is inquisitive about the defects of the people should commence this task with himself". Imam Ali does not consider the fault-finders to be fit for friendship and warns the people against them in these words: "Refrain from associatig with the fault-finders, because their friends, too, cannot remain safe from their harm". (Ghurarul Hikam).

Mockery

Mockery means finding fault in respect of a defect which is not optional and possible to remove, for example a rich person mocks a poor person, a beautiful person mocks an ulgly person or a strong person mocks a weak person. This indecent act i.e. mocking others sows the seeds of enmity because the person who is mocked at is lowered in the eyes of the people and his sentiments are injured.

The holy Qur'an says: *Believers, let not a group of you mock at another. Perhaps they are better than you.* (Surah al-Hujurāt, 49:11)

This is so because in Islam the criterion of virtue and excellence is not wealth, strength, beauty etc. but the honour and respect which one enjoys before Allah.

Islam, which is desirous of respect and honour for all the Muslims, does not permit that the honour and respect of anyone of them should be transgressed and tarnished.

Islam which considers the Muslims to be brothers of one another and is desirous of the development of their mutual relations has campaigned against this indecent conduct and has warned its followers against such acts.

Usually two types of persons mock the people: Firstly, those who are selfish, proud and jealous. The desire to show themselves to the people as great and respectable and others as insignificant and worthless. Secondly, those whose vocation is to ridicule others and whose object is to amuse the people and make them laugh. Persons belonging to this group are the meanest members of the society.

Imam Sajjad has called the clowns and the jesters as *'mubtil'* (worthless person). Once a jester snatched his cloak from his shoulder and ran away. The Imam remained quiet. His companions ran after the man, recovered the Imam's cloak and brought it back. The Imam asked "Who was he?" He was informed that the man was a jester who amused the people. Thereupon the Imam said: "Tell him that Allah has fixed a day (viz. the Day of Judgement) to assess the good and bad deeds of the people and those who indulge in such absurdities will be the losers on that day". (Manāqib ibn Shehr Āshūb, Vol. II)

Those who pay attention to the jesters and laugh upon those who are ridiculed should remember that they, too, are partners in this indecent behaviour, because unless they laugh, the jesters cannot make their trade brisk by harming the people.

What has been said above is a brief sketch of the Islamic injunctions by which the mutual relations of the individuals become pleasant and auspicious and the society is identified with a human touch.

The point which must be hinted at in the end is that Islam invites the people to acquire good qualities for the sake of Allah and virtue. They should shun mean qualities and become honest, benevolent and polite for the sake of humanity and not to earn material gains and laying hands on worldly pleasures. It is for this very reason that those trained under the guidance of Islam do not, in any circumstances, deviate from their conduct which is compatible with the teachings of Islam and the vicissitudes of life do not bring about any change in them whereas the conduct of those trained in other schools undergo a change as and when vacillations between hope and fear take place in their lives because the morals and training without a support and security for enforcement do not last permanently.

It is necessary for those who are interested in the welfare of the society should endeavour to acquaint the individuals with the duties which Islam has prescribed for them so that with the grace of Allah, the Islamic society should become superior to all other human societies. The holy Qur'an says: *You will surely prevail if you are true believers.* (Surah Ale Imran, 3:139)

Quotations
1. Believers! have patience, help each other with patience, establish good relations with one another and have fear of Allah so that you may have everlasting prosperity. (The holy Qur'an)
2. One who commences his day and does not make any effort for the welfare of the Muslims is not a Muslim.
3. A Muslim is he from whose hands and tongue other Muslims remain safe.
4. The person most liked by Allah is he who is more useful for the people. (The holy Prophet)

* * * * * *

SOCIAL ETIQUETTE

The thing which is of paramount importance in the social life of human beings is the existence of good relations, sincerity and serenity between individuals.

The greatest problem of the present day world is not with regard to bread, clothes and shelter but it pertains to cordial relations between individuals and the societies. This problem is faced by the countries as to how they should maintain their relations with other countries and it is also faced by the individuals as to how they should put up with others.

Unfortunately the phrase 'peaceful co-existence' has not also solved the problem and no sign thereof can be seen except in the lectures and articles of some persons.

Every day flames of war kindle in different parts of the world which devour a number of human beings and make many families distressed and helpless.

The small differences which take place between the people of the same city or the same locality and at times between the members of the same family all indicate this problem.

In fact so long as the mutual relations of human beings are not established on faith and spirituality the crux of the problem will continue to exist and it will not be possible to solve it.

Islam which is a Divine and heavenly religion has paid full attention to the training and reformation of the individuals to solve this problem and it has also laid the foundation of this training on faith in Allah and the strengthening of the spirit of virtue and humanity.

The regulations of Islam in this behalf are so effective and minute that if the people act according to them the mode and complexion of their life will become bright and their associations and contacts will assume a humanitarian characteristic.

In the first intance Islam has endeavoured to make the people understand the fact that all of them are the descendants of one father and one mother and none of them enjoys any distinction vis-a-vis others. The white, black, yellow and red race and as a general rule the colour of the skin of the body and the face cannot be the means of one nation being superior to another. Difference of languages and dialects cannot make one nation superior to another. But according to Islam, faith, piety, knowledge and integrity can be the source of the superiority of an individual or a society.

The holy Qur'an says explicitly: *Men, We have created you male and female and have formed you into nations and tribes so that you may recognize each other. He who has more integrity has indeed greater honour with Allah. Allah is All-Knowing and All-Aware.* (Surah al-Hujurāt, 49:13)

In another verse it says: *Allah will raise the position of the believers and of those who have received knowledge. Allah is well-aware of what you do.* (Surah al-Mujādilah, 58·11)

The holy Prophet says: "No Arab enjoys any superiority over a non-Arab (and no race is superior to another race) except on acount of piety".

As and when the human beings realize this reality most of the differences and distinctions which crop up from selfishness and foolish egotism will disappear and their relations will assume new shape. This remark is correct at the national and international level and will also eliminate the inimical relations and the consequences arising out of them in domestic affairs.

What needs attention in this discussion is that the Muslim families and individuals should be acquainted with the social teachings of Islam so that by acting upon them they may derive greater and better advantages so that mutual relations may be established between them.

There are many persons who wish to associate with others but on account of their not being aware of the social duties they are obliged to sequester themselves from others and thus they do not find a place for themselves in the society.

It is in itself something very important as to how mutual understanding and friendly relations should be maintained with the people in all walks of life. We know some persons in the society who are extraordinarily popular and wherever they go people show inclination and heart-felt attachment for them. On the other hand we see another group to whom nobody pays any attention and they are not liked by the people.

In order to reply to the question as to why some persons are so popular and others are not we may content ourselves by saying that the individual characteristics and disposition of every person are different from others and it depends upon the natural disposition of a man whether he is popular or otherwise. However, the psychologists do not consider this reply to be correct and believe that it depends on the conduct of different persons as to whether they are popular or not. It is the persons themselves who must build their character by good conduct and perform their duties while associating with others so that they may enjoy friendship and love of people.

I. Showing Respect to the People

One of the most important points in the social code is respect for the personality of the people which has been taken into account in the Islamic moral code and the distinguished leaders of Islam enforced it strongly.

The holy Prophet of Islam took into account even the most insignificant matters in according respect to the people and did not fail to perform even the smallest duty in this behalf. As and when a person came to see him he accorded him due respect and often spread his cloak on the ground for the visitor to sit on it and also gave him his own pillow. (Bihārul Anwār)

One day the holy Prophet was sitting alone in the masjid. A man approached him. The holy Prophet stepped aside. The man said: "O Prophet of Allah! The masjid is vacant and much space is available. Why have you stepped aside?" The holy Prophet replied: "A Muslim has a right on th other Muslim that when he wants to sit near him the latter should step aside by way of respect". (Bihārul Anwār, Vol. VI)

"When some persons happened to be present before the

holy Prophet, he, in order to ensure respect for all of them, cast a cordial glance at everyone of them equally. (Rawzatul Kāfi)

Whenever the holy Prophet arrived in any gathering he used to sit down at any place which was vacant and did not pay any heed for the prominent place.

Whenever he met his companions, the sitting arrangement was made in a circular position so that there should have been no position of elevation for anybody.

If a stranger arrived in the assembly of the holy Prophet he could not identify him, because he could not be distinguished from others. That man was, therefore, obliged to enquire as to who the Prophet of Allah was.

The round table which is utilized by the dignitaries and distinguished men of the world in these days is a specimen of the assemblies of the holy Prophet with one difference that the purpose of the present-day round table gathering is exactly the opposite of what the holy Prophet had in view while organizing his meetings.

The holy Prophet organized his meetings in a circle, because he did not wish to enjoy any distinction upon others and that anyone should sit at a place lower than his, whereas the round table conferences of the present times is arranged for this reason that none of the participants wishes that he should sit at a place lower than that of others and that someone should enjoy a higher position than his.

The holy Prophet endeavoured with all the strength at his command to eliminate tribal distincitions, racial discrimination and other similar anomalies. He tried his utmost to do away with the false standards which the people had invented to become superior to one another and made integrity and sublime human qualities the standard of virtue and excellence.

The respect which the holy Prophet accorded to the personality of others attracted everyone towards him. All classes enjoyed his immense love and none was despised or disregarded by him. He himself said explicitly: "I have been appointed by Allah to carry the good morals of the people to their zenith".

During the period of his rule Imam Ali happened to be the fellow-traveller of a non-Muslim. That man did not know Imam Ali. He asked: "Where are you going?" The holy Imam replied: "I am going to Kufa". When they reached the cross-section that man went on his way, but on the contrary he saw, that Imam Ali was also coming with him. He, therefore, asked: "Do you not intend going to Kufa?" The holy Imam replied: "I do". Thereupon the man said: "That road leads to Kufa". He replied: "I know". The man then asked: "Why are you not proceeding towards your way?"

Imam Ali said: "In order that association and companionship may end properly it is necessary that one should escort one's fellow-traveller up to a certain distance and this is the direction which has been given to us by our holy Prophet. This sincere honour and respect impressed the non-Muslim much and he asked: "Has your Prophet directed you thus?" Imam Ali replied: "Yes". The man said: "Those who followed the holy Prophet of Islam were enamoured by his moral teachings and kind behaviour". Then he abandoned the way he was going and accompanied Imam Ali to Kufa. He had a talk with him regarding Islam and eventually became a Muslim". (al-Kāfi, Vol. II; Kurbul Asnad; Bihārul Anwār, Vol. LXXIV)

Showing respect for the people is so important in the social code of Islam that the holy Qur'an recommends to the holy Prophet thus: *Tell my servants only to speak words that are good, verily Satan sows dissensions among them. Indeed he is the sworn enemy of mankind.* (Surah Bani Isrā'il, 17:53)

The holy Prophet says: "Do not despise and belittle any Muslim, because a Muslim, howmuchsoever small he may be, is great in the eyes of Allah".

Imam Muhammad Baqir says: "Respect your friends and consider them to be honourable and do not interfere with one another in an impolite manner".

Some persons behave with their friends in a so-called friendly manner and ignore the duty of mutual honour and respect on the pretext of friendship, although this very attitude weakens the foundation of friendship and creates dissension.

Imam Ali says: "In order to preserve the friendship which exists between you, never violate the rights of your friend because a person whose right is violated by you, will no longer remain as your friend". (Bihārul Anwār, Vol. LXXIV)

Some ignorant persons think that one of the means to

cement friendship between two persons is that they should use the most abusive languge for each other and should not desist from any severe criticism. They consider this method to be the means of maintaining closest friendly relations, although ridiculing and belittling friends is in no way commendable and these two indecent acts cannot be treated as a fun or the proof of close friendship.

Aristotle says: "To ensure the maintenance of friendship it is necessary that the friends should recognize the virtue and worth of each other and should look at it with respect. If two friends do not recognize the merits and worth of each other and do not respect them how can they claim to be sincere and worthy of friendship?

Politeness does not do any harm to a person but carries many benefits. The objects which cannot be achieved by spending wealth can be achieved by means of politeness.

A man named Zuhari came before Imam Sajjad, with a sullen face and a broken heart. The Imam enquired from him about the cause of his distress. He replied: "O son the Prophet of Allah! I am engulfed in grief and distress. The envious people who cannot tolerate my living in comfort cause me sorrow by their behaviour. My enemies and malevolent persons provide means of my sadness; and there are persons whom I have served and expect friendship from them, ridicule me".

The holy Imam said: "O Zuhari! Guard your tongue and do not speak out everything which comes to your mind so that you may not lose your friends and make them your enemies".

He said: "O son of the Prophet of Allah! I am serving those people and doing good to them by way of good sayings".

The Imam said: "It is not so. Avoid saying things which the minds of the people are not prepared to accept". Then he added: "O Zuhari! Whoever does not possess perfect wisdom is ruined due to the smallest thing".

Then the holy Imam gave the following basic instruction to Zuhari by acting whereon a person is not grieved due to the treatment meted out to him by the people: "O Zuhari! What is the harm if you consider all the Muslims to be your family and kith and kin? You should consider the aged persons to be your fathers, those who are younger than you to be your children and your coevals to be your brothers. When you take such a decision whom will you be prepared to harm or curse? Will you like that anyone of them should be disgraced?

O Zuhari! If the idea crosses your mind that you are better than such and such person you should make this suggestion to yourself: If he is older than you remind yourself· 'He enjoys precedence over me in the matter of Islam and faith and has done more good deeds than myself'. If he is younger than you, remind yourself: 'He has committed lesser sins than me'. And if he is of your age remind yourself: 'I know my own sins but am not aware of those committed by him'.

If people honour and respect you, say: 'It is on account of the magnanimity of the people themselves'. And if they are unkind and cruel to you, say: "It is due to some blunder committed by me". If you adopt this attitude your life will become pleasant and you will make many friends and the number of your enemies will decrease.

You should also remember that the people respect that person most who does more good to them and does not seek anything from them". (Bihārul Anwār, Vol. LXXIV)

In accordance with what has been stated above one of the most important secrets of success in social life from the viewpoint of Islam is to show respect for the people and to be polite to everyone. A large number of traditions have come down in this behalf and we quote below a few of them.

II. Treating the People with Courtesy

One of the social instructions of Islam is that one should treat the people gently and kindly. The holy Qur'an says thus about the conduct of the holy Prophet: *Only through Divine Mercy that you (Muhammad) have been able to deal with your followers so gently. If you had been sterm and hard-hearted they would all have deserted.* (Surah Ale Imran, 3:159)

In this sacred verse it has been explained that one of the reasons for the people being attracted to the Prophet of Islam was his mildness and undoubtedly the hearts of the people are attracted towards one who possesses this quality.

People hate rude and hot tempered persons and such persons are obliged to lead a secluded life.

Usually people commit blunders while associating or coming in contact with one another or do things which are opposed to human inclinations. It is in such circumstances that remission and indulgence should step in and prevent rudeness and harshness.

Imam Ja'far Sadiq was asked: "What are the conditions of good behaviour? He replied: Being kind and gentle, speaking good and decent things and meeting one's brethren-in-faith with a cheerful face".

Imam Ali while making recommendations to his son, Imam Hasan said: "Prepare yourself that as against the faithlessness of your friends and breaking off relations by them, you should remain faithful and should retain your relations with them and as against their coldness, severity and remoteness you should be forgiving and friendly and should seek their proximity and as against their rudeness and harshness you should observe gentleness and mildness and in case they commit mistakes you should accept their excuse and should behave with them in such a way as if they had a right over you. However, you should be careful to adopt this policy in respect of yourself and should perform it only with regard to those persons who are deserving".

Losing temper and hurting the people by one's anger becomes the cause of one's failure to maintain good relations with his friends.

It is but natural that due to his instinctive drive for domination, man punishes others for their faults but commonsense dictates that such a course of action is not rational as on the contrary punishment does not yield the desired results.

It is not possible to punish and reform others with harshness and if there is any method to achieve this end it is the same which has been suggested by the holy Qur'an and has also been recommended by the leaders of Islam. The method directed by them is to deal with people mildly and gently and guiding them by means of kind words and good deeds.

The holy Qur'an says that on their having been commanded to guide Pharaoh the following orders were given to Prophet Musa and his brother, Aaron: *Go both of you to the Pharaoh; he has become a rebel. Both of you must speak with him in a gentle manner so that he may come to himself or have fear of Allah.* (Surah Taha, 20:43 — 44)

Dale Carnegie says: "If your anger is aroused and you utter angry words you will feel relieved on account of your having discharged your feelings of anger. But what about the other party? Will he also experience the same enjoyment as you do? Will your revengeful tone and inimical behaviour make matters simple for him so that he may become friendly with you? Woodrow Wilson says: "If you approach me with a clenched fist I assure you that I too shall clench my fist immediately. However, if you come to me and say: 'Come, let us sit together and discuss matters and if we have any differences let us find out why these difference have cropped up and what the exact nature of those differences is; we will soon find out that we do not differ much and the points of difference are very trivial and insignificant and on many points we agree with each other. We can and should agree with each other only with patience, sincerity and feeling of reconcilliation". (How to win friends and influence people)

A man came in the assembly of Imam Sajjad where persons belonging to different classes were already present. On account of the grudge which he harboured in his heart against the holy Imam he began using abusive language and said many unbecoming things and then left the place. A moment after his leave the Imam turned to those present and said: "You have seen how rude this man has been with me and what words he uttered! Now I wish to go to him along with you and to give a reply to what he said". All of them agreed to this.

The holy Imam with his companions proceeded to the house of that man. All of them were thinking that the holy Imam would reprove him very harshly. They, however, saw that he was reciting the following sacred verse in a low tone: *And those who harness their anger and forgive the people. Allah loves the righteous ones.* (Surah Ale Imran, 3:134)

On hearing this they realized that the holy Imam had no intention of taking revenge. After having reached the house of that man they called him. When he came to know that the holy Imam had come along with a group of his companions he became sure that he had come to punish him. He also prepared himself for every eventuality and stepped out of the house. However, contrary to his expectation, he found the face of the holy Imam to be kindly and cheerful. The holy Imam said to him: "An hour ago you came to me and uttered indecent words. I have now come to tell you that if you have spoken the truth and the evils which you have attributed to me do exist in me I pray to Allah that He may forgive me, but if you have told lies and attributed things to me unjustifiably I request the Almighty that He may forgive you and overlook your sin".

That man found himself helpless before this generous attitude and apologized to the holy Imam and said: "O son of the Prophet of Allah! None of the bad things imputed by me to you exists in you. In fact I am more deserving of possessing them". In this manner the holy Imam obliged his antagonist to become friendly with him and thus he set an example before his followers to remain calm under provocation and overlook the highhandness of the transgresser. (Irshād-i Mufīd, Vol. II)

In fact this lesson is one of the most important methods in the field of social conduct and which has been paid much attention in the teachings of Islam. The followers of the holy Qur'an ought to develop the habit of this desirable conduct so that they may enjoy its great benefits.

III. Being Gentle and Modest

One of the things which produces good results of good social behaviour which makes one popular among the people is humility and modesty.

Not only that humility does not damage the position of a person but it also becomes the cause of its betterment. What makes the people hate a person is his pride and self-conceit because these thing prevent a man from showing respect to others and which sows the seeds of hatred and enmity.

While praising the pious the holy Qur'an says: *Among the servants of the Beneficent are those who walk gently on the earth and when addressed by the ignorant ones, their only response is peace be with you.* (Surah al-Furqan, 25-63)

It means that the noble and magnanimous slaves are they who lead their lives on the face of the earth with dignity and modesty and without egotism and formalities and when they hear unbecoming words from the ignorant persons they do not reply indecently and do not behave like the ignorant persons. (Tafsir Majam'ul Bayan, Vol. IV, p. 178)

The conduct of the holy Prophet and the respectable members of his family was based on this very principle. They associated with persons belonging to weak and indigent classes, sat along with them for dinner and treated them like brothers.

The holy Prophet campaigned vehemently against the egotism and selfishness of the people and, as and when the circumstances demanded, taught them the lesson of modesty and gentleness. One day when he was sitting in his assembly and the companions were sitting in a circle, a Muslim who was penniless and was wearing tattered clothes arrived and, as in accordance with the Islamic tradition when a person, whatever his social position may be, arrives in an assembly he should sit down wherever he finds a vacant place and should not look for a particular place suited to his social status, cast a glance on different sides of the assembly, saw a vacant place and sat down. By chance, at that place he happened to sit by the side of a rich man. It would appear that the rich man felt uneasy on account of that poor man sitting by his side, he, therefore, gathered his clothes together and pulled himself aside so that a distance was created between him and the poor person.

The holy Prophet who was watching the behaviour of the rich man turned to him and said: "Did you fear that something out of his poverty might stick to you?" He replied: "O Prophet of Allah! No". Then the holy Prophet asked: "Did you fear that something out of your wealth might be transferred to him?" He replied: "O Prophet of Allah! No". The holy Prophet asked further: "Did you fear that your dress might get soiled by touching his dress?" He replied "O Prophet of Allah! No". Upon this the holy Prophet asked: "Then why did you keep yourself off from him?"

The rich man replied: "O Prophet of Allah! I admit that I have committed a blunder and now, in order to make amends for this blunder and to atone for this sin, I am prepared to give half of my wealth to this brother Muslim of mine".

When the poor man heard his words he said: "O Prophet of Allah! I am not prepared to accept his offer". Those present asked with surprise "Why?" He replied: "I am afraid that under the influence of wealth I too may be involved in arrogance and egotism and may one day treat one of my brother Muslims in the same manner in which this gentleman has treated me today". (al-Kāfi, Vol. II)

Plato says: "The best thing which is the cause of friendship is modesty and gentleness to a reasonable extent".

The great scholars of Islam have explained that arrogance and self-conceit are the most harmful things for friendship. One who is arrogant and self-concieted makes his friends shun him and very few persons seek his friendship. On the other hand gentle and modest persons attract friends by their conduct. A self-conceited person cannot befriend anyone, because people cannot tolerate arrogance and egotism.

The late Muhaddith Qummi says: "The self-conceit and egotism of the people becomes manifest at the following stages:

An egoist and self-conceited person always considers himself to be great and looks at others with contempt. He does not like to be equal to others in any matter. He wants to go ahead of others on the way and to sit at a higher place than others in a gathering. He expects others to greet him. If anyone tenders him an advice he gets annoyed and if he counsels anyone he torments him. If his word is not accepted he gets angry. If he teaches he belittles and insults his pupils and reminds them of the favour done to them and considers them to be his servants". (Safinatul Bihār, Vol. II, p. 459)

Now ponder over the matter and decide whether a person who behaves like this can befriend others in the society and whether people can pay any heed to such a person?

It is for this reason that Islam has campaigned against egotism and arrogance and the holy Qur'an says explicitly: *Isn't Hell the dwelling of arrogant ones.* (Surah az-Zumar, 39.60)

Imam Sadiq says: "There is extremely an uncomfortable place in Hell which is meant for the arrogants". (al-Kāfi)

The holy Qur'an has quoted the wise sayings of Luqman, which he advised to his son and says in this behalf: *Do not turn your face away from people scornfully. Do not walk around puffed-up with pride; Allah does not love the arrogant and boastful people.* (Surah Luqman, 31:18)

Imam Sadiq considers the psychological source of arrogance to be an inferiority complex and says: "No person suffers from the ailment of pride, except due to inferiority complex which he perceives within himself". (al-Kāfi, Vol. III)

After conducting a deep scientific investigations and studying the conditions of the arrogant persons the contemporary psychologists have also confirmed this view and consider inferiority complex to be the source of arrogance.

Mick Bryde says: "An individual or a nation seeking supremacy means humiliating and belittling other individuals and nations. The source of hatred, enmity and strifes of the present times is usually from inferiority complex. The root cause of such a thinking is in fact a sort of false compensation for inferiority complex, for otherwise no sensible and dignified person can imagine of any distinction or difference between himself and other classes and races". (Research on Mental and Moral Problems)

In the light of what has been stated, modesty and gentleness are closely related to the good of the society as has been already mentioned.

It has been instructed in the Islamic teachings that people should protect themselves from all sorts of egotism and adopt modesty so that they may acquire collective success and popularity in the eyes of Allah and the people.

IV. Keeping one's Promises

Man naturally feels that he should honour the promises made by him with others and should fulfil them. And as this is a matter which concerns the very nature of man, he realizes the necessity of keeping his promises, whichever religion he may follow, and considers the breaking of promises and agreements as something indecent and abominable.

In social life the honouring of one's promises has a wholesome effect as it ensures confidence and trust of the people in him. In other words it may be said that it is one of the main factors of prosperity of the society which is effective in all walks of life.

Every agreement which is made by two persons is a moral obligation although it may not carry any legal or formal sanction or the subject matter of the agreement may be insignificant.

The holy Qur'an considers fulfilment of promises to be a part of the conditions of faith and the qualities of the believers and says: *Successful indeed are the believers, who are humble in their prayers, who shun all frivolities. . . . . and those who are true to their trust, to their promise and who are steadfast in their prayers.* (Surah al-Mo'minun, 23:8)

In another verse the holy Qur'an says: *The righteous persons are those who honour the promises and covenants which they make with others.* (Surah al-Baqarah, 2:177)

The holy Prophet of Islam has been reported to have said: "A person who is not unjust while associating and dealing with the people and does not tell lies in his dealings and keeps his promises and honours his commitments is at the zenith of manliness and jutice and it is necessary that one should establish cordial relations with him". (Bihārul Anwār, Vol. LXXV)

Imam Muhammad Baqir, says: "There are three things which are incumbent upon a Muslim and Allah has not permitted anyone to deviate from them. (i) Returning of the property whether the owner be a righteous person or a sinner. (ii) Honouring of a commitment whether it is made with an honest person or a dishonest person. (iii) Doing of good to one's parents whether they be righteous or otherwise". (al-Kāfi, Vol. II)

Just as the honouring of promises creates a sense of confidence in the society and establishes discipline in different walks of life, in the same way breaking of promises and covenants leads to disorderliness and chaos.

If a person deviates from the path of piety and honesty and easily breaks his promises and tramples on his covenants, creates hatred and enmity in the hearts of others.

Breaking of promises is one of the great factors of disruption and dispersion in a society and if it becomes a thing of daily occurence it brings misfortunes and disaster to a society.

Unfortunately there are some individuals who not only do not keep their promises, but deem the breach of promise and deceit to be cleverness and a means of advancement and consider it to be a skill, although their action is not compatible with any moral and human principles and they undoubtedly are the treacherous enemies of the people and the society.

This was a brief description of the teachings of Islam as regards the mutual co-operation of the Muslims with one another and undoubtedly each one of these directions has a deep effect on creating friendly and sincere relations between the individuals.

Now at the end of the discussions, we invite the attention

of the readers towards the social etiquette of the holy Prophet so that we may, by the grace of Allah, become the true followers of that great leader and saviour of mankind.

The holy Prophet used to accept the invitation of everyone whether the person who invited him was a free man or a slave or a rich man or a poor one.

Whenever a needy person approached the holy Prophet he endeavoured to satisfy his need. If a person offered an excuse he accepted it. He did not retaliate the evil deeds of others, but ignored their errors. Whomsoever he met he greeted him first. He tolerated the disagreeable acts of the enemy with patience. He sat down on the ground without displaying any uneasiness. As and when it was necessary, he cobbled his shoes and darned his dress. He did not stare at the face of anyone. He visited the sick even though their houses happened to be at a distance. He shared his meals with the poor and was kind to them.

He did not believe in any personal liking for himself in the matter of food and dress. He used to shake hands with the Muslims and pressed their hands with warmth.

The person most liked by the holy Prophet was the one who helped the people most and sympathized with them. The gathering in which he sat used to be an assembly marked with forbearance, modesty, patience and honesty. He showed respect to the aged persons and kindness to the younger ones. He was always good natured and had a cheerful smile.

He was not strict. He did not entertain grudge for anyone in his heart. He did not shout. He never uttered anything bad and unbecoming even in respect of the infidels and the idolaters. He never slandered anyone. He did not interrupt a person while he was speaking. If his companions were absent he used to enquire about them. He did not stretch out his legs in the presence of anyone. He was kind to all the servants of Allah. He maintained good relations with his kith and kin and loved them. He was more particular than anyone else about fulfilling his promise. If anyone spoke to him he heard him carefully and did not content himself with only lending him ear but was wholly attentive to him.

These are a few specimens of the manners and morals of the holy Prophet which have been quoted by the historians and the traditionalists. It is hoped that his followers will succeed in emulating him and will become ideal followers in preaching the entire humanity to adopt good moral conduct for the betterment of mankind as a whole.

Quotations

1.   A person who is not unjust while associating and dealing with the people and does not tell lies while speaking and keeps his promises and honours his commitments is at the zenith of manliness and justice and it is necessary that one should establish cordial relations with him.   (The holy Prophet)
2.   Live amongst the people in such a manner that if you die they weep over you and if you are alive they crave for your company.   (Imam Ali)

* * * * * *

FRATERNITY AND BROTHERHOOD

One of the strongest and deep-rooted relationships among human beings is the relationship of brotherhood. Brothers love one another, they are sympathetic to one another and they consider themselves partners in weal and woe.

It is possible that at times differences may arise between brothers which may cause anxiety. But soon this anxiety disappears and the sad experiences are forgotten yielding place to love and sincerity again.

In order to strengthen the social order and to improve the relationship of human beings, Islam has utilized this strong relationship and has given all the true believers the status of a real brother to one another.

Just as two brothers are connected and joined with each other through blood having one common father, Islam considers the holy Prophet the father of the Ummah and all the Muslims his children and consequently brothers of one another.

No limit or barrier exists in the matter of Islamic brotherhood and all the Muslims, irrespective of race, country and language are covered by this rule and are recognized by Islam as brothers of one another.

The holy Qur'an speaks explicitly about this brotherhood and says: *Believers are surely brothers. So restore friendship among your brothers. Have fear of Allah so that you may attain mercy.* (Surah al-Hujurāt, 49:10)

History has witnessed innumerable enmities, contentions,

splits and differences existed before the advent of Islam. By means of the redeeming teachings of Islam, however, the spirit of sincere Islamic brotherhood was created among the Muslims.

The holy Qur'an says: *All of you as one unit, seek the protection of Allah and recall how He favoured you when your hostility to each other had torn you apart. He united your hearts in one faith and through His grace you became brothers. You were on the verge of falling headlong into abyss of Fire, but Allah saved you.* (Surah Ale Imran, 3:103)

In the teachings of Islam rights have been prescribed for the brethren-in-faith and all the Muslims have been made responsible to uphold them.

Imam Sajjad says: "The right of your brethren-in-faith is that you should always sincerely seek their welfare and be kind to them. As regards those who are bad amongst them you should be lenient and affable to them and should make efforts for their reform. And with regard to those who are good amongst them you should be thankful. It is necessary that you should pray for all your brethren-in-faith and help them collectively and assist everyone of them individually. You should consider the aged ones among them as your father, the young ones as your children and your coevals as your brothers. Whoever from among your brethren-in-faith comes to see you should be cordially received by you. You should behave with your brethren-in-faith in the same manner in which a brother behaves with his brother. (Bihārul Anwār, Vol. LXXIV, p. 12)

Imam Ja'far Sadiq says: "A Muslim is the brother of another Muslim. He is just like his eye (as he makes him see his good and bad qualities) and his mirror (which shows him his beauty and ugliness). He is his guide. A Muslim never misappropriates his brother Muslim's property. He does not oppress him. He does not tell him a lie and does not consider it permissible to slander or back-bite him. (al-Kāfi, Vol. II, p. 166)

The holy Prophet has said thus in connection with the rights which the Muslims enjoy over one another: "A Muslim should overlook and forgive the lapses of his brother Muslim. He should sympathize with him in his difficulties, keep his secrets within himself, overlook his faults, accept his excuse and defend him against the slanderers and back-biters. He should always give him advice and preserve his friendly relations with him. If he falls ill he should visit him to enquire about his health. He should accept his invitation and presents. He should reciprocate for his gifts. He should speak with him gently and thank him for his affection. He should be friendly with his friends. He should not leave him alone to face hardships. He should like for him what he likes for himself and should not like for him what he does not like for himself". (Bihārul Anwār)

Imam Ja'far Sadiq says· "Like that for your brother Muslim what you like for yourself. If you need something ask him for it and if he needs something do not withhold it from him. Do not restrain yourself or express sadness while serving him and doing him good and he, too, should not restrain himself from doing good to you. Be his supporter for he, too, is your supporter. Safeguard his honour during his absence. When he returns from his journey go to see him. Honour him and hold him dear. He belongs to you and you belong to him. If he is harsh to you do not break off relations with him but apologize to him. If he gains something thank Allah and if he is involved in some difficulty make haste to help him. If his enemies play a trick on him and want to involve him in difficulties, assist him and prevent him from getting into trouble". (al-Kāfi, Vol. III)

What has been stated above is a specimen of the rights of the brethren-in-faith regarding which orders have been given in the teachings of Islam. Besides these general orders there are many ther eciprocal duties of Muslims each of which has been discussed separately by the great leaders of Islam and their performance has been recommended emphatically.

Fraternity (Muwāsāt)

Muwāsāt means helping one's brethren-in-faith and rendering them financial support.

In the religious traditions *(ahādith)* much importance has been attached to this matter which is the means of the betterment of the lives of deprived classes and the creation of mutual love between the Muslims and it has been introduced as one of the necessary qualities of every Muslim and believer and the source of Divine reward.

Imam Ja'far Sadiq says: "Make yourself a favourite in the

sight of Allah by means of financial support to your brethren-in-faith". (Khisāl Sūdūq, Vol. I, p. 8)

The holy Prophet, in connection with the recommendations made by him to Imam Ali, says · "There are three best deeds, firstly, you should behave justly with all the people; secondly, you should render financial support to your brethren-in-faith; and thridly, in all circumstances you must remember Allah. (Bihārul Anwār, Vol. LXXIV, p. 392)

Imam Ali says: "Helping your brethren-in-faith and rendering them asistance for the sake of Allah increases one's means of sustenance". (Khisāl Sadūq, Vol. II, p. 94)

Wāqidi, who was one of the greatest scholars of the time of Caliph Mamun, has narrated the following event · "I had two friends one of whom was a Hashimite. The friendship of three of us was so sincere that we were in fact one soul in three bodies.

Once, during Eid season, I happened to be quite indigent. My wife said to me: 'You and I can tolerate all these hardships. However, I am very much grieved on account of the children, because they see other children wearing new dresses and adoring themselves for Eid whereas their own clothes are old and torn. Procure some money if you can so that I may make new clothes for them'. I reflected over the matter but could not think of any solution of the problem. At last I wrote a letter to my Hashimite friend and requested him to assist me to the extent possible for him.

My friend sent me a sealed bag and informed me that it contained 1000 dirhams. I had not yet opened the bag when a person sent by my other friend came. He informed me about his indigence and sought help for himself. I did not open the bag and sent it to him and went to the masjid with a heavy heart. As I felt ashamed to face my wife I spent the night in the masjid. However, when I went home in the morning she, contrary to my expectation, received me with a cheerful face and expressed pleasure for my having done good to my friend and having accorded him precedence over myself.

In the meantime my Hashimite friend arrived at my house and said to me abruptly: "Tell me the truth. What have you done with the bag of money which I sent you yesterday?"

I told him the whole incident. After hearing me he bowed down his head for a moment and then said: "Yesterday when you sent me a message and asked for help I had no money except this bag. I sent it for you and wrote a letter to our other friend seeking his help. He sent me my own sealed bag and I could not understand the matter till you explained it to me".

Wāqidi says: "The three of us divided the money amongst us and one hundred dirhams out of it were given to my wife. Mamun happened to hear about this strange incident. He called for me and enquired about the matter. I related the entire incident to him. Mamun ordered that 2000 dinars per head might be given to three of us and 1000 dinars might be given to my wife as a gift". (Mas'ūdi, Murujuz Zahab)

The incident which you have learned is an historical event which took place in connection with a few Muslims who received their training in the light of the teachings of the holy Qur'an. They acquired such sublime morals and human attributes under the auspicies of the teachings of Islam that the spirit of brotherhood had swayed their lives to such an extent.

If we study the history of the early days of Islam we can observe the spirit of brotherhood among the individuals.

"In the battle of Uhud which was one of the most fierce Islamic battles, the Muslims made great sacrifices. A number of them met martyrdom fighting bravely and many others who were wounded and half-dead were lying on the ground.

Seven Muslim warriors were lying side by side. They were wounded and were passing the last moments of their lives. All of them were weary and thirsty. The person who had been appointed to supply water to the soldiers approached them. The water available with him was, however, sufficient for one person only. He reached by the side of one of them and invited him to drink water. He, however, asked him to make the soldier lying by him to drink water. Then he went up to that man but he also did not drink water and asked him to take it to the next man. In this way six persons told him to take water to the other man. When he reached by the side of the seventh soldier he asked him to return and make the first man drink the water as he was the most thirsty.

He returned to the first man but found him dead. Similarly

the remaining six persons also passed away. In short all the seven persons died of dehydration and thus practically taught others the lesson of fraternity and self-sacrifice". (Majma'ul Bayān, Vol. IX, p. 260)

This was an example of the lesson which they learnt from the teachings of the great Prophet of Islam and put into practice in all walks of their life.

It is a matter of great regret that inspite of our possessing a valuable treasure of sublime teachings we have got involved in such a situation that the spirit of brotherhood and fraternity is gradually disappearing and a state of stinginess and indifference which is the gift of the West is taking its place. This point should, however, always be kept in view that this state of affairs is inconsistent with the teachings of Islam and a Muslim cannot remain indiffernent to the difficulties and inconvenience experienced by his brethren-in-faith.

The holy Prophet says: "A person who commences his day and does not endeavour to improve the condition of the Muslims is not a Muslim". (al-Kāfi, Vol. II, p. 164)

Imam Ja'far Sadiq says: "The best persons amongst you Muslims are those who are generous and forgiving and the worst are those who are miserly and narrow-minded. And one of the pious and desirable acts is being good to one's brethren-in-faith and to endeavour to satisfy their needs. Doing so makes Satan humble and one who performs this act remains away from the fire of Hell and gets nearer to Paradise and eternal prosperity". (Majālis Mufid, p. 179, Amāli Tusi, Vol. I)

Once a man approached the holy Prophet and complained about hunger. The holy Prophet sent someone to the houses of a few of his relatives to bring food for that man, but unfortunately food was not also available in those houses. The holy Prophet turned his face to those present and said: "Who from amongst you is prepared to entertain this man tonight?"

Imam Ali replied: "O Prophet of Allah! I take responsibility for this task". Then he held the hand of that man and took him to his house. He asked his wife, Lady Fatima Zahra. "How much food do you have in the house?" She replied: "Only a small quantity of food is available which will just suffice our children". Imam Ali said: "We must prefer our guest to ourselves and our children".

After the decision had been taken Lady Fatima made the children sleep. Imam Ali then carried the food to the guest and put out the lamp on the pretext of setting it right.

In the darkness the holy Imam invited the guest to take his meals. He himself also sat down by the side of the dining-cloth and, without eating anything, gave an impression to the guest that he, too, was busy eating.

That night Imam Ali, Lady Fatima and their children entertained their guest for the sake of Allah and themselves slept without taking meals. The Almighty Allah praised this self-sacrifice and magnanimity by revealing the following verse: .... *They give preference to them over themselves even concerning the things that they themselves are in need.* (Surah al-Hashr, 59:9; Vide Tafsir Safi, Vol. II, p. 684)

Evidently it is not possible for everyone to act in this manner and a person like Imam Ali the commander of the faithful is required to acquit himself of such a responsibility.

Islam, too, has not asked its followers to act in this manner as a matter of duty. On the other hand what has been recognized as a clear-cut duty is brotherhood and fraternity in this sense that a Muslim should help his brethren-in-faith when they are in difficulties and trouble; should spend a part of his wealth for the welfare of the indigent; should visit the sick and be kind to them and sympathize with them; should protect the orphans and helpless persons as far as possible; should partake in establishing centres for public utility.

A Greek remained in contact with Imam Ali for a long time and conducted studies about Islam. When his studies came to an end and he got convinced of the truthfulness of Islam, professed Islam at the hands of the holy Imam. While giving him necessary instructions regarding his future responsibilities, Imam Ali said to him "I recommend that you should observe fraternity with those who follow the holy Prophet and me and help them by means of the wealth which Allah has given you, meet their needs, solve their difficulties and behave with them in a cordial manner". (Ihtijāj Tabarsi, p. 114)

Imam Riza in connection with the rights of the brethren-in-faith says: "Out of the rights, which a believer has on his brother-in-faith is that he should love him sincerely, help him financially and observe fraternity with him and assist him if someone else is unjust to him. A true believer never oppresses his brother-in-faith nor deceives him, nor commits treachery with him, nor slanders him, nor tells him a lie". (Bihārul Anwār)

If a person presents a dress to a brother-in-faith, Allah will grant him a dress in Paradise in lieu thereof and if anyone makes a loan to a brother-in-faith to seek Divine pleasure, Allah will give him the spiritual reward for charity. And if a person removes the grief of his brother-in-faith, Allah will remove his grief in the Hereafter".

Safwān Jammāl says: "I was sitting in the assembly of Imam Ja'far Sadiq. In the meantime a resident of Makkah arrived and said that he was penniless and did not possess sufficient means to return home".

The holy Imam ordered me to tak necessary steps to help my brother-in-faith. I got up at once and solved his problem. The holy Imam asked: "What steps have you taken to assist your brother?" I informed him that by the grace of Allah his matter had been settled in a proper manner.

Thereupon, the holy Imam said: "Remember that if you assist one of your brethren-in-faith this act of yours is more pleasing for me than your performing recommended circumumbulation *(tawāf)* of the House of Allah for one week".

Imam Ja'far Sadiq further added: "A man approached Imam Hasan and explained his difficulty to him and requested for help. The Imam put his shoes at once and proceeded on the way along with that man. While going on their way they reached a place where Imam Husayn was offering his prayers. Imam Hasan then asked that man: "Why did you not approach Husayn to solve your problem?"

The man replied: "O son of the Prophet of Allah! I wished to approach him but was informed that he was observing *a'tikāf* (i.e. seclusion for the purpose of Divine worship). I did not, therefore, approach him". Imam Hasan said: "However, if he could help you it would have been better than offering *a'tikāf* for one month". (al-Kāfi, Vol. II, p. 158)

Imam Ja'far Sadiq says: "When a Muslim meets the need of a brother Muslim, Allah says: It is my responsibility to reward you for this act and I do not consider any reward sufficient for you other than Paradise". (Qurbul Asnād, p. 19)

A man named Abdul A'lā who was a distinguished Shi'ah proceeded from Kufa to Madina. The followers of Imam Ja'far Sadiq wrote down their problems and handed over the paper to Abdul A'lā to obtain their replies from the Imam. Furthermore, they asked him to request the holy Imam to narrate the rights which a Muslim has on his brother-in-faith.

Abdul A'lā says: "When I had the honour to approach the holy Imam, he gave replies to all the questions but did not say anything about the rights of the brethren-in-faith. Many days later I went in the presence of the holy Imam once again but even then he did not hint at this matter.

The period of my stay in Madina came to an end and I went to bid farewell to the holy Imam and said: "O son of Prophet of Allah! The question which I asked that day remained unreplied". The holy Imam said: "I did not give a reply thereto intentionally". I asked: "Why?"

Imam Sadiq said: "I am afraid lest I should tell you about the mutual rights of the Muslims and you may not act upon what I say and may go out of the limits of religion". Then he continued to say. "Certainly these three things are considered to be the most difficult things which Allah has made obligatory for His servants. Firstly, one should observe justice between oneself and others in this sense that one should behave with his brethren-in-faith in the same manner in which he wishes them to behave with him. Secondly, one should observe fraternity with his brethren-in-faith and assist them financially. And thirdly one should remember Allah in all circumstances. And when I say that he should remember Allah in all circumstances I do not mean that he should repeatedly say *'Subhānallāh'* or *'Alhamdulillāh'*. On the contrary what I mean is that when he is faced with an unlawful act he should remember Allah and refrain from doing it". (al-Kāfi, Vol. II, p. 170)

These teachings had influenced into the spirit of the followers of Islam in such a manner that as we have observed from the examples quoted above — and the history of Islam is also replete with instances of such fraternity — the conduct of no other nation can be compared with their conduct.

Now that centuries have passed since the advent of Islam

and humanity has, so to say, made amazing advancement in the fields of art and science, it is not that these sublime human morals are not visible in the advanced countries but quite the opposite of it is in observation.

One of the writers says about the mutual relationship of the Europeans: "The mutual relations of the people are cold and devoid of strong and deep-rooted sentiments. It may be said that heart-felt love, which is a sentimental tie and illuminates life has been crushed by the wheels of industrial machines. Normally self-sacrifice, indulgence and sympathy are unknown things and possibly the number of friends of a person does not exceed the number of the fingers of his hand.

At the time when I was confined to bed in a hospital, although the number of my visitors was not large, but at the same time it may be claimed that more persons came to see me than those who come to see the German patients in the ward and this very fact was astonishing for the workers in the hospital, because we saw very rarely that a German should have come even to see an ailing member of his own family".

It will not be out of place if we quote an interesting incident as an example so that you may realize the standard of love and sentiments of the advanced nations.

"A few years ago a German professor embraced Islam at the hands of the Chairman of the Islamic Association, Hamburg. Some time later the Muslim convert fell sick and was admitted into a hospital. On having learnt this, the Chairman of the Islamic Association went to the hospital to see him. However, contrary to his expectation, he found the professor very much depressed and dejected and enquired from him about the cause of his dejection.

The professor, who had remained quiet till that time and was absorbed in his sad thoughts, opened his lips and related his surprising and regrettable story in these words · "Today my wife and son came to see me. They came to know from the relevant department of the hospital that I am suffering from cancer. While bidding me farewell and leaving the hospital they addressed me said : 'According to the information which has since become available to us you are suffering from cancer and are not likely to live for more than a few days. We, therefore, bid you farewell for the last time and would like to be excused from coming to see you again'.

Then the ailing professor continued. "My acute distress and mental torture is not on this account that I have lost all hope of life. What has disturbed and troubled me extremely is the unjust and inhuman attitude of my wife and son".

The Chairman of the Islamic Association, who was very much moved by his pitiable condition, said, 'As visiting the sick has been recommended emphatically in Islam I shall come to see you as and when I can find time and shall thus perform my religious duty'. These words brightened his sad face with delight. Gradually his condition become serious and he breathed his last after a few days. Some Muslims went to the hospital and collected his dead body to perform the necessary burial rites.

However, the matter did not end here. At about the time of burial there came in great haste a young man, from whose face signs of nervourness were quite apparent, and asked: 'Where is th dead body of the professor?' In reply he was asked: 'Are you related to the deceased?' He said: 'Yes, he was my father. I have come to deliver his body to the hospital authorities for use of dissection purpose because a few days before his death I sold the dead body of my father to the hospital for thirty marks'.

Although he insisted very much that the dead body of his father might be delivered to him, but eventually abandoned the idea on meeting with strong opposition of those present.

Later, when the young man was asked about his profession, he replied: "In the morning I work in a factory and in the afternoon I do the job of tending the dogs".

This incident, which is very tragic, goes to show to what extent human sentiments are being destroyed in the advanced, modern, and civilized society!

During the present times the retrogression of humanity from the view-point of moral virtues and outburst of social evils is undeniable. While admitting this bitter reality the great thinkers talk about solving this problem and are very much pained on this account. They have fully recognized the ailment and feel the necessity of launching campaigns gainst selfishness and lack of restraint and to build a new world on the edifice of faith and virtues.

Those who are themselves immersed in this kind of life have realized that such a life is a hollow one and cannot at all make any contributain to the prosperity of mankind. It will be better if you hear this interesting and explicit confession from one of the Presidents of the United States of America which he made at the time of taking the oath of office: "We find ourselves rich in the matter of material goods, but have a shaky moral. We reach the moon with brilliant precision, but here on the earth we have been captured by shattering dispersion.

We are involved in wars and want peace. Dispersion has broken us up and we seek unity. We see empty faces around us and our life is hollow. As against the spiritual crisis which has overtaken us we need a spiritual remedy and for that we should look only to ourselves. As and when we lend our ears to the call of conscience we shall see that it hold dear only the simple and basic things like goodness, modesty, love and kindness".

When these realities are taken into account every just person bows his head before the Divine teachings of Islam.

It is Allah, the Creator, who has, keeping in view all the temporal and spiritual needs and the human instincts, enacted appropriate laws which are in harmony with the very nature of man and which satisfy all his needs.

These are the laws which have been practised upon for centuries and have produced satisfactory results.

These are the laws which were not on paper only but were enforced with their full import and did not face any difficulty even at the time of their enforcement.

The more we ponder over the confessions of the Western thinkers, the more we realize their spiritual and moral bankruptcy and still more we do appreciate and praise the sublime and Divine religion of Islam.

The thing which deserves attention at the end is that it is the duty of all Muslims to promote the teachings of Islam without any embellishments and should specially acquaint the young people with these teachings so that the spirit of brotherhood and fellow-feeling which has existed among the Muslims for centuries should become stronger and we should march forward towards peace, progress and prosperity under the umbrella of Islamic brotherhood.

FRIENDSHIP

Human beings need the friendship and company of others at all stages of their lives from birth till death.

On acocount of his inherent social nature man is obliged to live in society with the company of people and to avail himself of the assistance and co-operation of his friends.

Those who have bosom friends are never alone or helpless in the world, because their mutual and compassionate friends are their associates and helpers in every weal and woe.

Man naturally feels pleasure while in the company of his friends and becomes worried and unhappy when he is lonely and without a companion. Imam Ali considers the true friends to be a great asset in this world as well as in the Hereafter and says: "Procure friends for yourselves from amongst your brethren-in-faith because they are a great asset in this world as well as in the next world". (Wasā'ilush Shi'ah)

In another remark he considered sincere frineds to be as good as the most important part of the human body and says: "One who loses a noble-hearted friend who befriended him for the sake of Allah is like one who loses one of the main organs of his body". (Ghurarul Hikam)

The point which has always been the focus of attention of the leaders of Islam in the matter of friendship, is that friendship which could be valuable only when it is for the sake of Allah and only that companion is reliable whose friendship is based on spiritual consideration. The friendships which come into existence for the sake of wealth, position or beauty automatically end with the departure of these things and no material consideration can serve as a support for an everlasting friendship.

Another point to which much importance has been attached by Islam is the question of choosing a friend. From the point of view of Islam friendship cannot be established with any and every person, because there are some persons whose friendship is harmful and dangerous.

Undoubtedly every friend influences the material and spiritual affairs of his friend and each one of them penetrates intentionally or unintentionally into the beliefs, thoughts, morals and conduct of the other.

Experience has also shown that many friendshps changed the course of one's destiny and they influenced the very pattern of one's life.

Friends impress each other in the matter of conduct, thought and beliefs. The holy Prophet says: "The conduct of everyone will be according to the belief and principles of his friend". (Wasā'ilush Shi'ah, Vol. IV)

Prophet Sulayman has said: "Do not form an opinion about a person's being good or bad unless you have seen his friends, because everyone is known by the company he keeps and is thus identified by his friends and associates". (Mustadrakul Wasā'il, Vol. II)

A philosopher has said: "Tell me which persons you like so that I may tell you who you yourself are and what the standard of your intelligence, taste and morals is".

Friendship and association with decent persons is one of the main factors of happiness and prosperity and association with corrupt and wicked persons is considered to be one of the causes of adversity and disaster.

Socrates said: "All persons have their values. One desires wealth, another wants beauty and still another craves honour. I, however, believe that a good friend is better than all these things".

A renowned English author says: "One should be very careful in the choice of one's friends. Most of our hardship are the result of improper associations. When man steps from the cradle into his practicle life he gets acquainted with different types of people and accordingly he associated with one group or the other. It often happens that as a result of association with base persons he falls into the ditch of meanness. It is possible that the base persons may not have any bad intenions for their associates but as demanded by their nature they always sting others like a scorpion and inject their venomous influence into their spirit.

Some persons are so confident about their own chastity and virtue that they think that association with bad persons will do them no harm. They consider their character much above this that bad morals should affect it but ignore the fact that cotton lying near fire necessarily catches fire. Unfortunately corruption and wickedness influence the human soul very rapidly just like a heap of gunpowder explodes with a touch of spark and engulfs everything around into flames.

One who is proud of his virtue and does not refrain from associating with base persons is like one who builds his house on the course of flood-water under the impression that its force will not weaken the foundation of his house"

An Arabic proverb says: "A bad companion is like an ironsmith. Even if he does not burn you the smoke of his forge will harm your eyes".

Let us suppose that you are so self-possessed and magnanimous that association with bad persons does not affect your sublime character. But what opinion will the people form about you? Will they not place you in the category of bad persons on account of your associating with them?

In any case it should not be forgotten that association with good persons is a matter of good luck because there are many persons who are afflicted with miseries when they do not exercise proper care in the choice of their friends". (The Secret of Happiness)

The danger ensuing from bad friendship is not confined to one's life only. On the other hand such friendships will be a source of regret on the Day of Judgement as well.

Referring to a group of persons who will be subjected to Divine torture on the Day of Judgement the holy Qur'an says: *It will be a Day when the unjust will bite their fingers (regretfully) saying, would that we had followed the path of the Messenger. Woe to us! Would that we had not been friends with so and so. He led me away from the true guidance after it had come to us.* (Surah al-Furqān, 25:32)

Imam Ali says: "The good of this world and the Hereafter is combined in two things viz. keeping one's secret and friendship with good persons. And the adversity of this world and the Hereafter is summed up in two things viz. disclosing one's secrets and association with bad people". (Ikhtisās)

Sa'di, the renowned poet and saint, says:

"If a person keeps the company of bad persons he will be reckoned as one amongst them even if he may not be so. Similarly if anyone goes to a bar to offer prayers he will be considers as a drunkard.

You confirmed your foolishness by choosing a foolish person as your friend.

When I asked a wise man to give me a piece of advice he said, do not make friend with a foolish person".

The holy Prophet says: "The most fortunate person is the one who associates himself with noble and magnanimous persons". (Amāli Sadūq, p. 14)

George Herbert says: "Associate yourself with good persons so that you too may be reckoned as one of them".

A wise woman used to advice to her children: "Just as our body acquires strength from food which we eat, similarly our soul acquires virtues and piety or corruption and mischief on account of our associating with good or bad friends".

It is impossible that our association and friendship with the people around us may not leave deep impressions on our morals because man by nature is inclined to emulate others and therefore, every person is more or less influenced by the activities, behaviour and views of his friends and associates.

A wise man says: "There is a well-known proverb that a man is known by the company he keeps. Yet a sensible person does not associate himself with a drunkard, a scholar with an ignorant and a noble person with an ignoble one.

Associating with people of mean and bad character creates in man baser feelings and if his association with such people lasts for a longer time, he will completely be integrated as one such base people.

A wise man has said : "Even to converse with such persons

is harmful and dangerous, because even though association with them may be harmful only temporarily but even then it sows a seed in our brain which grows sometime later and takes its root".

Association with such persons is just like a plague which affects man immediately.

Association with well-behaved and able-minded persons is the best refresher of one's soul and on the contrary association and friendship with ignorant and bad persons become the cause of calamity and disaster.

A Spanish proverb says: "If you go to the wolves, it is howling which you will learn from them".

Friendship with base and selfish persons carries great dangers in its wake because their moral conduct influences and mars one's thinking and kills the spirit of manliness and high moral in him. And if friendship with them is continued one becomes cold and weak-hearted and the sense of advancement and dignity are eliminated. On the contrary, friendship with persons who are wiser, capable and more experienced is a valuable asset, because their company imbibes fresh spirit in man and teaches us the ways and manners of a successful life and improves our beliefs and opinions as compared with others and they make us share their knowledge, wisdom and experience.

Hence, nothing is more effective and useful for building up our morals than the establishment of friendship with active and wise persons, because association with them increases our spiritual strength and adds to our will power and makes our object in the world higher and sublimer and trains us to perform the individual as well as our social obligations.

Shaykh Sa'di says about the effect of association and companionship: "One day a piece of fragrant clay reached my hand in a bath-house from the hand of a sweetheart. I asked it : 'Are you musk or ambergris, because I am getting intoxicated by your enchanting fragrance'. It replied: "I was only worthless clay but for a long time I remained embedded with a rose. The sweet fragrance of my companion has influenced me, otherwise I am the very humble piece of clay that I am".

Imam Ja'far Sadiq says: "During the course of his sermons, my father said to me: 'My son! Whoever associates with bad persons cannot escape harm from them and whoever frequents unsuitable places earns a bad reputation and whoever does not have control on his tongue has to regret and repent". (Khisāl Sadūq, Vol. I, p. 80)

Imam Sajjad says: "Do not associate with persons belonging to five categories and do not also converse with them and do not accompany them in any case:

(i) Shun the liars because they are like a mirage. With their baseless words they depict matters different from what they actually are. WIth their lies they show a distant thing, to be near and a thing which is near to be far off and thus deviate you from the right path.

(ii) Avoid the licentious and the sinners because their friendship is not dependable and they will sell you for a morsel or even lesser then that.

(iii) Avoid stingy persons because at the time of need and difficulty these people will make you suffer humiliation.

(iv) Keep away from foolish persons because they may be desirous of doing you good but will involve you in hardship due to their ignornance and folly.

(iv) Shun those persons who have dissociated from their kith and kin and misbehave with them because these people have been cursed by Allah in the holy Qur'an". (Bihārul Anwār)

Imam Ali thus in connection with the recommendations made by him to his son, Imam Hasan, said: "Avoid centres of ill repute and seek distance from assemblies which are subject to suspicion and remember that a bad companion deceives his friend and encourages him to do evil deeds and eventually corrupts him. (Wasā'ilush Shi'ah, Vol. III)

Imam Ja'far Sadiq says: "Sincere friends who are attached to a person like brothers are of three kinds:

Firstly, a friend who is reckoned to be one of the positive necessities of life like food and one stands in need of him in all circumstances. Such a person is a wise friend.

Secondly, the person whose presence is just like pain and ailment. Such a person is the foolish friend.

Thirdly, the friend whose presence is like a life-saving drug. Such a friend is intelligent and very wise. (Tuhaful Uqūl)

Wise friends can save the people from great dangers at critical moments and those who have such friends possess a valuable asset and a great blessing.

Imam Ali has prohibited making friends with capricious persons and says: "There is nothing good in the friendship of fickle-minded and capricious persons because to whichever side the wind blows, they incline to that side along with the wind. They are generous and lavish when you do not need their wealth but if you stand in need of their wealth, they are stingy. Of course, when the friends are counted they are large in number, but the friends who come to one's aid in dire need are very few". (Diwān-i Imam Ali)

Imam Ja'far Sadiq says: "Avoid friendship with persons falling under three categories viz. a traitor, a tyrant and a rumour-monger, because on one day he will deceive others in order to benefit you and on another day he will also deceive you, and one who oppresses the people for your sake will also oppress you one day, and one who vilifies others before you will soon vilify you before others. (Tuhaful Uqūl)

In order to choose a suitable friend it is absolutely necessary that one should conduct an enquiry.

Mark Orwel says: "If you want to befriend a person, find out before everything else what the standard of his intelligence is, what is his opinion about good and evil? What importance does he attach to honour and insult? What constitutes good luck and adversity in his eyes? This is necessary so that you may not get surprised later on account of what you hear from him or what he tells you because you will see that all his actions are compatible with what he said and according to his line of thinking". (Friend and Friendship)

Experienced and wise persons are very particular about choosing a friend and in case they are desirous of establishing sincere friendship they act according to wisdom and logic and do not allow rash and inopportune sentiments to interfere in this matter. In the first instance they become familiar with the other person so that they may become aware of his way of thinking, morals and his antecedents. Thereafter they subject him to test on different occasions and befriend him if he is found to be suitable for friendship in all respects. Such friendship is free from any risk and it is firm and stable.

Imam Ali says: "If a person establishes friendship after scrutinizing, it will be firm stable". (Ghurarul Hikam)

While making recommendations to Ibn Mas'ūd, the holy Prophet said: "It is necessary that your friends should be pious and righteous and you should extend the hand of brotherhood and friendship to only those persons who are abstemious and virtuous, because Almighty Allah has said in the holy Qur'an that on the Day of Judgement all friends will become enemies of one another except the pious ones whose friendship will be stable". (Makaramul Akhlaq)

All the criteria, limits and qualities of a friend have been mentioned in the Islamic teachings which can serve as a guide for choosing and testing friends.

Imam Ja'far Sadiq says: "Friendship has certain limits and conditions. One who does not fulfil some of these conditions is not a perfect friend and one who does not fulfil anyone of them cannot be called a friend at all.

(i) His exterior and interior should be alike and whatever he professes about you by his tongue should come from his heart as well.

(ii) He should consider your good things to be his own good things and your bad things to be his own bad things. Similarly he should consider your honour to be his honour and your disgrace to be his disgrace.

(iii) If his financial condition improves and he amasses wealth or acquires a higher position he should not change his attitude towards you.

(iv) He should not fail to assist you to the extent of his capability and competence.

(v) He should not abandon you and leave you alone when you are involved in adversity". (Amāli Sadūq, p. 397)

Imam Ja'far Sadiq says: "When one of your acquaintances gets annoyed with you three times but does not say any unbecoming thing about you, you can extent the hand of friendship to him and establish companionship with him". (Safinatul Bihār)

Imam Ali says: "A person cannot be called a 'true friend' except when he protects the honour of his friend in adversity and at the time when he is not present and after his death".

Moderation in friendship is another important point which must always be kept in view because it is possible that immoderateness in friendship may result in irreparable losses and may place a person in a perilous situation.

During fiendship, confidence should be placed in a friend to such an extent that if separation takes place at a later stage due to differences he may not be able to do any harm.

Imam Ali says: "When you hold a person dear to your heart, express your friendship with him within the limits of moderation and expediency because it is possible that one day he may turn against you. And similarly be gentle towards a person whom you do not like because it is possible that one day your relations may cease to be strained and he may become your friend". (Tuhaful Uqūl)

Sa'di who has been mostly inspired in his poetic verses and writings by the sayings of the holy Prophet and the holy Imams says: "Do not divulge any of your secrets to your friend because it is possible that one day he may become your enemy and do not do any harm to your enemy because it is possible that some time later he may become your friend". (Gulistan)

An English author says: "Behave with your friends in such a manner that even if they become your enemies you may not be harmed and treat your enemies in such a way that if they become your friends you may not have to feel ashamed. There are many persons who do not observe this rule and are consequently always agitated and disturbed. They confide in their friends their most important secrets and the result is that when the friendship is broken and is replaced by enmity the same person who was his dearest friend till yesterday rises to ruin him with the weapon which he has already in hand. It was for this reason that when one of the greatest commanders was proceeding to the battlefield he said to Louis XIV: "Protect me from the mischief of my friends. I am not afraid of the enemies".

Imam Ali says: "Give your entire cordiality and love to your friend but do not place your entire confidence in him. Help him in all respects but do not divulge all your secrets to him". (Kanzul Fawā'id, Karāchaki)

At the first instance it is difficult to acquire reliable friends and it is still more difficult to maintain friendship. If rights and responsibilities are not observed in friendship its bond breaks up soon.

Imam Ali says: "The weakest among the people is the one who cannot acquire a friend and weaker than him is the one who loses his friends". (Nahjul Balaghah)

Shakespeare says: "Take care of your friend like your own llife".

Sinā'i says: "Consider that person to be bad who has few friends and to be worse than him who loses a friend after acquiring him".

There are many reasons which estrange friends and one of them is annoying and irritating one's friend.

The Commander of the Faithful, Imam Ali says: "When a person annoys and offends his friend he paves the path of parting and separation". (Nahjul Balaghah)

Another factor which can estrange friends is paying heed to back-biting of gossip-mongers.

Undoubtedly there are persons who feel grieved on account of the cordial and friendly relations of others and are always endeavouring to create differences between them. They carry talks from one friend to the other and cause to split their cordial relationship.

Imam Ali says: "Whoever lends his ears to the words of the gossip-mongers will lose his dear friend". (Nahjul Balaghah)

It is the duty of the people to refute and ignore what the mischief-mongers say so that they may refrain from this nasty habit and consequently do not lose their friends.

Finding faults with one's friends and attaching undue importance to their lapses and blunders is another factor which can eliminate friendship.

It is an admitted fact that everyone commits errors and blunders in his life nd it is the duty of a Muslim to overlook the lapses of his brethren-in-faith and of his dear friends.

Imam Ali says: "Accept the excuse of your friend (for the wrong done by him) and if he is not able to put forth an excuse for his wrong you should coin one for him". (Nahjul Balaghah)

One of the wise men says: "One should accept the excuse put forth by his friends even though it may be not convincing becaue the very fact that one has regretted and apologized goes to show that he has extended his hand for the continuance of friendship and it is the duty of a person that when the hand of friendship is extended to him he should hold it.

Sa'di says: "A friend does not get offended with a friend on account of any faults and if he does get offeded and still claims to be a friend, his claim is not correct".

Joking, mocking, belittling and ridiculing the friends are other causes of severence of friendly relations.

One day Hârith, son of A'war who was one of the companions of Imam Ali expressed his sincerity and devotion and said: "O Commander of the Faithful! I am your friend". When he made a mention of friendship the holy Imam explained a few things which friends must not do with regard to each other. He said, if you treat a person to be your friend:
- Do not dispute with him and do not be hostile to him.
- Do not ridicule him.
- Do not quarrel with him.
- Do not cut indecent jokes with him.
- Do not hold him in contempt or consider him to be humble.
- Do not claim precedence and supremacy over him.

These things are not suited for maintaining friendship". (Khisâl Sadûq, Vol. I, p. 296)

One of the wise men says: "Most of the people prefer sustaining a loss to hearing ridicule remarks".

A Latin proverb says: 'Mockey destroys friendship'.

We draw the following conclusions from what has been stated above:

(i) Friends exercise a deep influence and play an important role in the prosperity or adversity of each other.

(ii) Friendship should be based on faith and piety and should spring from spirituality. Other kinds of friendship are not reliable.

(iii) One should avoid the friendship of corrupt and depraved person because they will corrupt him.

(iv) Friendship has its limitations and it is necessary that before establishing friendship the requisite tests should be undertaken so that one may not have to regret later.

(v) Friendship of sincere friends should be appreciated and great care should be taken to preserve it.

Quotations

1. Do not associate with persons belonging to five categories and do not also converse with them and do not accompany them in any case:

Shun the liars because they are like a mirage. With their baseless words they depict matters different from what they actually are. With their lies they show a distant thing to be near and a thing which is near to be far off and thus deviate you from the right path.

Avoid the licentious and the sinners because their friendship is not dependable and they will sell you for a morsel or even lesser than that.

Avoid stingy persons because at the time of need and difficulty these people will make you suffer humiliation and abjectness.

Keep away from foolish persons because they may be desirous of doing you good but will involve you in hardship due to their ignorance and folly.

Shun those persons who have dissociated from their kith and kin and misbehave with them, because these people have been cursed by Allah in the holy Qur'an. (Imam Sajjad)

2. Friendship! mysterious cement of the soul! sweeter of life! and solder of society. (Robert Blair, The Grave)

3. Tell me the company you keep, and I'll tell you who you are. (Proverb)

4. A pleasant possession is useless without a comrade. (Seneca)

5. The only way to have a friend is to be one. (Ralph Waldo Emerson, Friendship)

* * * * * *

CLEANLINESS

One of the most important and attractive aspects of Islamic teachings is the one related to cleanliness.

Nowadays with the advancement of empirical sciences and procurement of facilities and establishment of various laboratories, the importance of the question of cleanliness and its direct effect on human health has become abundantly clear.

During the present age man has identified the microbes and viruses and has discovered the diseases caused by them.

Many of the problems which are now considered by man to be ordinary and of commonplace were unknown till a century ago and no one had any knowledge of them and if the contemporary scientists have explained the importance of cleanliness and recommended it to the people there is nothing strange or extraordinary about it.

They have observed the invisible enemies with the help of compound microscopes and have conducted numerous experiments on each one of them and now inform the people about the impending dangers arising from their existence.

It is interesting to note that until the 16th century of the Christian era, the Europeans were not only not acquainted with these matters but their life was also void of the very concept of cleanliness that everyone is astonished to know this fact.

Public bath-houses were not known in European cities and people were against building them and besides, the Christian priests also did not give their approval to build them.

Lavatories did not exist in the houses and the people threw their dirt in the streets and on the thoroughfares. These facts have been narrated by the great European research scholars.

Will Durant, the famous Christian writer, says about the conditions then prevailing in Europe: "The early Christians considered the Roman hot bath houses to be indecent and all similar centres to be pits for deviations and sexual anarchy. Furthermore, as Christianity generally spoke about body being abominable and fit for abandonment, observance of the hygienic rules could not be given due consideration".

At another place he writes: "In the thirteenth century the Parisians freely emptied their piss-pots from the windows on the thoroughfares and the only safeguard which the poor wayfarer has, was the warning given by the residents of the house who would say loudly: "Garl 'eau" (lest you may be drenched). Such unexpected occurrences became one of the commonplace jokes of the comedies which continued even up to the time of Moliere. Public lavatories were still a luxury.

In the year 1255 some public lavatories existed in San Gimignano, but they had not yet been introduced in Florence. People urinated in the courtyards, on the stairs, from the top of the upper chambers and even in the Louvre Palace. After the breaking out of the plague in 1531 a special order was issued requiring all the owners of houses and house-keepers in Paris to construct a lavatory for every house, but the majority of the people failed to comply with these orders". (History of Civilization, Will Durant, Vol. XIII, pp. 502 — 503)

The crusades which continued between the Europeans and the Muslims for a long time acquainted the Christians with bath houses and educated them about the importance of cleanliness.

Will Durant writes: "One of the good results of the Crusades was that in imitation of the hot bath houses of the Muslims, public hot bath houses became current in Europe. The Church was not, however, happy with the public bath houses". (History of Civilization, Will Durant, Vol. XIII, pp. 502 — 503)

Even in the present times in the lavatories of most of the European countries toilet papers are used instead of washing with water and the obnoxious body-odour is suppressed by means of eua-de-colongne and similar other things.

This was a specimen of the conditions of the European countries from the fifteenth century onwards till today.

Now we go a little backward and place ourselves in the dark world of fourteen centuries ago. It was the time when humanity was struggling in the darkness of ignorance and knew nothing about civilization, knowledge and wisdom.

At that time the leaders of Islam presented before the people the teachings which had a Divine origin and which were communicated through Divine revelation.

They made the slogan 'Cleanliness is a part of faith' reach the ears of the people, and introduced 'Allah likes those who repent and those who are pure' as the first step towards the purity of body and soul.

Imam Ali encouraged the people to remain clean and said: "The bath house is a good place. Its heat reminds man of the Fire of the Wrath of Allah and it also removes the dirt of the body". (Wasā'ilush Shi'ah)

In the Islamic regulations 'recommended' baths have been treated as a part of the 'recommended' act on Fridays, Eid festivals and on other auspicious days.

The first order to be complied with before visiting the holy shrines and the sacred tombs is that of taking a bath. These orders were issued in a country the residents whereof did not enjoy a satisfactory position in the matter of water and even now they draw water from the wells to meet their needs.

It was on account of these emphatic religious instructions that even during the Middle Ages when the Europeans were leading their lives in complete pollution, the Muslim enjoyed appreciable purity and cleanliness.

In a book entitled 'Muslim life in the Middle Ages', the French author has depicted the conditions of the Islamic countries, in the tenth up to the thirteenth centuries of the Christian era, in detail. He says: "After the advent of Islam the use of public bath houses became current and much time did not pass before some Muslims constructed big bath houses. In the cities there were one or two bath houses in every street and in the towns and the villages, bath houses were constructed in the neighbourhood of masjids. In the twelfth century there were about 5000 bath houses in Baghdad and 1170 in Cairo".

On account of the Muslims complying with the laws of Islam they became the most purified nation of the world.

Islam recommends that when the Muslims go to offer prayers in the masjids, they should wear their best dresses, apply perfume and restrain themselves from eating onions, garlic, etc. of bad odour.

It also recommends that before leaving their houses they should be smartly dressed, comb their hair and look at the mirror to reassure themselves about the condition of their dress and figure.

In the teachings of Islam attention has been paid to the most insignificant matters and necessary instructions have been given in detail to follow them.

The traditionalists say that the holy Prophet ordered his followers to remain clean and pure and encouraged them in this behalf. (Kanzul Fawā'id, Karāchaki)

One of the traditions of the holy Prophet which has come down in the form of an everlasting and beautiful slogan that, "Cleanliness is a part of one's faith and faith leads a person to Paradise". (Mustadrakul Wasā'il, Vol. I, p. 101)

Imam Ali says: "Cleanliness is half the faith". (Daʿā'imul Islam, Vol. I, p. 100)

Here we are not concerned with the religious duties which are related directly with the obligatory purification of the people and which the Muslims perform as articles of worship without the least negligence or remissness. For example, we are not concerned here with the question of ablutions *(wuzū)* which is performed a number of times by every Muslim during day and night to offer prayers and which brings about perfect cleanliness from head to foot.

We are also not concerned here with the obligatory baths which must be perforrmed by Muslim men and women every now and then as a religious duty and the entire body must be washed while performing them. And similarly we are not discussing here the duty of the Muslims to avoid impurities and to keep their body and dress clean from prescribed impurities.

Here we propose to discuss the directions which have only one aspect of guidance and wherein the details of the question of cleanliness have been attended to.

Islam has emphatically recommended the purity of body and dress and has asked the people to keep them clean.

The holy Prophet says: "Whoever wears a dress should always keep it clean and pure". (Makārimul Akhlāq, p. 117)

In shaded dresses, especially those with dark colours, dirt and pollution are not visible and as a consequence it is possible that the dirt may not be apparent in the dress of a person and he may not be knowing about it.

The holy Prophet says: "Among your dresses none are better than white dresses. You should choose a white dress for wearing". (Makārimul Akhlāq, p. 117)

A number of traditions have come down from the holy Imams regarding the washing and purification of dresses.

Imam Ja'far Sadiq says: "Clean and tidy dress humiliates one's enemy and the washing of clothes removes grief". (Da'ā'imul Islam)

As regards the residences it has been recommended emphatically in Islam that the Muslims should endeavour to keep them clean and tidy.

The holy Prophet says: "Sweep the space in front of your house and keep it clean and do not be dirty like the Jews". (Makārimul Akhlāq, p. 145)

Imam Ali says: "Allowing the spiders' webs to remain in the room brings poverty and keeping the rubbish in the house after sweeping, drags one to indigence". (Mishkātul Anwār)

The holy Prophet says: "After taking meal, leaving the dishes unwashed; allowing the spiders' webs to remain in the house, and leaving water containers without cover brings indigence". (Jāmi'ul Akhbār)

The holy Prophet also says: "Do not allow the sweepings and the rubbish to remain in your house during night, because they are the abode of Satan". (Makarimul Akhlāq, p. 490)

It is possible that it may be asked as to how the rubbish can be the abode of Satan. In order to explain this question it is necessary that we should first know its literal meaning and then see in what sense it has been used in the holy Qur'an and in the sayings of the leaders of Islam.

According to the Arabic dictionary the word *'Shaytān'* (Satan) carries many meanings, one of the them means, "Every rebellious and disobedient being whether it be a human being or a genie and whether it be a small living creature or a big one". (al-Munjid)

In the holy Qur'an also the word *'Shaytān'* has been used in different meanings: Firstly, about *'Iblis'* (Lucifer) who is the seducer of human beings. (Surah Ibrahim, 14:22)

Secondly, about the hypocrites who apparently embrace Islam but inwardly co-operate with the enemies of the faith. (Surah al-Baqarah, 2:12)

Thirdly, for those who joined the forces opposed to the holy Prophets. (Surah al-An'am, 6:112)

Fourthly, the persons who have gone astray are treated to belong to the party of Satan. (Surah al-Mujadilah, 58:19)

Hence every being which becomes the cause of deviation or adversity for human beings and pulls them towards corruption and misery is *Shaytān*, whether it be in the form of man, snake, a very small being or a microbe.

On this basis if in some cases we use the word *'Shaytān'* with regard to the microbes and the virus which cause ailments we will be saying something absolutely correct from the point of view of its lexicographical meaning. Now keeping these points in view if we say that some parts of human body are the places of flourishing of Satan, we mean thereby the places where backbiting, conspiracies and mischief are resorted to or some parts of the body like the armpits or the spots under the moustaches and the nails, we will not be saying something wrong in any of these cases. This is so because the assemblies in which conspiracies and mischief take place always consist of Satans who draw plans to harm others and in the moustaches and armpits and under the nails, Satans of another kind viz. harmful microbes settle down.

In the traditions of *Ahlul Bayt* (the chosen descendants of the holy Prophet) the word *'Shaytān'* has been frequently used for microbes. Fourteen centuries ago the people were not aware of microbes and their intellect, too, could not perceive these matters. And as it was necessary that the leaders of Islam should talk with the people in their language and according to the level of their intelligence they introduced these minute beings with *Shaytān*, a name with which they were fully acquainted with and considered it to be their dangerous enemy.

Hence if the holy Prophet says that the sweepings and rubbish which are collected from the nooks and corners of the house should be thrown out immediately and should not be allowed to remain in the house during night because they are the abode of Satan means that the harmful microbes which are a great cause of the ailment and sufferings of human beings settle down there and thrive. And if Imam Ali says that the spiders' webs, sweepings and rubbish bring poverty in the house it means that the microbes settle down at these places, multiply and make the inmates of the house sick. They are one of the great factors of indigence and ill health which make a person incapable of work and also burden him with expenses of medical treatment and usually when one becomes incapable of doing work and his expenses also multiply he becomes indigent.

Imam Ja'far Sadiq, says: "The most invisible way through which Satan acquires mastery over man is that it settles under his nails". (Wasā'ilush Shi'ah, Vol. I, p. 433)

The holy Prophet says: "Never allow the hair in your armpits to grow, because Satan settles there treating it as its asylum". (Wasā'ilush Shi'ah, Vol. I, p. 436)

The microbes grow and multiply in damp and dark places under suitable temperature.

In order to determine the kind of the microbes or to find out the method of campaign against them they are put in the laboratories in special containers wherein the food liked by them is also provided. Then the containers are placed in a dark and damp place which is ideal for the microbes and consequently they become mature in a short time and multiply profusely.

This method is a new one and not even a century has passed yet. However, the leaders of Islam made the matter clear fourteen centuries ago.

The spot under the nails is a suitable place for the growth of the microbes because on account of the hands touching food and other things sufficient quantity of food becomes available in them and the moisture of the hands and the natural heat of the body help their maturity and multiplication which expose man to danger.

The armpit also provides necessary conditions for the growth and multiplication of the microbes if the hair growing therein are long and as the light of the sun, too, does not fall on it and its washing also takes place after long intervals, the danger is aggravated.

Another tradition of Imam Ali has reached us wherein this matter has been hinted clearly. He says: "Do not keep greasy and meat carrying hankerchief or aprons in the house because these are the abode of Satan". (Wasā'ilush Shi'ah)

In the dark and damp inner folds of a handkerchief and a fleshy and greasy bag to which some foodstuff is also stuck, all the facilities of food, rest, moisture and darkness are provided and such places are considered to be suitable for the growth of the microbes.

Imam Ja'far Sadiq says: "One should not converse with a person suffering from leprosy except when there is a distance of about the length of a lance or a spear (one and a half meter approximately) between them". (Tibb-i Kabir)

In modern medicine, the bacteriologist have proved that while travelling a distnce of one and a half meter from the leper, the microbes of leprosy become weak and few in the atomosphere. (Tibb-i Kabir)

During the days when Imam Ja'far Sadiq prohibited the people from going near the lepers no one knew that very small beings are the agents of this disease and it is possible that it may also be communicated to them by physical contact.

Before the invention of microscope no information about these small organisms was available. The causes of the diseases had not been discovered and the efforts which were made for the treatment of the ailments were mostly erroneous.

After the invention of microscope, observation of the microbes which could not be seen with the naked eye, become possible and in the year 1683 the existence of bacteria was announced. About 200 years later i.e. in the year 1869 Louis Pasteur, the great French scientist proved that the microscopic beings cause diseases and was the first person to wage war against bacteria.

Pasteur, who was equiped with better facilities and prossessed extraordinary aptitude for scientific matters began studying the microbes and the diseases caused by them.

If we wish to judge justly we must admit that the leaders

of Islam have been inspired by Divine revelation and in those times an ordinary man could not understand these matters.

Imam Ali says: "If you are going to drink water from a container (which is broken) do not drink from the place which is broken and similarly do not drink from the side of its handle, because Satan settles at these two points. (Mahāsin)

In this tradition also the contaminations and the possibility of growth of macrobes at the broken part of the container and at the place where the handle is joined with the container have been hinted.

Emphatic recommendations have been made in the traditions of *'Ahlul Bayt'*, about the purity and cleanliness of hands, especially at the time of taking meals.

Hands are the only organs which have contact with us as well as with our enemies in the sense that they come in touch with our eyes and mouth and also come in contact with external polluted things. At one time they put a morsel of food or a fruit in our mouth and at another time they come in touch with the steering of an automobile, tables, chairs etc.

This exceptional condition of hands increases the possibility of their getting contaminated and also increases in the same proportion the possibility of infecting us.

Imam Ja'far Sadiq says: "A person who washes his hands before and after taking his meals will spend his life in ease and will remain safe from diseases". (Wasā'ilush Shi'ah, Vol. XVI)

Another point which is noticed in this behalf is that when the leaders of Islam washed their hands to take their meals they did not touch anything thereafter with their hands and did not even dry them with a towel or a handkerchief, because there also exists a possibility of a towel being contaminated.

Mazarim says: "I saw that as and when Imam Musa Kazim washed his hands before taking meal he did not dry them with a towel, but used a towel after he had taken the food and washed his hands". (Wasā'ilush Shi'ah, Vol. XVI, p. 577)

Once Imam Ja'far Sadiq happened to be present in a feast. At the time of taking meals he washed his hands and a servant brought a towel. The holy Imam did not, however, accept it an and said: "I have washed my hands of these very things" (Wasā'ilush Shi'ah, Vol. XVI, p. 572) i.e. the washing had taken place on account of the hands having touched external things and it is, therefore, necessary that after washing they should not touch anything, not even a towel.

Another subject which needs attention is the cleanliness of the mouth and the teeth.

"Innumerable microbes are found in the mouth the number whereof is considered to exceed the population of a city. These microbes take advantage of the presence of wounds, local wastages or general weak condition of the body do great harm to the mouth and the teeth and cause various diseases. Some cause dental caries and others bring about pyorrhoea with its dangerous consequences. Still others give birth to the bleeding and swelling of the gums and the mucous membrane of the mouth. These microbes enter the mouth by means of air and food or due to the proximity of hands and other things and find favourable conditions for their growth and multiplication. In the healthy persons vital equilibrium exists and the mouth defends itself against the attack of the microbes otherwise the vital equilibrium is disturbed and illness takes place". (Marzhā-i Dānish, Dr Mahmud Siyasi)

In the Islamic teachings, instructions have been given by which these dangers can be obviated satisfactorily.

The leaders of Islam have recommended that after taking meals the food particles should be removed from between the teeth by means of a toothpick.

The holy Prophet says: "Use a toothpick after eating food, because this act keeps the mouth healthy and protects the teeth from decay and destruction". (Mustadrak, Vol. III, p. 100)

The particles of food which come out from between the teeth by means of a toothpick should not be consumed but should be disposed of very carefully.

Imam Ja'far Sadiq says: "Never eat the particles of food which come out from between the teeth by means of a toothpick because they are the cause of internal ulcers". (Furu'-i Kāfī)

The holy Prophet says: "Whoever uses a toothpick after eating food should not devour what comes out by means of the toothpick". (Mustadrak, Vol. III, p. 277)

The space between the teeth is cleansed by means of a toothpick and the teeth should carefully be washed and purified by means of a tooth brush.

Imam Ja'far Sadiq says: "Brushing the teeth is one of the habits of the Prophets". (Wasā'ilush Shi'ah, Vol. I, p. 346)

The holy Prophet says: "If I had not been afraid that my followers might be faced with hardship and inconvenience, I would have made it obligatory for them to brush their teeth before offering daily prayers". ('Ilalush Sharā'i, Vol. I, p. 277)

As regards the method of using a truth brush, the holy Prophet has given the same instructions which are considered to be the best way of brushing the teeth by dental surgeons of the present times. He says: "Do not draw the tooth brush in the linear range, but draw it from upwards to downwards" (Mustadrak, Vol. I, p. 54) i.e. the space between the teeth should be cleansed and nothing should remain between the teeth.

One of the directions which has a great effect on the question of cleanliness is about the cleansing of the nose and the mouth.

When the microbes were discovered and their existence was announced, the people struggled hard to see them and went to the laboratories. On the one hand they saw these harmful organisms by means of microscopes and on the other hand they observed that the microbes died by heat and were destroyed by boiling. These people had come to acquire an eternal life or at least to remain safe from the mischief of the microbes. They preserved their food, garments, headwears and even their quilts by using disinfectants. Later they realized that dust brougtt sufficient number of microbes in contact with their bodies and it was also not easy to disinfect the air. And on the other hand by boiling the food-stuffs which resulted in loss of ingredients necessary for life, the statistics of the Department of Deaths suddenly showed a larger figure and announced that the deaths had increased due to the shortage of vitamins.

Let us not digress. What we mean is that there are a large number of microbes in the air and as man breathes about sixteen times per minute some air containing microbes passes through his nostrils. Hence, in the nostrils of man, rather in those of any animal which breathes, a number of microbes are available. Imam Ali Riza referred to this subject thirteen centureis ago in the following words: "Satan exists in the nostrils of every animal which breathes". (Bihārul Anwār; Awwalin Dānishghah, Vol. I, p. 55)

The holy Prophet says: "Every person must endeavour to perform *'mazmaza'* (rinsing of mouth with clean water) and *'istinshāq'* (drawing up water through nostrils) because this act purifies the mouth and banishes the foul odour (Satan). (Sawābul A'māl, p. 11)

Imam Ali says: *'Mazmaza'* and *'istishāq'* is an admirable religious practice which purifies the mouth and the nose". (Khisāl, Sadūq, Vol. II, p. 156)

What has been stated so far consists of very brief descriptions of the teachings of Islam about cleanliness and a more detailed study of the subject necessitates voluminous books.

As we all know the first chapter of the books on *"Fiqh"* (jurisprudence) which contains the most detailed account is about *tahārat* (purification). In this chapter the details of the question of cleanliness have been discussed very minutely.

The point which must be hinted at the end is, like all other matters Islam has paid attention to the cleanliness of the body as well as the soul and has invited people to maintain purity of body and piety of soul side by side with each other.

The holy Qur'an says: *Allah loves those who repent and those who purify themselves.* (Surah al-Baqarah, 2:222)

If we go deep into the teachings of Islam we find that impure things have been divided into two kinds and their purification also takes place in two ways.

Firstly, there are certain impure things which can be removed by means of water, fire, sunlight and *'istihāla'* (transformation of original form).

Secondly, the spiritual contaminations which can be purified and cleansed by other means. For example a person who calumniates a Muslim and endangers his position and honour should seek his forgiveness. One who transgresses the property of another and violates his right or becomes the owner of the property of others through gambling should return the property in question to its real owners. And one who deceives and misleads another person should guide him to the right path. Every such person should then repent for his misdeeds and make a firm determination not to repeat them in future.

In the sacred verse: 'Truly Allah loves those who turn to Him, and loves those who observes piety", the holy Qur'an has made a reference to these two points that is external and spiritual cleanliness and we learn from this verse that those who endeavour to maintain their body and soul pure and discharge their duties properly are the friends of Allah and He also loves them.

In the end we pray to the Almighty Allah to grant all of us necessary strength to act according to the teachings of Islam so that we may acquire real purity and cleanliness and be happy and successful in this world as well as in the Hereafter.

Quotations
1. Cleanliness is the sign of faith, and the faithful will enter into Paradise. (The holy Prophet)
2. Cleanliness is half the faith. (Imam Ali)
3. Cleanliness is, indeed, next to godliness.
(John Wesley, Sermon on Dress)

* * * * * *

CODE OF INSTRUCTION

In order to acquire real happiness and human perfection it is necessary to have trained and experienced teachers and to exercise great care and attention so that the talents of the individuals may develop and their harmful and improper inclinations may be suppressed.

Without education and training one cannot acquire the perfection deserved by human beings and one's intrinsic qualities cannot blossom and bear fruit.

As opposed to all other animals, which lead their lives with the help of inherent instincts and without any teacher or educator, man needs guidance, education and training.

The nurture and development of talents is not possible only by dint of speaking, hearing and reading, because there are many persons who recognize goodness but are not good themselves and understand what is bad but are still bad themselves.

A gardener looks after the flowers and trees every moment. He arranges them and gives them a good shape with all the means at his disposal. He removes the superfluous bushes and branches. At times he erects shelters for the saplings and utilizes all available facilities for their development and growth.

Able educators should take practical steps to educate the individuals. They should watch them at each step and guide them to the path of prosperity and virtue, because only lecturing and explaining and praising good deeds is not sufficient to build up individuals but training and practice is also necessary.

All know that in order to ride a bicycle it is necessary to hold the handle with two hands and to sit on the saddle and to rotate the paddles with one's feet. And in order to proceed to right or left the handle is to be moved to that side. However, merely knowing these things does not enable a person to ride a bicycle. On the other hand a good deal of practice is necessary to make use of this simple and comparatively trivial vehicle.

In the affairs of life also guidance by the educators as well as sufficient practice is necessary so that the individuals may perform their duty automatically in all circumstances.

The greatest drawback in our educational system is that our parents, teachers, preachers, instructors etc. place knowledge at our disposal and tell us about our duties, but there is not a single preceptor who may tell us at the time of action that such and such is the proper occasion for the application of the knowledge which he made known to us previously.

The method which the late Ayatullah Hāj Shaykh Ja'far Kāshiful Ghita employed for the instruction of the individuals was very instructive and effective.

For example, he wanted to make his son rise early and offer midnight prayers in such a way that he should continue to offer them with heartfelt ardour till the end of his life.

One day he went by the side of his son's bed before the call to dawn prayers, awakened him and said: "Get up so that we may go and pay homage *(ziārat)* to the sacred shrine of Imam Ali, the Commander of the Faithful".

The young man rubbed his drowsy eyes and said "Very well. You may please go and I, too, shall be coming".

The father, however, said. "No. I shall be waiting here so that we may go together".

The young man rose, performed ablutions and proceeded to the sacred shrine along with his father.

In front of the presincts of the shrine they saw a beggar sitting who had stretched his hand to the people. The father asked the son: "Why is this man sitting here?"

The son replied: "To beg and to seek help from the people".

The father asked: "Can you imagine how much money he can earn in this way?"

The son replied: "He may earn a few dirhams".

The father asked: "Is it certain that he gets this money?"

The son replied: "Nothing can be said with certainty. It is possible that he may get some money and it is also possible that he may not get anything".

When the father saw that the ground had been prepared for what he actually wanted to say, he said: "My son! You can see that this beggar has come here at this hour of night and has stretched his hand to acquire a probable worldly gain of which he is not certain. If you really believe in the spiritual reward fixed by Allah for early rising and offering night prayers and have faith in what the holy Imams have said, why do you act sluggishly in regard to it?"

The result was that the son did not give up early rising each night, and offering night prayers till the end of his life.

This result was due to the fact that the able preceptor and learned father created a lasting impression in his son's mind and acted as a stimulant to his performing that good deed.

The instructors should endeavour to make the individuals repeat decent acts so that they may develop their habit and consequently perform them without any inconvenience.

Imam Ali says: "Habit is second nature". (Ghurarul Hikam)

The role of habits in different aspects of life cannot be ignored, because individuals can perform with perfect ease some hard and tiresome jobs on account of their having developed the habit by regular practice.

If the social preceptors and educators by means of correct instructions and vigilance inculcate in the people the habit of performing good deeds, the people will naturally get inclined towards goodness and virtue.

It is evident that the educators can succeed in imparting proper instructions to the people only when they themselves act according to what they say and their conduct is actually an example for others, because if they invite the people towards human values and good deeds only by means of speech and writing, their actions will not be compatible with it and the result will be exactly the reverse of the desired one.

The holy Qur'an says: *Saying what you do not practice is odious to Allah.* (Surah al-Saff, 61:4)

Imam Ali has severely criticized the conduct of such preceptors and has condemned them. He says: "Allah's curse be upon those persons who invite people to good and decent acts but do not perform them themselves and Allah's curse be upon those who warn others against indecent acts but commit the same themselves". (Nahjul Balaghah)

The thing which is most effective for the education of the people is their following the examples in this sense that when young men or the people belonging to other classes observe with their own eyes the decent conduct of their preceptors and tutors they involuntarily become inclined towards good things and adopt sublime characteristics, the specimen whereof have been seen by them.

Hence, the leaders of Islam have recommended that the Muslims should practically invite others to piety and virtue.

Imam Ja'far Sadiq says: "Guide and preach the people by your action and behaviour and not by mere speech".

Advice which finds its way to the human heart through the ears is certainly effective, but its effect is limited and temporary. Hence if preaching and advice is not accompanied by an example so that the people may see the advice and preaching being acted upon practically and may follow it; mere preaching is not sufficient. Such an example sets the heart and soul of the people moving and awakens the dormant faculties which can be seen and felt by them with their very eyes. Such a suitable and effective example has a deep effect on one's heart and is reckoned to be one of the greatest instructive stimulants.

As explicitly stated by the holy Qur'an, the first and foremost assignment of the great Prophet of Islam was the reforming and training of the people of the world. The holy Qur'an says: *Allah granted a great favour to the believers by sending a messenger from their own people to recite to them Allah's revelations, to purify them of moral defects, to teach them the Book and to give them wisdom. Before this they were in manifest error.* (Surah Ale Imran, 3.164)

In this and other similar verses Almighty Allah has given training a precedence to education and it shows that the first step towards prosperity is the refinement and training of the individuals before education and teaching.

Knowledge and wisdom without religious instruction and

strengthening of spiritual bases is a dangerous thing as experience has also confirmed this view.

Nowadays the so-called civilized world is equipped with the tools and weapons of science and industry but lacks in spiritual training. The result thereof is conflicts, wars, bombardments, destruction, crimes and thousands of other calamities.

If those people who possess scientific knowledge and industrial equipments had possessed the kind sentiments and the strength of faith and spirituality they would have thought of human welfare rather than destruction and mischief and would have allocated all these stupendous expenses to the feeding of the hungry and the eradication of poverty and adversity of non-developed countries.

It is here that the able teachers and preceptors should, before anything else, direct their efforts to the training of the individuals and equip them with the strength of faith and spirituality before providing them the benefits of science and industry.

On account of his heavenly assignment, the holy Prophet resorted to the correct and comprehensive training of the individuals and explored all the possibilities in this behalf. He gave instructive lessons to the people by means of his own behaviour and conduct. He put politeness into practice, used to salute all and shook the hands of the people with warmth. He received the people with a cheerful and smiling face, heard their words most attentively, accorded respect to the new visitors, stood up before them and made them sit in his own place. He used to associate with the weak and indigent persons and shared the woes of the people. He sympathized with the people in their hardships and preferred others to himself.

Imam Ali, who was brought up under the guardianship of the holy Prophet and who himself is a great preceptor of the world of humanity, says: "I have never invited the people to do a good act unless, in the first instance, I have done it myself".

If he talked about justice, he himself was in the first place a just person and taught the lesson of justice to the people with his own just conduct. He strongly suppressed the oppressors and provided asylum to the deprived like an affectionate father.

He maintained equality among the Muslims in its full sense

and made the weak enjoy their rights and prevented the transgressors with all his might.

He prohibited the people from indulging in worldly pleasures and was himself also an image of piety and spirituality. He encouraged the people to work hard and he himself made diligent efforts to engage himself in useful work.

He overlooked the mistakes and bad conduct of the people and his followers also learnt these practical lessons from their magnanimous leader and preceptor and acted accordingly.

Mālik Ashtar who was a man of strong constitutions had received instructions from Imam Ali. One day while he was passing through the bazaar of Kufa an ill-bred tradesman who did not recognize him and was not aware of his strength and status threw some rubbish on him by way of fun and ridicule. His neighbour asked him : "Do you know this man on whom you have thrown the rubbish?"

The man replied: "No. He was an indigent passersby".

The neighbour said : "Woe betide you! He was Mālik Ashtar, the Commander of the Islamic forces".

The man began to tremble on hearing the name of Mālik. He became much disturbed and ran in all directions to find Mālik to make amends for his act. After some enquiries and search he found him in the Masjid of Kufa. He threw himself on Mālik's feet and apologized saying. "I did not recognize you. Kindly forgive me for the offence which I have committed".

Mālik showed him kindness and said to him with great magnanimity: "I had forgiven you and had come to the masjid to offer my prayers and to seek Allah's forgiveness for you".

This act of Mālik was a practical training and an unforgettable lesson which he imparted to that man and cautioned him against such slips for ever.

Plenty of the specimens of such practical lessons are found among those trained in the school of Islam and one of the most brilliant services rendered by the greatest Preceptor and Reformer of humanity and the last of the Prophets, Muhammad (peace be upon him and his chosen descendants) to the inhabitants of the world, was the opening of such a sublime school and the presentation of such teachings.

By means of his sublime conduct and guidance the holy

Prophet eradicated and suppressed the undesirable qualities in the people who received training from him and created in them desirable qualities and human traits.

He eradicated their pride, egotism, rancour, ill-naturedness, indecency, weakness and abjectness and replaced them by politenness, philanthropy, love, good-naturedness, piety, self-respect, strength and bravery.

Before the advent of Islam the people of Makkah were attacked by the Ethiopian army and notwithstanding the fact that the Ethiopian army did not deserve much consideration, the Makkans fled the city and did not even think of their homeland and their homes and hearths. However, with his proper and comprehensive training the holy Prophet of Islam gave a new life to that nation and created, out of those weak and timid people, a brave and warlike nation which made the great emperors of that time tremble.

Hence, the holy Qur'an has declared the teachings of Islam to be the source of life and vitality and has advised the people of the world to pay attention to these teachings and to act upon them meticulously in order to acquire the real worth of life. It says: *Believers, listen to Allah and the Messenger when they call you to that which gives you life.* (Surah al-Anfal, 8:24)

It should also be remembered that no instruction is as deep-rooted and reliable as religious instruction.

Dr Mahdi, Ki Niya says: "The Greek philosopher has rightly said, 'There is no art more Divine than the imparting of instructions'. It is because under the right method of instructions one can proceed to the exalted position human values and can become free from the captivity of ignorance, indigence and slavery". ('Ulūm-i Jinā'ī)

Georges Jacques Danton, the orator and notable personality of the French Revolution did not say vainly: "After bread and education, training is the first need of a nation. A society cannot acquire life without proper training and guidance".

No instruction can keep a society more safe from the mischief of wicked acts than religious instrucitions. The light of faith i.e. true belief which rests on rational basis and attention towards Allah guides a nation to the right path.

Real faith is the remedy for all moral ailments. If you want to keep a nation immune from the calamity of loose morals you should firmly establish faith in their hearts. Faith illuminates the heart of man with the light of hope, and the basic element of life is hope.

One can surmount the difficulties of life under the light of faith and the guidance of intellect and firm determination.

Henri Bergson, the French philosopher and writer has said "The well-being of man lies in his returning to God".

One whose attention is always directed towards his Creator does not stand in need of wine to endure hardships. And one who is always intoxicated with the mirth of faith does not find himself in need of the artificial and transient mirth of wine. Hence there is no reason why he should go to the tavern and lose his wisdom.

Dale Carnegie, the contemporary American writer, whose literary works have imensely impressed the people, says: "If thousands of persons who are faced with spiritual unrest and who are crying in mental hospitals had extended their hands to the All-Powerful Creator for help instead of fighting alone the battle of life, they would possibly have attained salvation".

If such instructions had been available in the first instance and the light of faith had illuminated their hearts, there would have been no possibility of superstitious ideas and spiritual torture having taken their roots.

Man should not keep himself aloof from the spiritual remedy and whenever one needs to overcome the backwardness of his spiritual awakening, he should resort to the remembrance of the Almighty Allah, the Lord and the Creator. Thus, illuminate the light of faith within your hearts as it is faith which eradicates all social and moral evils.

Islam rose to break the chain of groundless beliefs, superstitions, injustice, ignorance, indigence and slavery. It proclaimed the freedom of the people, which was based on prosperity, generosity, bravery, chastity, morality, love and affection. This was the freedom in the sense that man should become free from the internal domination of idols, lustful desires, wrath, avarice and all those evils which keep the man under bondage.

Some educated persons think that instructions without the backing of religion can deliver man from moral and social adversity and can guarantee the welfare of the society, but experience has shown exactly the reverse of it.

In the industrial and civilized countries of the West the principles of instruction are taught from kindergarten to the university level through trained and experienced teachers and inspite of this their collective and individual difficulties and misfortunes are increasing day by day and the position is such that even the governments are unable to find out a solution.

In 1962, John F. Kennedy said: "America has a dreadful future because the young people are immersed in lust and can no longer discharge their duties in a proper way and shoulder the responsibilities entrusted to them. As for example, out of every seven persons who are recruited for military service six prove to be incompetent and useless and it is because the excessive sensuality has diminished their physical and spiritual capabilities".

Like Kennedy, Khrushchev also in 1962 said: "The future of the U.S.S.R. is in danger and the young persons do not at all have a hopeful future because they have become irresponsible and have been captivated by lust".

According to a police report as many as 10,000 persons committed suicide in West Germany in 1967. During the same year more than 6,000 men and more than 7,000 women in Germany also attempted to commit suicide who were saved.

The use of narcotic drugs has spread among the Americans in an alarming manner. Recently New York police recovered the bodies of 38 persons whose ages ranged between sixteen and thirty five years and who had died as a result of the use of such drugs. Some of the victims of this curse did not get time even to take out the needle of the syringe from their bodies. Among those who are addicted to narcotics, the number of those who use heroin is the largest. In the present times in New York alone 100,000 persons are addicted to heroin in this sense that one out of every eighty persons uses morphine.

Among the wealthy classes the artists (actors, actresses etc.) occupy the first position. One of the New York physicians has said: "One of the famous American artists injects narcotic substance in his body ten times during every twenty-four hours and the price of every dose is about sixty dollars". The American physician has added: "Many well-known personalities whose death is officially treated to have occurred due to heart-failure actually die because of narcotic drugs". (Daily News Paper, Ittilā'āt, Issue No. 13015)

The materialistic society without the concept of Allah and religion has made life barren and unbearable for the people who possess all facilities of life and have become the champions of the world from the point of view of technique and industry.

The family life has lost its happiness and pleasantness and the ever-increasing rate of divorces is destroying the family life. Human sentiments have ceased to exist even among the fathers and the sons and crime has increased in an alarming manner.

Peace of mind, which is the most important base of the prosperity of man is very rare in the modern world, because such peace and tranquillity can be acquired only by means of faith and religion.

The holy Qur'an says: *Surely there is peace of heart in the contemplation of Allah.* (Surah al-Ra'd, 13:28)

Islamic instruction is based on the principle that strength of every kind as well as all instincts and sentiments should be refined and checked and should be utilized properly.

Islam controls the refractory inclinations and instincts of man by different means so that they may not prevail upon human intellect and assume the authority themselves. At the same time it considers permissible for the individuals a rational and decent share of enjoyment of their instincts.

Islam does not confine man within the four walls of material things and does not look at him from the economic view-point only. On the other hand it has taken all his natural needs into account and has based its instructional programme on the spiritual and moral principles which are the very basis of human values. At the same time it has not ignored the material and economic matters and has encouraged man to make correct efforts and achieve reasonable advancement.

A tradition has been quoted from Imam Ali: "Train your children with ways and manners other than your own, because they have been created for a time different from yours". If such a tradition exists; what the holy Imam means is that you should bring up your children with the knowledge, wisdom and manners of their own time so that they may go forward along with their time.

Some so-called intellectuals have taken undue advantage of this tradition and pretend to say that Imam Ali meant that if the time be that of dancing, obscenity and corruption, you too should bring up your children according to the conditions of the time, although to attribute such a statement to the holy Imam is a sin and blasphemy.

With his words as well as actions the holy Prophet encouraged and advised people to make efforts in all fields. At the same time he endeavoured that they should not get involved in improper and destructive excesses, lest love for wealth and position should prevail upon them or sensuality and voluptuousness should find way into their lives or they should sacrifice spirituality and morality for fleeting material gains.

This method of practical training was employed by all the leaders of Islam and as evidence by history its satisfactory effects were fully apparent in the society.

When the Muslims observed the human and heavenly behaviour of their leaders with their own eyes they were automatically attracted to their ways and manners.

When the people saw that notwithstanding the fact that Imam Ali was the Caliph and the Head of the State and the entire authority was centred in him, he was not severe or cruel even to his murderer and instead had made recommendation to his sons for his physical comfort, they certainly became inclined to justice and human values and this is the most sublime method of instruction which can only be found in the school of the Prophets and the pious devotees of Allah.

In the sixty third year of the Islamic era, the people of Madina revolted against the Caliphate of Yazid and his oppressive behaviour and created a chaotic situation. They expelled the governor of Madina and subjected the members of the Umayyad dynasty to extreme pressure. Marwān bin Hakam who was one of the elders of Bani Umayya and had a long past record of enmity with the family of the holy Prophet came under heavy pressure of the revolutionists along with the members of his family. Danger threatened him from all sides. He was extremely worried and was in search of a refuge so that he might save his wife and children from the revolutionists. He approached everyone of his former friends and requested them to provide asylum to the members of his family in their houses, but all of them gave him a cold shoulder. He went to Abdullah bin Umar bin Khattab but he, too, did not provide him the refuge.

At last he went to Imam Zaynul 'Ābidin, the fourth Imam, and with his past bad record and the harm which he had done to the progeny of the holy Prophet on various occasions he was not hopeful of any favourable response from the holy Imam and it was only the sheer desperation which had driven him to the Imam's doorsteps. However, quite contrary to his expectations, the holy Imam received him cheerfully and with great love. He gave a favourable reply to Marwan's request and sent the members of his family as well as his own to a house in Tā'if, which was owned by him and they lived under the holy Imams protection until the end of the revolution of Madina. (Kāmil ibn Athir)

No doubt this matchless instructional lesson influences every human being and prepares him to follow on the same path.

The leaders of Islam acted so meticulously and sympathetically in instructional matters that they influenced the mentality of the people in all aspects of life and attracted them towards good qualities and virtues. Even during their supplications and prayers to Allah they were not oblivious of this important duty that their supplications should be instructive for the hearers as well as the reciters.

In one of the supplications Imam Sajjad says:

"O Lord! Send your blessings on the souls of Muhammad and his chosen descendants and be my companion and helper in my difficulties. Give me strength so that this heavy burden may not exert pressure on my shoulders and may not prevnent me from doing my duties.

O my Lord! When I raise my head from the earth tomorrow (i.e. on the Day of Judgement) I shall be answerable for my words and deeds before Your court of justice. Destine it for me that I may think today about my tomorrow and may discharge my responsibility in the manner desired by You.

Destine it that my life may come to an end in your obedience and worship. Make me independent of the wealth of others and provide my abundant sustenance. Keep me safe from calamities and make my nature honoured and rich so that I may not covet the wealth of others.

O Lord! Destine it that my hands may work for the good and welfare of the people and similarly keep my efficacious hand safe from reminding someone of favour done to him and from vexing others and keep my tongue silent from self-praise and self-glorification.

O Lord! Reduce my position in my own eyes in the same way in which you exalt it in the eyes of the people and acquaint me with my hidden weakness in the same measure in which you bestow honour upon me in the society so that I may not at all forget my humble position and may not live beyond my means.

O Lord! Reform, with Your unlimited kindness, every indecent habit which You find in me so that it may become decent and take away from me every defect which implicates me in evil things and remove every shortcoming which prevents my soul from attaining perfection.

O Lord! Destine it that I may love all and may be righteous and benevolent towards all.

O my Lord! Bestow these gifts on me as well as on all the Muslims and all the faithful, whether male or female; keep the children of the people under the protection of Your Benevolence Mercy and Favour like my own children and keep them happy and prosperous in this world as well as in the Hereafter.

O Lord! Will it thus that instead of my indulging in bad and abusive language and finding faults and certifying falsehood and saying something opposed to truth and speaking ill of a fellow brother on his back and falsely accusing him in his presence, my heart may abound with thanksgiving to You and Your praise and remembering Your Bounties and the recitation of Your Glorious Name and let it be so that my heart and tongue may always remain illumined with Your remembrance.

O Lord! Let us enjoy Your Kindness in this world as well as in the Hereafter and keep the torture of Hell and Fire of Your Wrath away from us".

From what has been narrated in the above supplication, we draw the following conclusions:

- Without proper training man cannot acquire the perfection which he deserves.

- Besides imparting instruction verbally good preceptors should be a practical example of it.
- Only that instruction can be considered basic and reliable which is founded on religion and belief.
- Western system and method has not been able to solve the problems of the society.
- With their heavenly teachings and conduct the leaders of Islam gave the best instructional lessons to the people and brought the most developed societies into existence.
- In the end we invoke that Almighty Allah may bless all the Mulims with sufficient strength to follow the teachings of Islam and become the most advanced nation of the world.

* * * * * *

TRAINING OF CHILDREN

Only that society can be considered fortunate which is composed of pious, decent, responsible and faithful persons. In order to create such a society and to find such individuals it is necessary to resort to the proper upbringing and training of the children for the future.

Usually people look at the children superficially and do not pay attention to their proper training, although the fact is that the men of today are the children of yesterday and the children of today are the men of tomorrow.

A child who does not receive proper training during his young age cannot be expected to grow up as a pious man so as to be useful for his society.

The importance of the question of the training of children has received much attention in the modern world and the scholars have written numerous books on this subject.

According to the specialists in the field of training the children, the training should commence with the birth of the child and should continue gradually till the child reaches the threshold of perfection.

According to Islam the period of training begins at the time when man and woman enter into metrimonial alliance, as the future parents should feel themselves responsible for the upbringing of their children.

You may be wondering as to what the commencement of the training of the child means before it actually takes birth! However, after a little reflection importance of this direction becomes clear.

According to the law of inheritance which is accepted by the scholars most of the temporal and spiritual conditions and qualities are transferred from the parents to the child and this very thing prepares the ground for his good or bad future.

"All the physical and psychological conditions of a mother have their effect on her child, because in the womb the child is like a limb of the mother. Just as the physical conditions of the mother have their effect on the child in the same way her thoughts and manners affect its body and soul and at times it so happens that the child is affected more than the mother herself. For example, if during the period of her pregnancy a mother struck with terror the effect which this psychological condition has on her body is that her face becomes pale, but the child in the womb meets greater harm by this occurrence.

If during the period of pregnancy a mother is scared in such a way that her face turns pale and she begins to tremble, spots are seen on the body of the new-born which are called birth marks". (Dr Ghiyāthuddin, I'jāz-i Khorākihā, p. 172)

The sorrows, worries, anger, agitation, corruption, unrest, pessimism, malevolence and, in short, all the bad qualities of a mother and similarly her faith, piety, noble disposition, sincerity, love, sympathy, philanthropy, peace and tranquillity of mind, bravery and valour and consequently all the moral qualities of a mother have bad or good effect on the child and lay the foundation of his prosperity or adversity in the womb. As has been said by the holy Prophet: "The root of the prosperity or adversity of the people should be sought for in the wombs of the mothers. (Bihārul Anwār, Vol. III, p. 44)

The psychiatrists have proved that 60% of children who are suffering from mental diseases have inherited them from their mothers and if a mother is healthy and sound the nervous system of her child will also be healthy.

The holy Prophet says: "Select proper places for your seed".

Selection here means choosing the best spouse after studying a large number of similar persons. In this tradition the holy Prophet has explained that the womb of every woman is not fit to produce one's children and one should select the best and the most worthy woman for this important and delicate purpose.

In another tradition the holy Prophet says: "Stay away

from the verdure which grows by the side of rubbish-heap". The people asked: "O Prophet of Allah! What is it?" The holy Prophet replied: "It is a beautiful woman who has been brought up in corrupted family".

In order to prevent the Muslims from producing corrupt progeny Islam has taken all precautionary measures in the matter of marriage and has paid attention to all psychological, physical and moral aspects of man and woman. Islam has warned people against marrying insane persons, idiots and drunkards.

The holy Qur'an has treated woman to be a plantation for man and says: *Your wives are as fields for you, so cultivate your fields as you like.* (Surah al-Baqarah, 2:223)

Undoubtedly a person can acquire satisfactory produce from the cultivation when he cultivates crops in a favourable and proper land, because "A saline land does not produce hyacinth".

Centuries before biology appeared in the world as an independent science, the holy Prophet said: "Avoid marriage with dull and stupid women because association with them is grief and calamity and if they produce children they will be unworthy". (Mustadrak, Kitābun Niqāh)

As regards the effect of the milk which a child utilizes after its birth, the holy Prophet says: "Do not permit that your children should suckle from wicked and corrupt women and similarly from those women who are insane, because the manners, thoughts and conditions of the woman who suckles a child are transferred to that child". (Makarimul Akhlāq, p. 254)

It can be realized from the directions given by Islam as mentioned before that the responsibility of the training of children should be taken into account before marriage so that children who are fit to be trained should be born and great care should also be taken in the matter of suckling so that ground should be prepared for their elevation and advancement and the instruction imparted to them should be more effective.

The children who are born of healthy and pious parents are much more fit to receive training and instructions.

The period of childhood is the best time for the adoption of the right path of life because the power of imitation and acquisition and the sense of accepting things is much more intense in children than in the grown up persons and a child can retain all the acts, manners and words of his preceptor in his mind in the best possible way.

Imam Ali said to his son, Imam Hasan: "The heart of a young child is like a virgin soil which is void of any seed or vegetation. It accepts any seed you sow in it and nourises it. Dear son! I made use of your childhood and resorted to your training before your heart which was fit to receive instruction could become hard and your intellect could become occupied with other matters". (Nahjul Balaghah)

Just as the tutors pay heed to the physical health of the child so they should also attach importance to the development of his soul and feelings and endeavour that his body and soul should progress side by side with each other.

From the very early life of the child his tutor should teach him truthfulness, politeness, kindness, sense of responsibility and other good and decent qualities and they should set practical example before them by their good conduct.

The parents can exercise a great influence in the matter of the training of the children and can play an important role in laying the foundation of their prosperity. This can be done especially by the mother who is responsible to a very large extent for the nurture of the body, soul, sentiments and morals of the child and it is for this very reason that the lap of the mother is considered to be the first seat of learning for the education and training of her off-spring.

If a child receives proper training during the childhood, it may be said that he will remain happy till the end of his life and lucky are those children who are brought up properly by able mothers from the very outset and who acquire good qualities. On growing up, such persons utilize what they have learnt from their mothers without taking pains to build up their character.

In one of his speeches which Imam Husayn delivered on the last day of his life — the day of 'Āshura, he alluded to the importance of proper training and its deep effect on one's life and said: "O people! Be it known to you that Ubaydullah bin Ziyād, the illegitimate son of the bastard father insists on two things viz. war or disgrace (by accepting the oath of allegiance to Yazid). It will be very deplorable that I should submit to abjectness and humiliation. I am not permitted to do so either by Allah or by His holy Prophet, or that pious mother who brought me up or the very thought of my pious and celebrated fathers. None of them permits me that I should prefer humiliation to an honourable death".

In these few sentences the holy Imam actually meant to say that non-submission to mean persons is the result of the training of his worthy preceptors. He further says: "As I have suckled from a pure breast and have received training from pure, dignified and honourable fathers and preceptors I have inherited honour, dignity and freedom and cannot undergo abjectness and humiliation in order to live a disgraceful life.

These words are an instructive lesson which Imam Husayn has given to the various nations viz. that they should seek their honour, glory and prosperity by proper instruction.

Persons who have been brought up in exalted and honourable families have never experienced humiliation and are not prepared in any circumstances to undergo abjectness and disgrace for the sake of leading a disgraceful life.

Incorrect training kills the spirit of honour and freedom in the people and suppresses their aptitude for advancement and leadership and nourishes the spirit of meanness, flattery and abjectness in their nature and passes it to the future generations. This shows that how heavy the responsibility of the parents and the preceptors is!

If the upbringing of the children is limited to food, dress, personal hygiene and education, it will be something quite simple and easy. But the development of their talents and faculties and the strengthening of spiritual power is something very deep and sensitive and needs special care and attention.

Imam Ali, who is an ideal personality and a perfect example for humanity, explicitly recalls the training he received during his childhood under the guardianship of the holy Prophet and takes pride in having had such an able preceptor. He says: "You know well my kinship with the holy Prophet and the special position which I enjoyed in his esteem. I was a child of tender age. The holy Prophet used to make me sit on his lap. He embraced me. He pressed me to his bosom. At times he made me sleep in his bed. He caressed me and made me smell the fine fragrance of his body. On every rising day he showed a specimen of his moral qualities and directed me to follow his manners and morals". (Nahjul Balaghah)

If humanity has bowed its head before Imam Ali and considers him to be above man, and if the followers of religions other than Islam also praise this great benefactor of humanity with fervour and express devotion and admiration for him, one of the most basic secrets thereof is the very point which has been relied upon by Imam Ali himself.

One who has possessed the best physical and spiritual reserves from the point of view of inheritance and has been brought up in the noblest family and under the observation of the most worthy preceptor (viz. the holy Prophet) deserves, when he grows up, to be a distinguished personality and an excellent leader.

Islam has attached so much importance to the proper upbringing of children that it considers the established right of the child over his father.

Imam Zaynul 'Ābidīn says: "Your child enjoys the right on you that you should know that his being is a part of your being and his weal and woe in this world is related to you. You should know that you, in the capacity of his guardian, are responsible to bring him up by imparting him proper training and guide him to Almighty Allah and assist him in obedience to Him. You should be a father who knows his duty and responsibility. You should be a father who knows that if he does good to his child he will be rewarded for it and if he does him harm he will be punished for it". (Makārimul Akhlāq, p. 486)

It is the duty of the parents to create and maintain a pious environment in the house in which love, kind sentiments, conscientiousness, politeness, piety, righteousness and other good qualities and praiseworthy manners should prevail and which should make the children conscientious and polite.

A psychologist says: "The house and the family is the first social environment in which the child is brought up under supervision and guardianship. Hence it has more influence on the growth and gradual development of an individual than all other social environments and before the child comes under the influence of external social conditions he may remain under the influence of his family. The habits and views of the child commence from his house and a glance on these habits and views will make the importance of the influence of the family quite manifest. The child learns from the enviornment of his house all the habits like table manners, talking, walking and general way of dealing with the people as well as views regarding sex, property and rights of others, relations between man and woman, relations between parents and children and guardianship and the role and duty of a man in the family.

In short, as soon as a child arrives in this world and finds itself in the cradle, it is subjected to an environment which consists of the thoughts, feelings, ideas, hopes and aspirations of the family members.

The house is the place where the children learn the code of life in general and the culture of their parents in particular. The first person of the family with whom the child has direct contact is his mother and his life commences with the biological relationship between both of them in the sense that in the beginning the relationship of the child with his mother is based on the satisfaction of biological needs like food and sleep and he recognizes his mother only on account of nourishment and also wants her for it. Later, having grown up gradually he converts his physical and biological relationship into a strong mental and emotional attachments. Thereafter, he establishes his contacts with his father, brothers, sisters relatives and consequently the outside world of his society, and thus secondary influences come into play afterwards. It may, therefore, be said that the life of a child commences with the attachment of his mother and to become deprived of the mother's existence is in fact being deprived of life itself.

A child makes a model for himself and conforms his conduct with every action, whether good or bad, which he sees and with every word, whether decent or indecent, which he hears. And this unqualified imitation is made in the first instance of the parents, because in the family the child is influenced by his parents more than by anyone or anything else.

For this every reason Islam has, in its teachings, drawn the attention of the parents to the great responsibility and the delicate duty which devolves upon them and has given them necessary instructions in every case.

Imam Ja'far Sadiq says: "Love the children. Be kind to them. When you make a promise with them you should keep it by all means, because the children consider you to be their nourisher". (Wasā'ilush Shi'ah, Vol. V, p. 126)

Imam Ali says: "It is not proper that one should tell a lie seriously or in jest and it is not proper that one should make a promise to one's child and break it". (Wasā'ilush Shi'ah)

With perfect sincerity the child considers his parents to be the greatest and the noblest personalities on the face of the earth and does not acknowledge anyone other than them. He considers them a model for himself and follows in their footsteps.

If the parents tell him lies and do not honour the promise made with him, his sentiments are seriously injured and by acquiring this indecent behaviour he acts according to it throughout his life.

Just imagine that when we do not succeed in satisfying a child by usual and natural means we then deceive him, make false promises to him and intimidate him to a great extent.

There are many mothers who, in order to pacify a child who objects to their going out of the house, tell him that they are going to purchase toys for him. The child waits anxiously for their return but eventually finds that they have come back empty-handed.

"The car is ready. A father wants to go from the country house to the town. At the moment he intends entering the car his small son runs up to him and says that he too wants to go to the town. He insists. He entreats. And as the child has not yet learnt that 'no' means absolute refusal he continues to entreat and the father realized that it is not an easy job to dissuade him. He, therefore, quickly resorts to an excuse and says: "My dear! You cannot come to the town like this. Go, change your clothes and then come". On account of the faith which the child naturally has in his father he runs back to change his dress. However, on his return he does not find there anything except the dust left behind by the motor car. On observing this the child becomes impatient and loses temper. He shouts: "You are a liar! You are a liar!" He is right. His father is a liar and there are great chances that this child too, in his turn, will grow up to be a liar". (Mā wa Farzandān-i Mā)

Such actions and behaviour of the parents leave, to some extent, impressions on the innocent heart of the child and some of which are not effaced till the end of his life.

Islam has strictly prohibited the improper acts which spoil the habits of a child and create bad impressions.

Although Islam has made innumerable recommendations in the matter of the upbringing of a child, it has not permitted that he may be maltreated or tormented.

A man came to Imam Ali and complained against his son. The holy Imam said · "Do not cudgel your son and break off relations with him to correct him, and do not prolong the period of your anger but reconcile with him after a short time". (Biharul Anwar, Vol. XXIII, p. 114)

In this tradition the holy Imam has prohibited physical punishment and has directed that in order to correct a child his sentiments should be taken into consideration

A father is the only refuge for a child and when he is ignored by his father he suffers spiritual and sentimental punishment and this punishment can have a deep effect on the child.

After giving this direction the holy Imam recommended immediately that the father should not remain annoyed with his child for a long time, because if the anger of the father has a deep effect on the sentiments of the child its prolongation will cause nervous breakdown of the child. And if his anger does not have much effect on the child its duration will dwindle the personality of the father in his eyes and this corrective measure will not have much effect thereafter.

One day Imam Hasan called his sons and nephews and said to them: "Today you are the children of the society and it may be hoped that tomorrow you will be distinguished persons in the society. You should make efforts to acquire knowledge and wisdom and those of you who do not have a good memory and cannot retain useful matters should write them down and keep those writings in your houses for being utilized at the appropriate time". (Biharul Anwar, Vol. I, p. 110)

In this tradition Imam Hasan has adopted the method of encouragement for the training of the children and this too is one of the methods of utilizing the sentiments of a child.

By nature every human being possesses the instinct of self-love and what can be better than this that instead of administering physical punishment to the children they may be persuaded to perform their duties by rousing this instinct and encouraging them to work for their own bright future as well as for the advancement of the society.

In the modern world encouragement is considered to be one of the best and the most effective means of instruction and the teachers who are able to utilize this method for making the students acquire knowledge and do good deeds will be comparatively more successful in their field.

The holy Prophet says: "Accord respect to your children and behave with them in a decent manner". (Bihārul Anwār)

Harshness shown to the children can make them perform their duties for some time but it can never make them great men with strong character.

Just as the holy Prophet directed his followers to behave with their children respectfully he himself also followed this rule meticulously.

Ummul Fazl, wife of Abbas bin abdul Muttalib, who had the honour of working as a nurse for Imam Husayn, says: "One day when Husayn was in his suckling period, the holy Prophet took him from me and held him in his lap. The child made the dress of the holy Prophet wet. I took the child back from the holy Prophet's lap with a jerk and the child began to cry. The holy Prophet then said to me: "Be calm. Why have you made the child cry? Water can purify my dress, but is there anything which can remove the grief and dejection from the heart of Husayn?" (Hadyatul Ahbāb, Muhaddith Qummi)

A suckling, notwithstanding all his weakness, feels kindness and harshness. Kindness makes him happy and he laughs whereas harshness grieves him and he cries. And this happiness and grief have good and bad effect respectively on his character.

The holy Prophet behaved respectfully not only with his own children but with all the children. As written by the traditionalists, kindness towards the children was one of his praiseworthy attributes.

As and when the holy Prophet returned from a journey and saw the children of the people on the way, he stopped and asked his companions to bring the children to him. On their arrival he embraced some of them and made others sit on his shoulders and also advised his companions to embrace the children. The children became extremely happy on account of this kindness and love of the holy Prophet and they cherished it as a sweet memory after growing up and very often they remembered this incident as a pleasant reminiscence of their early life and felt proud of it". (Mahajjatul Bayzā)

The holy Prophet practically taught his followers to accord respect to the personality of the children so that they too should, in their turn, treat the children with respect and thus the foundation of proper training of the children should be laid.

A point which must be mentioned here is that we should not go to the extremes in the matter of love for children because proper bringing up of a child is that he should be prepared to lead a happy and prosperous life.

Ups and downs, bitterness and defeat and deprivations and failures exist willy nilly in the life of every person and an able preceptor is he who equips a child for facing and overcoming the difficulties of life. The children who enjoy too much love and whose parents surrender to all their desires unconditionally and give practical shape to all their good and bad inclinations, grow up to be obstinate and selfish. They expect and hope that all persons should behave with them like their parents and will obey them and when this hope of theirs is not fulfilled they become sentimental and pessimistic about everyone.

Imam Muhammad says: "The worst fathers are those who pamper and coddle their children more than what is necessary and the worst children are those who annoy their father due to disobedience and failure in the performance of their duties". (Tārikh-i Ya'qūbi, Vol. III, p. 53)

Welbert Robin says: "Undue pampering of a child results in severe emotional abnormality and domineering nature. Consequently the child takes power in his own hands and goes forward at a great speed. And although he has very sensitive nerves he acquires superiority by means of deceit and harshness. Spoilt children grow up as unfortunate, weak and aimless persons. If in the past when the people said to an easygoing mother mockingly: 'Your child is not spoiled but it has been ruined', they did not exaggerate but made a true prediction.

At times observing carelessness in the matter of bringing up of children makes one shudder because truly speaking, we can foresee the massacre of many innocent persons which could be avoided in all probability". (Tarbiyat-i Atfāl-i Dushwār)

Raymond Beech says: "It is necessary that we should mention some mistakes which are committed during the very early period of a child's life. The most current of these mistakes is the behaviour which spoils the child. Undue pampering and coddling at the very outset spoils the children. Parents actually desire the prosperity and success of their child and that is why they give extra attention to pampering. They flatter him and protect him from all pains and troubles even the most trivial ones. And when the child grows up gradually they provide him all means of recreation suited to his age. No doubt, these sentiments are apparently very praiseworthy but in reality they are extremely dangerous". (Mā wa Farzandān-i Mā)

The minute and delicate points related to the upbringing of the children are so numerous that their detailed study necessitates the writing of voluminous books. The scholars and psychologists have conducted extensive studies in this regard and have placed their findings before the people.

The main point, in the matter of upbringing of the children which is accepted almost unanimously by the scholars of the East and the West, is that, if the guardians and parents wish that their children should be brought up properly they should make use of the religious teachings and should acquaint the children with them at the very outset of their lives.

Raymond Beech further says: "No doubt a family is more responsible for providing moral and religious instructions to the child than for anything else, because training the child without moral consideration makes him nothing more than a clever criminal. On the other hand human mind does not incline towards morality without religion and if a person wants to learn the principles of morality without religion it is just like creating a living body which does possess spirit.

The first impression that is made about God on the mind of a child originates from his relations with his parents and similarly his first acquaintance with his father in the matter of obedience, generosity and truthfulness, depends on the behaviour of the family. It is necessary that all these matters should be accomplished during the early period of childhood, because during this period the mind of a child is more susceptible to retain than what he learns at a later part of his life.

Not only that the parents have time and opportunity of paying attention to the spiritual and intellectual guidance of their child, but they are under obligation to acquaint their children with God with all His Goodness and Power and with all His Determination and Greatness. For this purpose they can make use of religious teachings and natural phenomena.

The parents and the preceptors should remember that for the upbringing of a child religion is their strongest influence and power. Faith is such a torch which illuminates the darkest paths. It stirs up and awakens conscience and, wherever there is a deviated person, it easily guides him to the right path". (Mā wa Farzandān-i Mā)

The holy Prophet says: "May Allah save the children of the later time from the improper conduct of their fathers".

The people asked: "O Prophet of Allah! From the conduct of the fathers who are polytheists?"

The holy Prophet replied: "No, but from the conduct of the Muslim fathers who do not teach their children the religious duties and if the children resort to learning religious matters they forbid them from doing so and are contented with regard to them with insignificant material things. I am disgusted with them and they too are disgusted with me". (Mustadrakul Wasā'il)

Abu Abdir Rahman Salmi, who used to teach the holy Qur'an in Madina, taught Imam Husayn's child Surah al-Hamd, the first chapter of the holy Qur'an. When the child recited the surah before his esteemed father the holy Imam rewarded the teacher with valuable gifts and prizes.

Some persons criticized the action of the holy Imam in giving such big prizes to the teacher of his son for teaching one surah of the holy Qur'an. In reply to the objections raised by the people the holy Imam uttered a sentence which was more costly than all the aforesaid prizes. He said : "What comparison can there be between the present which I have given to the teacher of my child as against his teaching the holy Qur'an — the gift which he has given to my child?"

In his reply the holy Imam has called the prize given by him a 'present' and not a 'reward' and as regards the teacher's act he has given it the name of 'a benevolent gift' and has added that there can be no comparison between the two things.

By according so much honour to the teacher the holy Imam taught a lesson to the people that all the Muslims should attend to the religious instruction of their children and take interest in it and consider this matter to be important so that the children should get acquainted with their religious duties from the very begining of their childhood.

Imam Ja'far Sadiq says: "Make your children learn the Islamic traditions and religious commandments as early as possible before the opponents steal a march on you and fill the herrts of your children with misleading words". (al-Kāfi)

While commenting on the sacred verse: *Give glad tidings to the faithful.* (Surah al-Baqarah, 2:97) Imam Hasan Askari, the eleventh Imam says: "On the Day of Judgement Allah will give great reward to the parents of a child. They will say: 'O Lord! On what account has so much blessings and favour been bestowed on us? Our deeds did not deserve such reward! It will be said in reply: 'All these blessings are on this account that you taught your child the holy Qur'an and enlightened him with the commands of Islam and guided him towards the love for the holy Prophet of Islam, Muhammad and his successor Imam Ali and gave him instruction regarding their luminous teachings". (Mustadrakul Wasā'il, Vol. I, p. 290)

What has been stated above is a very brief specimen of the teachings of Islam regarding the bringing up of children, and history shows that the enforcement of these teachings in the first and second centuries A.H. was constructive in producing from among the Muslim children, men and women who were great and magnanimous, learned and able and brave and decent men who excelled all others in virtue and human qualities and women who were most eminent among the women of the world in the matter of modesty and chastity.

In the light of these very teachings and by the enforcement of this very vital instructions the Muslim society became the most advanced, refined and developed of all human societies and was, for many centuries, the torch-bearer of knowledge and civilization throughout the world.

From the day the Islamic system acquired Western colour and the vain and baseless behaviour of the foreigners served as a model for the superficial and characterless Muslims great difficulties and hardships commenced in all aspects of their life.

Nowadays most of the Muslims are ignorant of their most essential and vital religious teachings which guarantees their welfare and success.

The object of publishing these discourses is that the realities of Islam should be placed at the disposal of the intellects of the people without any embellishments and thus a step may be taken towards acquaintance with the religious instructions.

It is hoped that by paying attention and enforcing the Islamic teachings the Muslims will turn towards the right direction and make amends for their backwardness and downfall.

* * * * * *

GOOD LOAN

Islam considers individual ownership to be legal and recognizes every person who acquires property by lawful means to be its owner. At the same time it has enacted special regulations to prevent the accumulation of capital in some hands so that by their enforcement the Islamic nation should not at any time get involved in the individual and collective evils arising out of such accumulation like the modern capitalistic system.

Besides the legal and obligatory duties which devolve upon the wealthy Muslims regarding the payment of a part of their income for the welfare of the deprived classes, they have also been invited to perform a number of collective duties and from the moral and conscientious point of view have been promised, in lieu thereof, reward in this world as well as in the Hereafter.

One of the duties prescribed for the wealthy persons on which Islam has laid emphasis is advancing loan to the needy, which has been given the name of *'qarzul hasnah'* (viz. money advanced without interest and repaid at the pleasure of the borrower).

In the case of such loans on realization of anything by way of interest over and above the principal amount has been disallowed and usury has been declared to be unlawful.

This type of loan which may be given the name of 'Islamic loan has an aspect of purely social service and is at the same time treated to be a religious duty — so much so that in Islamic traditions such loans have been declared to be superior to giving of alms. This is so because it is possible that alms may be given to a person who may not really stand in need of them but a loan is usually given to one who actually needs it and only that person involves himself in loan who requires the money for some urgent and important purpose. (Safinatul Bihār, Vol. II, p. 424) Not only this that such a loan is not injurious for the society and does not destroy the good order of the families like usury, but it is very helpful for solving the financial problems of the people and plays a very important role in cementing their relations and creating friendship between them.

Islam has attached much importance to assistance of this sort which, while improving the conditions of the people, is quite distinct from supporting beggary. It has encouraged the Muslims to take such steps and thereby to serve the society and help the believers.

Imam Ja'far Sadiq says: "Every Muslim who fulfils the need of his brother-in-faith is declared by Allah thus: Your reward lies with Me and I do not like a reward for you lesser than Paradise". (Sawābul A'māl)

The holy Prophet says: "Allah will eliminate the worry and grief, in both the worlds, of a person from whose hands the problem of a brother Muslim of his is solved".

Ibn Abbas says: "Imam Hasan had observed *i'tikāf* (seclusion for worship) in Masjidul Harām and was performing *tawāf* (circumumbulation) of the holy Ka'bah. In the meantime a faithful approached him and said: 'O Son of the Prophet of Allah! I owe some money to such and such person. Kindly pay my debt, if possible'. The holy Imam said: 'I am sorry to say that just at present I don't have the required amount of money with me'. The man said: 'Then please ask him to give me some time as he has threatened me that if I failed repay the loan he will throw me into prison'. The holy Imam discontinued his *tawāf* and accompanied him with a view to see the creditor and ask him for time.

Ibn Abbas says: 'I said: O son of the Prophet of Allah! Have you forgotten that you have decided to observe *i'tikāf* in the masjid? (Because a person who observes *i'tikāf* is not entitled to leave the masjid before the prescribed period ends). The Imam said: 'I have not forgotten this thing. However, I heard from my father that the holy Prophet said: 'Whoever meets the need of a brother believer is like one who may have worshipped Allah and remained awake at night for many years". (Safinatul Bihār, Vol. I)

Imam Muhammad Baqir says: "If a person advances money to a needy person and allows him time (for repayment) till his financial conditions improve, his property amounts to zakat and the angels pray and seek blessings for him till the day he gets back the loan". (Man Lā Yazuruhul Faqih, p. 361)

Imam Ja'far Sadiq says: "The famous word *ma'rūf* (good deeds) which occurs in the sacred verse consists of advancing loan to the people. The Almighty Allah says: *No good come from their talk unless it is for charity, justice or for reconciliation among men or for seeking the pleasure of Allah for which He will give a great reward"*. (Surah an-Nisa, 4:114; Vide Man Lā Yazuruhul Faqih, p. 361)

Imam Sadiq further says: "When a man gives a loan to a Muslim and set a time-limit for its repayment but the debtor is unable to repay the debt in time and if the moratorium is allowed by the creditor Allah will recompense him for the reward of a charity for every single extended day". (Sawābul A'māl, p. 76)

The holy Prophet says: "If I lend twice 1000 dirhams out of my property to my brethren-in-faith I consider it better than spending that amount at a single instance for the sake of Allah". (Tahzib, Vol. II, p. 61)

These emphatic directions have been given with this object in view that the Muslims may solve the problems of their brethren-in-faith by means of their wealth and provide means of their welfare and prosperous life without coveting for material gain and without getting involved in usury.

Usury is Prohibited

Only that person becomes entitled to these Divine virtues and rewards whose object in advancing the loan is not the realization of interest but who undertakes this work for the welfare of the nation and to seek the pleasure of Allah.

If interest is fixed and realized against a loan it ceases to be good loan and falls under the category of usury, which is considered by Islam to be one of the major sins — rather one of the greatest sins.

In connection with the interpretation of the verses of surah al-Baqarah, Allama Tabātabā'i says: "In these verses the Almighty Allah has been severe with regard to usury to an extent to which he has not been severe in respect of any other branch of faith, except relations with the enemies of Islam. Although the tone in which other major sins like adultery, drinking wine, gambling and even murder have been mentioned is very harsh, yet it is not as harsh as that relating to these two curses. This severity is due to the fact that whereas other sins do not affect more than one or a few persons but the evil effects of these two sins ruin the foundations of religion, destroy the organization of the society and corrupt human nature.

The course of history proved the correctness of the view of Islam regarding the dangers ensuing from these two curses, because relation with the enemies of Islam and inclination towards them pulled the Muslims to such a dangerous precipice that all virtues departed from among them and their condition became such that they ceased to be the owners of their own wealth, life and honour and began struggling between life and death. Usury and profiteering also became the cause of centralization of wealth and the division of the people into two groups viz. the rich and the poor. At last the world war took place and a disturbance became a foot which pulled down the mountains, shook the earth and threatened humanity with annihilation. And what happened eventually is well-known". (al-Mizān, Vol. II)

Islam has endeavoured to establish the spirit of co-operation, sincerity, mutual help and kindness between the Mulims in the best possible manner. Usury is a sort of economic exchange which weakens these ties and sentiments, sows the seeds of extensive enmity and grudge in the hearts and pollutes the atmosphere of the society with the feeling of revenge.

The system of usury is based on this principle that in all conditions, that is whether the borrower gains or loses by utilizing the loan, the lender must get interest on the principal amount. He is not at all concerned with the loss, if any, sustained by the borrower. Even if the poor borrower becomes bankrupt or insolvent he must pay the total interest without any remission, though this pitiable condition does not harmonize with the standard of equity, justice and human values.

Justice demands that if the usurer takes interest from the borrower on account of the profit earned by him he must also share the loss which he sustains. This position is evidently inequitable that he should always be after gain and should have nothing to do with the loss sustained by the other party. Such a transaction is not based on anything other than a cent per cent attitude of personal gain.

The borrower knows that the usurer has made money the means of exploitation of the poor class which does not possess any capital. Although he agrees to such a transaction under the force of circumstances yet he does not forget the unjust and inhuman nature of the usurer.

In the usuary system a stage usually arrives when the debtors feel the severest grip of the clutches of the usurer on their throats. What position will arise when the debtor is not able to earn any profit from the loan but the interest accumulates in such a manner that it becomes many times as much as the principal amount and the very existence and life of the poor debtor is endangered? On such an occasion what can be expected from the debtor except that he should curse the usurer and become thirsty of his blood!

It is in such critical conditions that scores of dreadful and tragic crimes are committed. It has often been seen that the debtors who become absolutely helpless kill the creditors in a very ruthless manner and leave their families in utter distress without a supporter. Many of them are so much tired of their lives that they find no solution other than ending their lives and commit suicide. The courts of justice have so far witnessed many bloody scenes of these tragic suicides and also in the daily press one sees many instances of such man-slaughters and suicides which are caused due to usury.

Let us look at a usurer from the point of view of spiritual and moral considerations. He is a person who has bade farewell to morality. He thinks only of his profit and is ready, for this reason, to exert every kind of pressure on the debtor. He is devoid of human sentiments. Cruelty of a special kind awakens in the minds of these people. They look at everything from the view-point of material gain. Their entire spiritual and human personality may be summed up in profiteering. This love for profit does not permit them to realize the dangerous consequences of usury so far as the debtor is concerned. Their power of moral assessment is suppressed.

The holy Qur'an thus depicts the condition of the usurers: *Those who take usury will stand before Allah (on the Day of Judgement) as those who suffer from a mental imbalance because of Satan's touch.* (Surah al-Baqarah, 2:275)

Usury does not only affect the morality of the usurer but on the other hand it is the cause of many social, moral, economic and other evils and it is for this very reason that Islam treats it as a revolt against Almighty Allah. The holy Qur'an says: *Believers, have fear of Allah and give up whatever rate of interest you still demand from others, if you are indeed true believers. If you will not give up the rate of interest which you demand, know that you are in the state of war with Allah and His Messenger. But if you repent, you will have your capital without being wronged or having done wrong to others. One who faces hardship in paying his debts must be given time until his financial condition improves. Would that you know that waiving such a loan as charity would be better for you.* (Surah al-Baqarah, 2:278 − 280)

It further says: *Do not exchange your property unjustly but trade by mutual consent.* (Surah an-Nisa, 4:29)

Imam Muhammad Baqir says: "What is meant by the word *bātil* (unjustly) in this verse is usury, gambling, deluding the buyer and doing injustice". (Tafsir Majma'ul Bayān)

The holy Qur'an has condemned the Jews for committing sins, taking interest on money and violating the rights of one another in matter of property. It says: *We made unlawful for the Jews certain pure things which had been lawful for them before, because of the injustice which they had committed, their obstructing people from the way of Allah, their taking usury which was prohibited for them and their consuming other's property unjustly. For the unbelievers among them, We have prepared a painful torment.* (Surah an-Nisa, 4:161)

The exegetists says: "The Jews, while acting as judges, took bribes and wrote books themselves and told the people that they were from Allah and collected money from them on that account".

Giving Gift to the Lender

It is necessary to make it clear that the interest which is unlawful consists of that thing which at the time of giving the loan the lender may stipulate with the borrower that he will repay something over and above the principal amount of the loan. However, if the lender advances money as 'good loan' without any condition of over-payment and the debtor, while making repayment, gives something in addition to the principal amount it is not only not unlawful but his action will be a recommendably lawful act.

Imam Ja'far Sadiq says: "Profiteering from loan is of two kinds, one of which is lawful and the other is unlawful. The kind which is lawful is that one may give money as loan with the hope of getting profit, but without any condition or stipulation. If, in that case, the borrower gives him something (over and above the principal amount) it is lawful for him, but he is not entitled to any Divine reward and recompense. And the unlawful profit is that the lender may stipulate that the borrower would pay him something over and above the principal amount. This action is illegal and unlawful.

Imam Muhammad Baqir was asked: "A man has advanced a loan to another and the borrower sends a gift to the lender. Is it permissible or not?" The holy Imam replied: "It is permissible and there is no harm in taking it". (Mustadrak, Vol. II, p. 492)

Islamic traditions on this subject are numerous and it is learnt from all of them taken together that it is possible to set up a correct banking system in accordance with which the rights of those who provide the capital should remain safe and the borrowers, too, should not have to face distress and adversity as a result of payment of exorbitant interest.

It is evident that the wages and expenses of the employees and the preparation of bills and other related documents will have nothing to do with 'interest'.

For further information on the subject refer to *Iqtisāduna* (Our Economics) and *al-Bank al-lā Rabawi Fil Islam* (Interest-free Banking in Islam) written by the Martyr, Sayyid Muhammad Baqir Sadr and similarly other books written by Muslim scholars.

Apart from the recommendations made by Islam about advancing good loan and refraining from taking usury, the

From what has been stated above we draw the following conclusions:
- Islam is strongly opposed to usury, especially when it is to the detriment of the people.
- Good loan is a great social service and a valuable religious deed amounting to worship of Allah.
- Usury is not permissible on any account and under any title and amounts to revolting against Allah.
- The Muslims are under obligations to honour the rights of one another and not to be negligent in repayment of loans.
- If the creditors know that the debtors are in distress financially they should give them extension in time so that their circumstances may improve.
- It is not permissible to take over the residential house and the necessities of life of a debtor in the realization of debt.

In the end we invite our Muslim brethren to study the economic system of Islam exhaustively written on the subject so that they may become more orientated with the magnanimity of Islam and its eternally viable regulations. And simultaneously with the studying of the economi system of Islam they should also put it into practice so that with the grace of Allah, a valuable service is rendered to the society and a forward step is taken towards prosperity in both the worlds.

* * * * * *

CAMPAIGN AGAINST CORRUPTION

Numerous invisible powers have been so endowed in the human body that everyone of which plays a great role in man's life. Although many of these powers have not been perfectly identified yet but their effects have been discovered to some extent by the psychologists.

The spirit of justice, sincerity, equity, manliness, philanthropy, compassion, love for goodness etc. exist in the nature of man. Similarly instincts like selfishness, egotism, love for supremacy, vengeance, love for comfort etc. are also found in him.

These hidden powers pull man to piety or to corruption. If the seeds of good qualities which have been given to all human beings are allowed to nourish properly under favourable conditions, it will bear fruits and by which man acquires the desired perfection and if the baser instincts and disposition become strong and dominate the affairs of life the result is nothing but corruption and destruction.

Man by his very nature wants to enjoy without any restrictions the pleasures of worldly life but the position is that he indulges in unlawful enjoyments which damage the prospects of his prosperity and put him into trouble.

The unlawful acts which are called 'sins' in the terminology of religion undoubtedly bring about inauspicious incidents and irreparable losses in different walks of life.

According to the leaders of Islam all individual and social misfortunes and many sufferings faced by the people are the result of their sins and loose morals.

Imam Muhammad Baqir says: "Injustice is of three kinds:
(i) The injustice which cannot be forgive on any account and that is making anyone partner of Allah.
(ii) The injustice which can be forgiven consists of the sins which a person commits against his ownself and the matter is between him and Allah only.
(iii) The injustice which is not forgiven by Allah, consists of the rights of the people and the debts owed by the person concerned". (Khisāl Sadūq, Vol. I, p. 134)

In order to safeguard the rights of the people Islam provides that if a deceased person is indebted the debts should be the first charge on his property after meeting expenses with regard to his shrouding and burial.

The holy Prophet says: "If a person dies, first the expenses of his funeral should be met out of his property and then his debts should be repaid. Thereafter his will, if any, should be executed and if anything is left it should be distributed among his heirs". (Mustadrakul Wasā'il, Vol. II, p. 491)

The Shi'ah jurists *(mujtahids)* are unanimous on this point that if a borrower is in a position to repay his debt and the lender also demands it, the borrower is not entitled to offer his prayers when the time is sufficient for it unless he should first repay his debt and then offer his prayers.

In this connection the verdicts of the jurists are given below:

"If a person is offering his prayers within prayer time and the lender demands the repayment of the debt he should repay it during prayers, if he can repay it in that condition. In case, however, it is not possible to repay it without breaking the prayers he should break the prayers, repay the loan and then offer the prayers". (Tawzihul Masā'il Muhashshi, Article — 1170)

"If a borrower is in a position to repay his debt and the lender demands its repayment, it is unlawful for the borrower to offer prayers during the early time of prayer before repaying the debt". (Shaykh Bhā'i, Jāmi' Abbāsi, p. 144)

"If the repayment of a debt demanded by the lender depends on breaking the prayers it is obligatory for the borrower to break the prayers during the prayer time and repay the debt. ('Urwatul Wuthqā, p. 252)

House of the Debtor Should not be Occupied

Although Islam has made strong recommendations regarding the rights of the people and repayment of debts and has considered negligence in the matter of repayment of debts to be injustice, treachery and sin, it has at the same time asked the lenders to allow time to the borrowers for repayment and not to subject them to hardship and distress.

The holy Prophet says: "Just as it is not permissible for your debtor to neglect repayment of the debt when he is in a position to repay it, in the same way it is not permissible for you to subject him to pressure when you know that he is in adverse circumstances". (Wasā'ilush Shi'ah, Chapter 25, debt)

According to the regulations of Islam it is not permissible for a creditor to take himself or put to sale the residential house of the debtor and similarly the necessities of his life like dress, carpet, utensils etc. in order to realize his debt.

Imam Ja'far Sadiq says: "A residential house cannot be sold against debt, because it is necessary for everyone to possess a place to live in". (Furu'ul Kāfi, Vol. I, p. 35)

Muhammad bin Abi Umayr was a draper and a faithful follower of Imam Ja'far Sadiq. As a result of the oppression of the Abbasid Caliphs his financial position became very weak and he lost his entire capital and became confined at home.

One of his acquaintances owed him 10,000 dirhams. When he saw the unenviable condition of Muhammad bin Umayr, he sold his residential house and brought the money to him. Muhammad asked the man: "What money it is? He replied: "It is the amount which I owe you". Muhammad asked: "Has something come down to you by inheritance?" He replied: "No". Muhammad asked: "Has someone given you this money as a gift?" He replied: "No". Muhammad asked: "Did you own some real estate which you have sold?" He replied: "No. It is none of these things. On the other hand on seeing your condition I have sold my house and have brought the sale proceeds to discharge my debt". Muhammad said: "Although I need every dirham of this money, I will not take even one dirham out of it, because my leader, Imam Ja'far Sadiq has said: 'Do not turn out a man from his house to realize your debt'. Pick up this money and get back your house". (Wasā'ilush Shi'ah, Vol. II, p. 622) borrowers have also been told to try their utmost to pay back their debts.

According to the Islamic regulations a loan is of two kinds: The first kind of loan is that for the repayment of which a time has been fixed. In such a case the lender has no right to claim repayment of the loan before the due date except in the event of the death of the borrower he becomes entitled to claim and realize the amount of loan before the inheritance is divided. The second kind of loan is that for the repayment of which no period has been fixed. In such a case it is incumbent upon the borrower to repay the loan immediately as and when the lender asks for it, even though he may have to sell for this purpose some of his belongings which are not the necessities of life and if he is negligent in making repayment he is guilty of sin.

The holy Prophet says: "If a person is negligent in paying his debts inspite of his being in a position to pay them ten times sins is recorded in his deed-sheet for every single day of the period of delay". (Wasā'ilush Shi'ah, Chapter on debt)

Imam Ja'far Sadiq says: "One who obtains a loan and does not intend repaying it is just like a thief". (Furu'ul Kāfi)

Imam Sadiq further says: "One who approaches another person for a loan and intends not to repay it is a cold-blooded thief". (Man LāYahzuruhul Faqih, Vol. II, p. 60)

Imam Muhammad Baqir says: "Martyrdom in the path of Allah makes amends for every sin except for indebtedness to the people which cannot be compensated by anything except that the debtor himself or his executor or guardian repays it or the lender forgoes it". (Wasā'ilush Shi'ah, Vol. XIII, p. 83)

Mu'awiya bin Wahab says: "I said to Imam Ja'far Sadiq: 'I have heard that a man from amongst the Ansar had passed away after owing two dinars to a person. The holy Prophet declined to offer his funeral prayers and told his relatives to go and offer the prayers themselves. They, however, undertook to repay the debt and it was only then that the holy Prophet offered his funeral prayers".

Imam Ja'far Sadiq said: "This tradition is authentic and the holy Prophet took this step so that people should honour the rights of one another and should not consider their debts to be something light but should repay them".

Imam Muhammad Baqir says: "The first drop of the blood of a martyr which falls on the earth is an atonement for his sins, except for his debts the atonement wherefor is their repayment and nothing else". (Wasā'ilush Shi'ah, Vol. XIII, p. 85)

Abi Thumāma reports that he said to Imam Muhammad Taqi: "I have decided to settle in Madina and Makkah. However, I am indepted to some persons. What is your view in the matter? The holy Imam replied: "Return to your home town and remain there until you repay your debts and you should try to ensure that you are not indebted to anyone on the day you meet Allah (on the day of your death), because a true believer does not commit treachery. ('Ilalush Sharāya', p. 178)

In this tradition the ninth Imam has considered negligence in the matter of repayment of debt and failure to pay the rights of the people to be treachery, just as the holy Prophet has called it 'oppression'.

Imam Ali says: "I heard the holy Prophet saying that a Muslim who can afford to repay his debt and neglects to do so commits oppression upon the Muslims". (al-Kāfi)

In these two traditions failure to pay the rights of the people has been described to be treachery and oppression upon the Muslim society and this is an undeniable reality because in a society the economic condition of the people is interdependent with another like a necklace of beads. Just as one person is indebted to another it is possible that the lender may be indebted to a third person and he, in turn, may be indebted to another person. If one of these persons is dishonest and fails to repay the debt it is possible that the second person, too, not be in a position to repay what he owes to the third person and so on. Hence, on account of the dishonesty of one person, a group of Muslims becomes involved in difficulties. Moreover, the Muslim society has been founded on mutual confidence and respect for the rights of one another and if any person betrays public confidence with a cowardly act, that is by ignoring the rights of the people, he is guilty of treachery and injustice done to the Muslim society.

Islam considers violation of the rights of others to be injustice and an unpardonable sin and the acceptance of repentance for this sin depends upon there payment of the rights.

The holy Qur'an considers the destruction and extinction of many nations of the past which lived in this world for sometime and nothing except their names are now extant in history to be the result of their evil deeds and sins and thus it says: *They rejected the revelations of Allah and because of their sins His retribution struck them.* (Surah al-Anfal, 8:54)

Similarly the holy Qur'an considers 'sin' to be the cause of loss of blessings and it says: *Allah does not change the favour that He has bestowed on a nation unless that nation changes its state.* (Surah al-Anfal, 8:55)

Imam Muhammad Baqir says: "Allah has proclaimed descisively that when He bestows a blessing on someone He does not take it away from him unless he commits a sin as a result whereof he deserves that the blessings may be taken away from him". (al-Kāfi, Vol. II, p. 209)

Imam Ja'far Sadiq says: "Certainly sin becomes the cause of one's being deprived of his daily portion and becoming involved in indigence". (al-Kāfi, Vol. II, p. 208)

Dr Alexis Carrel, a renowned physiologist says: "It will not be wise if we wish to forget the existence of sin because as a matter of principle, sin is harmful. As we know, life destroys, sooner or later those who commit it".

"Sin consists of trampling down the laws of life intentionally or unintentionally and the laws of life, too, are unbreakable like the laws of the mixture of gases or the fall of bodies. However, as the punishment for sin comes very late man has not yet realized the seriousness of the consequences of sin. Every sin becomes the cause of appearance of irreparable organic, mental and social disorders. Just as it is not possible to remove the physical ailment of a habitual drunkard by his repentance or the defects inherited by the children in the same way it is not possible to eradicate the maleficent effects of jealousy, slander, grudge and back-biting. Sooner or later sin culminates in the over-throw and the ultimate death of the sinner or his progeny or the nation. Hence one should properly distinguish a bad person from a good person and should know where the invisible line has been drawn between right and wrong in the realm of reality. (Rāh wa Rasm-i Zindagi)

Imam Ali Riza considers the commission of every new sin

the cause of a new calamity, and says: "When people commit a new sin which they have not committed before, Allah subjects them to a new calamity which they have not experienced before". (al-Kāfi, Vol. II, p. 211)

Imam Ali says: "By Allah! It has never happened that a nation may be living in welfare, comfort and blessings and that comfort and blessings may be taken away from it except on account of the sins which its members commit. This is so because Allah never oppresses His servants". (Nahjul Balaghah)

In the holy Qur'an the people have been asked to travel over the world and study the conditions of the past nations and discover and understand the realities about their overthrow and extinction which were due to their sins. The holy Qur'an says: *Say, 'travel through the land and see how terrible was the end of the criminals'* (Surah an-Naml, 27:69)

It also says, *Haven't they travelled through the land to see the terrible end of those who lived before them. They have been mightier than them in power and in leaving their traces on earth. Allah punished them for their sins. They had no one to save them from Allah's torment.* (Surah al-Mu'min, 40:21)

History tells as how sin subjects man to adversity and makes him proceed to the world of obscurity.

The following event has been narrated in *A'lāmun Nās:*

"A minister of the Abbasid Caliph, Mu'tasim, who enjoyed all the facilities of life, built a very magnificent multi-storeyed palace. He used to sit in the top floor of the palace and peeped into the houses of the people through the windows and looked at their women and young girls.

One day his eyes fell on a very beautiful girl and he madly fell in love with her. He made enquiries to find out as to who the girl was and eventually came to know that she was the daughter of one of the merchants of the city.

He asked for the hand of the girl but her parents declined to accept his wish. He made many efforts in this behalf and made some notables and distinguished persons intercede in the matter, but did not meet with success.

He made the matter known to one of his friends and asked him to suggest a solution of the problem. He replied: "If you place 1000 dinars at my disposal I shall make arrangements for the attainment of your desired object".

returned to Allah and has repented for his sins". (Rawzatul Jannāt, Fuzail)

The thing which prevented this man from committing sin and changed his destiny was a reminder. Of course, he did possess beliefs and faith, although weak, so that the reminder could impress his heart and brought about a revolution and a change in him.

Hence, the first step towards combating with sin and corruption is that the people should be acquainted with the realities of religion and the faith in Allah, the Day of judgement, accountablility for good or bad deeds and spiritual reward or punishment thereof etc. may flourish in their hearts and bear fruit.

Dr Ki Niya says: "Kindle the fire of faith in the hearts of the people, because faith is the most effective weapon for fighting against all social and moral evils". ('Ulum-i Jinā'i, Vol. II)

Another step which Islam has taken for fighting against sin is limiting the implements and factors of sin.

As we are all aware, in order to eradicte a disease, the hygienic organizations besiege all the factors of the cause of the disease and make efforts to destroy it by different means. They vaccinate the people, introduce compulsory quarantine and place at the disposal of the people necessary medicines in sufficient quantity to enable them to prevent the disease. Similarly, for the eradication of sin, it is necessary that the people should be equipped with the strength of faith to enable them to commit sin and at the same time the environments should be cleared of the pollution of sins and whatever becomes the cause of sins should be checked and circumscribed. Islam has taken steps on these lines for fighting againnst alcoholic beverages, gambling, theft, adultery, manslaughter, usury etc.

In the first instance, making use of the faith and religious beliefs of the Muslims, Islam has declared these deeds to be unlawful and their commission to be the cause of Divine wrath and on the other hand by fixing individual and collective duties of the Muslims it has prevented the coming into existence of favourable ground for the appearance of sin.

The holy Qur'an makes the following recommendation to the Muslims: *Co-operate with each other in righteousness and piety, not in sin and hostility.* (Surah al-Maidah, 5:3)

Propagating One's Sins

In order to keep the environments pure, Islam does not permit the people to be inquisitive about the sins of one another and gives clear orders to this effect: *Believers, stay away from conjecture; acting upon some conjecture may lead to sin. So do not pry into other's secrets and do not back-bite. Would any of you like to eat a dead brother's flesh?* (Surah al-Hujarat, 49:12)

If at times a person becomes aware of a hidden sin of another he is not allowed to give it a publicity and to mention it before other people, because doing so will result in his being disgraced and as a result thereof he will become more bold in the matter of commission of sins.

Spreading the news about the lapses, crimes and lack of restraint of the people makes sin something light and trivial in the eyes of the society and becomes the cause of the prevalence of sin. The holy Qur'an has warned of severe torture to those who assist in the propagation of sin by spreadinng news and it says: *Those who like to publicize indecency among the believers will face painful torment in this world and in the life to come.* (Surah an-Nur, 24:19)

The holy Prophet says: "The sin of one who spreads the news of a bad deed among the people is like the one who has actually committed it". (Safinatul Bihār, Vol. II, p. 295)

Imam Ja'far Sadiq says: "If a person becomes aware of the sin committed by a believer and does not conceal it and does not seek his forgiveness from Allah but makes it public and spreads it among the people his sin before Allah is of the same magnitude as of the person who has committed it". (Safinatul Bihār, Vol. II, p. 296)

National Supervision

One of the methods which Islam has prescribed for campaign against sin and various kinds of evil is the law of social supervision.

This law permits all Muslims — rather makes them responsible that they should exercise supervision for the enforcement of Divine laws and if they find anyone breaking the law they should not remain indifferent but should try to reform him in a wise and proper manner, restrain him from doing anything unlawful and thus prevent the commission of sin.

they may be, are transient and usually we have to suffer many times more than their real worth. So why should we involve ourselves in everlasting loss for a temporary pleasure?

These transient pleasures are a dangerous lightning which shines in the darkness of life and its lustre dazzles the eyes of the ignorant. However, very soon its flame burns the harvest of auspiciousness and good fortune and makes some helpless persons sit on the heap of its ashes with regret and despair.

Base enjoyments are like a mirage which manifests itself in the sandy region of the world from a distance and as soon as we reach near it we find nothing except hot and burning sand. The deceitful pleasures which attract the young persons are like fog and mist which covers the sky in the morning. A wise person does not attach much importance to it and knows that this mist will soon disappear due to the heat of the sun".

Dr Alexis Carrel says: "An unrestrained person is not at all like an eagle which flies in the limitless space of the sky. On the other hand he resembles more a dog which has run away from its abode and for fear of being caught runs around in the buzzing noises of the automobiles".

Many sinners get involved in sins due to carelessness and ignorance about their consequences and undoubtedly if they had been aware of the harm done by sins to one's body and soul and in this world and in the Hereafter they would have taken care of themselves and would have refrained from the harmful pleasures which have been made unlawful by Allah.

It is evident that only those persons can refrain from sin for the sake of Allah who possess faith and religious beliefs. As regards faithless sinners nothing can prevent them from committing sins except force.

Hence, in the Islamic teachings the question of faith has been given priority to everything and utmost effort has been made that by studying the religious realities the Muslims should acquire strong faith so that the strength of faith should keep them from committing sins.

The command of this invisible strength, the headquarters whereof is the depth of the hearts and souls of the people, is so penetrating and effective that at the time of the appearance of the danger of sin it saves the individuals from degradation and deviation. This very strength under Divine inspiration makes the people resort to beneficence, piety kindness, justice, public service and other human virtues.

Experience has shown that if a person possesses the strength of faith, howmuchsoever weak it may be, he will save himself from falling into the ditch of sins by his act of remembering Allah.

It is recorded in history that Fuzail bin Ayāz was a notorious dacoit. He used to attack the caravans and rob the property of the people. The caravans which used to pass through Sarkhas region took all necessary precautions so as not to fall under Fuzail's trap.

This dangerous outlaw fell in love with a girl and decided to go to her house at night and meet her. At midnight he went and ascended the wall of her house. However, he had not yet entered the house when he heard a very pleasant voice of a person from the adjacent house reciting the verse of holy Qur'an: *Is it not time for the hearts of the believers to become humbled by the remembrance of Allah?* (Surah al-Hadid, 57:16)

By hearing the sacred verse, Fuzail felt a sudden change and he said, "O Lord! The time for that has now come". He then descended the wall immediately and refrained from committing the sin which he intended to commit. This very reminder became the cause of Fuzail's forsaking all the evil deeds. During the same night when the said change came within Fuzail he chanced to pass by an inn where a caravan had arrived and unloaded its merchandise. Fuzail crept into a corner and began regretting his ignoble past. At that moment he heard the members of the caravan talking about the hour of their departure. One of them said: "My friends! Don't move from here tonight and let the atmosphere become favourable, because, according to the available information, Fuzail is on the highway and posses a threat to the caravan".

This panic-striken conversation of the people of caravan kindled a fire in the heart of Fuzail. He was extremely grieved to learn that his crimes had worried and distressed the people to such a great extent. He rose from his place instantly and said: "Gentlemen! You should know that I am Fuzail bin Ayāz and you should rest assured that Fuzail will no longer commit robbery and I will no more intercept the caravans. He has

The minister said: "I am prepared to spend even 100,000 dinars for this purpose". He then handed over 1000 dinars to that man immediately.

The man took 1000 dinars and went to ten well-known persons whose evidence was considered reliable by the judge. He explained the matter to them and said: "I want you take from me 100 dinars per head and depose before the judge that the minister has married this girl. You will not be committing any sin by giving such evidence, because, firstly the life of a human being is in danger and secondly the minister will give her thousands of dinars as dowry. Furthermore, the father of the girl wants to prevent her from marrying and by giving such evidence you will be doing something lawful. And consequently your position will be enhanced in the eyes of the minister and he will ever remain grateful to you throughout his life".

For the sake of money and the promises made with them the ten persons agreed to adduce false evidence, which is one of the major sins and the cause of Divine wrath.

After having obtained the agreement of the ten persons the minister lodged a complaint with the judge saying: "I have married the daughter of such and such merchant and have also fixed such and such amount as dowry for her. This matter is known to ten reliable persons. But my father-in-law is detaining her in his house and does not agree to surrender her to me".

After hearing the evidence of the witnesses the judge ordered that the girl should be transferred to the house of the minister forcibly and no heed should be paid to the opposition of her father.

The girl was transferred to the house of the minister, but her father, too, did not sit still and continued his efforts and campaign. Unfortunately, however, the only person who could interfere and get the girl restored to him was the Caliph Mu'tasim and the merchant had no source to approach him. After a good deal of investigation he came to know that the Caliph was getting a new palace built and went at the site every day for an hour or so to see the construction work in progress.

The merchant put on the dress of a labourer engaged on construction work, joined the group of such labourers and began doing work. When the Caliph arrived, the merchant started crying and complaining. The Caliph enquired from him as to what the matter was. He related the entire incident. Thereupon the Caliph summoned the minister at that very place.

The minister came and confessed his guilt under the hope and impression that the Caliph would forgive him.

Then the witnesses were summoned and they also pleaded guilty. The Caliph then ordered that all the witnesses should be hanged at the threshold of the palace. As regards the minister he was wrapped in a cover and was beaten so much with the iron maces that his entire body was reduced to minced meat.

Then the Caliph told the merchant to take away his daughter to his house along with the entire dowry, as was mentioned by the witnesses". (A'lāmun Nās, Atlidi, p. 190)

This historical event is one of the instances which can show the evil consequences of sin and if we look into the history of the ancients and even into the lives of our contemporaries we shall come across many such instances.

So many families have been destroyed on account of being polluted with sin. So many men and women have gone down the precipice of sin and their dignity and status have been stained. The health and prosperity of many young men have been sacrificed for unlawful enjoyments and transient sensuality. In order to ensure the prosperity of the people and to save them from the misfortunes arising out of sin, Islam has explained the grave consequences of sin and advised the people to abtain from it.

As most of the people are unaware of the consequences of their sins and are impatient about carnal desires, Almighty Allah has warned them against this wrong conduct and says: *You may not like something which, in fact, is for your good and something that you may love, in fact, may be evil. Allah knows, but you do not know.* (Surah al-Baqarah, 2:216)

Lord Iboury, the famous British author writes: "Dangers are involved in voluptuous life which, if taken into account, make it advisable for us to shun transient pleasures which cost us so extraordinarily dear. We should always keep this point in view that life is linked with pains and hardships and if, at times, we violate this established law and surrender ourselves to alluring enjoyments we will soon see the result of this obstinacy.

Physical pleasures, howmuchsoever charming and agreeable

The holy Qur'an says thus in this behalf: *You are the best nation that ever existed among men. You command people to follow the law and prohibit them from committing sins and you believe in Allah.* (Surah Ale Imran, 3:109)

The leaders of Islam have impressed upon the Muslims that if they desire that mischief, corruption, sins, oppression and other evils should not prevail in the society and it should not be driven to annihilation and adversity they should not forget the law of social supervision and should always act upon the two important principles viz. enjoing good and forbidding evil.

While quoting the recommendations made by Luqman to his son the holy Qur'an says: *My son, be steadfast in prayer, make others do good, prevent them from doing evil and be patient in hardship, patience comes from faith and determination.* (Surah Luqman, 31:16)

The holy Prophet says: "So long as my followers enjoin good and forbid evil and co-operate with one another in good deeds they will remain blessed and prosperous. And if they forsake this duty they will be deprived of blessings and some of them will prevail over the others and as a result of which they will become shelterless and helpless and no one will come to their aid from anyside". (Tahzib, Vol. II, p. 58)

If we reflect a little on these two important principles viz. enjoining good and forbidding evil we realize that this law is one of the greatest miracles of the holy Qur'an, because during modern times, after the passage of fourteen centuries of the advent of Islam, the civilized nations have enacted and enforced similar laws and consider them to be the basis of democracy and their own advancement.

Ibrahim Khwaja Nuri writes. "However, this is also an undeniable fact that in order to ensure justice it is necessary, for example, like the Swiss nation, that every individual of our society should be the guardian of justice and, as laid down in their constitution like the sacred heavenly verse · 'Immediately upon observing the smallest injustice it is obligatory upon all the members of the society not to sit still till that injustice has been rectified'. As you can observe, this is exactly the same obligation which has been imposed by Islam on all the Muslims. No doubt if this practice becomes usual and customary, justice will be ensured automatically and opposition thereto will naturally become impossible". (Taqiyya, Chapter, Enjoining the good)

Imam Ali stressed upon this important and vital matter in his historical will made on his bed of martyrdom. He said: "Do not abandon enjoining good and forbidding evil, because if you do so the wicked persons will dominate you and you will pray and invoke Allah to eliminate their mischief, but your prayer will not be accepted". (Nahjul Balaghah)

Punishment for the Sinners in the Hereafter

In the holy Qur'an and Islamic traditions the bad luck and adversity of the sinners in the Hereafter has been analyzed and explained at length and this in itself is a method of fighting against sin. The holy Qur'an says: *Would that you could see (on the Day of Judgement) that criminals with their heads hanging down before their Lord, saying, 'Our Lord, we have seen and heard. Send us back to act righteously, now we have strong faith'. Had We wanted, We could have given guidance to every soul, but My decree, that Hell will be filled-up with jinn and men, has already been executed. They will be told, 'Suffer on the Day of Judgement and for your having ignored it. Suffer the everlasting torment for your evil deeds'.* (Surah al-Sajdah, 32:12)

In another verse the holy Qur'an says: *A sinner will wish that he could save himself from the torment of that day by sacrificing his children, his wife, his brother, his kinsmen who gave him refuge (from hardship) and all those on earth. By no means! For the flames of the Fire will strip-off the flesh and drag into it anyone who has turned away from obeying Allah.* (Surah al-Mā'ārij, 70:11 — 15)

These and other similar verses invite the attention of the sinners to the dreadful future which awaits them so that before being subjected to Divine punishment they should seek a remedy and take steps towards salvation and good fortune by means of repentance and atonement for their misdeeds.

Punishment for the Sinners in this World

Islam has prescribed punishments, for those who oppose or violate law, by the enforcement of which corruption and crime can be uprooted from the society or reduced to the minimum.

As the penal laws of Islam have been enacted by Allah, the penalties have been fixed exactly according to the standard of the offences i.e. they are neither so light and mild that the offenders should be encouraged to commit crimes nor so harsh and cruel that they should not be compatible with reason.

These laws have been discussed in the books on 'Islamic Jurisprudence' under the title of *Hudūd*. Those desirous of becoming acquainted with the depth and greatness of these laws and regulations should refer to the detailed books on the subject.

What has been stated above is a specimen of the profound and basic compaigns of Islam against sin, corruption and crime. We hope that by paying attention to the auspicious rules of Islam and their proper enforcement, the Muslims of the world will be able to set up a pious and ideal society free from corruption and sin and will acquire prosperity in this world as well as in the Hereafter.

* * * * * *

THE RIGHTS OF SPOUSES

A man alone is an imperfect being and similarly a woman alone is also an imperfect being. This defect in them is on this account that for the continuance of race and existence of life both of them depend on each other. Permissible and legal marriage eliminates their defect and it makes their life fruitful.

Besides the question of the continuance of race the formation of a family is necessary for every man and woman from the point of view of the health of body and soul and proper enjoyment of the privileges of life.

Women and men who lead single lives are mostly threatened by nervous and mental ailments, because if they suppress their sexual instinct it results in dreadful diseases and if they become unrestrained and satisfy this instinct illegally the risks involved are still more grave.

Marriage and formation of family, with the fulfilment of its necessary conditions is the command of nature and the law of creation and violation thereof involves heavy punishments. The man and woman who perform this vital duty by contracting marriage mus t also keep in mind the duties and responsibilities attached to this relationship to lead a happy life. They should not lay the foundation of marriage on sensuality and satisfaction of carnal desires and should not also marry for the sake of wealth or beauty, because such ties are weak and such marriages are without solid foundation. They must not forget the great objective which they must keep in view while taking this step and should select the future spouse or partner of their life from amongst faithful, wise and able persons after very careful consideration.

Man and woman do not enjoy any precedence over each other on account of being man or woman. In the eyes of the Creator both are human beings and enjoy respective rights.

The Almighty Allah says in the holy Qur'an: *Man, We have created you from male and female and formed you into nations and tribes so that you may recognize each other. The most honourable among you in the sight of Allah is the one who is most pious.* (Surah al-Hujurāt, 49:13)

Like any other organization the existence of a guardian and a responsible person is necessary in the organization of a house, because a company or an organization which does not possess a responsible authority must get involved in chaos and disorder.

Keeping in view the interests of this organization, let us see as to who should be entrusted the responsibility. Should it be man or woman or both of them?

Undoubtedly the control by both of them will not only solve the problem but will increase the difficulties, because experience has shown that presence of two chiefs in an organization is more harmful than not having any chief at all and a country which has two independent rulers is always faced with anarchy and chaos.

If there are differences between the father and the mother about control over the affairs of the house the result is chaos and disorder. Besides this, according to the psychologists, the children brought up in such a house are faced with spiritual and nervous complications and mental abnormality.

In view of the above-mentioned difficulties there is no doubt that the responsibility for managing the affairs of the house should be entrusted either to the man or the woman and it is also undeniable that from the point of physical constitutions and mental faculties man is more suited to shoulder this duty.

According to expert opinions held by the intellectuals and specialists, woman enjoys superiority over man as far as sentiments and emotions are concerned while man is superior to her in the matter of thought and wisdom. As for the administration of affairs there is more need of reasoning and intellectually sound judgement, commonsense demands that the administration and organization of the family which involves great responsibility should be placed on man and the supervision and guardianship should be entrusted to him.

This view of Islam is also the same as of the law of nature. Allah says thus in the holy Qur'an: *Men are the protectors of women because of the greater preference that Allah has given to them and as they financially support them.* (Surah an-Nisa, 4:34)

The guardianship of man with regard to his wife is accepted in all the countries of the world and women are also happy with this arrangement.

According to the 213th Aticle of the new law of France, guardianship, control, and supervision of the family rest with man and according to the laws and regulations of other nations also the position is the same. (Huqūq-i Zan, p. 134)

Allah has entrusted the guidance and supervision of the family affairs to man. This is on account of the fact that man is physically more strong and more fit to do hard work as well as to protect the members of his family.

From the physical and spiritual aspect woman possesses a special elegance and she has tender sentiments and feelings. Moreover, during her monthly period and pregnancy and during the years she suckles her child, woman is not only not fit for physical exertion, she needs particular care and attention also.

The authority to be exercised by man over the family is not in this sense that he is the master of its members and they are his slaves but it means that as against the financial support and physical and mental protection that he provides to his family members, he will naturally be acting as a chief. But limitations of his power and authority have been ordained by Allah so that he may not exceed his limits.

It must also be noted that while giving man the position of a chief in the family, Islam has not ignored the woman's aspirations of having a mental pleasure of superiority and in this connection she has been entrusted the responsibility of managing the household affairs.

The holy Prophet says: "Every individual is independent and a chief. Man enjoys independence and authority in family affairs and woman enjoys the same position in household affairs". (Huqūq-i Zan, p. 134)

The holy Prophet further says: "All of you are guardians and watchmen according to your responsibilities and all of you are answerable for that for which you have assumed responsibility. The ruler and the Imam are answerable for the nation, man is answerable for the family, woman is answerable for the household affairs and the children and everyone is answerable to the extent of the authority enjoyed by him and is under obligation to carry out the duties entrusted to him by Allah". (Sahih Bukhāri, Vol. III, Chapter on Marriage).

Furthermore, the Almighty Allah has clearly reminded men in these words: *Always treat them reasonably. If you dislike them you could be disliking that which Allah has filled with abundant good.* (Surah an-Nisa, 4:19)

Sa'd bin Mu'āz was one of the faithful companions of the holy Prophet who received much attention from him. When he passed away, the holy Prophet personally attended his funeral ceremonies and said that the angels also escorted his funeral. The holy Prophet offered his funeral prayers and when the dead body was placed in the grave he entered the grave, put it in order and closed the gaps between the bricks. Thereafter he said to his companions: "Although I know that this grave will be ruined soon, but Allah likes that when his slaves perform any task they should perform it firmly and meticulously".

The grave was covered with sand and it was levelled with the ground. Sa'd's mother, who had been present throughout the funeral rites and has seen the special attention paid by the holy Prophet, said to her son involvuntarily· "O my son! May Paradise welcome you!"

The holy Prophet said to Sa'd's mother: "Keep quiet! What do you expect from Allah? Just now the grave has shrunk and has pressed Sa'd hard. She asked: "O Prophet of Allah! Why?" The holy Prophet replied: "Because in his house he maltreated his wife". (Tabaqāt Ibn Sa'd, Vol. III)

Imam Ja'far Sadiq, says: "May Allah bless the man who lays the foundation of his relations with his wife on goodness and kindness". (Man Lā Yahzuruhul Faqih, Vol. II, p. 142)

The holy Prophet says: "The best person among you is he who behaves well with his family members and I treat my family members in a better way than anybody else". He also says: "One who violates the rights of the members of his family deserves to be cursed". (Wasā'ilush Shi'ah, Vol. VII, p. 122)

Evidently, as it has been impressed upon men in Islam to

behave well with their wives, the women have also been asked to carry out their duties with regard to their husbands and to prove themselves to be capable and worthy spouses.

Imam Musa Kazim says: "Jihād (holy war) of women is that they should perform their marital duties properly". (Furu'ul Kāfi, Vol. II, p. 60)

During the early days of their married life Imam Ali and his honourable wife Lady Fatima approached the holy Prophet to specify the duties of each one of them. The holy Prophet entrusted all out-door jobs to Imam Ali and the household affairs to his daughter, Fatima". (Qurbul Asnād, p. 25)

With right and wise conduct men and women can lay the foundation of a prosperous life and can avoid such actions as may damage their happiness. At times small and insignificant things become the source of love and kindness and similarly at times trivial matters become the cause of strife and separation.

The holy Prophet says: "It is proper that the woman should kindle the lamp of the house and prepare food and when her husband comes home she should receive him at the door and welcome him and should bring water and towel to assist him in washing his hands and should not refuse any of his wishes without just cause". He further says: "A man who marries a woman should endeavour to honour her and hold her dear". (Mustadrak, Chapter 68, 65)

"Do not mention the lapses of your wife before your children and even if they complain about their mother you should set their minds at rest in this regard and establish respect for their mother in their minds. Of course, it is also the duty of the mother to impress upon her children to respect their father". (Ā'in-i Kāmyābi, p. 116)

It is the duty of husband and wife to keep themselves neat, clean and attractive before each other and to avoid filthiness and remaining in an abominable condition.

Hasan bin Jaham says: "I saw that Imam Musa Kazim has dyed his hair. I wondered and asked him the reason for doing so. He said: 'If a man adorns his face and hair and wears neat and tidy dress it enhances the chastity of his wife' (because if a woman loves her husband she will not pay heed to other men). Many women deviate from the path of chastity on account of the carelessness and inattention of their husbands. Then he said: "Would you like to see your wife in a deplorable condition?" I replied: "No".

He said: "She, too, is like you and does not like to see her husband dirty and untidy. Of course, cleanliness, use of perfume and keeping one's head and face in good shape are the ways of the holy Prophet".

During the time of one of the Caliphs a woman complained to the Caliph against her husband and requested that he might be summoned and asked to divorce her. The Caliph enquired about the reason for this request. The woman replied: "I don't like my husband and it is intolerable for me to pull on with him".

The Caliph was inquisitive and questioned her further to find out the cause of her dispiritedness. He said to her: "Does your husband neglect to meet your expenses?" She replied: "No". He said: "Does he beat and torture you?" She replied: "No". The Caliph asked: "Is he indifferen to you?" She replied: "No. There is none of these things. My husband is a good man but I do not like him".

The Caliph ordered that the husband of the woman might be summoned. After some time the officials brought a man before the Caliph who was very dirty and untidy. His hair were ruffled, his nails were long and his dress was torn and shabby.

The Caliph assailed the man with questions so as to ascertain the cause of the dispiritedness of the woman but could not find any clue to it. However, it occurred to him suddenly that possibly the reason for the woman's discouragement was the shabby condition of the man. He, therefore, said to her: "You should go away today and come tomorrow along with your husband so that divorce may be made effective".

The woman went away. Thereafter, as ordered by the Caliph, her husband's hair were cut and he was bathed and provided a neat and tidy dress. The Caliph then ordered him to depart and to come on the following day along with his wife.

On the following day the Caliph kept waiting but none of them turned up. He then sent someone to bring them. On their arrival he said to the woman. "We are now prepared to order for your divorce". The woman said with much agitation and fear: "I do not at all wish to leave my husband. I love him and regret what what I said yesterday. The Caliph smiled and encouraged them to lead a happy marital life".

The Caliph had guessed correctly. Abominable condition of man or woman may become the cause of discouragement and unkindness and even divorce and separation.

Imam Muhammad Baqir says: "A woman should not remain without an ornament for her husband's sake even though it may be only a necklace worn round her neck". (al-Kāfi)

If a woman is particular about these very matters which apparently seem to be unimportant and adorns herself and keeps the house in order she can make her disgusted and discouraged husband take interest in herself and the house and can make the atmosphere of the house replete with sincerity and love.

Dale Carnegie says: "When the house is well-decorated and the rooms are in proper shape as to make the house attractive and the woman feels pleasure on her husband's presence in the house, the husband, instead of going here and there along with others, comes to his house and gradually he becomes attached to it. This is so because in the first instance the husband feels proud of his condition and later becomes interested in the house. Let the husband be free in the house. Let him sit wherever he likes, eat whatever food he likes, smoke and read newspapers and have perfect comfort". (Ā'in-i Shauhar dāri)

Peace and happiness are not the commodities that one can buy from the market. It is available only in the good marital relations of husband and wife.

Imam Sajjad says: "Good words increase the wealth and sustenance of man, prolong his life, become the cause of his being loved by his wife and children and lead him to Paradise". (al-Ziwāj Fil Islam, p. 198)

The western scholars have expressed views about the responsibilities of the spouses to some of which we shall allude here. It must, however, be pointed out here that there is a difference between the commands of Islam and the views of the scholars viz. the Islamic teachings originate from Divine revelations and are immune from mistakes and errors of all kinds whereas the views of the scholars, which have been formed by them on the basis of experience and personal observation are not free from mistakes. For this very reason there are many differences between the views of the scholars on various problems. Furthermore, many views of the past scholars are treated to be incorrect and are replaced by new ideas. However, even after the lapse of fourteen centuries since the time when the laws of Islam were enforced they continue to exist with full force and credit and are confirmed by the modern scholars.

Here is a short account of the views of the western scholars: Samuel Smiles says: "Although the qualities and distinctions of man are linked with his intellect and the merits and specifications of woman are related with her heart, it is necessary that man should train his heart like his intellect and it is also necessary for woman that she should train her intellect like her heart. Like an ignorant and simple woman a man with a corrupt and depraved heart is of no value or consequence in a civilized society. Men and women who are desirous of possessing healthy and good manners should endeavour to train and nourish their thinking and morals as a whole, because man is a humble, worthless and selfish being without the sense of companion and regard for the condition of others, and woman, howmuchsoever beautiful she may be is a dressed doll unless she possesses intelligence and sagacity. There is no doubt about the fact that the most sublime qualities and merits of a woman are manifested at the time of her relationship and contact with others and by means of her sentiments and kindness.

Woman is a nurse who has been appointed for the nurture of mankind and it is for this reason that she looks after weak and helpless children and brings them up in the lap of love and kindness on account of her inherent instinct.

Woman is the angel which protects the house and provides by means of her good nature and conduct peace and tranquillity in the family which is the best tonic and nourisher of morals and superior habits. On account of her nature and physical build, woman is gentle, kind, patient and self-sacrificing and the light of hope and confidence shines from her eyes filled with kind feelings, which provides hope to the helpless and consolation to the grieved and the afflicted, wherever it shines.

In order that a society may always have a congenial atmosphere, it is necessary that there should be a balance between the training of man and woman because the virtues and chastity of woman and the virtues and piety of man are correlated with each other and the moral laws apply equally to both of them. Hence, if a society desires to be pure and clean and free from moral defects it is necessary that both of its men and women should be pious and virtuous and should unanimously avoid every action which is opposed to the dictates of conscience and morality. Both of them should consider it as equivalent to a fatal poison as when once it enters the body, it does not leave it and its evil effects destroys the prosperity and welfare of one's future life.

In order that man may lead a happy and prosperous marital life it is necessary that he should have mental affinity with his wife. However, the woman should not at all be a variant of the man and should not imitate him in everything, because as the woman does not wish that her husband should be effeminate in the same way the husband also does not wish that his wife should possess the ways and manners of man.

The virtues and merits of woman lie in her heart and sentiments and not in her reason and intellect and man utilizes and enjoys her kindness and not her wisdom and knowledge".

Oliver Wendell Holmes says: "We are always inclined more to a woman who possesses heart and sentiments rather than to a woman who possesses rational and intellectual faculties.

At times men get so much weary of themselves that they are prepared to praise all sorts of qualities and habits of another person which may be different from their own". He further says: "If anyone asks me to furnish proof of the goodness of the Almighty I shall say in reply that the best proof of His kindness towards us is the wonderful difference which He has kept between the disposition of man and woman so that by this means they can put up with each other in peace and happiness".

Henry Tubelov says: "A good woman must possess such qualities and habits that she should be able to make the house a place of tranquillity and comfort for the man. And to achieve this end it is necessary that the woman should possess the ability to relieve the man of the trouble of running the house and should especially protect him from evil effect of borrowing. The woman should appear pleasing and agreeable before the eyes of her husband and according to his taste, because his taste is in conformity with his nature and no love can beget without it. If in life which is mixed with sufferings and hardships the house is not the place of love and affection. It will certainly not be the place of tranquillity and comfort, because peace of mind can possibly be acquired only under the protection of love and affection.

Man expects more of intelligence, sagacity, pleasant disposition and open mind from his wife than coquettishness and simulation and is more desirous of her kindness of heart than her extravagant love and refractory sentiments and feelings.

The rule of the life of married persons is "patience and steadfastness". Marriage also necessitates a special policy like government and a married person must give and take, should yield and refuse and should be patient and persevering. It is not necessary that one should be blind as against the feelings of others and should not notice them. The only thing which is required is that he should have the strength to overlook and should ignore whatever he sees with leniency and kindness.

From amongst all the qualities and good habits, moderateness is more useful, more necessary and more durable in married life and if this decent habit is joined with self-control it makes a person accustomed to patience and forbearance and it habituates him to face hardships and misfortunes with fortitude, not to give a reply to the harsh words which he may hear but to sit in such a calm and quiet manner until the anger of the other party subsides.

The remark that 'a soft reply extinguishes the flame of anger' applies more appropriately to conjugal life than to any other occasion. A well-known English proverb says: "The girls are adept in making snares, but their interest lies in that they should know how to make cages".

Usually men can be ensnared very easily like birds but their safe custody is also very difficult like that of birds. If the woman cannot keep the house tidy in such a way that the man may not be able to find a place more neat and pleasing than that and may return to it with pleasure after toiling throughout the day the poor man deserves to be pitied and should in fact be considered to be homeless and vagrant. No wise man marries a woman only for the sake of her beauty. It is true that in the beginning beauty is a very effective means of attracting and enamouring man, but later it ceases to have any effect on his life. Of course, we do not want to blame or despise beauty or to diminish its value becaue beauty of the face and the body is usually the sign of healthy constitution. On the other hand what we mean is that marrying a beautiful woman who lacks moral and spiritual virtues is a grave error for which no amends can be made and no compensation is possible.

External beauty fades and becomes commonplace very soon whereas the spiritual beauty and goodness, in whichever frame it may be, is always fresh and attractive and with the pasage of time, instead of decreasing its lustre, always increases its value and worth. When about a year passes after the marriage neither the man nor the woman is very keen about the facial beauty of the other. On the contrary both of them take into consideration the manners and behaviour of each other".

Duo Tow Copule says: "During his life man cannot acquire a better support than a good-natured and virtuous wife. During my life I have seen comparatively weak persons who displayed great virtues and noble characteristics in social matters and the reason for this had been that they had good-mannered and chaste wives who rendered them with inspirational drive for performing their duties in marital life and who saved them from slips and errors".

What has been stated before is an illustration of Islam in connection with the rights of the spouses. Now in the end we propose to enumerate the rights of husbands and wives. As regards other rights we would advise the readers to refer to the books on relevant subject:

(i) It is obligatory for the husband to meet the expenses of his wife as may be customary. These expenses include dress, food, household effects, servant, and other necessities according to the status of the woman.

(ii) He should not subject the woman to difficulty and distress in the matter of necessities of life and should provide means of comfort to her.

(iii) He should honour and respect the woman and should not oppress her and hurt her feelings.

(iv) He should not compel her to do jobs which are not suitable for a woman (for example, trade, farming etc.) and not even the household tasks like washing clothes, cooking food and keeping the children neat and tidy. Of course, it is 'recommended' that woman should perform household jobs and services related to her husband and children.

(v) He should overlook the mistakes and blunders of the woman and should forgive her and in case she is ill-mannered at time he should be patient and tolerant and should not unnecessarily entertain misgivings against her.

(vi) He should be careful in keeping his body and dress neat.

(vii) He should say good things and should give good replies to her queries.

(viii) He should persuade the woman to do good things and should restrain her from doing evil things.

(ix) If the woman gives birth to a daughter he should not maltreat her and should not consider it a bad luck.

(x) He should not separate from her.

(xi) It is obligatory upon the woman not to misbehave with her husband and not to hurt his feelings by her rudeness, sourness and abusive language.

(xii) It is recommended for her to assist her husband in varous jobs and should especially take over the responsibility of running the household affairs such as cooking of food etc.

(xiii) She should hold her husband dear to her and should not fail to accord him due respect and honour.

(xiv) She should adorn herself for her husband only.

(xv) She should not spend her husband's property without his permission not even by way of alms and charity.

(xvi) She should safeguard her husband's honour in his presence as well as in his absence.

Acting according to these instructions makes the life of spouses happy and the prosperity of their family is ensured.

Experience has shown that almost all the misfortunes of the families are the result of the ignorance of husband and wife about their mutual obligations or failure on their part to perform their duties.

Faithful men and women who believe themselves to be under obligation to carry out Divine orders, act according to them unhesitatingly and are consequently endowed with blessings in this world as well as in the Hereafter.

THE STATUS OF TEACHER

If the worth of individuals is assessed on the basis of the worth of their work, the teachers will undoubtedly acquire one of the most distinguished positions, because persons belonging to this class perform the most important and most delicate responsibility and the result of their work can be compared with that of very few other classes.

To the highest grade, belong the Prophets of Allah, who undertook this responsibility and were entrusted the task of educating and training the people.

The teacher of the Prophets is Allah and this fact has been stated explicitly in the holy Qur'an a number of times.

The disciples and companions of Prophet Isa called him 'the teacher of goodness' and this phrase has no doubt been used to glorify him.

For those who are responsible, in one way or the other, for the education and training of others it is a sufficient honour that their work falls within the range of the work of the Prophets and if one day the human beings are classified from the view-point of their work they will form part of the class of the greatest benefactors of mankind.

The Prophets, while undergoing great hardships and not expecting any reward fom the people, endeavoured to pull the servants of Allah towards good deeds and virtues and to equip them with the armour of knowledge and faith. They did not spare any effort in this regard and had no aim other than the guidance of the people.

Prophet Isa, son of Maryam, behaved with his disciples very meekly, made them sit by himself like friends and imparted instructions to them.

"After they had mastered what he taught them he sent them to different areas so that they might teach others what they had learnt. No teacher does this, even if he has a religious assignment. A teacher usually tries to teach the people personally and to have personal contact with all the students in the class. For example, when Socrates wanted to teach something to a person he did so personally. Of course he had disciples who had attained the position of a teacher but it was never heard that he deputed them to different directions to teach others". (Gilbert Height, The Art of Teaching, p. 175)

Prophet Isa, son of Maryam, said to his disciples: "I stand in need of something from you and ask you to perform it". All of them said: "We shall do whatever you ask us to do". Prophet Isa rose and washed their feet. They said: "O Prophet of Allah! It would have been proper that we should have washed your feet". He replied: "A learned man is more suited than anyone else to serve the people and I have shown this humility and meekness to you so that you may also practise humility like me with regard to the people". (Wāfi)

Other Prophets also taught and guided the people with humility and kind behaviour and made them learn human virtues and goodness in a practical manner.

The holy Prophet of Islam who had combined education with training availed himself of every opportunity to guide the people during day and night and whether he was journeying or staying somewhere.

The verses of the holy Qur'an and the remarks of the holy Prophet were the lessons which were infiltrated into the ears of the people and these lessons brought about a great revolution in the world of that time in a period lesser than a quarter of a century which changed the destiny of the nations, rescued the people from idol-worship, killing of daughters, murders, crimes and thousands of other adversities and guided them to the path of prosperity and humanity.

Imam Ali, the true successor of the holy Prophet, also pursuade the same method. Nahjul Balaghah (See: Peak of

Eloquence, ISP, 1984) consists of a part of the lessons which he taught the people on appropriate occasions. Everyone of the aphorisms, wise words, letters, precepts and other traditions which have come down from him is a treasure of knowledge and virtues from which not only his contemporaries but all his disciples have benefited in all times up to the present day.

With the sentence: 'Ask me whatever you wish before I am not with you,' Imam Ali encouraged the people to propound their questions and ask him whatever they wished. After the martyrdom of Imam Ali the domination and rule of Bani Umayya became the cause of the limitation of the activities of the holy Imams, their staying at home and the suspension of their teaching sessions continued till the time of Imam Muhammad Baqir. Inspite of all the pressures and limitations, however, the great leaders of Islam availed themselves of every opportunity to educate and train the people.

During the last years of the life of Imam Muhammad Baqir, Bani Umayya became weak and Bani Abbas, too, had not yet attained to power. The Islamic territories were burning in the fire of revolution and this very interval between the rule of Bani Umayya and Bani Abbas was the opportunity which was availed of by Imam Baqir and Imam Sadiq to educate and train the people and to propagate the realities of Islam and they established their teaching sessions in the Masjid of Madina.

In the school of Imam Ja'far Sadiq more than 20,000 scholars were trained out of whom 4000 commenced their studies at one and the same time.

The importance of the school of the Holy Imam lay in that he trained his disciples in the first instance and educated them afterwards. The first lesson taught by him was that knowledge should be gained to act upon it and wisdom should be acquired to serve the religion and the society and to exalt one's soul.

About 4000 narrators have narrated traditions from Imam Ja'far Sadiq. They undertook compilation of books during his lifetime and wrote 400 books on jurisprudence which are known as '400 principals'.

The four books entitled *al-Kāfi, Man Lā Yahzuruhul Faqih, al-Tehzīb* and *al-Istibsār* have been obtained from them.

Jābir bin Hayyān, one of the distinguished students of

Imam Ja'far Sadiq, was the famous chemist who left, as his memorial, a book consisting of 1000 pages containing the text of the lectures of the holy Imam.

Muhammad bin Talha Shāfi'i (d. 654 A.H.) writes thus while giving an account of the life of Imam Ja'far Sadiq: "Very valuable pearls became available from the boundless ocean of the knowledge of the holy Imam. Looking at him reminded one of the Hereafter and hearing his speeches taught one the lesson of piety and virtue. His merits and talents were countless. He had combined knowledge with moral excellence and this conduct is peculiar to the Prophets and the saints of Allah". (Matālibus Su'ul, p. 81)

Notwithstanding the fact that the Abbasid Caliphs had completely restricted their activities, other Imams also endeavoured on proper occasions to guide and train the people.

When the unfavourable circumstances of the time did not permit the holy Imams to establish educational assemblies, they taught the lesson of virtue and piety to the people by their conduct and practical education which is certainly more effective than verbal education.

Imam Ali says: "It is necessary for a person who designates himself as the leader and guide of the people to educate himself before educating others. He should guide the people in the first instance with his decent conduct and thereafter with his tongue. And one who undertakes his own education, training and reforms, is worthy of more honour and respect than a teacher who reforms the people". (Nahjul Balaghah)

The secret of the success of the Prophets who were the teachers of mankind lay in that, they did themselves what they enjoined others to do and refrained from that which they forbade others to do. They had full faith and confidence in what they said and as their words originated from their hearts they also settled on the hearts of others.

Undoubtedly the education and training by the teachers and preceptors who are themselves endowed with virtues make a very good and lasting impression on the students.

Rights of Teacher

In Islamic traditions various rights of a teacher have been mentioned, some of which are as detailed below:

Imam Sajjad, the fourth Imam says: "The right enjoyed by your teacher on you is that you should always look upon him with respect and honour and hold it dear to associate with him and hear his words attentively and sit facing towards him and refrain from raising your voice in his presence. If a person asks him a question you should not give a reply thereto and should let the teacher answer it. You should not converse with anyone else in his presence. You should not speak ill of anyone before him and should defend him if a persons slanders him in his absence. You should conceal his defects, praise him before the people and refrain from associating with his enemies or being inimical towards his friends. If you act according to these instructions the angels will testify that you have paid the right of your teacher and have benefited from his knowledge to seek the pleasure of Allah". (Bihārul Anwār, Vol. II. p. 42)

The holy Prophet says: "One who makes a Muslim learn a problem becomes his master". The companions asked: 'O Prophet of Allah! Can he sell him?' The holy Prophet replied: "No. But he can give him orders and can restrain him from doing any act". (Bihārul Anwār, Vol. II)

Imam Ali says: "The right of a teacher is that the student should not ply him with numerous questions and should not give a reply unless the teacher asks him a question. He should not insist on him in any matter and should not compel him to continue the discussion if he gets tired. He should not make a sign to him with the movement of his hand or eye. He should not speak ill of anyone before him and should honour him in his presence as well as in his absence. If he arrives in his assembly he should wish all those present generally and the teacher specially and should accord him respect. He should sit before the teacher very respectfully and if the teacher needs something to be done he should endeavour to meet his need before others. If the speech of the teacher becomes lengthy he should not show signs of weariness. Indeed, the teacher is like a date-palm tree and the student should wait to benefit from him when the appropriate time arrives". (Bihārul Anwār, Vol. II)

The holy Prophet says: "All the reptiles of the earth, the living creatures of the air and the inhabitants of the heavens and of earth pray to Allah for the salvation of a teacher who guides the servants of Allah to the path of goodness and prosperity". (Bihārul Anwār, Vol. II, p. 17)

A Muslim woman of Madina came before Lady Fatima Zahra and said: "My mother, who is very old and weak, has become doubtful about some matters relating to prayers and has sent me to you to get the position clarified".

Lady Fatima said: "You are welcome to ask any question".

The woman questioned Lady Fatima about a problem and she gave a reply. Then she asked another question and received a reply. She continued to ask questions till she asked ten of them and received replies thereto.

The woman then felt ashamed and said: "I do not want to trouble you any more".

Lady Fatima said very kindly: "You may ask whatever you like. Do you think that if a man who is promised 100,000 dinars for carrying a heavy load to the roof of a house will feel tired of the job keeping in view the handsome reward?"

The woman replied: "No".

Lady Fatima said: "As against every problem which I am explaining to you I am getting reward for it thousands of times more than that and it is only appropriate that I should not get wearied or fed up. I heard from my father, the holy Prophet of Allah, that on the Day of Judgement the Muslim scholars will present themselves before Allah and everyone of them will be given a great reward keeping in view the extent of his knowledge and the efforts made by him to guide the people to the right path". (Tafsir Imàm Hasan Askari; Bihārul Anwār, Vol. II, p. 3)

Imam Ali says: "There are three things of which one should not feel ashamed viz. entertaining a guest, standing up as a mark of respect to one's father or teacher and claiming of one's right, although it may be small". (Ghurarul Hikam)

Imam Ja'far Sadiq says: "If a person teaches a good deed to another a share of the spiritual reward for the good deed done by the latter shall also be given to the teacher".

The narrator said he asked the holy Imam: "Will the first teacher share the spiritual reward if that person imparts the knowledge to another?" The holy Imam replied: "Even if he imparts the knowledge to all the people the first teacher will share the spiritual reward with all of them".

The narrator asked: "Will he share the reward even if he has passed away?" He replied: "Yes". (Basā'irud Darajāt)

The important point to which the teachers and preceptors must pay perfect attention is that the human brain, inspite of its small size is the abode of intellect and reason as well as the centre of feelings and sentiments.

If we employ only reason and intellect and try to strengthen it and do not pay attention to sentiments we will undoubtedly be using only one half of the brain and will be paralyzing and wasting the other half.

Nowadays in most of the countries a great difficulty has arisen that the schools and educational centres take care of only the rational and intellectual aspect of the children and young people only endeavour to pour into their brains the scientific, historical and other theories and formulae and they also teach the views of the scholars like a tape recorder, but no effort is being made to make use of their sentiments.

Dr Alexis Carrel, the famous French physiologist says: "The first essential is not the nourishment of intellectual faculties but the construction of the texture of sentiments within oneself which should serve as support for all internal factors. Necessity of moral sense is in no way lesser than the need for the senses of sight and hearing. It is necessary for us to develop the habit of distinguishing good from evil in the same way in which we distinguish light from darkness and sound from silence and then we should make it our duty to avoid evil and adopt goodness. However, avoiding evil needs a good mental and spiritual base. The final growth of the body and the soul is not possible without self-refinement.

The intelligent, learned and wise people follow the principles of good life. Those who want to seek spiritual exaltation, no irregularity is permissible for them. Self-discipline always gets its reward. This reward is strength. Strength brings pleasure, which cannot be described fully and which becomes the bliss of life. Although this physiological and psychological condition may seem strange to the modern teachers and sociologists of the West still it forms a necessary element of one's personality and is like an airport from which the soul can take off".

The treasure of knowledge amassed by man can be the

source of his prosperity when it is accompanied with moral virtues. The holy Prophet of Islam, who is the greatest preceptor of humanity has summarized the aim of his mission in one sentence. He says: "I have been appointed to the prophetic mission to perfect good morals". (Safinatul Bihār, Vol. I, p. 411)

The Prophets who were entrusted the task of education and refinement of humanity laid the foundation of their teachings on self-purification and they attached more importance to moral and sentimental matters than to anything else.

While explaining the mission of the holy Prophet of Islam, the holy Qur'an mentions the self-purification should be attained before education and says: *It is He who has sent to the illiterate a Messenger from among their own people to recite to them His revelations and purify them. He will teach the Book to them and he will give them wisdom.* (Surah al-Jumu'ah, 62:2)

Before reaching the age of twenty years Abu Ali Sina had learnt all the sciences and arts prevalent in his time and was an expert in every field. One day he arrived in the study circle of Abu Ali Maskuya, who was a very learned man and a well-known intellectual of his time and was specially proficient and clear-sighted in ethical and instructional matters. *Taharātul A'rāq* is one of the books written by him. Abu Ali Sina rudely threw a walnut, which he was holding in his hand before Maskuya and asked him to calculate its surface.

Abu Ali Maskuya handed over a part of *Kitabul Akhlāq* (Book on Ethics) to Abu Ali Sina and said "Young man! You are more in need of reforming your morals. Go and reform your morals first and then come back to me so that I may calculate the area of the surface of the walnut for you".

He did not forget this advice throughout his life and by keeping it in mind and acting thereon never stepped down from the right course of life". (Tārikh-i 'Ulum-i 'Aqli dar Islam)

The French scholar H. Mossiear says: "It should be proved to the students that there are other valuable things also besides knowledge and there are other means of classification also for the individuals and the nations besides education".

"Aptitude for technical work, acquiring of wealth and means of public welfare, ability for administration or invention and many other factors which have great social value. Above all these and also above knowledge there exists another factor which consists of virtue and piety". (Parvarish-i Zahn)

Imam Ali said to his son Imam Hasan: "Indeed wisdom enjoys the greatest freedom from wants and the greatest indigence is ignorance and foolishness. The most dreadful fear is self-conceit and the most valuable character consists of good morals". (Nahjul Balaghah)

The Role of Teacher

Andre Maurois, the great French writer, writes thus about his teacher, Emil Chartier: "I do not consider myself as much indebted to my father as to this teacher and whatever I know is the result of the education imparted by him".

The confessions made by this great writer and other distinguished personalities about the deep impression made by a teacher and many historical events manifest fully the important role played by the teachers.

A teacher who is aware of his important responsibility and performs his duty meticulously can leave a lasting impression on the people as a memorial and which serves as a guidedline as a well-known English proverb says: "If Christ brought the dead persons to life a teacher can vitalize a nation".

History shows that the rulers who receive proper education and training during their childhood and youth from competent and faithful teachers adopt decent conduct during the period of their rulership.

Umar bin Abdul Aziz, inspite of his belonging to the Umayyad dynasty followed, during the period of his Caliphate, policies different from those of other Umayyad Caliphs and, as confessed by him, it was due to the teachings of his tutor that he avoided most of the deviations and wrong acts. He says: "I was engaged in my studies at Madina and was attached to Ibn Mas'ud. He had heard that I also abused Imam Ali like other members of the Umayyad family.

One day I visited my tutor. He was offering prayers. I sat down and waited till he finished the prayers. He then turned to me and said: 'When did you come to know that after being pleased with the Muslims who fought the battle of Badr and took the oath of allegiance to the holy Prophet at Hudaybiya,

Allah became angry with them?' I replied that I had not heard any such thing. He said. 'Then how is it that I have heard this about you in respect of Imam Ali?' I told him that I sought forgiveness from Allah as well as from himself and from that day onwards I ceased abusing Imam Ali". (Kamil ibn Athir, Vol. V)

The conversation which took place between the teacher and the pupil was very brief and neither of them imagined that these few words would become the source of a great revolution in the territories of Islam. However, the words uttered by the teacher on that day got imprinted on the heart of the child and impressed him very much. A few years passed. The child grew up and found his place among the persons of distinction in the society. Unexpected developments and various events brought about great changes in the country, placed the child of that day on the throne of the Caliphate and gave the administration of the affairs of millions of persons in his hands.

The remark of the teacher was a seed which was sown in the heart of the child on that day. The facilities provided by rulership and chiefdom nourished that seed and eventually it assumed the shape of an auspicious harvest from which millions of persons benefited and are delivered from the shameful heresy of abusing Imam Ali". (Kudak, Vol. II, p. 32)

This was one illustration of the great effect of the remark of a teacher and many such events are found in history.

We All Should be Teachers

The honour which has been accorded to the position of a teacher in the statements of the leaders of Islam is not confined to the persons who are engaged in the profession of education. On the other hand it applies to everyone who makes another person learn something useful.

It is evident that the word 'teacher' applies openly to those who are engaged in imparting education. However, everyone, in whatever conditions he may be, can and ought to be a teacher. He should teach others what he knows, show them the paths of prosperity and happiness and try to guide his fellow-beings and brethren-in-faith so that he may be blessed with Divine reward in this world as well as in the Hereafter.

The holy Prophet says: "There are four things which are

necessary for the wise men among my folllowers: (i) Listen to wise words; (ii) commit them to memory; (iii) put them into practice and act upon them and (iv) to teach others what he has learnt". (Kanzul Fawā'id, Karachaki)

The holy Prophet also says: "Amongst the alms which people give none is as valuable as imparting knowledge and wisdom to others". He further says: "No gift is more valuable than that one should tell his brother Muslim a true word by means of which he is guided to the path of Allah and gets rid of perversion".

Imam Ali says: "Thanksgiving by the learned men for the blessings of knowledge which Allah has given them is that they should impart their knowledge to those who deserve it".

Imam Ja'far Sadiq says: "On the Day of Judgement, Allah will summon the 'ulema' and the scholars and similarly the pious and the devout persons in His presence. Then the pious persons will be told to go to Paradise and the scholars will be ordered to wait and intercede for the people for the sake of the troubles which they bore in the path of their guidance and reformation". (Bihārul Anwār, Vol. II, p. 16)

Sa'di, the renowned Persian poet says: "A pious person left the monastery and came to a religious institution, abandoning the idea of associating with the ascetics. I asked him: 'What is the difference between a scholar and an ascetic that You have chosen this path in preference to that?' He replied: 'That the ascetic wants to pull only his own cloak out of the sea-waves whereas the scholar endeavours to rescue a drowning person".

What has been said above is a brief and concise account of the position of a teacher and his delicate duty and effective role in the society as well as the reward fixed by Almighty Allah for the compassionate and benevolent teachers. We hope that keeping all these matters in view all of us shall perform our duties with regard to the guidance, education and training of our fellow-beings and especially the guidance of children and young persons in an appropriate manner so that we may enjoy Divine blessings in this world as well as in the Hereafter.

* * * * * *

RESTORATION OF TRUST IN ISLAM

Islam was not only a source of a change in the life of man or the basis for a human movement or the cause of leap towards development and perfection. On the other hand it gave a new life and a new existence to humanity and, in fact, with the advent of Islam, man took a new base of life.

Man existed in the world even before Islam. However, he was a being far removed from civilization and was engulfed in numerous discriminations, excessive pollution, polytheism and idol-worship, crime and fratricide and thousands of other individual and social vices.

A brief comparison between the condition of man before Islam and his condition after the advent of Islam tells us how he acquired a new life.

During a period lesser than a quarter of a century, Islam brought up individuals who became a sublime specimen of humanity and an object of pride for the human society. The spirit of piety and virtue was blown into the people. Fratricide and bloodshed were replaced by beneficence and philanthropy. Fellowship and brotherhood took the place of discriminations and egotism. Justice, equity and respect for the rights of others replaced oppression and aggression.

The Islamic training taught the most excellent lessons to the Muslims and the holy Prophet invited the people practically to justice, restoration of trust and other decent qualities.

Restoration of trust to their owners which is the subject

we propose to discuss is one of the matters which has undeniable influence on the advancement and prosperity of human societies and Islam has attached great importance to it.

The thing which makes the restoration of trust a vital matter is its effect on the individual and social life.

At one time or another during his life every person either entrust something with another person or receives something as a trust from others and the needs of the people demand that they should occasionally keep the trust of others in safe custody or hand over their own things to others for being kept in safe custody.

If the people are particular about the safety and restoration of the trust to their owners and mutual confidence exists in the society the welfare of the people will be ensured and if honesty and righteousness is replaced by dishonesty and treachery the mutual confidence of the people is destroyed and consequently numerous difficulties take place.

In a number of its verses the holy Qur'an has made it obligatory for the Muslims to restore the trust to their owners. In one of these verses it says: *Allah commands you to return that which had been entrusted to you, to the rightful owners.* (Surah an-Nisa, 4:58)

The holy Qur'an further says: *Triumphant indeed are the believers who are submissive to Allah in their prayers......and those who are true to their trust and to their promise.* (Surah al-Mu'minun, 23:1, 2 and 8)

In these verses the Almighty Allah declares that only the believers are entitled to deliverance in this world and salvation in the Hereafter and also to enjoy eternally the bounties of Paradise. He also mentions their characteristics.

One of the characteristics of the true believers mentioned in these verses is that they take care of the things entrusted to them and adhere to their covenants and honour them.

Besides the above-mentioned two verses there are other verses also in the holy Qur'an wherein proper care of the trust and their restoration has been recommended. Restoration of trust has also been recommended in many sermons and sayings of the leaders of Islam.

When the holy Prophet appointed Mu'āz bin Jabal as the

governor of one of the provinces of Yemen, he explained his basic duties to him and said *inter alia:* "O Muʻāz! I recommend it to you to observe piety and truthfulness in your speech and to honour your covenants, restore the trust to their owners and forsake treachery". (Nasikhut Tawārikh, Vol. V, p. 267)

The holy Prophet has been reported to have said: "Whoever is guilty of dishonesty in misappropriating the thing entrusted in trust is not amongst us". (Wāfi, Vol. III)

In another tradition *(hadith)* the holy Prophet criticizes carelessness with regard to a trust and says: "One who considers the trust of the people to be a trifling thing is not one of us and one who misappropriates the property of a Muslim is also not one of us". (Mustadrak, Vol. II, p. 505)

Imam Muhammad Baqir says: "It is incumbent upon you to be chaste and to endeavour to perform your duties and to be truthful and to restore the trust to the person who has reposed his trust in you, whether he be a good man or a bad man. Indeed, if the murderer of Imam Ali entrusts something to me, I shall return it to him in perfect condition". (Tuhaful Uqūl)

Abdur Rahmān bin Siyāba says: "When my father died one of his friends came to my house to condole his death and after consoling me enquired about my financial position. I told him that my father owned nothing at the time of his death and I too did not have anything. He gave me 1000 dinars and said: 'Start business with this money and meet your expenses from the profit earned by it and take proper care of it'.

His behaviour pleased me much. I went to my mother and told her how Allah had solved our financial problems. Both of us slept very happily that night.

On the following day I went to the bazaar and met a man who had been a friend of my father. He purchased some cloth for me which I started selling it at a corner there.

I continued selling clothes and began to earn more than my household expenses and my business flourished.

Hajj season came and I decided to go on pilgrimage to the House of Allah to perform the ceremonies of Hajj. I, therefore, mentioned my intention to my mother. My mother said: 'You have to perform still a more important duty before you go to Hajj and it is that you should restore 1000 dinars to that man which he entrusted to you and to free yourself from the debt'.

I arranged for the money and went to hand it over to him. He said: 'What has brought you back with this money? If it is insufficient I shall give you more. I said: 'No. The fact is that I want to proceed to Makkah for Hajj and considered it expedient to return your money before going on to the pilgrimage'. Then I made necessary preparations and proceeded to Makkah.

After performing the ceremonies of Hajj I went to Madina. There I had the honour to present myself before Imam Ja'far Sadiq. There was a group of people present there and I, being a young man, sat at the corner.

People placed their problems before the Imam one after the other and departed after receiving replies. When all of them had left the holy Imam asked me: 'Have you any business with me?' I introduced myself. He enquired about my father and I told him that he had passed away. He said: 'Did he leave any wealth for you'. I replied in the negative. Then he asked: 'Where from have you procured the expenses of Hajj?' I told him about the friend of my father who had given me 1000 dinars to engage myself in trade.

The holy Imam enquired from me anxiously: 'What did you do with the money of that man?' I replied: 'I returned it to him'. He said: 'Exellent! You have done a nice thing'. Then he said: 'May I tender you a piece of advice?' I told him that it would be very kind of him'. He said: 'You should be truthful in what you say and should restore the trust to their owners. If you behave with the people in this manner you will share their wealth". (Wāfi, Vol. III, p. 112)

The holy Prophet says: "One who commits breach of trust and does not restore the entrusted property to its owner will be treated at the time of his death as not being one of my followers and will become subjected to Divine wrath". (Man Lā Yahzuruhul Faqih, Vol. II, p. 198)

The holy Prophet says: "Whoever purchases a property which has been acquired by means of breach of trust becomes involved in the disgrace and sin of the person who has committed the breach and whoever purchases a property knowing it to have been stolen also becomes involved in the disgrace and sin of the thief". ('Iqābul A'māl, p. 47)

Breach of Trust

In many traditions a mention has been made of the serious consequences of breach of trust so that the Muslims may pay more attention to this matter. The Commander of the Faithful Imam Ali says: "If one out of four things makes its appearances in a house it ruins that house and deprives it of prosperity and blessing. (i) Breach of trust (ii) Theft (iii) Drinking wine and (iv) Adultery and unchastity. (Khisāl Shaykh Sadūq, Vol. I)

The holy Prophet says: "Safe custordy and restoration of a trust to its rightful owner increases one's wealth and its misappropriation brings about poverty". (Qurbul Asnād, p. 55)

People develop faith in the persons who are upright and honest and as a result of that faith they can easily overcome the difficulties of life and their business flourishes. On the contrary no one relies upon the persons who are dishonest and wicked. They are expelled from the society and become involved in affliction and poverty which is the result of dishonesty.

The pages of history can also assist us in understanding clearly how dishonesty and breach of trust results in ruination:

During the time of 'Azudud Dowla of Daylami, a wealthy young man who had spent many years of his life in sin, drinking and revelries fell ill and was confined to bed. When he lost all hope of life he made a promise to Allah that if he recovered he would give up vices and would turn towards piety.

Allah restored his health. He also kept his promise, threw away the tools of gambling and amusements and the wine which he had in his house and decided to go for the pilgrimage of the House of Allah.

He had 30,000 gold dinars which he entrusted to the judge of the city, who enjoyed good reputation for his honesty, and proceeded to Makkah.

His journey was prolonged. He met with some accidents on the way and suffered many hardships. After a long time he returned to his hometown, very much tired and distressed.

Notwithstanding all these sufferings and hardships he was happy that he owned 30,000 gold dinars in cash and it would be possible for him to overcome all the difficulties by means of that money. However, when he approached the judge for the restoration of the money the latter said: 'I do not know you and have not taken any money from you'.

All the beseechings and entreaties of the man proved to be in vain. Eventually the judge threatened him that if he disturbed him any more he would give the verdict that he was insane and would send him to the lunatic asylum where he would remain till the end of his life.

Overcome by despair and perplexity the man went to the jungle where he wept and cried on account of his bad luck.

One of the officials of 'Azudud Dowla met the man and came to know about the incident. He related the same to 'Azudud Dowla.

'Azudud Dowla sent the man to Isfahan for a few days. Then he summoned the judge and said to him : 'As you can see I have grown old and the world, too, is very unreliable. I have young sons and daughters and am afraid that if I die suddenly and the kingdom falls in the hands of my enemies my children will get involved in difficulties and afflictions. As a precautionary measure, therefore, I have decided to deposit more than a million gold dinars of the treasury with you as you are a decent and honest man, so that you may give this amount to my children after my death and they may not have to face difficulties. Now I want you to construct a basement in your house so that one night I may transfer the money there secretly'.

The Judge expressed his willingness to perform this task and took his leave of the king. He was extremely happy and from that very moment began preparing plans in his mind to appropriate one million gold dinars.

A few days after the judge had built up a basement in his house for the transfer of gold, 'Azudud Dowla summoned the oppressed person and said to him : 'Go to the judge now and ask him to repay your money. If he declines to do so threaten him by saying that you are going to lodge a complaint with me'.

The man acted as he was directed by the king. When the judge heard his threat he feared that if the matter reached the ears of 'Azudud Dowla he would not dpeosit the money with him. He, therefore, spoke affably to him and restored to him the total amount which was contained in two copper receptacles. The man brought the money to 'Azudud Dowla and informed him of the developments.

As ordered by the King the officials went and brought the

judge, with bare head and feet before the King, dragging him in a very insulting manner. There was no occasion for denial. Everything was quite evident and patent.

The King said: 'Let there be the curse of Allah upon you! You have grown old. You have reached the end of your life. You were appointed to the exalted position of a judge, but inspite of this you misappropriated the property entrusted to you by the Muslims. I have realized now that you have accumulated this property and wealth by means of bribes and dishonesty and all of it belongs to the Muslims'.

Then, as ordered by the King, the entire property belonging to the judge was confiscated and he was removed from his office". (Siyāsat Nāma, Khawaja Nizamul Mulk, p. 87)

This man had to meet a tragic end and lost his wealth, position, dignity and everything else on account of the breach of trust committed by him in respect of the amount which was entrusted to him. It is in this very sense that the holy Prophet says: "Respect for trust makes one free from wants and breach of trust brings about poverty and affliction".

Restoration of Trust is a Human Obligation

It is possible that some persons may think that restoration of trust is necessary only when the owner is a pious Muslim and if the position is otherwise it is desirable to misappropriate it. However, if a little attention is paid to the regulations of Islam it becomes apparent that restoration of trust is a duty which the Muslims must perform irrespective of the nationality, faith or race of the owner.

According to the Islamic regulations there are a number of duties which the Muslims are required to enforce upon themselves and which are not applicable to people belonging to different creeds. A number of duties have also been prescribed for the Muslims by the teachings of Islam which they must perform in respect of all the people whether good or bad and whether Muslims or non-Muslims, for example restoration of trust and honouring the promises and covenants.

Imam Ja'far Sadiq says: "There are three things for which there is no alternative and which must be done in all circumstances. Firstly, it is the restoration of trust, whether its owner be a good man or a bad man. Secondly, it is the keeping of a promise whether the other party is good or bad. And thirdly, it is doing good to one's parents whether they be good persons or bad ones". (Mustadrak, Vol. II, p. 505)

Imam Ali, the first successor to the holy Prophet of Islam says thus while making recommendations to Kumayl bin Ziyād: "O Kumayl! Know and beware that we do not permit anyone to show negligence in the matter of restoration of trust to its rightful owner and if any person has quoted me as having accorded such permission he has told a lie and will be punished with the Fire of Divine wrath for this lie. I swear that a short while before his passing away the holy Prophet said thrice: "Restore the trust to their owners whether they be good or bad persons and whether it is big or small. Perform the duty of restoring trust to its owner even though it may be as insignificant as a needle and a thread". (Mustadrakul Wasā'il, Vol. II)

A man said to Imam Ja'far Sadiq: "One of your companions happens to hold trust belonging to Bani Umayya and he considers it lawful to misappropriate it".

The holy Imam said: "Restore the trust to their owners even if they happen to be Magi". (Wāfi, Vol. III, p. 112)

A man asked Imam Musa Kazim: "A man has entrusted something valuable to one of your companions as a trust. The owner of the property in question is malicious, irreligious, devilish and impure. The person who has taken the trust is in a position to retain it and is not likely to suffer any harm by doing so. Can he restain that property?"

The holy Imam replied: "Tell him to restore the trust to its owner, becaue the latter considered him to be honest and thus entrusted the thing to him for his piety". (Wāfi, Vol. II)

Imam Ja'far Sadiq says: "Be pious and it is necessary for you to restore the trust to their owners. Indeed, if the murderer of the Commander of the Faithful Imam Ali entrusts something to me as a trust I shall surely restore it to him". (Mustadrakul Wasā'il, Vol. II, p. 505)

Misappropriation is a Sign of Faithlessness

It has been quoted from Imam Musa Kazim that the holy Prophet said: "Whoever is not particular about the restoration of trust does not possess faith". (Mustadrakul Wasā'il)

Imam Ja'far Sadiq, says: "Any person in whom there is anyone of these three qualities is a hypocrite even though he may offer prayers and keep fast:
(i) A person who tells lies during his conversation.
(ii) A person who makes a promise but does not keep it; and
(iii) A person who misappropriate trust". (Tuhaful Uqūl, p. 316)

Imam Ali says: "Misappropriation of trust is the root of hypocrisy. Breach of trust is the proof of faithlessness and impiety". He further says: "Refrain from misappropriating of trust because it is the worst sin and one who commits it will be subjected to the torture of the Fire of Hell". (Ghurarul Hikam)

Islam has prohibited the Muslims from committing breach of trust even in respect of those persons who are themselves guilty of this sin and has not permitted them to retaliate, because dishonesty and breach of trust is an indecent act and it is not worthy of a Muslim to do indecent things.

Imam Ja'far Sadiq says: "If a person has considered you to be trustworthy and has entrusted something to you, you should return his trust in perfect condition and if a person has committed breach of trust with you and betrayed you, you should not betray him". (Wāfi, Vol. III, p. 122)

The holy Prophet says: "Do not commit breach of trust with a person who has committed breach of trust with you, because in that case you too will be like him". (Mustadrakul Wasā'il, Vol. II, p. 505)

Kinds of Trust

Trust is not confined to money only and that is why in the Qur'anic verses the word has been mentioned in plural form *Amānāt* that is trusts.

Allama Tabarsi says: "Trusts are of two kinds: (i) Divine trust which consist of religious duties like prayers, fasting etc. and (ii) The trust of the people like cash deposits, loans, transactions, evidences etc". (Majma'ul Bayān, Vol. VII, p. 98)

On this basis we become aware of a series of trusts which it is our duty to protect and restore.

The holy Qur'an is a trust which Allah and His Prophet have placed before the Muslims so that, by acting according to its orders, we may achieve the blessings in this world and in the

Hereafter and besides acting according to Allah's commands may communicate the same to the people and explain to them the merits of this sacred law.

We should esteem our women and children as they are the trusts of Allah and should guide them to the right path.

We should not neglect advising our brethren-in-faith and sympathizing with them as this act of giving advice to others is also a trust of Allah.

We should safeguard the secrets of the servants of Allah and should not endanger their reputation, because secrets of the people are the trust violation of which is reckoned to be a sin.

Imam Ja'far Sadiq says: "A person cannot be treated trustworthy unless he is tested in respect of three things as trust: (i) Property (ii) Secrets and (iii) Honour. If he is successful in two cases but commits breach of trust is not trustworthy".

In some traditions the holy Prophet treated the meetings of the friends to be a trust and said: "The meetings are trusts". (al-Kāfi, Vol. IV, p. 49)

Imam Sadiq says: "The meetings are trusts and nobody has a right to divulge any matter which the person concerned does not wish to be divulged, except that it may be with his permission or the hearer is a reliable person or what is said is in praise of that man". (al-Kāfi, Vol. IV, p. 49)

The students are trusts in the hands of their teachers and it is the duty of the latter in that capacity to endeavour for their training, education, refinement of morals and strengthening of their beliefs with extreme sympathy and interest and to bring up and deliver them as pious and useful persons.

Factories and industrial workshops are trusts in the control of the directors, engineers and managers who should keeping in view their duty as a trustee, supervise and maintain them and benefit from them in an appropriate manner.

All administrative and other occupations and posts are trusts and those holding positions should, keeping in view the duties which they owe to Allah and his servant, carry out their responsibilities with perfect truthfulness and honesty.

A driver who drives an automobile, a worker who is concerned with an agricultural or industrial machine and a mechanic who is entrusted the task of repairing engines are all trustees, who are responsible before Allah for the safe custody, upkeep and proper maintenance of the trusts in their charge.

The assets of the Islamic countries, whether public or private wealth are trusts and whoever controls them is duty-bound to take care of them and restore them to the rightful owners.

In the end we refer to the legal aspect of the matter, as listed below:

"It is 'recommended' that trust may be accepted from the people, but when they are accepted it is obligatory that proper care thereof should be taken". (Jāmi' Abbāsi, p. 234)

"Only that person is entitled to accept trusts from the people who can keep them in safe custody. One who accepts a trust should provide usual conditions and facilites for its safe custody. If the owner of a trust fixes a place for his trust the trustee cannot transfer it to another place.

If a trust is detstroyed without any mistake or negligence on the part of the trustee he is not responsible for the loss.

If safety of a trust from a thief or an oppressor is dependent upon telling a lie or taking a false oath it is permissible, rather obligatory upon the trustee to tell a lie or to take a false oath and if he fails to do so and the deposit is destroyed as a consequence thereof he is responsible for it.

When the owner of a trust asks for the restoration of the trust it is obligatory for the trustee to surrender it to him, even though he (the depositor) may be an infidel.

If the trustee fears that the trust, while with him, will be destroyed he should return it to the owner or his agent". (Wasilatun Najāt, Chapter of Wadi'ah, Āyatullah Isfahāni)

What has been said above is a specimen of the emphatic directions of Islam regarding the importance of the preservation and restoration of trust.

An interesting point which deserves attention in this connection is that while arranging this discussion scores of books on ethics written by the Western authors were consulted, but it was observed that notwithstanding the importance of the question of restoration of trust no reference thereto had been made in those books. After much investigation we came to the conclusion that like many other vital matters this proposition is also an outstanding aspect of Islam which has probed all its dimensions with impressive and instructive statements and guided the Muslims in this behalf.

It is hoped that by paying attention to this vital duty and enforcing it dutifully the Muslims in general will be recognized to be reliable, trustworthy and honoured nation among the nations of the world and will also be endowed with the blessings of the Almighty Allah in both the worlds.

* * * * * *

MORAL CODE

Just as man has an exterior which can be seen with the eyes and is called his figure, he also possesses an interior which is called his character. And similarly as it is possible that the outward appearance of a person may be beautiful or ugly it is also possible that his character may be good or bad.

The exterior of man is formed by his limbs like head, face, hands, feet, eyes, ears etc. and his interior is formed by his morals, habits and nature. If a person has proportionate limbs which are harmonious with his face and body it is said that he possesses a beautiful figure and if his limbs are unusual and undesirable his figure is said to be ugly.

Similarly, if a person possesses decent behaviour like love and affection, honesty and sincerity, piety and virtue, tolerance and fogiveness, meekness and humility, he is said to be possessing a decent character and if he is fierce, spiteful, selfish, ambitious and rebellious his character is said to be bad.

Praiseworthy habits are called 'good conduct' or 'good morals' and indecent habits are called 'bad conduct' or 'bad morals'. Thus 'good conduct' consists of having an open countenance, dealing with the people in good spirits and being mild and gentle in association and discourse with others.

Although, in many cases good and bad morals have an acquisitive aspect and they are those very good and bad habits which appear in man and gradually assume the shape of disposition and conduct, he can change them with a little care and attention and bring about a transformation in his morals.

Commonsense as well as religion appreciate a person possessing good morals and reproving one having bad habits because each one of them is capable of changing one's mode of conduct and if that had not been the case there would have been no occasion for either praise or criticism.

Keeping this fact in view that every person can possess good or bad morals with his own will, it is imperative for every one that he should first of all take steps to refine his morals and should abandon bad habits and adopt good ones by means of incessant efforts and attention.

One of the methods which assist us in reforming our morals is paying attention to the extraordinary value of good morals as well as the value of those who possess them and similarly to the meanness and indecency of bad morals and of one who possesses them.

The moral code of the great leaders of Islam is our best guide in these matters. It reminds us of the deep effect of morals in our present life as well as in the Hereafter.

In one of his traditions the holy Prophet has mentioned the importance of good morals in these words: "If the people had known what importance good conduct has and what influence it exerts on their prosperity they would have found themselves in need of possessing good morals". (Biḥārul Anwār)

Some persons are negligent of the benefits of good morals and think that they do not stand in need of them. Especially those persons who consider themselves superior to others in the matter of wealth, knowledge, status etc. treat good morals to be something superfluous and useless, although in fact none of these privileges can take the place of good morals and one who lacks good morals lacks human values and attributes.

In other words if a person lacks wealth, status and knowledge but possesses good morals he is far better than the persons who possess everything except good morals, because these very morals guide and assist him to acquire other privileges.

The holy Prophet says: "Indeed, one who possesses good morals acquires prosperity in this world as well as in the Hereafter". (Jāmi'us Sa'ādāt, Vol. I, p. 273)

Comfort in life is one of the blessings which can be acquired by means of good conduct and immoral persons deprive themselves of this great blessing by their own conduct.

Imam Ja'far Sadiq says: "No life is more agreeable and delightful than the one led with good conduct". ('Ilalush Sharāya)

He also says: "He whose morals are bad involves himself in worry and torture". (Jāmi'us Sa'ādāt, Vol. I, p. 271)

Imam Ali says: "Good conduct is the best companion of man in life". (Bihārul Anwār, Vol, LXXVII, p. 396)

People like to associate themselves with persons possessing good morals as good conduct has an attractive charm which pulls others towards itself.

The holy Prophet of Islam possessed the best morals and Allah has praised his morals in the holy Qur'an in most eloquent terms and says: *(O Prophet!) You have attained a high moral standard.* (Surah al-Qalam, 68:4)

Allah has also explained in another verse the reason for the people becoming inclined to the holy Prophet and has considered it to be the result of his excellent morals, kindness and good behaviour: *Only through the Divine Mercy, you (Muhammad) have been able to deal with your followers so gently. If you have been stern and hard-hearted they would all have deserted you a long time ago.* (Surah Ale Imran, 3:159)

The treatment meted out by the holy Prophet to the people, even to the idolaters and polytheists, was based perfectly on kindness, good morals and human values. The traditionalists have thus written about his morals:

The holy Prophet associated himself with the people and did not turn away anyone from his presence. He accorded respect to the elders of every nation. If any person requested him for something he met his needs and if this was not possible he satisfied that person with great kindness. He met every one cheerfully. He became annoyed for the sake of Allah but was never angry on his own account. He had always a sweet smile on his lips. He was not hot-tempered and severe. He never used abusive or indecent language. He never found fault with anyone.

Anas bin Mālik says: "I served the holy Prophet for ten years. During this period he was never harsh with me. If I did something he never objected to my having done it and if I failed to do something he never asked me as to why I had not done it. On many occasions he broke his fast only with a little milk or bread soften in water.

Once by chance, the holy Prophet was late in coming home. Under the impression that he might have gone to a dinner that evening I utilized the milk myself. He arrived after a while and I asked his companions who had come with him whether he had broken his fast and they replied in the negative. I was very much grieved and was also afraid lest he should ask for his food. He did not, however, say anything in this regard till the call of the dawn prayers and he kept his fast for the following day without having anything to eat.

The holy Prophet behaved with his companions like close friends. He sat and conversed with them in friendly manner. He was kind to their children and made them sit on his knees. He enquired after the health of the sick. He did not believe in any discrimination between himself and his slaves and bondswomen in the matter of food and dress.

If he was mounted he did not allow anyone to walk along with him. Either he made him mount or said to him: "You may go and we shall meet each other at such and such place".

One of the residents of Madina invited the holy Prophet and five of his companions to a feast. When they were going to the house of the host they met a man on the way and he also accompanied them. When they reached near the house of the host the holy Prophet said to that man: "The host has not invited you. You should stay here so that I may have a talk with the host about you and may obtain permission from him for your partaking in the feast".

If he shook hands with someone he did not withdraw his hand until the other man had withdrawn his and if a person sat by his side he did not get up from his place until the other man had got up. He never outstretched his legs in front of any one. He wished everyone. He honoured everyone who came to see him and at times spread his cloak for him to sit on. He called his companions by those names which were liked by them". (Safinatul Bihār, Vol. I, p. 415)

"A large number of the polytheists embraced Islam on account of their being impressed by the sublime morals and manners of the holy Prophet.

In order to escape from Islam 'Adiy bin Hātim Tā'i ran away to Syria and settled there with his co-religionists. His sister who was a wise woman encouraged him to go to Madina and meet the holy Prophet.

'Adiy says: "When I reached Madina I went to the masjid and presented myself before the holy Prophet. After having identified me he got up from his place and took me to his house. An old and weak woman chanced to come before him on the way. For quite some time the holy Prophet stood on his feet and heard what the woman said and replied to her in kind words. I said within myself: 'By Allah! The behaviour of this man is not that of an ambitious ruler'. When we reached the house he spread a quilt stuffed with date-palm fibre and asked me to sit on it. I asked him to sit on it himself but he did not agree and made me sit on it and himself sat on the ground. I said in my heart: 'By Allah! He cannot be called a king'.

When we sat down he began to speak and mentioned some secrets of my life of which nobody was aware. Taking all these matters into account I became convinced about his being the Prophet of Allah and embraced Islam at his hands". (Sīrah Ibn Hishām, Vol. IV, p. 580)

"An old and indigent woman used to sweep the masjid in which the holy Prophet offered his prayers. She usually slept in a corner of the precincts of the masjid and food for her was arranged by the persons who came to offer prayers.

One day the holy Prophet came in the masjid and did not see the woman. He, therefore enquired as to where she had gone. The people replied that the woman died the previous night and was buried and it was imagined that she was not so much important that the news of her death might be communicated to the holy Prophet.

The holy Prophet was quite displeased on hearing this and reprimanded them. He then desired that he might be taken to the grave of the woman. He was guided to that place and went there along with some companions. He stood in front of the grave of the woman together with his companions and offered funeral prayers for her salvation". (Dāstānhā-i Az Zindagi-i Paygambar-i Mā, p. 121)

Throughout his life the holy Prophet was not seen to have been harsh with anyone or to have uttered any unbecoming words or to have treated anyone with contempt or insolence.

Undoubtedly such behaviour attracts the people to the person concerned, because man is naturally inclined towards those who possess good morals and manners.

Luqman, the wise, says: "A good-natured person is a relative of the strangers and an ill-natured person is a stranger to his relatives". (Amthāl wa Hikam, Dehkhudā, Vol. II)

The question of morality is so important in the eyes of Islam that the Great Saviour of humanity — the holy Prophet of Islam has declared the perfection of the moral principles to be the object of his appointment to the prophetic mission and says: "I have been chosen by Allah to perfect good morals". (Safinatul Bihār, p. 41)

In order to make this heavenly assignment fruitful the holy Prophet resorted, orally as well as practically, to the refinement of the morals of the society and discharged his duty with indefatigable efforts.

Before the appointment of the holy Prophet to the prophetic mission the morals of the society had deteriorated so much that they had totally lost their human colour and animal savagery was prevalent among the people.

The holy Prophet taught lessons in morality with his words and provided practical examples by his conduct.

The holy Qur'an says: *The Messenger of Allah is certainly a good example for those of you who have hope in Allah and in the Day of Judgement and who remember Allah frequently.* (Surah al-Ahzāb, 33:21)

In accordance with this clear verdict of the Qur'an the Muslims were under obligation to follow the holy Prophet in all walks of their lives and make his conduct an example for themselves. As a result of this the ethical school of Islam, with such a distinguished teacher and such trained disciples, was able to bring about a great revolution in the moral fibre of the people.

In Islamic traditions, consisting of different wordings and expressions, good morals have been reckoned to be the means of prosperity in this world and in the Hereafter and immorality has been treated to be the cause of being subjected to different kinds of afflictions.

A person inquired the holy Prophet: "O Prophet of Allah! Such and such woman observes fast during daytime and spends the night in the worship of Allah and offers mid-night prayers, but she is ill-mannered and hurts her neighbours with her tongue". The holy Prophet replied: "She is worthless and she is one of inmates of Hell". (Bihārul Anwār, Vol. LXXVII)

In this tradition the holy Prophet has considered observing fast and offering prayers throught the night to be useless for the one who is ill-mannered and who hurts the people and has declared him to be deserving of the Fire of Hell.

Imam Ja'far Sadiq says: "One who is not self-composed at the time of anger and is not well-behaved with his associates and friends is not one of us". (al-Imam al-Sadiq wal Mazāhibul Arba'ah, Vol. II. p. 350)

The holy Prophet says: "Be good-natured because it leads to Paradise and refrain from being ill-tempered because it decidedly drags one to Hell". (Wasā'ilush Shi'ah, Vol. II, p. 221)

Imam Ja'far Sadiq says: "Performing good deeds and having a cheerful countenance are the means of receiving love of others and deserving of Paradise, and stinginess and bad temper drive a person away from Allah and pulls him towards the Fire of Hell". (Jāmi'us Sa'ādāt, Vol. I, p. 273)

A few polytheists who had come to Madina with the intention of murdering the holy Prophet and his companions were arrested. When their guilt was proved, they declined to repent. The holy Prophet ordered that one of them might be set free and the others should be put to death.

The man who was realsed asked with much surprise: "O Muhammad! What was the reason for your releasing only myself and putting others to death?"

The holy Prophet replied: "Just now the Archangel Jibrīl brought information to me from Allah that you possess five qualities which are liked by Allah and His Prophet: (i) You are very particular about your honour and dignity. (ii) You are a generous man. (iii) You are truthful. (iv) You are brave and (v) You are well-behaved.

The man who knew more about himself than anybody else did, confirmed what the holy Prophet had said. He then acknowledged the Prophethood of the holy Prophet, joined the ranks of the Muslims and made many sacrifices for the advancement of Islam". (Amāli Sadūq, p. 163)

The holy Prophet says: "A person whose morals are better and who is more humble is more dear to me than all others and he will be nearer to me on the Day of Judgement". (Qurbul Asnād)

The holy Prophet further says: "The greatest testimony, which will pull my followers to Paradise and eternal bliss, is piety and good behaviour". (al-Kāfi, Vol. II, p. 100)

Good behaviour is a valuable and precious asset which is superior to all other things. It is an asset which also produces good results in the material life of man.

Imam Ali says: "Treasures of sustenance are hidden in good behaviour and cheerfulness". (Safinatul Bihār, Vol. I)

Imam Ali further says: "The overpowering effect of contentment and the everlasting benefit of good behaviour are quite sufficient for man". (Nahjul Balaghah, Vol. II, p. 195)

Luqman, the wise, advised to his son to preserve this treasure and said: "Dear son! Even if you happen to lose the material gains with which you can do good to your relatives and friends, do not lose the wealth of good behaviour and cheerfulness because if a person possesses the trait of good behaviour, the good people love him and the bad ones support him". (Safinatul Bihār, Vol. I, p. 410)

The holy Prophet says: "You do not at all possess so much capital and wealth that you may be able to relieve the people of indigence and pressures of life. Hence, equip yourselves with the wealth of morality and alleviate the burden from the hearts of others by means of good behaviour and cheerfulness". (Amāli Sadūq, p. 9)

Islam considers good behaviour to be one of the conditions of faith and an important article of worship and it says that one who possesses this trait will be favoured with Divine recompense.

The holy Prophet says: "The faith of a person, whose morals are better, is more valuable". (Amāli Sadūq, p. 126)

Imam Ja'far Sadiq says: "The faith of a man who possesses four traits is perfect, although he may be immersed into sins. They are: Truthfulness, restoration of trust to its rightful owner, modesty and good behaviour". (al-Kāfi, Vol. II, p. 99)

The late Allama Majlisi says thus in explanation of the above tradition: "The Imam's remark: 'although he may be immersed into sins' means excessive sins on the part of the person concerned and it is possible for us to interpret it as 'minor sins', because one who possesses the aforesaid outstanding traits will certainly not persist in committing major sins and these qualities themselves restrain one from committing sins. For example truthfulness restrains one from committing breach of trust in respect of the property of the people and the rights of Allah. Feeling ashamed of one's conduct before the people restrains one from demonstrating one's sins and feeling ashamed before Allah restrains one from committing major sins intentionally. And good behaviour restrains one from hurting the the people, misbehaving with one's parents, breaking of ties with relationship etc. In short if a person possesses the aforesaid four traits he automatically remains immune from a number of sins and on account of these very traits Allah provides him an opportunity to repent and make atonement for his sins and he leads a prosperous life and has a good future". (Bihārul Anwār)

Imam Ja'far Sadiq says: "Good behaviour exalts its possessor to the position of those who fast during daytime and pray at night and also provides him with spiritual reward similar to theirs". (al-Kāfi, Vol. II, p. 103)

The holy Prophet says: "When the deeds of the people will be evaluated on the Day of Judgement nothing will be superior to that of his good behaviour". (al-Kāfi, Vol. II, p. 99)

Just as the recommendations made by the dignified leaders of Islam with regard to good behaviour and its effects on the prosperity of the people in this world and in the Hereafter, they have also condemned bad and base conduct.

Imam Ali says: "There is repentance for every sin and everyone who repents can hope for the acceptance of his repentance except an immoral person who, before he repents for a sin, gets involved in a worse sin". (Safinatul Bihār, Vol. I, p. 424)

The holy Prophet says: "Bad conduct destroys the good deeds of man in the same manner in which vinegar spoils honey". (Majmu'a-i Warrām, Vol. I, p. 90)

Imam Ali was asked: "Which person involves most in worries and grief?" He replied: "One whose morals are worse than others". (Jāmi'ul Akhbār, p. 107)

Sa'di says: "An ill-natured person is caught in the hands of such an enemy that wherever he goes he cannot get rid of it.

If an ill-natured person escapes to the sky from affliction he will remain afflicted even there on account of his bad nature".

A man who had the honour of presenting himself before the holy Prophet asked him to give him an advice. The holy Prophet advised him *inter alia:* "To meet people cheerfully and with good honour". (al-Kāfi, Vol. II, p. 84)

Imam Ja'far Sadiq says: "Beneficence and good behaviour make the country prosperous and prolong the lives of the people". He was asked: "What are the limits of good behaviour?" He replied: "You should behave with people gently, say good things and meet others with a cheerful countenance".

A Few Note-worthy Points
(i) The moral code of Islam, specimens whereof have been quoted above, were communicated to the people fourteen centuries ago through the holy Prophet of Islam and his real successors viz. the Commander of the Faithful Imam Ali and his eleven infallible descendants (peace be on them) have had no source other than Divine revelation.

If during the modern age the Western writers have paid attention to morals and have published books and articles in this behalf the source thereof, like many other sciences, is in the Orient and in the valuable works of the Muslims.

(ii) Islam has laid the foundation of morality on faith. Hence, change in the conditions and circumstances of a Muslim does not bring about a chance in his morals which are always firm and unalterable.

In the societies in which morals are based on profiteering and material gains they are likely to collapse and change at any moment and such morals cannot be permanent.

(iii) One of the reasons for the backwardness of the Muslims is their moral degradation and their involvement in mean and indecent acts.

It is now the duty of every wise Muslim to pay more attention to Islamic moral code and to endeavour by all possible means to refine the morals of their brethren-in-faith and especially the young persons so that in future we may become the best and the foremost nation of the world.

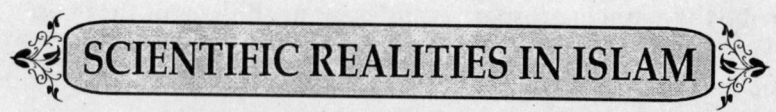
SCIENTIFIC REALITIES IN ISLAM

As human knowledge increases and the scientists take new steps towards the discovery of the mysteries of creation value of the teachings of Islam and the greatness of its leaders become more apparent.

The laws, which have been enacted by Allah, the Omniscient Creator are in conformity with nature and can never become obsolete. The well-informed and unbiased researchers who have conducted studies and investigations of the reules and regulations of Islam have humbly bowed their heads before it and praised it.

Some of them have adopted this sacred faith and considered it essential for themselves to follow it till the end of their lives. (See · Why I Became a Muslim)

Some others have, with their far-sightedness, considered Islam to be the future religion of the world.

George Bernard Shaw, the famous British writer said · "I have always held the religion of Muhammad in the highest esteem because of its wonderful vitality. It is the only religion which appears to me to possess the capability of assimilating and controlling diverse conditions and changing circumstances of life and facing different ages. I can foresee — and the signs thereof are apparent even now — that the religion of Muhammad will be accepted by the Europe of tomorrow. As a result of their ignorance or partiality the clergy of the Middle Ages presented a dark picture of the religion of Muhammad. They, due to rancour and religious animosity considered him as an opponent of Jesus Christ. I have conducted studies about this man — this extraordinary man — and have come to the conclusion that not only that he is not opponent of Jesus Christ but he ought to be acknowledged as the saviour of mankind. If a man like him becomes the ruler of the modern world he will be successful in solving the problems and difficulties of the world in such a way that the peace and prosperity which is desired by all human beings will be guaranteed". (KhudāParasti wa Afkār-i Roz, p. 21)

The monuments which have survived from the holy Imams and the distinguished leaders of Islam astonish every researcher.

We, who believe the leaders of Islam to be the Divine Imams (leaders) and consider their knowledge to be branched out from the Divine knowledge are not surprised when we come across their scientific predictions. However, the non-Muslim researchers who wish to study everything on the basis of physical and human sciences are so much surprised, when faced with these predictions, that they cannot hide their surprise.

Some time back the magazine named *'Khwandanihā'* translated and published a book entitled 'The Reflective Brain of the Shi'ah World'. This book was compiled and published by a group of scholars and researchers of Islamic Studies Centre, Strasbourg* who are mostly Christians. This book is the biography of Imam Ja'far Sadiq, the sixth Imam, and his wisdom has been studied and analyzed. The scholarly authors of this book, everyone of whom is a specialist in one branch of learning or another, have compared the remarks of Imam Ja'far Sadiq with the modern sciences and discoveries and are surprised and perplexed as to how the holy Imam acquired information about all these sciences! We reproduce below some extracts from the said book by way of specimen.

Teaching of Medical Science

"There are two versions, one positive and the other negative, about the teaching of medical science in the educational centre of Muhammad Baqir. Some say that the medical science was taught there whereas others deny that Muhammad Baqir

---

*Strasbourg, which is a city of France and the capital of the province of Alsace, is situated on the bank of the river Roun. Its population is 1,95,000 and it contains very magnificent and splendid churches.

imparted instruction in this science. However, there is no doubt about the fact that when Ja'far Sadiq himself imparted lessons on medical science and his scientific opinions influenced this science and the physicians of the second and third centuries of the Hegira era benefited from his views on the subject of medicine.

We have said that we are not aware whether or not Muhammad Baqir taught medicine and whether or not his son learnt this science from him. However, we do not have any doubt that Ja'far Sadiq himself taught medical science and introduced things in it which had not till then been introduced by the physicians of the East. And by 'East' we do not mean Arabia, because Arabia did not possess medical science and it reached there from other countries after the advent of Islam. If we admit that Ja'far Sadiq acquired this knowledge from his father it is necessary that his father, in his turn, should have acquired it from somewhere and we do not know from where he acquired it.

We know that Ja'far Sadiq did not belong to the medical profession so that he might have acquired perfection in this branch of knowledge. Hence, it would appear that he learnt them from his father and then the question arises again as to wherefrom his father learnt them?

Earth and Air are not Simple Elements

One day Ja'far Sadiq, while taking lessons from his father, reached that part of Aristotle's* 'Physics' wherein he says that there are only four elements in the world namely earth, water, air and fire. Ja'far Sadiq objected to this and said: 'I wonder how a man like Aristotle neglected this thing that earth is not one element but there are many elements in it and every metal available in earth should be treated to be a separate element'.

There was a distance of 1000 years between the time of Aristotle and that of Ja'far Sadiq and during this long period the four elements as specified by Aristotle were reckoned to be one of the fundamentals of physics and there was none who might not have believed in the idea and it did not occur to anyone to oppose it. It was after 1000 years that a boy who was

---

*Aristotle (384 — 322 B.C.), Greek philosopher and scientist, and founder of the technique of organized research and classification.

not yet twelve years of age said that earth is not one element but it is composed of many elements.

When the same boy himself began teaching others he also rejected the idea of air being a simple element and said: 'Air is not one element but it is composed of a number of elements'.

Eleven hundred years before the European Scientists of the 18th century of the Christian era discovered and separated the component parts of air, Ja'far Sadiq said that air was not one element but it had come into existence by the combination of a number of elements.

Even if after reflection and reasoning it was admitted about earth that it is not one element but a number of elements, no one had any doubt about the air being an element.

The most distinguished physicists of the world after Aristotle did not know that air was not a simple element. Even in the 18th century A.D. which was one of the brilliant centuries from the point of view of advancement in science many scholars thought, till the time of Lavoisier* that air was a simple element and did not imagine that it was composed of a few elements. And when Lavoisier separated oxygen from other gases available in the air and showed what great effect oxygen has on breathing and burning, all the scientists acknowledged that air is not a simple element but is composed of a few gases. And one day in the year 1794 A.D. the head of Lavoisier was severed from his body with the blade of the guillotine and the father of modern chemistry, who might have made some more discoveries if he had lived, was sent to the other world.

Hence, Ja'far Sadiq who declared that air is not a simple element preceded his own time by 1100 years.

The Shi'ah say that Ja'far Sadiq gathered this and other scientific realities by means of Divine Knowledge the knowledge bestowed upon him in the capacity of an Imam.

Nowadays this matter appears to us to be something common because we know that there are 102 elements in the world. However, in the 7th century A.D. and 1st century Hegira it

---

*Lavoisier, Antoine Laurent (1743 — 94), French chemist. He discovered the properties of oxygen, explained the process of combustion and demolished the phlogiston theory. He formulated the law of the Conservation of Matter.

was a great revolutionary idea and human intellect at that time could not agree that air was not a simple element. We may add that at that time and during the following ages till the 18th century A.D. Europe did not possess the capacity to hold this scientific and revolutionary belief and to believe in other things said by Ja'far Sadiq which will be mentioned in the following chapters......

Oxygen

While delivering his lecture, he (Imam Ja'far Sadiq) said: 'Air has some component parts. One of these parts is absorbed by some bodies and brings about changes. And out of the many parts of the air it is that very part which helps burning. In case that help had not been available, many things which are inflammable would not burn.

This idea was expounded by Ja'far Sadiq himself and he said in his later lectures: 'If the thing in the air which helps burning is separated from air and is acquired in a pure form it is so effective in burning things that even iron can be burnt with it'.

Hence, 1000 years before Priestley* and earlier than Lavoisier, Ja'far Sadiq clearly described oxygen and only did not give it the name of oxygen. Although Priestley discovered oxygen yet he could not realize that it can burn iron.

Lavoisier, notwithstanding the fact that he deduced some properties of oxygen by means of experiments, could not understand that gas could burn iron, but Ja'far Sadiq realized this 1000 years earlier.

We know now that if a piece of iron is made so hot that it becomes red and is then thrown in pure oxygen it burns with a luminous flame. Just as in the oil or kerosene-lamps of the past the wick burnt with glowing light in the same manner a lamp can be provided with an iron wick and dipped in liquified oxygen and the wick is heated in such a way that when it becomes red hot it will then emit dazzling light turning the night in day light.

It has been narrated that one day, while teaching a lesson,

---

*Priestley, Joseph (1733 — 1804), English clergyman and scientist. He discovered oxygen and carbon monoxide.

Muhammad Baqir, father of Ja'far Sadiq said: 'With the help of science fire can be lit by means of water which normally extinguishes fire'. If this remark was not interpreted as a poetic fancy it appeared to be meaningless and for a long time those who heard this narration thought that Muhammad Baqir had said something fanciful. However, from 18th century onwards it was proved that with the help of science, fire can be lit by means of water and that fire would be hotter than the fire which is lit by means of wood and coal, because the heat emitted by hydrogen (which is one of the two components of water) when burnt by means of oxygen reaches a temperature of 6664 degrees. The process of burning hydrogen in the presence of oxygen is called 'oxidization' and is utilized a good deal in the industry to weld metals or to analyse the pieces of metals.

Rotation of Earth on its Axis

Henry Poincare,* who died in the year 1912 A.d. at the age of 58 years, was the greatest mathematician of his time and the date of his death also shows that he lived up to the beginning of the 20th century. Inspite of this even this great scientist used to say: 'I do not believe that the earth rotates on its axis'.

When a scientist like Henry Poicncare doubted in the beginning of the 20th century whether or not the earth rotates on its axis it is evident that the people of the second half of the first century and of the second century A.H. could not accept the proposition that the earth rotates on its axis.

The rotation of the earth on its axis could not be proved by perception until the time when man landed on the moon and observed the earth from there.

Even in the early years of exploration of space, the astronauts could not observe the rotation of the earth with their eyes because during those years they did not have a stationary base and were confined to airships, everyone of which revolved round the earth once in every ninety minutes or a little more. And while the astronauts were themselves revolving round the earth at such a speed they could not realize the movement of the earth itself.

*The famous French philosopher and mathematician (1854 — 1912).

However, on the day on which they landed on the moon and turned their film-taking telescopes towards the earth they saw in the photographs that the earth rotated slowly on its axis and on that day the rotation of the earth on its axis was proved visibly. . . . . . In view of the fact that Galileo* knew very well that like all other planets of the solar system the earth revolves round the sun it is possible that he might have guessed that like other planets the earth also rotates on its axis. However, we do not find any trace of such a guess in his writings. . . . . . Not only this that Galileo did not talk during his lifetime about the earth's rotation on its axis, but even after his death nothing was found in his writings which might show that he had become aware of the earth's rotation on its axis.

In the sixteenth century of the Christian era another astronomer named Tikhubraha lived in Denmark who believed that the earth revolves round the sun.

As opposed to Copernicus‡ of Poland, who had to go without meals at times, Tikhubraha belonged to the aristocrats of Denmark and lived a luxurious life and arranged magnificent feasts in his palace. He died in 1601 A.D. i.e. in the first year of the 17th century. He was a man whose astronomical studies helped Kepler,* the German scientist, a good deal and without Tikhubraha it would not have been possible for Kepler to discover his three famous astronimical laws relating to the movement of the planets, including the earth's revolution round the sun.

Inspite of this Tikhubraha could not realize the rotation of earth on its axis and if he had realized it he would have confirmed it openly like the earth's revolution round the sun. . . . . .

---

*The famous Italian philosopher, mathematician and astronomer. (1564 — 1642) He made the first astronomical telescope.

‡Copernicus, Nicolaus (1473—1543), Polish astronomer. He revolutionized thinking and laid the foundation of modern astronomy with his conception of the Universe. This was that the planets, including the earth, revolved around the sun, the stars are infinitely distant and the Universe spherical.

*Kepler, Johannes (1571 — 1630), German astronomer. An assistant of Tycho Brahe in Prague, he founded the science of optics with his work *Dioptrics*. His most important works are *New Astronomy* and *The Harmonies of the World*.

With the discovery of the three laws relating to the movement of the planets, Kepler, who died in 1630 A.D., not only won applause from the scientific world of that time, but even today, whoever studies his three laws, praises him. That great scientist who proved his genius by discovering the three astronomical laws, could not realize the rotation of the earth on its axis.

However, Ja'far Sadiq discovered twelve centuries earlier that the earth rotates on its axis and the reason for the successive appearance of day and night is not the revolving of the sun round the earth (the theory which he considered to be irrational and unacceptable) but the rotation of the earth on its own axis by which one half of the earth receives daylight and the other remains in darkness.

The ancients who believed the earth to be spherical knew that there was always night in one half of the earth and day in the other half, but they considered day and night to be the outcome of the movement of the sun round the earth.

How did it happen that twelve centuries earlier Ja'far Sadiq realized that the earth rotates on its axis and consequent to it day and night come into existence.

Notwithstanding the fact that the scientists of the 15th and 17th centuries of the Christian era, names of some of whom have been mentioned above, discovered some laws of astronomical mechanism had not realized that the earth rotates on its axis, how then did Ja'far Sadiq, residing at a remote point like Madina which was far away from the centres of learning of those times came to know that the earth rotates on its axis?

The Genesis

Ja'far Sadiq thus said about the creation of the world: 'The world came into existence with a single particle and that particle had two opposite poles and these two opposite poles became the cause of the birth of atom and then matter came into being and matter acquired variety and the variety of matter arises from the deficiency or excess of its atoms'.

This theory is not at all different from the modern atomic theory regarding the coming into existence of the world. The two opposite poles are the two charges — positive and negative — in the atom. These two charges became the cause of the coming into existence of atom and atom also brought matter into existence. And the difference which is seen in matter (i.e. the elements) arises from the deficiency or excess of things which are available in the atoms of the elements.

The Shi'ah say that all the things which Ja'far Sadiq said about the coming into existence of the world, astronomy, physics, elements, chemistry, mathematics and other things became known to him on account of his knowledge as an Imam i.e. the knowledge bestowed upon him by the Almighty Allah... We have commenced the study of the learning of Ja'far Sadiq in respect of geography, astronomy and physics under the main subject of the creation of the world and shall continue the discourse with regard to his physics and shall thereafter discuss other subjects. And we say in this connection that Ja'far Sadiq said things about physics which none had said before him and none was in a position to say the same after him till the middle of the 18th century and in the 19th and 20th centuries.

Parts of Human Body

Ja'far Sadiq used to say like other Muslims that man has been created from earth. The difference between him and other Muslims was that he said things about the creation of man from earth which were unintelligible to the Muslims of that age.

Even during the later ages no Muslim possessed knowledge about the structure of human body which might match that of Ja'far Sadiq and if anyone said anything directly or indirectly it was that which he had heard from the disciples of Ja'far Sadiq.

He (Imam Ja'far Sadiq) said: 'All the things available in earth are also found in the body of man. However, the quantity of all of them is not the same. Some of them are in a great quantity in human body and others are in a little quantity'.

The quantity of the things which are much more in human body is also not equal and some of them are lesser than others. He said: 'There are four things in a human body in good quantity and there are eight things which are lesser and there are another eight things which are still lesser'.

This view about the structure of the human body which has been expressed by Ja'far Sadiq is so peculiar that at times one thinks whether, as the Shi'ah believe, he possessed the knowledge of Imamate and gained this idea from that knowledge and not from the human sciences. This is so because one's understanding cannot accept the position that only a scholar who possesses human qualifications should have become aware of these realities twelve and a half centuries ago. . . . . . Ja'far Sadiq, irrespective of whether, as believed by the Shi'ah, he possessed the knowledge of Imamate or according to the view of those who believe in intuitional knowledge he depended on intuition or, according to the view of Bergson* he benefited from his supernatural knowledge he has said things about the structure of human body which prove that so far as the knoledge of human body is concerned he was unique among the people of his own time as well as of the later ages, because after twelve and half centuries the correctness of his view has been proved scientifically and there is no doubt about it. And Ja'far Sadiq did not mention the names of the elements available in the body of man.

It may be pointed out that just as Ja'far Sadiq has said whatever is available in earth is also available in the body of man. Whatever is in earth has come into being by means of 102 elements and these 102 elements are available in the body of man. However, the quantity of some of these elements in the body of man is so small that it has not so far been possible to determine them exactly. . . . . . As we have said above the correctness of this view has since been proved.

The eight elements in the human body which according to Ja'far Sadiq are in a very small quantity are as follows:
(i) Molybdenum   (ii) Selenium   (iii) Fluorine   (iv) Cobalt
(v) Manganese (vi) Iodine (vii) Copper (viii) Zinc

The eight elements which are available in a large quantity in the body of man as compared with those mentioned above are as follows:
(i) Magnesium (ii) Sodium (iii) Potassium (iv) Calcium (v) Phosphorus (vi) Chlorine (vii) Sulphur (viii) Iron

*Bergson, Henri (1859 — 1941), French philosopher and winner of the Nobel prize for literature (1927). His most celebrated work is *Creative Evolution* (1907). He held that all evolution and progress are due to the workings of the *élan vital* or life force; and that to attain philosophic truth we must use not Reason but Instinct.

The four elements which are available in the human body in a larger quantity consist of the following:

(i) Oxygen (ii) Carbon (iii) Hydrogen (iv) Nitrogen

Knowledge about the availability of these elements in the body of man was not acquired in a day or two. This work was started in the 18th century of the Christian era with the dissection of human body, and in anatomy the two nations, the French and the Austrians, took the initiative in this behalf. In other countries anatomy was not practised and in the European countries the Orthodox, Catholic and Protestant Churches opposed it. However, in Austria and France anatomy was practised without defying the orders of the Church openly. Inspite of this, anatomy did not expand in France till the time of Marat* and was almost a secret. Incidental to anatomy Marat, with the assistance of some other French scientists including Lavoisier who was guillotined in 1794 A.D., used to analyze the tissues of human body to find out the elements with which it is composed.

After Marat, his pupils continued his work and, incidental to anatomy, analyzed the tissues of human body and this work continued throughout the 19th century and the early part of the 20th century and expanded.

Anatomy, which was almost confined in the beginning of the 18th century of the Christian era to France and Austria, became current in other European countries and then in the countries of other continents and is now practised everywhere except in a few countries which do not have colleges which may impart instruction in medicine and surgery. Wherever anatomy is practised research is carried out about the elements of which human body is composed. At times the results of the research conducted by two centres differ from each other to a very small extent but there are no big differences between them and the ratio which Ja'far Sadiq mentioned is intact in all the countries in respect of all healthy persons.

---

*Marat, Jean-Paul (1743 — 93), French revolutionary, doctor and scientist. He was a leading opponent of the Girondists, and was assassinated by a Girodist adherent, Charlotte Corday.

Oxygen and Hydrogen in Water

The miracle of Ja'far Sadiq was not that he moved a mountain but his miracle was that he came to know about the existence of oxygen twelve and a half centuries ago and came to know at the same time that there was something in water which burns. On this very account he said that water can be transformed into electricity.

It is said that the most outstanding trait of a prophet is his speech because he does not say anything which has no base. . . . It is just as when we hear today that in the first half of the second century of the Hegira era Ja'far Sadiq discovered the existence of oxygen (in water) we admit in our heart that it is a miracle. One is astonished to think as to how Ja'far Sadiq or his father (Muhammad Baqir) became aware of hydrogen gas when it is not available in nature in its true form and does not also have colour, odour or taste.

Ja'far Sadiq or his father became aware of the existence of hydrogen in water but they could not isolate it without analysing water.

Analysis of water also necessitates the use of electric current, because water cannot be analyzed without it. And it is also unacceptable that anyone of them could utilize electric current for analysing water.

During the present time the first person who succeeded in separating hydrogen from water was the English scientists Henry Cavendish (1731 — 1810). He endeavoured for years to analyse water and when he succeeded in discovering hydrogen he gave it the name of 'inflammable gas' and when it was inflammed for the first time he himself and his house were about to burn. . . . . Hydrogen gas was discovered at a time when use of electric power had advanced so much that it was possible to utilize it for the analysis of water.

During the time of Ja'far Sadiq, however, the use of electric power was limited to the use of straw and amber which was considered frivolous activities. A piece of amber was rubbed with a woollen cloth and brought near straw and it attracted the blades of straw towards itself.

Did Ja'far Sadiq or his father, Muhammad Baqir, use a facility to separate hydrogen from water which is not yet known to the scientists? And were they able to separate hydrogen from water by a means other than electric current?

From the day on which Cavendish was successful for the first time in obtaining hydrogen till today the only means of separating hydrogen from water has been the electric current and the scientists have not been able to separate hydrogen from water by any other means.

Pollution of the Atmosphere

During the time of Ja'far Sadiq industries were limited to artisanship and not even one factory resembling the modern factories did not exist. Metals were melted in small furnaces and as all metals, even iron, were melted with wood, it did not pollute the atmosphere. However if iron was melted with steam coal the quantity of the products was not so large that the atmosphere might be polluted. Even when from the beginning of the 18th century iron and steel began to be produced in large quantities in Germany, France, England and other European countries, the atmosphere was not polluted although all the foundries in Germany, France and England were burning steam coal and the emission of smoke from the chimneys of the factories did not stop for even a moment from the beginning of a year till its end.

Inspite of this the atmosphere was not polluted with the smoke of steam coal, not to speak of the time of Ja'far Sadiq when not even one factory resembling those of the modern times existed and none burnt steam coal. Even then Ja'far Sadiq, like one who could see the conditions of the present age, said 'Man should lead his life in such a way that he should not pollute his environments, because if he does so a day will come when it will be difficult and perhaps impossible for him to live on account of pollution'.

The problem of the pollution of the atmosphere of life did not exist even about forty years ago. This problem cropped up from the time when the first atomic bomb was exploded and polluted the atmosphere in the zone of its explosion.

If man had contented himself with these first explosions the atmosphere would not have been polluted. However, the countries which possessed atomic weapons continued the experimentation of those weapons and simultaneously with these experimentations the factories producing electricity began working with atomic energy and pollution of the atmosphere increased due to the radio-active materials.

At the same time industries, especially in America and Europe, also polluted the atmosphere and water of some rivers, for example of the river Roun in Western Europe got so much polluted that the species of the fish was destroyed. Similarly the species of the fish have become almost extinct in the big lakes of Northern America, which contain soft water. And the pollution of the water of the oceans is more dangerous than the pollution of the atmosphere of land, because the microscopic unicellular living organisms, called planktons which live on the oceanic water surface provide 90% of atmospheric oxygen to the earth, will die on account of the pollution of the ocean and with their death and extinction the quantity of oxygen in the atmosphere of the earth will be reduced to 10% of the present quantity. This quantity is not sufficient either for the breathing of the living creatures including human beings or for the breathing of the plants. As a consequence of this the species of plants and living creatures on the earth will become extinct. This is not a mere theory so that the possibility of its being right or wrong may be debated. On the other hand it is a scientific calculation and keeping in view the manner in which the oceans are being polluted at present the number of planktons on the surface of the oceans will be reduced to 50% during the next 50 years and the quantity of the production of oxygen will also be reduced in the same ratio.

A child who is born today will breathe after 50 years (if he lives till that time) in the same manner in which a mountaineer breathes while scaling the top of the Himalayas, the highest mountain of the world, without the use of breathing apparatus.

If the pollution of water of the oceans continues during the next 50 years the manner of breathing of all human beings and other living creatures will be the same as that of persons who are supposed to be suffering from palpitation.

After 50 years if a person will strike a match to light a cigarette or to kindle an oven in his house the match will not catch fire because there will not be sufficient oxygen in the air to set it on fire. This remark is not a myth but a scientific reality. . . . . . In order to understand how by ignoring the recommendation made by Ja'far Sadiq (to the effect that man should not pollute his atmospheric environments) involves a rich nation in difficulties, we take the example of Japan.

Today Japan is the foremost nation in the world, after U.S.A., from the point of production of automobiles, computers and acrylic fibre cloth and is reckoned to be the foremost nation so far as the manufacture of ships, radios, cassettes, televisions, cameras and motor cycles is concerned.

If we narrate how Japan acquired such a high position in industry and trade, in so short a time, commencing from zero we shall be deviating from the matter under discussion viz. pollution of the environments of life. It may be said briefly that two real factors became the cause of Japan achieving this position in a very short period: (i) Good management and (ii) Sincerity of the Japanese workers, with regard to their work. However, as this wealthy and efficient nation failed to keep the environments unpolluted it is now faced with a great difficulty so much so that the health of its people has been endangered and as a consequence of the pollution of the atmosphere, diseases have appeared in Japan which have no precedent in the history of medical science. Mankind has realized only recently the dangers of polluting the environments, especially land, rivers and seas.

However, the wise men of the past, like Ja'far Sadiq had realized 1200 years ago that man should lead his life in such a way that he does not pollute his atmospheric environments.

Keeping the Infant on the Left Side of the Mother

One of the demonstrations of the scientific genius of Ja'far Sadiq was his recommendation to the mothers that they should make the sucklings lie on their left side.

For centuries this recommendation appeared to be superfluous or inopportune. The reason for this was that none understood the benefit inherent in this recommendation and some persons considered it dangerous to act upon it. They thought that if a child was made to lie on the left side of the mother it was possible that while changing sides during sleep she might crush her child under weight.

Muhammad bin Idris Shāfi'i who was born at Ghazah in 150 A.H., two years after the death of Ja'far Sadiq, died at Cairo in 199 A.H., was asked whether a mother should make a suckling lie on her right side or on her left side. He replied: 'There is no difference between the right side and the left side. A child should be made to lie on whichever side it is more comfortable for the mother'.

At times some persons considered the remark of Ja'far Sadiq to be contrary to sound judgement, because according to their view right side was more dignifiable than the left one and thought that a mother should make her child lie on her right side so that he may benefit from the blessings of the right side.

Nobody attached any importance to the said recommendation of Ja'far Sadiq either in the East or in the West so much so that even during the Renaissance when every scientific topic was studied with a critical eye nobody attached any importance to the remark of Ja'far Sadiq nor did any person think of finding out whether or not it had any value or utility from the scientific point of view.

The 16th, 17th and 18th centuries A.D., which were the centuries of the period of Renaissance passed and the 19th century arrived. During the second half of that century the Cornell University was established in the U.S.A. and started functioning.

Ezra Cornell, the founder of the University, who had suffered many hardships as a suckling and as a boy decided to set up a special Institute in the University for research about the new-borns and sucklings.

This Institute was established by the Cornell University during its first acadamic year and was affiliated to the Medical College. It is more than a century now that it has been engaged in research about the new-borns and the sucklings.

There is nothing related to the affairs of the new-borns and the sucklings which has not been investigated into by this Institute and no scientific centre in the world matches it in the matter of possessing information with regard to the new-borns and the sucklings.

It is impossible that there should be a topic related to the new-borns and the sucklings which this Institute may not have investigated into. Even the tableaux on which the pictures of the new-borns and the sucklings have been drawn have been the subject of research by the Institute.

During the first half of this century (20th Century) the researchers of this Institute looked at tableaux related to the new-borns in the museums of the world and from the 466 tableaux which they saw in the famous museums of the world they found in the majority of the tableaux that the mothers were carrying their children on the left side.

In 373 tableaux the mothers were carrying the children on the left side and in 93 tableaux they were carrying them on the right side. Hence, in 80% of the tableaux in the well-known museums it was seen that the mothers were carrying their children on the left side.

In New York State some maternity hospitals are attached to the Research Institute of the new-borns and sucklings of the Cornell University and the doctors who work in those maternity hospitals communicate the results of their studies and observations to the said Institute.

From the reports which were received in the Institute from those doctors covering a long period it was concluded that in the early days after birth the child feels more comfortable when he lies on the left side of his mother than when he lies on her right side and if he is made to lie on her right side he wakes up after short intervals and start crying.

The investigators of the research centre did not confine their studies to the white Americans, but planned to find out whether or not the same position was true in respect of the black and the yellow races.

After a long study tour in respect of other races it was found that the same position was true in respect of all nations and everywhere the new-borns felt more comfortable, especially during the first few days after their birth, if they were laid on the left side of the mothers rather than on their right side and this is a universal reality and is not peculiar to the white race.

The research centre of Cornell University continued studies in this subject. For hours the doctors of the research centre subjected the pelvis of a pregnant woman to examination by means of X-rays to see the foetus in the womb of the mother.

However, observance of the foetus did not add anything to their information till holography* was invented.

After the invention of holography the doctors of the research centre planned to take photographs of the foetus in the womb of the mother when the X-ray had thrown light on it. At that time they observed that the waves of the sound of the beatings of the heart of the mother which are distributed in her entire body reach the ears of the foetus.

After this stage and in order to acquire further information it was necessary for them to know whether or not a pause in the beatings of the heart of the mother brought about a reaction in the foetus. As they could not halt the heart of a mother because this would have resulted in her death they continued their experiments on mammalian animals and every time they stopped the working of the heart of an animal carrying a foetus in the uterus they saw that a reaction took place in the foetus.

Repeated experiments on some mammalian species proved that when the beatings of the heart of a mother stop a reaction takes place in the foetus and after the death of the mother the foetus also dies, because the foetus feeds on the blood of its mother through placenta and when the heart of the mother ceases to work the food does not reach the foetus and it dies.

After conducting many experiments the scholars of the research centre of Cornell University came to the conclusion that the child in its mother's womb not only gets habituated to hear the beatings of her heart but those beatings are also related to its life and when the beatings are discontinued the child dies of hunger in the mother's womb.

The habit of hearing the heart-beats of its mother which the foetus acquires before its birth becomes so much ingrained in it that even after its birth it feels uneasy if it does not hear

---

*In simple words 'holography' means photography of very tiny things and three-dimensional photography. Nowadays not only the photographs of very tiny things are taken by means of holography but even sound is photographed and the waves of sound appear on the photographic film in the shape of well-arranged circles and eclipses. Holography is so powerful in taking photographs of tiny things that a white or red globule in the blood appears as big as an elephant.

its mother's heart-beats and the intelligence of a new-born child can very well discern these beatings. It is for this reason that when a new-born child lies on the left side of its mother it hears the sound of the beatings of her heart and becomes comfortable, but if it is made to lie on the right side it does not hear that sound and, therefore, becomes uneasy.

If the founder of the Cornell University had not established a research centre related to the new-borns and the sucklings and the centre had not conducted incessant research the philosophy of Ja'far Sadiq's recommending to the mothers to make their sucklings lie on their left side would not have become known.

Nowadays in all the nurseries attached to the research centre of the Cornell University an appratus has been provided for in the room in which the sucklings lie which creates the sound of the beatings of the heart of a mother and there is a receiver in the bed of every new-born child which communicates the artificial beatings of a mother's heart to its ear.

The heart of an adult person, whether man or woman, usually beats 72 times per minute.

In the nurseries which are attached to the research centre of the Cornell University it has been experimented a number of times that if the number of the artificial beatings of the heart of a mother reaches 110 or 120 per minute all the children begin crying. It is, therefore, necessary that number of such artificial beatings should be 72 per minute so that the children may not become uneasy and may not cry.

In the nurseries attached to the research centre the following experiment has been made a number of times.

Some new-borns were placed in a room in which the sound of the artificial beatings of the heart of a mother did not reach their ears and some other new-borns were placed in a room in which they could hear that sound. Every time this experiment was made it was found that the weight of the children in the room in which the sound of the artificial beatings of the heart of a mother could be heard increased more rapidly than that of others although same food was provided to the children in both the rooms.

The fact is that the children in the room in which the sound of the artificial beatings of the heart of a mother is heard eat their food with more appetite whereas the others eat it with lesser appetite.

Research was also conducted in the nurseries attached to the research centre of the Cornell University in respect of the intensity of the sound of the artificial beatings of the heart of a mother and it was found that if that sound is more intense than the natural sound of the beatings of a mother's heart the children become uneasy and start crying.

During his journeys in different continents of the world one of the doctors of the research centre of the Cornell University noticed carefully as to how mothers in different countries carried their children on roads.

This doctor named Dr Lee Salk who is working at present in the said research centre says: 'Most of the women in all the continents of the world carry their children on their left side while walking on roads. The women who carry their children on their right side are mostly those who work with their left hands. They carry their children on their right side especially when they have to carry a basket or groceries so that they may carry the same easily with their left hand'.

In the maternity hospital attached to the research centre Dr Lee Salk puts this question to all the women after parturition who leave the maternity hospital and carry their new-borns on their left sides: 'Do you know why you are carrying your new-borns on your left side?' However, none of them has told Dr Lee Salk that they are doing so because heart is located on the left side of the breast and it is useful for the new-borns to hear the sound of its beatings. Mothers carry their children on their left side without knowing why they prefer that side.

Even the women of black-skinned African tribes carry their children on the left side of their breast as and when they do not carry them on their back. In all black-skinned African tribes the women know that when a new-born is placed on the left side of the breast it sucks milk better and the appetite of a new-born for sucking milk from the left breast is more as compared with the right one.

Dr Lee Salk has heard from mothers that when the child feels hungry at night it locates the left breast of the mother in darkness with surprising quickness, places his mouth on it and sucks milk.

They wonder as to how it happens that the child sees the breast of his mother, without the light of a lamp, and places his mouth on it quickly.

Dr Lee salk explains to the mothers that the child is guided to the breast of the mother in darkness by the beatings of her heart. As soon as he hears the sound of those beatings he locates the breast without any hesitation and places his mouth on it'.

Light — a Means of Transmission of Disease

...... One of the views of Ja'far Sadiq which proves his scientific genius is the view according to which a disease can be transmitted by means of some kinds of light.

Ja'far Sadiq said: 'There are some lights which, if thrown from a sick person to a healthy person, can possibly make that healthy person sick'.

It should be noted that what is being talked about here is not the atmosphere or the transmission of microbes about which people were not at all aware during the first half of the 2nd century of Hegira but it is about light. And then it is not being said that all lights have the characteristic of making a healthy person sick if they fall on him from a sick person but it is said that only some lights can possibly do so.

The scholars of biology and medicine considered this view to be something extravagant because they believed that the agents of transmission of illness from a sick person to a healthy one were microbes or virus, whether the means of transmission of the disease were reptiles, water, air or physical contact between a sick person or a healthy one.

Before the existence of microbes and virus became known, odour was considered to be the means of transmission of disease and all steps taken in olden times for the prevention of the transmission of diseases were based on the prevention of spreading odour so that a healthy person might not catch a disease by contagion from an ailing person. No one said during any period that if some lights fall from an ailing person to a healthy person they make him ill. However, it was Ja'far Sadiq who said this.

As we have said above that all the scientists considered this view to be something extravagant till the modern scientific research proved that it is a reality and there are some lights which make a healthy person sick if they fall upon him. It was the U.S.S.R. who realized this reality for the first time.

In the city of Novo Sabirisk which is situated in the Soviet Union (in Siberia) and is one of the greatest centres of research in medicine, chemistry and biology it was proved scientifically and undeniably that in the first instance rays radiate from the cells of the ailing person and secondly there are some rays which radiate from the cells of an ailing person and make the healthy cells sick as and when they fall on them without the slightest contact between the ailing cells and the healthy cells and without the transmission of microbes and virus from the ailing cells to the healthy ones.

The line of action adopted by the scientists who were busy in research at Novo Sabirisk was this: They selected two groups of cells of the same shape from a living being and separated them from each other and saw that some kinds of photon* were radiating from those cells.

After selecting two groups of similar cells from a living being and dividing them into two parts they made one of those groups sick to observe whether or not rays radiated from them in the state of sickness and found that photons radiated from the cells even when they were sick.

The scientists placed the cells of the second group which were healthy in two chests. One of these chests was made of quartz and the other was made of glass.

Quartz has the characteristic that any kind of photon i.e. any kind of ray cannot pass through it except the ultra violet rays. Common glass has the characteristic that every kind of photon i.e. every kind of rays can pass through it except the ultra violet rays.

After some hours when the healthy cells placed in the Quartz and glass chests were exposed to the rays of the sick cells it was observed that the healthy cells in the quartz chest fell sick whereas those in the glass chest did not fall sick.

This experiment was repeated 5000 times during a period of 20 years with various ailments and similar and dissimilar cells, because the scientists concerned did not wish that there

*Unit of quantity of energy in light is called photon.

should be the least doubt about the results arrived at. In all 5000 experiments the final result was the same viz. the ailing cells radiate certain kinds of rays including the ultra violet rays. Furthermore, as and when the healthy cells are exposed to the ultra violet rays which are radiated by the ailing cells (and not other ultra violet rays) they fall ill. Moreover, their disease is the same as that of the ailing cells.

During all this experimentation which lasted for 20 years there was no proximity or contact between the healthy cells and the ailing ones so that it might be imagined that virus or microbes of one group were communicated by contagion to the other group and the scientists came to know for certain after 5000 experiments that the agents for the appearance of disease in the healthy cells are the ultra violet rays which radiate from the ailing cells and fall on them.

From the experiments conducted by the Soviet scientists it may be concluded that every cell of our body is like a sender and a recipient which radiates rays and is also affected by the rays and retains them......

It is evident that this scientific reality which has been proved with 5000 experiments spread over a period of 20 years has opened a new field for the biologists and physicians for treating various diseases.

Research has been carried out in this field in the United States as well and the results obtained are similar to those obtained by the Soviet scientists and have been reported in the American scientific magazines. One of the research scholars named Dr John Oat has also written a book on this subject.

From what has been stated above it may be concluded that the view held by Ja'far Sadiq in the first half of the second century Hegira to the effect that some lights cause diseases (and which had so far been held to be something extravagant) is a reality and we know now that as and when the ultra violet light rays travels from the ailing living beings to the healthy living beings it makes them sick whereas other ultra violet rays and most important of all the ultra violet rays of the sun do not cause any disease when they fall on the living beings.

In case the light of the ultra violet rays of the sun falls on the bodies of the living beings without the medium of air and there is no obstacle between the body and those rays they will be fatal for the living beings. However, when these very rays reach the earth after passing through the medium of air they do not make any living being sick.

In any case the modern biological and medical discoveries have proved the correctness of the view of Ja'far Sadiq after the lapse of a period of 1250 years.

Sciences of Other Worlds

Another question which Ja'far Sadiq was asked was this: 'Who can be considered to be omniscient and at what stage does man feel that he has learnt everything?' Ja'far Sadiq said to the questioner: 'You should divide this question in two parts and should ask me each question separately'.

The first part about which you can enquire from me is as to 'who can be considered to be omniscient?'

'I tell you in reply that no one who may be omniscient exists except the Almighty Allah and it is impossible for any human being to be omniscient. It is so because knowledge is so vast that no one can understand all knowable things even though he may live for thousands of years and may remain busy in acquiring knowledge throughout that period. After living for thousands of years he may perhaps become acquainted with all branches of knowledge relating to this world. However, beyond this world there are other worlds and sciences exist in those worlds. Hence one who has learnt all sciences of this world will be an ignorant person when he arrives in other worlds and will have to commence his studies *de novo*, so that he may become acquainted with the sciences of those worlds.

It is only the Almighty Allah who is Omniscient because no human being can acquire knowledge about everything'.

The disciples of Ja'far Sadiq then asked the second part of the question viz. when does man feel that he has learnt everything? Ja'far Sadiq replied: 'The first reply given by me covers the reply to this question also, because I have told you that even if man lives for thousands of years and studies continuously he cannot learn all knowable things.

Hence, a time never comes when a man may feel that he does not need any more knowledge. Only the ignorant persons feel that they do not need knowledge and whoever is ignorant considers himself to be independent of knowledge'.

Ja'far Sadiq was asked as to what was meant by the science of the other worlds. He replied: 'Besides the world in which we live there are many other worlds which are much bigger than this and in those worlds there are sciences which are different from the sciences of this world'. Ja'far Sadiq was asked: 'What is the number of other worlds?'

He replied: 'Nobody other than the Almighty Allah knows the number of other worlds'.

He was asked: 'How does the learning of other worlds differ from the sciences of this world? Is knowledge not learnable? And how is it possible that which is learnable should be different from the sciences of this world?'

He replied: 'In the other worlds there are two kinds of sciences. Sciences of one kind are similar to the sciences of this world and if anyone goes from this world to those worlds it will be possible for him to acquire them. However, in some other worlds there are sciences which is not possible for the people of this world to understand because their intellect cannot comprehend them'.

These words of Ja'far Sadiq became a riddle for the later generations. Some persons did not consider them to be acceptable and said that what he had said was not well-founded.

One of the persons who doubted the correctness of the remark of Ja'far Sadiq was Ibn-i Rāwandi of Isfahan. He said that human intellect was able to comprehend everything which was science — whether it was a science of this world or of other worlds.

However, the disciples of Ja'far Sadiq accepted the words of their teacher and believed that in some other worlds there are sciences which cannot be learnt by human beings because human intellect is not capable of comprehending them.

However, during the present century Einstein's Theory of Relativity opened a new and unprecedented chapter in physics and later the theory of essence (anti-matter) passed from the stage of theory and arrived at the stage of science and the scientists came to know for certain that 'anti-matter' exists. In the light of these developments the remark of Ja'far Sadiq that in some other world there are sciences which are not comprehensible for man, becomes intelligible, because in the world of anti-matter the physical laws will be different from the physical laws of our world and besides this there may be laws of logic and reasoning in those worlds which it may be impossible for our intellect to formulate or comprehend.

The world of anti-matter is a world in which electron charge in the atoms is positive whereas proton charge (in the nucleus of the atom) is negative, but in our world the electron charge in the atom is negative and the proton charge (in the nucleus of the atom) is positive.

It cannot be said what physical laws govern the world in which the charge of the electrons of the atom is positive and the charge of the protons is negative.

According to our logic and reasoning the "whole" is better than "a part" but it is possible that in that word "a part" may be better than the "whole" and our intellect is not in a position to understand or accept this poroposition.

In our world when we throw something heavy into water it becomes lighter according to the law discovered by Archimedes,* but it is possible that in that world the thing may become heavier when thrown into water or another liquid.

In this world, according to the law discovered by Pascal,‡ when pressure is exerted on one point of a liquid in a receptacle it is on all the points of that liquid. It is in the light of this very law that hydraulic brakes are prepared for automobiles and especially for the heavy vehicles and when the pressure of the foot of the driver on the pedal of the brake exerts some pressure on oil the pressure comes on all the points of oil and consequently the pressure on the wheels of the truck is one thousand times more which brings it to a standstill in a moment.

However, it is possible that this physical law may not be

---

*Archimedes (287 — 212), an outstanding Greek mathematician, physicist, engineer and inventor. He was the most celebrated scientific thinker of the ancient world.

‡Pascal, Blaise (1623 — 62), French mathematician and religious writer. He was one of the outstanding minds of the 17th century.

applicable in the world of anti-matter and the pressure which comes on one point of the liquid may not come on other points.

If a person belonging to this world arrives in the anti-matter world it is possible that gradually he may get reconciled with the physical laws of that world which are unusual and strange for him just as the astronauts get reconciled with weightlessness.

However, the things which man cannot accept in the anti-matter world are those which are inconsistent with the laws of his logic and reasoning. If in that world he sees "a part" superior to the "whole" or finds that the people of that world do not observe the prescribed rules in the matter of addition, subtraction, multiplication and division or feels that in that world heat freezes water or coldness evaporates it without there being even any vacuum he cannot understand these irrational phenomena. This is the right occasion when the view of Ja'far Sadiq seems acceptable to the effect that in some worlds there are sciences which it is not possible for man to acquire.

The conclusion which can be drawn from the above discussion is that firstly Ja,far Sadiq considered knowledge to be unlimited and secondly he believed that there are sciences in other worlds which man cannot comprehend with the intellect and wisdom with which he learns things in this world and now, as already stated above, when Einstein's Theory of relativity and the idea of anti-matter which have crossed the limits of theory and have arrived at the factual stage of science it may be said that Ja'far Sadiq had presented a correct idea twelve and a half centuries earlier than today". (Khwandanihā)

The above specimens which show only a drop out of the boundless sea of the knowledge of the progeny of the holy Prophet and the leaders of Islam, make this point clear that they acquired their knowledge from a source which is is beyond the reach of ordinary people and it is also not possible for anyone to benefit from that source except through the chosen dsescendants of the holy Prophet's Household.

These specimens also bear witness that we should not under any circumstances neglect to enforce the teachings of Islam and never to be negligent to act upon its redeeming orders, because every order and command thereof has a philosophy behind it and if we disobey them we may get involved in difficulties which may at times be irremediable and may destroy the very foundation of our prosperity.

In the end we pray to Almighty Allah that He may assist the Muslims to follow the orders of Islam thoroughly under the guidance of the chosen descendants of the holy Prophet's Household (Peace be on them).

* * * * * *

KEEPING ONE'S PROMISE

Keeping promises and fulfilling covenants is one of those qualities the need wherefor is realized by the nature of every human being.

The value and necessity of keeping one's promise and similarly the indecency of violating pacts and disregarding the promises and covenants is recognized by every person to whichever race or nation he may belong and whatever creed and religion he may follow so much so that even children, following the dictates of nature, consider the conduct of their parents, who make promises with them and do not honour them, to be indecent and unfair and condemn it with their child-like protests.

The importance of keeping promises becomes evident when its social effects are taken into account and the dangers ensuing from breaking promises and violating covenants are kept in view.

Honouring pacts and promises has a direct and undeniable effect on all the aspects of life of every individual, community and nation. A society which honours its pacts and covenants leads a comfortable life and commands respect in the eyes of other societies.

Financial and economic matters are the most important and basic pillars of the life of every society. If the people honour their commitments in financial matters the wheel of the economy of that society rotates properly and the economic activities assume a good shape. The debtor repays his debt on the appointed date and the creditor also places his goods at his disposal with confidence and faith. In this way everyone can make plans for his future and make agreements with others.

In such a society verbal promises can serve the purpose of most authentic statement and mutual confidence creates a proper order in the economy of the society. Hence, if a nation loses this great moral and human value it gets involved in irremediable calamities and unbearable difficulties.

Thousands of persons are homeless and are on the look out to take houses on lease and thousand of houses are vacant and their owners wish to put them out to lease. However, as mutual confidence does not exist the landlords prefer keeping their houses vacant to leasing them out to persons who are not prompt in paying rent and do not keep their promises.

A good deal of capital is stagnant and its owners are looking for a partner to start a joint business. There are also persons who are ready to undertake business activities but do not possess money. They too are in search of a partner who should possess capital for investment. However, as mutual confidence does not exists, the owners of capital prefer its remaining stagnant rather than to have a dishonest partner.

When these matters are kept in view the value and importance of honouring the promises and agreements becomes quite clear. However, this valuable asset can be acquired only by that person who has received religious training because the only factor which makes people honour their promises is the strength of faith and religious training.

The holy Qu'ran and the Islamic traditions have attached so much importance to the honouring of promises that one can realize its standard only by referring to the explanations and remarks of the dignified leaders of Islam.

In Islam honouring of promises has been recognized to be one of the bounden duties of every Muslim and one of the distinguishing signs and qualities of faithful persons.

The holy Qur'an says: *Successful indeed are the believers, who are submissive to Allah in their prayers. . . . . . and those who are true to their trust and to their promise.* (Surah al-Mu'min, 23:1, 2 & 8)

Further the holy Qur'an says: *Keep your promise; you will be questioned about it.* (Surah Bani Isra'il, 17:34)

Imam Musa Kazim quotes the holy Prophet as having said: "One who does not honour his promises has no faith". (Nawādīr-i Rāwandi, p. 5)

The holy Prophet says: "If a person who believes in Allah and the Day of Judgement and make a promise with anyone he should keep that promise". (Wāfi, Vol. I, p. 157)

Even while he was in the prime of his youth and had not yet been appointed to the prophetic mission, the holy Prophet always honoured the promises and agreements made by him with others.

"A man named Ammar who was a shepherd in Makkah says: 'I took my sheep every day to the forest of Makkah for grazing. Muhammad (peace be on him) also brought his sheep. One day I said to him: 'There is a green valley between those two hills which is very suitable for the grazing of the sheep. If you agree both of us shall take our sheep to that place tomorrow'. Muhammad (peace be on him) expressed his willingness and then we returned home in the evening. In the morning I took my sheep to the appointed place and saw that Muhammad (peace be on him) had already brought his sheep there but was not allowing them to graze. On my enquiring about the reason for this he said: 'I had made a promise with you that we shall graze the sheep in this locality together. I did not, therefore, like to let my sheep graze before your arrival'. (Bihārul Anwār)

The holy Prophet says· "On the Day of Judgement the persons nearest to me will be those who speak the truth, endeavour more to restore the trusts to its owner, who are faithful in honouring their promises, who possess good morals and who keep cordial relations with the people". (Amāli Tusi, Vol. I)

The leaders of Islam have considered honouring one's promise to be one of the pre-requisites of nobility and justice and have said that one who honours his promises is worthy of respect, friendship and brotherhood.

Imam Ali Riza quotes the holy Prophet as having said: "If a person does not do injustice to the people in the matter of transactions and does not tell lies and honours his promises he is noble and just and is fit for friendship and brotherhood and it is unlawful to backbite him'. ('Uyūnul Akhbār, Vol. II, p. 30)

One of the freed slaves of Imam Sajjad acquired some capital as a result of hard work. At one time the holy Imam was faced with financial difficulties. He asked the said freed slave to lend him 10,000 dirhams to be returned at his convenience. He asked for security. The Imam pulled a piece of thread from his cloak and gave him saying. 'This is my surety which should remain with you till the repayment of the debt'. It was hard for the lender to accept such a trifle thing as a surety. However, keeping in view the personality of the holy Imam and his remarks he handed over the money to him and taking the thread of his cloak kept it in a small locket. By chance the financial condition of the holy Imam imporved soon. He, therefore, brought 10,000 dirhams to the lender and said to him: 'Here is your money. Bring my surety'. He said· 'I have lost the thread of the cloak'. The holy Imam then said: 'In that case do not take back the amount of debt from me. My personal guarantee should not be treated to be insignificant'.

The man was, therefore, obliged to bring the locket and saw that the thread of the cloak was in tact. He surrendered the thread to the holy Imam. He gave him the money, took the thread from him and threw it away". (Bihārul Anwār, Vol. XI)

A thread of a cloak does not carry any value by itself, but when that thread is the token of the guarantee and obligation of a noble and virtuous person, it becomes so valuable that it can serve as a surety for large amount of money and the creditor accepts it with full confidence and recovers his debt at the appointed time.

Honouring the promise is one of the attributes of the Almighty Allah. He says thus clearly in the holy Qur'an· *Allah does not disregard His promise.* (Surah al-Ra'd, 13:31)

A person who is steadfast in keeping his promise is endowed with one of the Divine Attributes and this in itself is a sign of his degree of perfection and virtue.

After the battle of Siffin a party named *Khawārij* (khārijites) came into existence. Rash persons who were ignorant of the fundamentals of knowledge and faith joined that party and were engaged in heinous crimes for many years. The governments of the time also combated with them in different ways. During the time of Hajjāj bin Yusuf some persons were arrested on the charge of associating themselves with this party and brought before him for being awarded punishment. Hajjāj examined the case of each one of them and fixed his punishment. When the turn of the last man came the mu'azzin proclaimed the time of prayers. Hajjāj got up and entrusted the accused to 'Anbasa and said to him: "Keep him in your custody during the night and bring him to me in the morning so that I may award him punishment".

'Anbasa obeyed the order and left the Governor's House accompanied by that man. On the way the accused said to him: "Can any good be expected from you?" He replied: "If you want to say something let me hear it. It is possible that I may be able to tread the path of beneficence and goodness". The accused said. "By Allah I am not a Khārijite. I have not attacked any Muslim, nor have I revolted against anyone. I am perfectly innocent of the offence of which I have been accused. Although I have been arrested without my having committed any offence. I believe in the Mercy of Almighty Allah and am sure that He will be kind to me and I will not be tormented without any fault. My request to you is that you may be kind enough to let me go tonight to my wife and children so that I may bid them farewell, make my will, pay the rights of the people and then return to you early tomorrow morning".

'Anbasa says: "To hear such a request from an accused under surveillance evoked my laughter and I did not give him any reply. He repeated his request and his words appealed to me. I said to myself that it would be good to rely on Allah and accept that man's request. I, therefore, took a decision accordingly and said to him: "You may go but you must promise that you will return tomorrow morning".

He replied: "I promise that tomorrow I shall return early in the morning and I call Allah to witness this promise".

Then he went away and disappeared from before my eyes. When I came to myself I felt very agitated and uneasy on account of what I had done. I said to myself · 'What a foolish thing I have done! Why have I exposed myself to Hajjāj's wrath unnecessarily?' I went home very much disturbed and related the story to the members of my family. They also reproached me.

I did not sleep the whole night and remained uneasy like a person who is bitten by a snake or a woman whose son has passed away.

Morning came. The man kept his promise and came back during the early hours. I wondered at his return and said to him: "Why have you come back?" He replied: "Whoever is blessed with the knowledge about Allah and recognizes Him with all His Might and Perfection keeps his promise when he calls Allah to witness it and does not violate that promise".

'Anbasa took him to the Governor's House before Hajjāj at the appointed time and related the entire story of the previous night to him. Hajjāj wondered at the faith and fidelity of the accused and said to 'Anbasa· "Would you like that I should make a gift of this man to you?" 'Anbasa replied: "I shall be very grateful if you are kind enough to do so".

Hajjāj made a gift of the accused to 'Anbasa. He brought him out of the Governor's House and said with great kindness: "You are free and may go wherever you like". The man went away without expressing any gratitude to 'Anbasa.

'Anbasa was grieved to observe this coldness and ingratitude of the man. He said to himself that possibly he was insane. However, he came to see 'Anbasa on the following day and expressed much gratitude and thankfulness. He said· "My Saviour was Allah and you were the means in the matter. If I had thanked you the other day I would have made you a partner of Allah in the bestowing of His blessings which would have been unlawful. I, therefore, decided to thank Allah in the first instance and have come today to express my gratitude to you". Then he thanked Anbasa very sincerely for his kindness, apologized for the invonvenience suffered by him and went away". (Kūdak, Vol. II, p. 18)

In the Islamic traditions no exception has been mentioned to the honouring of one's promise. It means that the Muslims are under obligation to honour the promises made by them with anyone, even with the unbelievers.

Imam Ja'far Sadiq says· "There are three things which Allah has not permitted anyone to forsake (i) Doing good to one's parents, whether they be good or bad persons, (ii) Honouring one's promise whether the other party be a righteous person or a licentious and (iii) Restoring a trust to its rightful owner whether he may be a good or bad". (Khisāl, Sadūq, Vol. I, p. 63)

A point which must be explained here is that keeping one's promise is obligatory when it does not involve making lawful things which have been made unlawful by Allah and vice versa.

In such cases the obligation to keep one's promise lapses and nobody is entitled to perform any such deed.

The holy Prophet taught the Muslims practically the lesson of keeping promises and himself honoured all the promises, pacts and covenants made with all the people including the unbelievers and his enemies.

Huzayfa was one of the persons who did not participate in the Battle of Badr and missed this great blessings. He himself narrates his story of this deprivation in these words: "My companion Abul Hasbal and I came out of Madina to join the holy Prophet and the Muslim warriors who were on the war front. By chance we came face to face with a group of the polytheist Quraysh. They asked us whether we were going to join Muhammad. Having been afraid of them and in order to escape their mischief we replied in the negative and added that we were going to Madina. They took a promise from us that if they set us free we would not go to assist Muhammad and would not fight against them. We made the promise and became free.

From there we went to the holy Prophet, informed him of the incident and sought permission to participate in the battle. The holy Prophet replied · "No, you have made a promise with them and should not ignore it. You should abide by your promise and go away. We too seek help from Almighty Allah". (Islam wa Sulh-i Jahāni, p. 264)

The holy Prophet made agreements with many communities and tribes as for example the Treaty of Hudaybiya which he signed with the infidels of Qurayhsh or the non-aggression pact which he concluded with the Jews of Madina. And it was never seen that he might have disregarded or violated any agreement.

When that great Prophet made promises with the people he considered their fulfilment to be obligatory for himself and as good as a formal debt.

Imam Ali Riza says: "We are a family who believe in the fulfilment of promises made by us to be as good as a debt, the repayment wherefof is obligatory. It is just as the holy Prophet acted. (Bihārul Anwār, Vol. LXXV, p. 97)

Imam Ali said that he heard the holy Prophet saying: "A promise which a true believer makes with another person is as good as a vow with this difference that there is an atonement for violating a vow but there is no atonement for violating a promise". (Kashful Ghumma, Vol. III, p. 92)

Imam Ali in his advice to Mālik Ashtar said: "Avoid reminding your subordinates of the favour done to them, and treating your favours to be great, and violating the promises made to them, because reminding others of the favour done to them destroys the good deed and considering a good deed to be a big one eliminates the light of reality and violating a promise invites the wrath of Allah as well as of the people". (Nahjul Balaghah)

At another place in the same testament he made the following recommendation to Mālik Ashtar: "If you conclude an agreement with your enemy or grant him protection, you must fulfil your promise and respect the shelter given to him, because amongst the things made obligatory by Allah nothing is so important and respected by the people as much as the fulfilment of a promise, inspite of all the differences among them in their beliefs and views".

"During the time of the Caliphate of Ma'mūn a resident of Damascus, who was accused of revolting against the government, was arrested and sent to Baghdad. The caliph summoned Abbas, the police chief, and handed over the accused to him and said with much emphasis: "Be careful about him lest he should escape, because he is dangerous".

Abbas says: 'I handed over the man to my officials and sent him to my headquarters. At night, however, I felt anxious lest the officials should become negligent and the accused might escape. I, therefore, ordered that he might be brought handcuffed to my special room so that I might keep him under my own vigil'. He was brought in my room and made to sit in a corner. When the officials left and both of us were alone in the room I decided to know more about him and to find out what offence he had committed. I asked him: 'Where are you from?' He replied: 'I belong to Damascus'.

I had been a government officer in Damascus for a long time and had also an unforgettable remembrance relating to those days. I, therefore, asked him: 'Do you know such and such person?' He replied: 'I know him but how do you know him?' I said: 'There was an incident which concerned both of us'. He said: 'Please let me know what that incident was and then I shall relate my story'. I said: 'Some years ago I was serving in Damascus with the Governor. The people of Damascus revolted against the Governor and besieged the Governor's House. The Governor jumped from the roof of the palace into the street by means of a rope and ran away. I also escaped from another corner. The people pursued me and I was likely to be caught when, in one of the streets, I saw a man sitting in front of his house. I took refuge with him and requested him to hide me in his house'.

He took me into his house and accommodated me in a room. He also directed his wife to remain in the same room and to ensure my safety. The people poured into the house and conducted a search throughout the house till they reached the room in which I was hiding. My legs were tembling on account of intense fear and it was even difficult for me to sit.

When they reached in front of the room the woman stood opposite the door and shouted upon them saying: 'Don't you feel ashamed of attempting to enter my room?'

The people felt ashamed on hearing her words and went away. When the danger ceased to exist the man and his wife consoled me and said: 'Don't worry. Hereafter nobody will interfere with you'. They placed a room at my disposal and showed much love and kindness to me'.

One day I said to the man: 'I want to go out of the house to gather information about my slaves'. He permitted me to go out but took a promise from me that I would return to the house after completion of my job'.

I came out of the house and tried my best to locate my slaves but in vain. I, therefore, returned to the house of that man. After some days I decided to proceed to Baghdad. When I mentioned my intention to the man he said: 'I don't like that you should travel alone. A caravan is likely to leave Damascus for Baghdad after three days. You should stay here till then and proceed to Baghdad along with the caravan.

I agreed and stayed there for another three days. During this time he showed me much kindness and at the time of my departure presented to me a suit, a pair of shoes, a sword, a belt, a horse, a mule and a slave and also placed a sum of 5000 dirhams at my disposal.

I thanked him and made a promise with Allah that I would never forget his love and would compensate him for it in whatever way it was possible. However, it has not been possible for me so far to render him any service.

Till that time the accused was sitting still under the burden of the shackles and was hearing me. When I stopped talking he said: 'Will you be able to recognize that man if you see him?' I replied in the affirmative. He said: 'The man you are looking for is sitting before you and is your captive'.

I stared at his face. He also mentioned other signs and I was convinced that the poor captive was my kind and self-sacrificing host.

I got up from my place and kissed him profusely. Then I summoned the officials who removed the shackles from his hands and feet and thereafter asked him to narrate his story. He told me everything in detail. I was convinced that he was innocent and had fallen pray to the conspiracy of his enemies.

Then he said to me: 'If you want to keep your promise and be good to me send someone to bring my slave who is at such and such place so that I may make a will to him, because when I was taken into custody I was not permitted to bid farewell to my wife and children or to make a will'.

I sent someone immediately who brought his slave. On seeing the slave he began to weep and then started making his will. I summoned my deputy and ordered that a few horses and slaves and other provisions for the journey might be made ready for the man and his departure from Baghdad during night might be arranged.

The man said: 'Don't do so, because my offence is grave in the eyes of the caliph and he is very much annoyed with me and will put me to death'.

I said: 'You need not bother about the caliph. Necessary arrangements for your journey have been made and you should, therefore, depart and save your life'.

He said · 'This is impossible, because if I go away you will be faced with danger. Now that you have taken this descision you should send me to a safe place so that if my appearance before the caliph becomes necessary tomorrow you may be able to produce me'. I agreed and transferred him to a safe place.

I had not yet finished my dawn prayers on the following day when the officials sent by the caliph came and told me that the caliph had desired that the captive might be produced before him.

I myself went before Ma'mūn. When he saw that I was coming alone he said: 'If you say that the man has escaped I shall put you to death in his place'. I replied: 'No. He has not escaped and is still within the control of the caliph. I, however, seek permission to narrate his story'.

Ma'mūn accorded permission. I narrated in detail the incident of my hardship in Damascus as well as what had taken place during the previous night and said: 'I now want to fulfil my promise. If my master wishes to put me to death in his place I am already wearing a shroud under my dress and am absolutely ready to meet this fate and if he forgives me he will have done a great favour to his slave'.

When the caliph heard the story he said: 'May Allah not bless you! He did not know you and did good to you and you know him and want to do good to him. Why did you not tell me about it earlier so that I might have rewarded him for his goodness?' I said: 'O Commander of the Faithful! He is in this city at present and although I insisted him last night to escape but he declined to do so and said on oath that he would not leave Baghdad unless he was satisfied about my future'. The caliph said: 'This is even a greater favour which he has done to you. Bring him to me'.

I immediately reached the place where he was staying. I assured him that the caliph had forgiven him and had sent me to take him in his presence.

On hearing this good news he offered two *rak'ats* of prayers and thanked Allah and then both of us went to the caliph.

Ma'mūn showed much love and kindness to him and he had his luncheon with the caliph. At the time of his departure the caliph offered him the Governorship of Damascus, but he excused himself. Then Ma'mūn said: 'Henceforth you should remain in Damascus and write to me regularly about the conditions in Syria'. He accepted this proposal. Thereafter, as ordered by the caliph, a number of horses and slaves and some bags of money were given to him. The caliph also wrote a recommendatory letter about him to the Governor of Syria and sent him to Damascus with great honour". (Thamaratul Awrāq, Hamawi)

In order that the Muslims may not have to suffer the shame of violating promises it has been recommended in the Islamic teachings that every person should, before signing an agreement, assess his own capability and if he is unable to honour it he should decline to make a promise at the very outset.

Imam Ali says: "Do not make a promise at the very outset if you cannot fulfil it and do not undertake initially to perform a job which is beyond your control". He further says: "Do not make a promise about which you are not certain whether it will be possible for you to fulfil it". (Ghurarul Hikam)

Now that the importance and necessity of honouring a promise, as viewed by the leaders of Islam, has become evident to some extent, it is necessary for the revival of this great trait that the children should get acquainted with this matter during their childhood when they begin to perceive the meaning of 'pledge' and should learn the lesson of fulfilment of promises from the words and deeds of their parents and guardians so that it may become their second nature.

If the environment of a house and the family, which is the first and the basic school, is an atmosphere of piety and virtue the children undoubtedly learn the lesson of piety and virtue and adopt proper ways and manners of life.

The leaders of Islam have paid great attention to this important matter in their discourses and considered it a duty of the Muslims to keep their promises in the family environments.

The holy Prophet says: "Love your children and be kind to them and when you make a promise with them honour it, because they consider you to be their sustainer". (Wasā'il)

Imam Ali says: "It is not proper that one should tell a lie either in jest or seriously and it is also not proper that one should make a promise with his child and should not fulfil it". (Wasā'il, Vol. III, p. 232)

The holy Prophet says: "When anyone of you makes a promise with his small child he must honour it". (Mustadrak)

All this emphasis laid on honouring the promises made with the children is on this account that the actions of the elders are imprinted on the minds of the children and have an undeniable effect on their future.

If the children find that their parents and elders break the promises made by them they too will adopt the same conduct when they grow up and will prove to be dishonest persons.

In the end we pray to Almighty Allah to enable us to fulfil our promises and to train our children on the basis of Islamic teachings which are the source of the prosperity and perfection.

* * * * * *

MODERATION

Moderation is the basis of all teachings of Islam and going to extremes has been prohibited in all its orders and regulations. Moderation has been recommended in the matter of worship, acquisition of knowledge, food, dress, friendship, enmity and all other affairs of life. The holy Qur'an says: *Thus We have appointed you a middle nation.* (Surah al-Baqarah, 2:143)

The above verse means that in Islam there is no such thing as going to the extremes and as opposed to the followers of other religions, the Muslims follow those rules and regulations which have been promulgated by the Law-giver who is aware of all the natural needs of the human beings and has had in view every aspect of the material and spiritual life of man.

A large number of persons, in order that they may not be obliged to follow any religion or creed, pay attention to their body only. All their efforts are directed towards strengthening their carnal desires and they do not care for anything other than material life, free living and seeking pleasure. They do not pay any heed to moral virtues and sublime human qualities and they do not believe in Origin *(Mabda')* and Resurrection *(Ma'ād)* they get involved in all sorts of spiritual contaminations. Their life is like the life of animals.

There are people (like Christians) who follow a religion which has warned them against paying attention to the body and partaking in the enjoyments of this world and has invited them only to strengthen the soul and to forsake the world and lead the monastic life. These people, too, in order to ignore the body, have failed to attain the prosperity and perfection for which man has been created by the Almighty Lord.

However, Islam is a moderate religion and lies between these two extremes. It neither permits its followers to lead a monastic life and forsake the world nor agrees to their leading an animal life.

"Islam recommends the golden mean and the path of moderation in this sense that a Muslim should pay attention to the strengthening of his body as well as his soul, because man does not consist of body only just as he does not possess soul only, but he is the combination of both and in order to attain real prosperity one must protect and strengthen this combination". (Allama Tabātabā'i, Tafsīr al-Mizān, Vol. I, p. 319)

Islam orders the Muslims that in order to attain the lofty human position they should moderate their inclinations and instincts. They should keep their faculties within proper limits and utilize them after correct and wise assessment.

Islam praises bravery which lies between fear and rashness.

Islam considers generosity to be proper for a Muslim, which stands between stinginess and prodigality.

Islam recommends the establishment of justice, which lies between cruelty and deprivation.

The Almighty Lord has praised the high morals of the holy Prophet and reckoned them to be magnificent. And the admirable morals, which all the wise men of the world praise and honour one who possesses them, consist of 'good nature'. Good nature means that all the inner faculties and qualities of man should be within moderate limits and should not go beyond them". (Safinatul Bihār, Vol. I, p. 211)

There are various instincts and inclinations within man each one of which contradicts the other. If these instincts are not moderated and everyone of them is not utilized after proper assessment, the prosperity of man is endangered.

As regards the brain of man, which is a strange and wonderful creation, Imam Ali says: "More wonderful than man himself is that part of his body which is connected with his trunk with muscles. It is his brain (mind). Look what good and bad tendencies arise from it. On the one hand it holds treasures of knowledge and wisdom and on the other it is found to harbour very ugly desires. If a man sees even a tiny gleam of success, then greed forces him to humiliate himself. If he gives way to avarice, then inordinate desires ruin him, if he is disappointed, then despondency almost kills him. If he is excited, then he loses temper and gets angry. If he is pleased, then he gives up precaution. Sudden fear makes him dull and nervous, and he is unable to think and find a way out of the situation. During the times of peace and prosperity he becomes careless and unmindful of the future. If he acquires wealth, then he becomes haughty and arrogant. If he is plunged in distress, then his agitation, impatience and nervousness disgrace him. If he is overtaken by poverty, then he finds himself in a very sad plight, hunger makes him weak, and over-feeding harms him equally. In short every kind of loss and gain makes his mind unbalanced". (See Peak of Eloquence, Saying — 107, p. 686, ISP, 1984)

The only means, which can eliminate the contrariety of inclinations and satisfy every natural human desire in its own place with correct assessment, is the moderation of inclinations and limiting the inner desires.

The question of shunning egotism and moderating one's carnal desires is not only a positive Islamic duty. Rather the necessity of controlling one's inner inclinations is a definite and inviolable principle from the rational, scientific, educational, moral, hygienic and social view-point and in short from the point of view of the need for life.

In order to lead a healthy and tranquil life man is obliged to ignore his undue desires and to rerfrain from inhuman acts.

"Man cannot let his inclinations free, without imposing any condition and criterion, in his individual and social life and at the same time acquire the means of deliverance". (Adabun Nafs, Vol. I, p. 26)

Imam Ali has said - "If we suppose that there is no hope of Paradise and no fear of Hell and also that no spiritual reward or punishment will be awarded on the Day of Judgement even then it is necessary that we should demand good morals and human qualities from ourselves because acquiring good qualities and putting them into practice is an effective means of deliverance and the real source of prosperity and happiness in the life of man". (Jawān az Nazar-i 'Aql wa Ahsāsāt, Vol. I, p. 308)

Moderation in Worship

Just as it is the duty of man to observe moderation regarding the inner faculties and inclinations and consequently to acquire good morals and human qualities, he is under obligation, in the same way, not to forsake moderation in other affairs of life.

Uthman bin Maz'ūn was one of the distinguished companions of the holy Prophet and a devoted Muslim. One day his wife came before the holy Prophet and said: "Since long my husband Uthman has forsaken worldly affairs and has dedicated himself to the worship of Allah. He fasts every day and spends his nights in offering prayers and worshipping Allah".

The holy Prophet who always preached moderation and campaigned against all sorts of extreme actions was very much annoyed on hearing this and went immediately to the place which had been selected by Uthman for worship.

Uthman was offering prayers. When he saw the holy Prophet he ended his prayers quickly and paid his respects to him. The holy Prophet said to him: "O Uthman! Allah has not ordained monastic life and renunciation of the world in my religion. On the other hand He has appointed me to the prophetic mission with a pure, simple and liberal religion. I, who am your Prophet, also observe fast and offer prayers and also pay attention to my wives and the affairs of life. Whoever likes my religion should follow my ways of life and one of my ways is marriage and formation of a family and paying attention to one's wife and the affairs of one's life". (Safinatul Bihār, Vol. II, p. 574)

Islam treats those who turn away from worshipping Allah to be deserving of punishment and has promised them the same and at the same time it has warned them against the renunciation of the world and monastic life.

The holy Prophet has said: "Islam is a sound and firm religion. Take firm steps in carrying out its orders and do not make the worship of Allah wearisome and annoying for His creatures (as a consequence of extravagance). If you do so you will be like a hasty camel-rider who does not reach his destination and also makes the camel collapse". (Bihārul Anwār, Vol. LXXI, p. 211)

In this tradition the holy Prophet has alluded to the undesirable effect which excessiveness in worship has on others.

Such excessivenesses are harmful for the person who practises them as well as for those who watch such practices. They are harmful for those who watch them because they prevent them from inclining towards religion and subjecting themselves to the obligations prescribed by it. They think that if a person wishes to become the slave of Allah and observe the religious duties he must wash his hands of the affairs of his life and deprive himself of all sorts of activities, enjoyments and comforts and it is only then that he can become a responsible Muslim. However, if the people see that the Muslims, too, look after the affairs of their life and also worship Allah and perform their religious duties they will undoubtedly incline towards Islam and achieve the prosperity and happiness of this world as well as of the Hereafter.

Imam Sadiq says: "Do not make yourself reluctant in the matter of Divine worship i.e. do not over-burden yourself with 'recommended' articles of worship and thus tire yourself because as a result thereof you will become reluctant in the matter of worship". (al-Kafi, Vol. II, p. 86)

Imam Ali, in connection with his precepts to his son at the time of his death, said: "My son! Be moderate in the affairs of life and also practise moderation in the matter of worship of Allah in such a way that you may always be able to continue it". (Amāli Tūsi, Vol. II, p. 67)

Imam Muhammad Baqir, the fifth Imam, said to his son: "O my son! Always choose a desirable way which lies between two wrong and undesirable ways. His son asked: 'Which is that desirable way?' Imam Baqir said: 'We read in the holy Qur'an that extravagance in expenditure and stinginess are both despicable and between these two is the desirable way which is moderation and the golden mean. It is necessary for you to observe moderation". (Tafsir 'Ayāshi, Vol. II, p. 319)

The Divine leaders of Islam have considered stepping beyond the limit of moderation to be the consequence of ignorance.

Imam Ali says: "It is seen that the ignorant persons are either extravagant or fatigued in all matters and moderation is never observed in them". (See · Peak of Eloquence, ISP, 1984)

It needs no explanation that in the matter of worship those persons are extravagant, who, without performing obligatory rituals, engage themselves in recommended rituals to such an extent that their life is paralyzed and they cannot perform their various duties. There are very few such persons in the modern society and unfortunately most of the people lag behind in the matter of worship and do not even perform the obligatory rituals.

Moderation in Expenditure

To make necessary assessment and to exercise moderation in expenditure is one of the inevitable duties of every Muslim. This moderation has nothing to do with the meagreness and excess of income. Of course, the persons whose income is meagre feel the importance of moderation all the more. However, Islam recommends it to its followers to observe moderation in expenditure in all circumstances.

Imam Muhammad Baqir says: "Three things ensure the deliverance of man: (i) Fearing Allah openly and secretly. (ii) Moderation in expenditure at the time of affluence as well as indigence. (iii) To say the right thing at the time of happiness as well as anger". (Safinatul Bihār, Vol. II, p. 431)

It is possible that excessive expenditure may not be onerous for the rich and some of them may perhaps consider moderation to be something wrong. However, this point should be kept in view that no one has guaranteed that those who are rich today will remain rich till the end of their lives, because the vicissitudes of time reduce many rich persons to poverty and if they develop the habit of extravagant expenditure at the time of affluence they suffer hardship at the time of poverty.

Furthermore, the rich should also keep the future of their children in view, because there is no guarantee that the children of the rich will also continue to live in affluence. It has often been seen that the children of this class of society get involved in hardships. If the rich inculcate the habit of moderation in their children the possible hardships will not make them helpless.

Extravagance prepares the ground for the adversity and bad luck of the people whereas moderation and proper assessment ensures their future.

Imam Ali says: "The affluence of one who exercises moderation will continue for ever and the policy of the golden mean will make amends for the difficulties and hardships of his life".

"One who exercises moderation, at the time of affluence and indigence, prepares himself for the vicissitudes of time".

"Destruction and adversity do not exist in moderation i.e. whoever chooses the middle path between two extremes and refrains from improper extravagances does not get involved in adversity". (Ghurarul Hikam).

Moderation in Food

Eating and drinking is also one of those matters with regard to which people go to extremes and, of course, mostly towards the side of excessiveness.

No doubt man needs food to live and it is necessary that food should reach the cells of the body so that they may continue their life. However, the important question is, as to how much food is needed by one human being and whether excessive food is good or harmful for him.

Imam Raza says: "You should know that human body is like a fertile land. If moderation is exercised in the matter of its development i.e. if necessary quantity of water is provided to it which should neither be so excessive that the land should drown in the water and change into swamp and bog nor so scanty that it should remain thirsty and dry, such land gets developed and yields much produce. However, if that land is not looked after properly it becomes barren". (Risālatuz Zahabiya)

Human body, too, is like this. When proper care is exercised in the matter of edibles and beverages and correct assessment is made the body remains healthy and sound.

"During the period of the caliphate of Harūn Rashid, once a famous Christian physician, who lived in the city of Baghdad, had a meeting with one of his contemporary scholars named Waqidi and had the following discussion on the subject of medicine: He asked Wāqidi: 'Is there anything about medicine in your Qur'an?'

Wāqidi replied: 'Yes. There is a brief verse *'Eat and drink but do not be extravagant'* (Surah al-A'rāf, 7:31) wherein Allah has ordered the Muslims to make use of the edibles and the beverages but not to indulge in excessiveness'.

The physician asked: 'Has your Prophet said anything about medicine?'

Wāqidi replied: 'Yes. Our holy Prophet has said: "The stomach is the seat of all ailments and restricting oneself and eating less is the best of all medicines". (Bihārul Anwār, Vol. XIV) The Christian physician said: 'The Imam and the Prophet of Islam have not left anything for Galen to say on the subject of medicine and have stated in most brief sentences the basic rules for the prevention and cure of ailments". (Barnāma-i Zindagi)

The famous scholar Victor Dean says: "We eat much and as a result of gluttony we lose the vital energy which should work to ward off waste matter. Consequently we are faced with the dilatation of the stomach and the liver and weakness of the kidney. The Uric acid is scattered in the body and makes us suffer from rheumatism and swelling of the joints. Fat accumulates on the heart. The flow of blood is retarded. The digestive organ is weakened due to excessive activity and one develops dyspepsia.

The famous physician and theist Dr Alexis Carell says: "Gluttony, besides creating much disorder in one's physical constitution, weakens the nerves, especially the nerves of the brain, and brings about a sort of nervous and mental disorder the effects whereof appear in the shape of indisposition, gloominess, laziness, indifference, condition of consternation and sleep, grief, domination of thinking, dreadful dreams and groundless fears". (Tibb wa Bahdāsht, p. 47)

Imam Ali says: "Do not extend your hand to food unless you are perfectly hungry and stop eating before you are fully satiated. Chew the food completely and soften it in your mouth and under your teeth and off-load your bowels before you go to sleep. If you follow these four rules you will not need the services of a physician". (Khisāl Sadūq)

Some doctors say: "One third of what you eat is beneficial for you and the remaining two third provides for the livelihood of the physician. All ailments take place due to the contamination of blood. Hence there is one remedy for all of them viz. finding out the cause of this contamination and removing it by means of restricting oneself and taking proper food in small quantity". (Tibb wa Bahdāsht, p. 142)

"Every limb which does not take rest tires and becomes weak gradually and this fatigue reduces its age i.e. it nullifies its usual function and the organic changes subject it to various diseases. The stomach, too, is not an exception to this rule. Those who eat something or the other throughout twenty four hours are oblivious of the fact that a stomach which is full is always at work and excessive daily work weakens it. Effort should, therefore, be made that firstly the stomach is not filled fully at any time and one should stop eating before picking up the satiating morsel, and secondly the stomach should be allowed some rest after eating so that it may get ready for the next meal. One's own sense of hunger is the best guide for taking meals and effort should be made that meals are not taken unless one feels hungry". (Ṣad Dars-i Salāmati)

Imam Ali says: "It seldom happens that one may eat his fill and may not fall ill. Being always satiated gives birth to various ailments". (Ghurarul Hikam)

To know that human stomach has a specific limit and capacity and cannot accept foodstuffs beyond that capacity is the real condition of health and something extremely wise.

"It is natural that those who do not follow this principle and eat too much and do not even observe any order in this regard fall victims to dilatation and inflammation of the stomach. When beverages are taken in excess of what is necessary they not only cause dyspepsia but also increase dilatation of the stomach and may possibly cause intestinal diseases. And to make amends for this gluttony and excessiveness one has to restrict oneself in the matter of eating and drinking and to be on special diet for quite a long time". (Dastūrāt-i Pizishki Barā-i Hamā, p. 396)

The holy Prophet says: "Do not kill your hearts with intemperance in the matter of eating and drinking, because human heart is like a sown field which decays and dies if it is watered too much".

Luqmān Hakim said to his son: "Dear son! When the stomach of man is full his faculty of thinking goes to sleep and his tongue of wisdom becomes dumb and his limbs fail to worship Allah". (Jāmi'us Sa'ādāt, Vol. II, p. 3 — 4)

There are many traditions and narrations wherein excessiveness in the matter of eating has been condemned, some of which have been mentioned above as a specimen. The point which deserves consideration is that the traditions condemning gluttony or praising hunger do not mean that excessiveness in eating less is praiseworthy, because, as has been stated earlier, Islam does not approve any kind of excessiveness or lagging and the traditions in which satiety has been condemned and hunger has been praised accord with a special policy which is known to those who are conversant with the traditions of *Ahlul Bayt*.

Islam strongly condemns everything which human nature desires in excess. In such cases those who look at the matters superficially think that Islam desires the other extreme but the learned persons are aware that what Islam desires is the golden mean. For example, when human nature desires continual gluttony and satiety the traditions should recommend continual hunger so that what nature desires should come face to face with what religious law prohibits and man may be able to remain within proper limits. Or when hunman nature desires wealth and position the traditions should overwhelmingly condemn worldliness and love for wealth so that attraction on one hand and prohibition on the other should create a state of moderation in the individuals.

Moderation in Friendship and Enmity

Although Islam supports the bonds of friendship which exist between the Muslims and considers these friendships to be a very valuable asset, it prohibits excessiveness even in this regard. Imam Ali says in one of his sermons: "Your friendship with your friend should be within the limits of moderation, because it is possible that one day that friend may become your enemy". (See: Peak of Eloquence, ISP, 1984)

Excessiveness in friendship becomes the cause of one's telling his friend about the secrets of one's life. In that event if that friend changes his attitude and becomes an enemy he can utilize against us those very secrets which we ourselves have imparted to him. In case, however, a friendship is established on the basis of moderation one tells his friend about those secrets only which pose no danger to him even if they are divulged. Furthermore, such friendship is permanent, whereas experience has shown that some extremist friends have, after mutual friendship for some time, adopted the path of extreme enmity and stood up to fight with each other, although acute and extreme enmity, too, is despicable in the eyes of Islam.

After recommending moderation in the matter of friendship Imam Ali continues to say: "You should also be moderate in your enmity with your enemy and should not go to the extreme, because it is possible that the same enemy may change his attitude one day and become your friend". (Tuhaful 'Uqūl)

If one has not gone to the extreme in the matter of enmity with his enemy he does not have to feel ashamed when they decide one day to establish their relations on the basis of friendship. On the contrary if he has gone to the extreme in the matter of enmity and used all his sources against his enemy, he feels ashamed when they decide to become friends.

Moderation Recommended Once Again

As we have explained in the beginning of this chapter that Islam recommends moderation in all things and all tasks and it is interesting to note that it is not oblivious of even minor matters so that the Muslims may exercise moderation in everyday affairs as well as in important and vital ones.

Luqmān Hakīm says to his son: *Be modest in your gait. Neither walk slowly and listlessly nor too quickly and rashly. And do not make your voice loud but speak moderately and make your voice reach others to the extent necessary.* (Surah Luqmān, 31:20)

What has been narrated above consists of brief specimens of Islamic teachings in the matter of moderation and if we study other Islamic rules and regulations we find that this principle has been kept in view in all matters and an extreme course has not been adopted in any one of them.

It is hoped that keeping this important fact in view will apprise us of our rational duty regarding unconditional submission to the orders of Islam and acting in all matters of life according to the guidance provided by this Divine religion and paying special attention to moderation in all walks of life so that, with the Grace of Allah, we may acquire prosperity in this world as well as in the Hereafter. Amen.

RESPONSIBILITY OF THE RICH

The rich are the trustees and depositaries of the Almighty Lord and their assets are His trusts and deposits.

Just as the Almighty Creator has been kind to the rich and has given them distinction among His Creatures in the shape of wealth He has also subjected them to certain responsibilities and asked them to perform some duties.

Just as the rich lead a comfortable life by means of the wealth given to them by the Almighty they can and should also ensure prosperity in the Hereafter by utilizing this wealth.

Contrary to what some ignorant persons think it is not only that Islam does not oppose wealth, but it considers it to be a means of the permanence of the society (Vide: Surah an-Nisa, 4:5) without which it can have no strength. On the other hand the economic regulations of Islam which are observed in the text of the holy Qur'an and the traditions of the Divine leaders of Islam indicate the value and worth which wealth enjoys in the eyes of Islam. And if it had been otherwise i.e. if wealth had been despicable in the eyes of the Lord He would not at all have spoken about it and would not also have prescribed limits and regulations for it.

If wealth has been condemned in some verses of the holy Qur'an or in some traditions, the object has been to warn the people against the dangers to which their prosperity may possibly become subjected on account of wealth.

It is, no doubt, possible that wealth may make the individuals suffer from the ailments of pride, egotism, selfishness, stinginess, greed, exploitation, injustice etc. and consequently their prosperity as well as that of the society may be jeopardized.

In the narrations of the leaders of Islam the question of wealth has been analyzed with all its dimensions, effects and specifications and in every case necessary recommendations have been made. Islam says: Wealth is a means and not an end, and people should attain the prosperity of this world as well as the Hereafter by means of wealth.

In the society wealth is like blood in the body of man. Just as blood must circulate in the entire body and should flow in all the veins and blood-vessels so that each limb, part and cell of the body should utilize it according to its need, wealth should also circulate in all the strata of the society so that all the individuals may utilize it and their lives may be secured.

If blood is corrupt or stops at one point of the body or ceases for a moment to circulate, the limb which does not receive blood is threatened by ailment and death and very often it culminates in the general death and annihilation of the body.

As regards wealth also if it is acquired from unlawful sources or is concentrated in a few persons and the common people are deprived of it, it poses grave dangers to the society and leads it to decay and destruction.

From the economic point of view the most prosperous society is that which is ruled by economic equilibrium and all the individuals enjoy the benefits of the wealth of the country according to their respective shares.

The Rich are the Pillars of the Society

The rich should utilize their assets for the welfare and betterment of the deprived classes of the society and should make the indigent benefit from their wealth.

Imam Ali considers the rich to be a pillar of the palace of the prosperity of the society provided they do not neglect to carry out the responsibilities which the Almighty Allah has prescribed for them and do not suffer from the ailments of greed and stinginess. He said to Jābir bin Abdullah Ansāri: "O Jābir! The faith and the society exist due to the presence of four sorts of persons:
(i) The scholar who puts his knowledge into practice and kindles the path for the people with the light of his knowledge.

(ii) The ignorant person who is aware of his ignorance and does not hesitate to acquire knowledge.

(iii) The kind person who is not stingy in spending for the welfare of the society, the wealth which Allah has given him.

(iv) The poor who bears the hardship of poverty and neither loses patience nor sells the Hereafter for the sake of this world.

If in a society the scholars waste their knowledge and do not utilize it properly the ignorant people will turn away from acquiring knowledge and if the rich do not spend their wealth for the welfare of the society the indigent will lose patience, ignore their self-respect and sell the Hereafter for this world.

O Jābir! The people have to depend more on the person who is given a larger share of Divine blessings. And the rich man who performs his duty and acts according to the commands of Allah ensures his affluence and one who spends his wealth corruptly and prodigally and shows stinginess in spending for the sake of Allah and welfare of the people, places his wealth and prosperity in jeopardy". (Nahjul Balaghah, Fayz p. 1251)

A man came before Imam Sadiq and began to speak ill of the rich and subjected them to attack and criticism. Imam Sadiq said to him: "Be quiet. If a rich man observes relationship and helps his relatives with his wealth and does good to his brethren-in-faith, Allah gives him double reward, because He says in the Qur'an: *Your wealth and your off-spring are not the means of your access to Allah except for one who possesses faith and does good deeds, such persons will get double reward and will remain safe from every harm in the upper chambers of Paradise".* (Safinatul Bihār, Vol. II, p. 327)

Warning to the Rich

The rich should promote the welfare of the weak classes with their financial resources in a correct and calculated manner and should take basic steps to meet their needs and to solve the problems of their life. Imam Ali says: "The Almighty Allah favours some of His slaves with the blessing of wealth so that others may benefit from them. However, he places this wealth at their disposal till the time they spend it for the welfare of the people. In case, therefore, a time comes when they fail to perform their duties Allah takes away the wealth from them and places it at the disposal of others". (Nahjul Balaghah, Fayz, p. 1275)

It is possible that some rich persons may take this warning of Imam Ali perfunctorily and may imagine proudly that their wealth is indestructible and everlasting. However, the history of the ancients shows that this is an undesirable fact and the rich persons who spent the God-given wealth for sinful purposes or resorted to uncalled for extravagance and dissipation and did not pay the dues of Allah and His creatures were reduced to poverty one day and Allah took away His blessings from them and placed them at the disposal of others.

The holy Qur'an relates the story of Korah as an example for the rich and warns them against the fate similar to his.

Korah belonged to the tribe of Prophet Musa and was one of his near relatives. In the beginning he was a pious man. (Vide: Surah al-Qasas, 28 -76) However, when the period of the stay and wandering in Tiyah* of Bani Isrā'il was prolonged Korah left his people and engaged himself in alchemy and making gold. By means of this act he accumulated much wealth and treasures of gold. A few strong men used to carry the keys of the treasures of Korah.

Wealth and treasures make Korah rebellious and proud and drove him to the precipice of adversity. He looked at the believers with disdain and considered himself to be superior to them on account of his wealth. When the short-sighted persons saw how luxurious a life Korah was leading they envied him and said to themselves: 'O that we too had wealth and facilities like Korah, for he is enjoying his life fully'.

The wise men of the tribe said to them: 'Woe betide you! Do not envy Korah for his outwardly attractive life. No doubt the Divine reward is much greater and more valuable than this'.

When some enlightened persons of Bani Isrā'il saw the extravagances of Korah they admonished him and said to him: 'O Korah! Do not be happy on account of these yellow and red things of the world, because Allah does not like such persons. With the immense wealth and the innumerable blessings which

---

*Tiyah is a desert in the Sinai peninsula wherein Bani Isrā'il kept wandering for forty years on account of their disobeying the Command of Allah.

Allah has granted you, you should make provision for the Hereafter and should take steps for the sake of Allah. Profit by the world and be kind to the slaves of Allah in the same manner in which He has been kind to you. Do not tread the path of evil and do not make mischief because Allah does not like the mischievous'. Korah replied 'I have myself accumulated this wealth by means of the science which I know as if he did not know that Allah had destroyed many nations on account of their sins, who were stronger and more affluent than him and it is also something very easy for the Lord to destroy him''. (Qaṣaṣul Qur'an, Vol. I, p. 148)

The disobedience and rebellion of Korah continued and he went his own way till the day Allah decided to destroy him and as clearly stated in the holy Qur'an, he and all his treasures were buried in earth as commanded by Allah.

The holy Qur'an says clearly: *Those who do not utilize properly the wealth which Allah has bestowed upon them should not think that it is better for them. No, it is the source of their adversity and a collar of torture which they will have round their necks on the Day of Judgement. Allah's is the heritage of the heavens and the earth, and Allah is aware of all you do.* (Surah Ale Imran, 3:180 — 181)

It also says: *You will not attain to prosperity until you spend in the path of Allah of the wealth you love. And whatever you do, Allah is aware of it.* (Surah Ale Imran, 3:92)

Two Brothers in Two Different Poles

'Alā bin Ziyād Hārithi was one of the nobles of Iraq and a rich person. He was the commander of a garrison in the army of Imam Ali. When this brave officer was bed-ridden on account of having been wounded in a battle Imam Ali went one day, accompanied by some dignitaries of Kufa, to inquire about his health. When he stepped into his house he found it to be a magnificent palace which covered a large area and consisted of beautiful rooms. On that day Imam Ali, the great leader of Islam, addressed his sick officer in these words:

"What are you going to do with such a spacious house in this world? What you really require is a spacious abode in Paradise where you are going to stay permanently. If you sincerely desire to own a house there also like this and as big as this one, then make this house a centre of your hospitality, treat your relatives well, go to their help; be particular about doing your duties and fulfilling your obligations, then only you will achieve your aim.

Hearing this 'Alā requested the Imam to advise his brother also, whose name was 'Āsim bin Ziyad and against whom 'Alā had to make a complaint. Imam Ali enquired what was wrong with him and how he was behaving. He said, "Sir, wearing a coarse woolen cloak he has renounced this world and is leading the life of a hermit". Imam Ali replied, "Bring him to me". When he came, Imam Ali said to him, "O enemy of your ownself! The Devil has misled you. Do you not feel pity on your wife and children and on other members of your family? Why do you not look after them? Why do you think that Allah will be displeased with you if you eat, consume and use all those things which have been allowed by Islam and which you have earned with honest and pious means? Why renounce all that? You are living far below your standard; you will be questioned about this renunciation".

Upon these remarks of Imam Ali he replied: "O Amirul Mo'minin! I am following your example. Look at your dress, how coarse, rough and cheap it is even the poorest of us would not care to wear it. Look at your food, it is dry and stale bread without even a pinch of salt". Imam Ali said, "Alas friend! You are mistaken, you are not like me. Allah has made it incumbent upon true and just Imams to keep themselves on the level of the poorest and humblest of men, so that those poor and humble persons may not feel shame and humiliation on account of their condition, may not lose heart, may not give way to frustration and grief and may maintain their self-respect". (See: Peak of Eloquence, Sermon — 214, ISP, 1984)

Right of Wealth

Imam Sajjād says thus in connection with the rights which a Muslim owes: "The right which wealth enjoys upon you is that you should not earn it by unlawful means and should only spend it in a rightful and lawful manner. Obey the orders of Allah in the matter of your wealth. Do not refrain from spending and utilizing it in a proper manner, because if you do so you will be faced with regret and Divine punishment". (Tabarsi, Makārimul Akhlāq, chapter XII)

While comparing affluence with indigence and indicating as to which of them is better for the prosperity of man the holy Prophet says: "Indigence is better than wealth except in the case of a wealthy person who pays the debts of the distressed and indebted persons from his own pocket and relieves them of debt and the pressure of life or helps the poor and distressed Muslims with his wealth. Indigence is better than wealth, because a poor Muslim does not owe any responsibility to the deprived and needy whereas a wealthy Muslim is under obligation to spend out of his wealth for the benefit of the society and to use it for the welfare and comfort of his brethren-in-faith". (Bihārul Anwār, Vol. LXXII, p. 56)

Imam Ali says: "Almighty Allah has made obligatory and specified the sustenance of the poor in the wealth of the rich and wherever a poor man is hungry it is due to the fact that a rich man has not paid him his due. However, Allah will call the rich to account in this behalf". (Nahjul Balaghah, Fayz, p. 1232)

The value of the words of Imam Ali can very well be assessed in the modern world when millions are faced with hunger and poverty and wealth has heaped up and concentrated in the hands of a small group of persons.

According to the view of the experts and the available statistics 85% of the wealth of the world is in the hands of 15% of its population and the sociologists predict that if a revolutionary change in the present conditions does not take place and wealth continues to accumulate by milliards the above ratios will change after 20 years to 90% and 10% respectively.

The following table shows how wealth has amassed at certain points and as against this how millions of indigent human beings on the face of the earth are on the threshold of death and destruction:

	Population(%)	Income of the world(%)
Advanced countries	30.2	75.5
Western bloc	19.7	58.7
European communist block	10.5	16.8
The third world	69.8	44.5

The above table shows the distribution of the wealth of the world in the middle of 1960.

There is no doubt about the fact that so long as the rich people of the world do not realize their human duties and do not feel themselves responsible before Allah and do not take basic steps for the just distribution of wealth the conditions will remain as they are — rather they will become more dreadful.

Spending in the Path of Allah

The rich should not keep their funds stagnant and should not make treasures of money for themselves by means of bank deposits or in other ways. The holy Qur'an says: *Those who hoard up gold and silver (and wealth given by Allah) and do not spend in the way of Allah (and do not utilize it for the welfare of the Mulims), give them tidings of a painful doom.* (Surah at-Taubah, 9:34)

Imam Sadiq says: "Allah holds an oppressive rich man and an aged adulterer and a proud beggar to be His enemies". Then the Imam asked those present: 'Do you know who a proud beggar is?' They replied. 'It is an indigent person'.

The Imam said: "No. A proud beggar is a rich man who does not take a step towards the pleasure and nearness of Allah by spending his wealth in His path. The Almighty Allah says in the Qur'an. *And let not those who possess wealth among you be negligent in giving to the kin and to the needy and to the Muhajirs (immigrants) for the cause of Allah. The believers should be magnanimous and should forgive and show indulgence. Don't you wish that Allah may forgive you? Allah is Forgiving, Merciful".* (Khasā'ilus Sadūq, Vol. I, p. 43)

In Nahjul Balaghah Imam Ali has mentioned some duties of the rich. He says: "If Allah grants wealth and prosperity to a person, he should show kindness to his deserving kith and kin, should provide relief to the poor, should come to the assistance of those who are subjected to calamities, misfortunes and reverses, and should assist honest people to liquidate their debts. Thus by performing his moral duties patiently bearing difficulties to relieve others of their afflictions, he should qualify himself for Rewards and Blessings of Allah, because only these merits will carry him to the zenith of virtues in this world, and to the height of excellence in the Hereafter". (See: Peak of Eloquence, ISP, 1984)

Rendering Help to the Needy

Islam has conducted a strong campaign against begging and does not permit those persons to beg who can do work and if they beg, their act is in contravention of law and the money earned by them is unlawful.

Imam Ja'far Sadiq says: "If a person begs without need Allah will make him distressed and dependent upon begging and will fix his place in the fire of Hell". (Furu'ul Kāfi, Vol. IV, p. 19)

The holy Prophet has cursed those who do not work inspite of their being strong enough and depend upon others.

However, it cannot be denied that in every society there are certain collapsed, weak, aged and retired persons who are not strong enough to do any work and do not also have enough income to support themselves. The wealthy are under obligation in respect of such persons to make good the deficit as regards their food, dress, lodging, medical treatment etc.

Imam Sadiq says: "Our wealthy Shi'ah are our trustees in respect of our needy Shi'ah. Then the holy Imam recommends to the wealthy Shi'ah: 'Preserve the respect due to us in respect of our needy Shi'ah so that Allah may preserve you". (Safinatul Bihār, Vol. II, p. 378)

The holy Prophet of Islam says: "Whoever maintains brotherly relations with the poor and the needy and lets them partake in his wealth and behaves justly with the people is a real believer". (al-Kāfi, Vol. II, p. 119)

Imam Ali says: "If a person spends the wealth given to him by Allah for good purposes and in His path, Allah will compensate him in this world for the expenditure incurred by him and will also give him additional reward in the Hereafter". (al-Kāfi, Vol. II, p. 123)

When Imam Riza sat by the dinner-cloth to have his meals, he used to keep a big dish near his hand and put some of the best foods of different kinds in it and sent the same to the needy. Then he used to recite this verse: *But he could not scale the steep ascent* (Surah al-Balad, 90:11) and said: 'Allah knew that everyone is not in a position to set free a slave. He, therefore, opened for them a path to Paradise so that by feeding the hungry and the needy they might attain eternal Paradise". (Furu'ul Kāfi, Vol. IV, p. 52)

If the rich desire that their wealth and blessings may last and Allah may not turn away His favour and kindness from them they should spend in His path and make the routine to help the needy families.

A man came before Imam Ja'far Sadiq and said: "Some Muslims are well-to-do and their income exceeds their expenses. And there are others who are hard up and zakat, too, is insufficient to meet their needs. Is it permissible in these difficult circumstances that the rich should remain indifferent to their brother Muslims and whereas they themselves may eat their fill and allow their brothers to remain hungry?

The Imam replied : "A Muslim is the brother of a Muslim. He does not oppress or humiliate him. He does not deprive him of his wealth. It is proper that the Muslims should perform their duties of brotherhood diligently and should strengthen its bond and help one another. They should be kind to the needy and should display human sentiments and follow as they have been ordered by Allah thus: They are kind to one another and have mercy on one another". (Furu'ul Kāfi, Vol. IV, p. 5)

Imam Muhammad Baqir says: "If I support a Muslim family and procure food and dress for them and preserve their honour in the society, I consider it to be better than performing seventy recommended pilgrims". (Furu'ul Kāfi, Vol IV, p. 20)

The Effects of Alms

As helping the humble and giving alms to the needy is a means of Divine pleasure, it produces deep and prosperous effects some of which are related to the Hereafter and a large portion of it pertains to this world itself.

In the traditions of the Divine leaders of Islam these effects have been alluded to and some of them are mention below:

Imam Ja'far Sadiq has said: "I owned a piece of land in common with an astrologer who possessed skill in astrology and decided to divide it so that the share of each one of us might be specified. My partner, the astrologer, however, dilly-dallyed and was regularly endeavouring to find out a moment which should be auspicious for himself and inauspicious for me so that at the time of division he should get the more desirable portion.

At last he fixed a day on which we divided the land. However, contrary to his expectation and forecast I got the desirable portion and he got the undesirable one.

He wrang his hands with much sadness and annoyance and said: 'I have not so far seen a worse day than this'. I asked him: 'What is the matter?' He said· 'According to my calculations this was an auspicious hour for me and an inauspicious one for you but now I find that the best part of the land has fallen to your share'. I said to him: "Let me narrate before you the tradition of the holy Prophet: The holy Prophet has said: 'Whoever wishes that Allah may keep the inauspiciousness of the day away from him should give alms in early morning and whoever wants that Allah may keep the inauspiciousness of the night away from him should begin his night with giving alms'.

Before I came here for the division of the land I took the first step with giving alms. If you, too, had acted according to the orders of the holy Prophet it would have been more beneficial for you than depending on astrology". (Furu'ul Kāfi, Vol. IV)

Imam Muhammad Baqir, says: "Performing good deeds and giving alms protects a man from becoming indigent, his life is prolonged and his remains immune from tragic death".

Guardianship of Orphan

Guardianship of the orphans and management of their affairs is one of the irrevocable duties of the rich. The children who have lost their guardians deserve the love and kindness of all and especially of the rich. It is necessary that they should lead respectable life and food, dress and lodging should be provided to them.

In his last precepts, addressed to his children and all his followers while he was on death-bed and in which he explained important Islamic matters, Imam Ali spoke thus about the orphans: "Fear Allah when the question of helpless orphans arises. You should never let them starve. So long as you are there to guard and protect them they should not be ruined or lost. The holy Prophet had always advised, cautioned and reminded us of this responsibility, so much so that we often thought that the Prophet of Allah might on the next occasion assign them a share from our heritage". (See: Peak of Eloquence, Letter — 47, p. 617. ISP, 1984)

The holy Prophet says: "Whoever undertakes the guardianship of an orphan and meets his expenditure will be my companion in Paradise and will sit by my side". (Safinatul Bihār, Vol. II)

Meeting the needs of orphans is a social necessity and if the rich neglect this vital matter such children are faced with psychological complexes and create irremediable dangers for the society in future.

According Respect to the Indigent

One of the matters to which the rich should pay special attention is to accord respect to the deprived and indigent classes. In the following Islamic laws and the traditions of the leaders of Islam this matter has been emphasised much and has become the object of attention in various narrations:

The holy Prophet says: "Whoever accords respect to an indigent Muslim will appear before Allah on the Day of Judgement in such a condition that the Almighty Lord will be pleased with him". (Safinatul Bihār, Vol. II, p. 379)

"Be it known to you that if a person despises and belittles an indigent Muslim he considers the right of Allah to be insignificant and in order to punish him for this bad conduct Allah will subject him on the Day of Judgement to despise and humiliation except that he should express regret for what he has done and repent before Allah". (Amali Sadūq, p. 257)

Imam Ali says: "What a nice and good thing it must be that in order to get reward from Allah the rich should be humble before the poor and respect them". (Nahjul Balaghah)

Apart from the religious aspect, showing disrespect to the indigent is opposed to good morals and humanity and gives birth to complexities and enmities between the rich and the poor which at times culminate in undesirabl incidents.

Display of lavishness, prodigalities and extravagances by the rich kindles the fire of enmity and grudge in the hearts of the needy. At times the food prepared for a feast exceeds the requirements and the residents of the house, not caring that it is Allah's bounty, throw the balance food in the dust bins. On the one hand they waste Divine bounty and thus commit a major sin and on the other hand when the poor and hungry passers-by see this state of affairs they get annoyed and perhaps curse the owners of the food.

In some houses of the rich the windows of the kitchens open on the side of the road and the pleasant flavour of the food constantly fills the atmosphere of the road and the passers-by who certainly include poor men and women and hungry orphans pass by the side of those houses with regret and undoubtedly entertain unfavourable feelings in their hearts for their owners.

At times when the children of the rich go out of their houses they carry with themselves fruits, sweets, dried fruits etc. and begin eating them before other children whereas the poor children keep looking on them with much regret.

Such acts are blameworthy from the moral and human point of view and according to Islam also such deeds are bad and indecent.

No doubt there are many good and responsible persons among the Muslims and the effects of their social and religious services are visible everywhere. Such rich persons enjoy the respect of the masses and good wishes of the people are the guards of their lives and according to Allah's promise they will also enjoy prosperity in the Hereafter.

* * * * * *

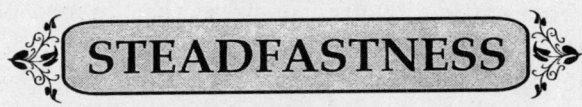

STEADFASTNESS

Success in every task is lined with steadfastness and no one can succeed in any matter without it.

If a person wishes to become a scholar he must bear the hardships of acquiring knowledge and sit respectfully before the teacher constantly and patiently. He should not get tired of studies, should avail himself of every opportunity of acquiring knowledge and should not waste his time. It is in this way that he can gradually acquire knowledge and wisdom and attain the position of a learned man.

One who wants to earn wealth must work hard and must not refrain from effort and struggle. If he meets with failure at the initial stage and suffers a loss he should not get disheartened but should continue his efforts so that he may gradually accumulate wealth.

An ailing person who wants to get cured must tolerate the bitterness of the treatment and proper restricted diet and should at times bear the operation fees with perseverance so that he may be restored to health.

One who wants to reform himself and to replace his bad habits by good ones should stand steadfastly in the face of sensual inclinations and misleading passions and should control his temptations and achieve his object with steadfastness.

One who wants to work as a reformer and guide his society to peace and prosperity should not be disheartened on account of the opponents' activities and should not withdraw himself from his activity. On the other hand it is the pre-requisite of his mission that he should bear all hardships and should observe patience in the face of all inconveniences and should display perseverance and steadfastness.

A Muslim who wants to safeguard his faith must stand firmly before the derision and scorn of the unbelievers and should bear hardship and torture with patience. He should also show constancy in the face of love for wealth, rank and passions, should put up with hardships, should tolerate deprivations and should refrain from getting involved in sin so that he may be able to safeguard his faith.

The conditions mentioned above are the specimens of different problems of material and spiritual life in which man feels intense need of steadfastness and in other fields also it is not possible to achieve success without steadfastness.

Hence, steadfastness is the most eminent trait of man, because by this it is possible to acquire all human qualities and material and spiritual advancement.

By means of steadfastness an ignorant person becomes a scholar, a miser becomes a generous man, an egotist becomes a god-fearing person and a poor man becomes rich.

Besides this one must also be persevering for safeguarding the capital available with him, because just as steadfastness is necessary to achieve one's object it is also necessary to safeguard that object when it has been achieved.

Imam Ali says: "If you are desirous of deliverance and prosperity you should push aside carelessness, forsake absurd things and make hard work your motto". He further says· "It is necessary for you to tread the path of steadfastness because this path provides you leadership and greatness and keeps you safe from the reproaches of the people". (Ghurarul Hikam)

Sakkāki was one of the distinguished scholars of the seventh century of Islamic era. During his youth he worked as an iron-smith and made much headway in this profession.

Once he manufactured a very elegant iron box along with a small lock and presented it to the caliph.

The beauty, elegance and lightness of the box immensely impressed the caliph and his courtiers. They praised and encouraged Sakkāki for his workmanship.

In the meantime a scholar arrived. The caliph stood up as a mark of respect to him and then sat before him on his knees.

Sakkāki enquired as to who the man was who had been accorded so much respet by the caliph and was informed that he was a scholar. Sakkāki said to himself: 'I worked hard for a long time to manufacture this elegant box and the only thing that I earned was praise and encouragement. Why should'nt I pursue knowledge so that I may too attain that position.

When he came out of the caliph's court he went straight to a school and requested the teacher to teach him. At that time he was thirty years old.

On the first day the teacher taught him a problem of jurisprudence with instructions to repeat it on the following day. But when he repeated the problem he did so in such a distorted manner that all other students began laughing heartily. The teacher restrained the students from laughing and taught Sakkāki another lesson. He pursued his studies for ten years but all his efforts came to nothing. At last, having got tired and losing all hope he went to the jungle and sat down at the foot of a mountain. While sitting there he began reflecting on his unenviable position. In the meantime he saw that drops of water were falling from above the mountain on a stone, one by one, and they had made a hole in the stone.

He said to himself: 'My heart is not so hard as this stone'. He then got up immediately, went back to the school with a renewed determination and occupied himself with studies.

Eventually, this thirty years old untalented iron smith became, by means of constancy and perseverance, one of the distinguished scholars of his time and attained high position". (Rawzātul Jannāt, p. 747)

Imam Ali says: "Whoever employs his strength and capacity will achieve his objects". He also says: "If a person continues knocking at a door and shows steadfastness in doing so, the door will be opened for him". (Ghurarul Hikam)

The point which must be kept in mind is that steadfastness which is one of the most sublime human qualities, consists of this that man should conduct reflection and studies without interference by false sentiments and prejudices and should ascertan the correctness of his object and display constancy and steadfastness for the achievement of that object for its protection. However, if one persists for the achievement of an illegal, irrational and false object it cannot be called 'steadfastness'. On the other hand it is 'obstinacy', which is one of the worst and base qualities and the cause of perversion and destruction.

Another point is that steadfastness is desirable for all proper causes and legal and rational objects, but the cause which really deserves steadfastness and bearing hardships is in the cause of Allah and the protection of faith and the spreading of spirituality in the society. This is so because the only result of steadfastness in material matters is that one achieves material objects whereas the result of steadfastness in the path of Allah is success in achieving prosperity in both the worlds.

The holy Qur'an promises eternal bliss to those who adopt such steadfastness. It says: *Those who have said, 'Our Lord is Allah' and are steadfast in their belief need have no fear or grief. They will be the dwellers of Paradise forever as a reward for what they have done.* (Surah al-Ahqāf, 46:13)

The conduct of the holy Prophet of Islam is the best example for his followers in this behalf. The holy Qur'an says: *(Prophet) Be steadfast on the orders given to you.* (Surah Hud, 11:112)

Under the command of Allah the holy Prophet undertook the guidance and reformation of the people when he was devoid of any apparent strength and material support. His greatest asset in this path was faith in Allah and steadfastness in the face of all difficulties. He had absolute faith in Allah and His guidance and did not mind sacrificing his wealth and life in this path.

Relying on Allah the holy Prophet did not give himself away in the face of the threats and pressure of the infidels and stood firm with perfect peace of mind. He also succeeded in training a group of persons who did not fear mishaps and dangers and faced all emergencies with great force and strength.

"Ayyāsh bin Abi Rabi'ah and his wife Asmā' bint Salāmah were among the persons who embraced Islam during the early years of the holy Prophet's prophetic mission and were subjected by the unbelievers to severe persecution on this account and faced it with perfect steadfastness.

'Ayyāsh was the brother of Abu Jahl and Hārith from his mother's side. When he embraced Islam he was about thirty and his wife was twenty. The members of 'Ayyāsh's family were much annoyed on account of his having embraced Islam and subjected him to severe torture to make him abandon his religion. Their punishment did not, however, prove effective and he remained steadfast in the path of Islam.

'Ayyāsh and his wife migrated to Ethiopia, along with some other Muslims, with the consent of the holy Prophet. They, however, returned to Makkah earlier than others and once again became subjected to persecution by the polytheists. This state of affairs continued to exist till the migration of the holy Prophet when the Muslims also followed him to Madina and became free from torture by the enemies.

When the mother of 'Ayyāsh came to know about his migration she made a vow that until he returned to Makkah she would neither use oil in her hair nor would sit under a shade. Abu Jahl and Hārith then visited Madina, met 'Ayyāsh and telling him about his mother's vow said: "From amongst her children you are the most dear to your mother and you are the follower of a religion which recommends goodness to one's parents. You should, therefore, return to Makkah, where you may worship your Lord in the same way in which you worship Him in Madina".

'Ayyāsh was very much moved to learn about the condition of his mother and agreed to accept the suggestion made by his brothers. He took a promise from them that they would not betray him on his return to Makkah and then departed from Madina along with them.

When they reached at a distance from the city, torture and persecution commenced. The brothers tied the hands of 'Ayyāsh behind his back and brought him to Makkah in the same condition. They entered Makkah in broad day light and said aloud: "O people of Makkah! Treat your ignorant ones who have embraced Islam in the same harsh manner in which we have treated this silly person of ours. Then they imprisoned him in a room which had no roof and breaking all the promises made with him subjected him to severest possible treatment.

'Ayyāsh remained imprisoned in Makkah for a few years and endured torture. During that period, however, not the least signs of weakness or spiritual breakdown appeared in him. He had his contact with the Almighty Allah and faced all the hardships and inconveniences with the strength of his faith.

The holy Prophet prayed for him repeatedly in Madina and all the Muslims were worried on that account. Eventually one of the Muslims arrived in Makkah secretly and secured the release of 'Ayyāsh by means of a dexterously drawn out plan. Then both of them returned to Madina together". (Shabāb-i Quraysh, p. 128; Jawān, Vol. II, p. 161)

Other persons who were trained in the school of the holy Prophet — the last of the Prophets of Allah, were also endowed with appreciable steadfastness.

Perseverance of the holy Prophet

The perseverance of the holy Prophet in the path of Allah was a practical lesson for his followers and they learnt the ways and manners of steadfastness and perseverance from his conduct.

The idolaters of Makkah did not spare any means to extinguish the light of Islam. In the first instance they adopted the path of discussion and alluring promises. They approached Abu Talib and said to him: "Have a talk with your newphew, Muhammad, and ask him what his real object is in campaigning against the idols and inviting the people to the worship of an unseen Deity. If he wants money we shall place a large amount thereof at his disposal. And in case he desires authority we are prepared to accept him as our ruler".

Abu Talib conveyed the message of the idolaters to the holy Prophet. In reply thereto the holy Prophet said· "Dear uncle! Tell the people of Makkah that I have been entrusted with responsibility by the Almighty Allah which is necessary for me to perform and my object is nothing other than the pleasure of Allah and the enforcement of His Commands. Even if the people of Makkah place the sun on my right hand and the moon on my left hand I shall not abandon my call".

When the Makkans met with disappointment they commenced their campaign in earnest and in a headstrong manner they resorted to persecution, abusive language, slander, conspiracies and harsh treatment in different ways.

The pressure and persecution assumed such dimensions that the Muslims had to migrate to Ethiopia and afterwards the holy Prophet also migrated to Madina. Even after that the conflict continued in the form of the battles of Badr, Uhud,

Ahzāb etc. However, none of these battles affected the firm determination of the holy Prophet and he remained steadfast in the face of all these conflicts. As a result of this he succeeded in spreading the sacred religion of Islam in the world of those days and in turning those semi-wild people into an advanced nation which was endowed with all human qualities.

The point which must be mentioned here is that it should not be thought that steadfastness should be coupled with harshness. In case, therefore, a steadfast man is likened to a mountain it is on account of the capacity of a mountain to withstand the storms and floods and not on account of its hardness. And the holy Prophet who was a perfect and manifest specimen of steadfastness possessed very gentle manners and kind disposition and the same mildness was one of the factors of his success.

One of the important and basic matters related to one's personality and the adaptability to the environment is the flexibility with regard to collective events. Persons who face the events wisely and refrain from obstinacy and unjustified resistance can overcome the difficulties very easily and can demonstrate their personality. On the other hand the persons who are obstinate and hard-hearted resort to uncalled for resistance and consequently break up their personality and are often faced with unbearable difficulties and sufferings.

The holy Prophet says: "As against the storm of events a believer is like a ripe bunch (of grapes) which bows down on earth when the wind blows and assumes its former position when the wind ceases to blow. By doing so it conforms itself with the circumstances and remains safe from mishaps. However, the silly unbeliever stands against the storm of events unknowingly and unjustifiably like a pine tree and is eventually uprooted". (Tafsir-i Rūhul Bayān, Vol. IV, p. 356)

A healthy person who possesses flexibility and the power to return to his usual position can bear every failure. He rises on his feet once again and commences his efforts afresh. And as he has many arrows in his quiver, he goes another way when he finds one way closed and selects a new target. On the other hand a sickly soul does not see more than one target and one way in the world and if there is an obstacle on that way he is distressed and loses all hopes. The more a person is endowed with the power of flexibility the lesser he is afraid of breaking down. He controls the field of success in a better way and makes it a good ground of his aspirations, talents and ambitions. And if a person is devoid of this power he quits the field of competition very soon and surrenders himself to failure.

Steadfastness should always be coupled with self-possession and mildness so that it may lead one to success and victory.

During the lifetime of the holy Prophet it often happened that polytheists behaved with him harshly. And notwithstanding the fact that he was in a position to chastise any such person he did not permit his companions to deal with him harshly. On the contrary he himself talked with him with an open countenance and unusual kindness and eventually succeeded in winning him over to Islam.

The holy Qur'an says thus: *Only through the Divine Mercy have you (Muhammad) been able to deal with your followers so gently. If you have been sterm and hardhearted they would all have deserted you a long time ago. Forgive them and ask Allah to forgive (their sins) and consult with them in certain matters. But when you reach decision trust Allah. Allah loves those who trust Him.* (Surah Ale Imran, 3:159)

It is necessary to explain here that in the above verse Allah has directed the holy Prophet to consult his companions and his consultation pertains only to common matters like war, peace etc. As regards the laws of Islam and their enactment, however, it was not only that the companions could not interfere with them but even the holy Prophet had no say in the matter. These laws were sent to the holy Prophet by Allah and he communicated them to the people.

Steadfastness in Good Behaviour

One of the matters with regard to which steadfastness is necessary for all persons is the acquisition of good manners and habits and abandonment of bad habits.

At the time of his birth a human being has neither good qualities and habits nor bad ones. Gradually, he acquires habits and qualities, whether good or bad, under the influence of his parents and preceptors and of the society.

Good habits and qualities must be protected and steadfastness is necessary for their preservation. If a person does not make efforts for their protection he loses them soon. Thus efforts and steadfastness is also necessary for abandoning bad habits and manners so that good habits and qualities may be implanted in their place.

If anyone thinks that undesirable habits and qualities cannot be changed he is sadly mistaken. Experience has shown and the psychologists also admit that all the qualities of man can be changed with determination and resolution. Hence, if on account of undesirable upbringing in the family and corrupt social atomosphere a person has not grown up to be a good man and cannot put up with the society, he should not despair and should not think that he will be unlucky to be a failure in life. On the other hand he can reform himself with firm determination and can acquire a decent personality.

Such a person is duty-bound from the religious and educational point of view to campaign against his bad habits and to eradicate the indecent manners which are the source of his deprivation and to acquire means of his success by adopting decent qualities.

Imam Ali says: "Do not cease from making efforts to reform yourself, because nothing can help you in this task except effort and struggle". (Ghurarul Hikam)

He also says: "O people! Assume the responsibility of reforming yourselves and keep yourselves away from bad habits". (Nahjul Balaghah)

Imam Ja'far Sadiq says: "Restrain yourself from what is harmful before you breathe your last. And make efforts to ensure the freedom of your soul just as you make efforts to earn your livelihood because your soul is under the influence of your actions and it cannot be freed without your efforts". (Wasā'ilush Shi'ah, Vol. II, p. 40)

The habits which have become our second nature during the span of a number of years cannot be eradicated overnight. Fortunately, however, if we act according to the dictates of reason and logic with a firm determination and are not impatient, every deep rooted habit can be eradicated in a much lesser time than that in which it was acquired.

It is necessary in the first instance that we should understand the general laws which govern the human body. Thereafter we should try to understand our own selves as far as it is possible and find out as to which manners and habits need to be changed and which of them need to be developed. We should know especially which particular ability is available in us which can be the source of our success. When we have succeeded in making these assessments we should equip ourselves with the qualities of steadfastness and patience and should make it a point that unless we have reformed ourselves in the manner we wish we should not abandon our struggle and efforts.

It is evident that efforts and determination are necessary to eradicate the habits which have taken root in a man. However, it is an admitted fact that if a person commences a task with determination and patience he is bound to succeed.

Steadfastness in Adversity

Every person comes across difficulties and adversities in life which cannot be overcome without patience and steadfastness. Hence, for the persons who are equipped with the trait of steadfastness it is easy for them to overcome difficulties and they can overcome the hurdles from their path.

The holy Qur'an advises the people that in difficult and adverse circumstances they should seek assistance from patience, steadfastness and prayers. It says: *Believers, solve your problems through patience and prayers; Allah is with those who have patience.* (Surah al-Baqarah, 2:153)

Steadfastness and seeking help are necessary because man cannot solve the problems of life alone. And as in fact there is no real helper of man except Allah, help should be sought from Him alone and it becomes available by means of steadfastness, patience and remembrance of Allah which is nothing but prayers. In fact these two — patience and prayers — are the best means of overcoming difficulties, because patience and steadfastness reduce great difficulties into something very small and directing one's attention towards the Almighty Allah and seeking refuge in Him awakens the strength of faith in man and tells him that during the difficult circumstances he is not unprotected and enjoys a strong support viz. that of the Almighty". (Allama Tabātabā'i, Tafsir al-Mizān, Vol. I, p. 152)

Imam Ali says: "Wear the dress of patience and faith as it guards both in prosperity and in adversity". (Ghurarual Hikam)

"Life of man has two conditions. At times there is adversity and inconvenience and at other times there is peace and comfort. Sometimes man is immersed in blesings and sometimes he is drowned in adversities. If time is unkind to an enlightened and wise person he can adopt steadfastness and patience. If I am faced with an adversity I shall remain firm and resolute like a rock". (Imam Ali)

As history tells us Imam Ali had to face great difficulties throughout his life, because right from the age of ten when he resolved to serve Islam and the holy Prophet, to the last moment of his life, he experienced thousands of difficulties and dangers and remained firm and steadfast on every occasion.

On the day he slept in the bed of the holy Prophet — the Prophet migrated during that night from Makkah to Madina.

On the day when he was made responsible for the safety of Muslim ladies, — he escorted them safely to Madina.

On the day when he fought against the spiteful Quraysh in the Battle of Badr — he killed several of enemy warriors.

On the day when during the Battle of Uhud he was left alone to defend the holy Prophet and received as many as ninety wounds by fighting the enemies — he earned the distinction of receiving the acclamation: "There is no champion except Ali and there is no sword except Zulfaqār".

On the day of the Battle of the Ditch when he fought against Amr bin 'Abd Wudd — he saved Islam from annhilation during those critical moments.

On the day when in the Battle of Khayber he entered the battlefield after Islam had suffered successive defeats due to the desertion of some pseudo-Muslims — he conquered the strong forts of the Jews.

On the day when he went to Makkah (before the conquest of that city) under the behest of the holy Prophet to recite Surah al-Barā't (Tauba) — he carried out this assignment in an environments which were beset with grave dangers.

And on the day when a plot was hatched in Saqifa Bani Sā'ida after the passing away of the holy Prophet, and the caliphate, which was the established and undeniable right of Imam Ali was usurped!

And on the day when Fidak which was indisputably owned and possessed by his wife, Lady Fatima Zahra, was taken away from her without any justification.

And on the day when 'Āyesha, in clear defiance of the text of the holy Qur'an started the 'Battle of the Camel' against Imam Ali.

And on the day when Mu'awiya started the Battle of Siffin against Imam Ali.

And on the day when the question of arbitration was raised against his will and permission.

And on the day when the Kharijites of Nahrawān revolted against him and started preparations for the Battle of Nahrawān.

And on many other days when Imam Ali was faced with serious problems and difficulties he remained firm at his place like a rock and performed his divine and heavenly duties.

In one of his sermons called the *Shiqshiqiyya**** Imam Ali hints at some of his sufferings after the passing away of the holy Prophet and speaks about his own patience and forbearance. He says: "By Allah, that man snatched the caliphate as if it was an insignia, which could be put on by him; though he knew very well that I was as indispensable to the caliphate as the pivot to the grind-stone (upon which its revolvings depend).

The eminence of my position among those men was such that I was like a fountain-head from which wisdom flowed and nobody could aspire to rise to the heights of my knowledge. But I was forced to bear this usurpation and turn my face away from the calamity; I was in serious straits. There were two alternatives before me; either to fight for my rights without the help of supporters, or to patiently endure the bereavement; the endurance was going to be of such a sad and long duration that during this period young men would become old, the old would lose their vitalities and the faithful would end their days unsuccessfully trying to improve the situation.

After thoughtful consideration I came to the conclusion that the wisest course for me was to face the disaster with patience and courage. I, therefore, bore it all patiently, though the very thought of usurpation of my just right was extremely painful and saddening to me.

*See: Peak of Eloquence, Sermon — 7, ISP 1984.

At last the First Caliph died, but while passing away he appointed someone else as the caliph. (Here Imam Ali cited a verse of the poet, in which the poet A'sha Hamdāni draws a comparison between the days when he was leading with his brother a happy and care-free life and again when he had to face difficulties alone).

"My days are now passed on the camel's back (in difficulty) while there were days (of ease) when I enjoyed the company of Jābir's brother Hayyān".

Is it not astonishing that during his lifetime the First Caliph was always badly in need of the help of others to compensate for his imperfections and defects and to cover his faults and failures, but at the time of his death he thought himself to be wise enough to fix and appoint somebody to carry on the duties at which he was a complete failure himself.

Boldly and unscrupulously he and his successor, in his turn, pillaged and plundered the wealth of the community leaving the State in such a sadly injured condition that the passage of time was increasing the intensity of the injury. It was almost impossible to undo the harm. And the danger of further repetition of the unscrupulous exploitations was apparent. But it was carried on under the guise of law and order and many lame excuses were offered to justify those irreligious and unholy arrogations and many more were repeated later.

Thus the situation was brought to such a pitch that whosoever took up the reins of the State or caliphate was in the unhappy predicament of riding an untrained and refractory she-camel; if desiring to keep the animal under control he had pulled the bridle hard, he would slit and wound its nostrils, and if he had allowed it a free run, the animal would rush itself and its rider to destruction.

I swear by Allah that people were misled and went astray; they missed the straight path of religion. But accepting the inevitable without reproving and with resignation I bore the long and painful period of the devastation of human rights and religion, till the second person also died; but before his death he left the question of the caliphate to the decision of a committee and he thought that I could also be on the panel of that committee (because he had himself nominated me).

O Allah! What had I to do with this select committee (I had nothing in common with any of its members). Did I ever have a doubt about my pre-eminence and superiority when compared to the first that I would accept to be one of the body of persons far inferior to him. But in the interest of humanity and religion I joined this select committee. I had to adjust myself to their level, to demand my just rights of them, as I had done at the time of those who were superior to them.

One of the members of this committee turned against me because of his hatred (by this the Imam meant either Sā'd or Talha), the other (Abdur Rahman bin Awf) had also got inclined the other way due to very obvious reason of kinship, besides a few other reasons which the world came to know later (he was brother-in-law of Caliph Uthman). Consequently the third proudly took charge of the caliphate, as if it was a private grazing-ground, and with bloated stomachs he and members of his clan (Bani Umayyah) started plundering the wealth of the Muslim world in the same recklessly gluttonous manner as characterizes a camel when it devours harvest grass. However, this man met an untimely death. The greed of his clan was the cause of his fateful end.

After his death people flocked around me imploring me to take up the caliphate. They gathered in such numbers and were so anxious to show their sincerity that both of my sons (Hasan and Husayn) were almost trampled and my dress was torn. They were simply falling upon me to accept their rulership and leadership. I would have turned down their request but I was afraid that with my refusal they would completely become out of touch with truth and religion.

When I accepted their rulership and made them follow the path of Allah — the same path as the holy Prophet (peace of Allah be upon him and his descendants) taught them to follow, they revolted. One party (Ummul Mo'minin Ayesha) broke the oath of allegiance; the second party (Kharijites) became apostates and the third adopted an equally wrong course and coveting the power and wealth which are part of such a rulership, they started tyrannizing the people and oppressing them into subjugation.

All the three groups behaved as if they had never heard the holy Qur'an saying, *Paradise is meant for those who neither create mischief nor do they oppress human beings: the eternal peace and happiness is for those who lead a pious life.* I swear by Allah that they were made to hear these words of Allah repeatedly and their meanings were clearly explained to them. But the vicious ways of life fascinated them and its luxuries, its pomp and show as well as its power and wealth enchanted them.

I swear by the Creator of this Universe that had they not sworn unconditional allegiance to me; had they not manifested profound gratitude in my accepting thair rulership; had not the presence of helpers and and supporters made it incumbent upon me to defend the faith; and had Allah the Almighty not taken a promise from the learned to put a check upon the luxurious and vicious lives of oppressors and tyrants as well as to try to reduce the pangs of poverty and starvation of the oppressed and downtordden; and had He not made it incumbent upon them to secure back the usurped rights of the weak from the mighty and powerful oppressors, I would even now have left the rulership of this State as I did earlier and would have allowed it to sink into anarchy and chaos. Then you would have seen that in my view the glamour of a vicious life of your world is no better than the sneezing of a goat".

These are the few specimens of patience and steadfastness of the Commander of the Faithful Imam Ali, as mentioned by him himself and wherein there is no exaggeration whatsoever.

A study of the life history of the Imam Ali teaches one the lesson of patience and steadfastness the example of which have been set by himself. (See · The Voice of Human Justice ISP 1982)

Imam Ali said; "One who is endowed with the quality of steadfastness and patience will succeed". (Ghurarul Hikam)

The lives of great men of history have always been blessed with patience and steadfastness in the face of difficulties and hardships in such a way that it may be said that patience and steadfastness were the prerequisites in their lives in the sense that none of them has succeeded in attaining greatness and supremacy without undergoing difficulties and hardships.

Anushirwān, the Sāsānian King, got displeased with his minister Buzar Jumhair and imprisoned him in a dark cell. He also ordered that the hands and feet of the minister might be tied together with iron chains. Quite some time passed and the great sage remained imprisoned and underwent great hardships.

One day Anushirwān sent a man to him to find out what his condition was and what effect the hardships had on his morale. That man met Buzar Jumair in the prison and, quite contrary to his expectations, found him strong spiritually and quite happy and well-contented at heart. He, therefore, said with surprise: "O great sage! Inspite of the very unfavourable and trying conditions in which you are living I find you quite happy, tranquil and contented. What is the reason for this?"

Buzar Jumhair said: "I have prepared a medicine which is composed of six things. I use that medicine and my present condition is due to this. The man enquired: "I would request you to let me know what that medicine is so that I may use it in difficult circumstances".

Buzar Jumhair replied: "The medicine is composed of these six items: (i) Reliance on Almighty Allah. (ii) One cannot escape predestination. (iii) Patience and steadfastness. (iv) If I do not observe patience what else should I do? And I am not prepared to accelerate my destruction with impatience and grief. (v) Conditions more hard and trying than my present condition also exist and (vi) One may hope for deliverance with the lapse of time.

The wise remarks of Buzar Jumhair were communicated to Anushirwān and he was also informed of his condition. He then released him from the prison and bestowed favours on him. (Dāstānhā-i Tārikhi, Safinatul Bihār, See, Sabr (Patience)

Conclusion
We draw the following conclusions from what has been stated above:
- Steadfastness is the secret of success in every task.
- To persist in endeavours for achieving wrong objective is obstinacy and not steadfastness.
- Steadfastness should be accompanied by mildness and not by harshness.
- The most valuable steadfastness is that which is in the path of Allah and spiritual attainment.
- Study of the lives of the leaders of Islam and benefiting from their sayings is the best lesson for acquiring steadfastness.

Steadfastness is the last lesson of this book because in actual fact patience and steadfastness have been the lifestyle of the Prophets and these are the cornerstone of human values. It is through these attributes that man can safeguard his belief and attain happiness and success in both the worlds.

The purpose of our discussing this point is that:

- We should affirm our faith in Allah and the holy Prophet and that our religion is Islam only.
- We should affirm that Islam, which has come as the Divine blessing for mankind and which ensures man's progress and prosperity, is nearest to our heart and that by our deeds we should prove that we are its true followers and propagate it by our speech and action.
- We should affirm that we would introduce Islam to the entire world, and in our own society we would establish it in its true form by all means.
- We should affirm that we would work for truth and justice and support the sublime principles of Islam for the unity of the Muslims without prejudice and narrowmindedness.
- We should affirm that we would emancipate the weak, downtrodden and oppressed, not only in our own society and country but in the entire world also, and for this purpose we would fight the evil forces and despotic rulers up to our last drop of blood.
- We should affirm that we shall never allow the infidels the hypocrites and the tyrants, who are Muslims in name only, or any such group of persons, to dominate and exploit any Islamic State or to expropriate it into their colonial domination.

In short we should affirm that under the blessings of Islam we will endeavour to establish justice, fairplay, equity and freedom, and that we will never bow our heads before anybody save Allah and that we will never tolerate any external domination.

The Almighty Allah says: *Surely the angels will come down to those who say, 'Our Lord is Allah' and then remain steadfast.* (Surah Hā Mīm Sajdah, 41:30)

May Allah be our Supporter and Helper.

The End

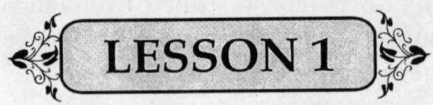

LESSON 1

1 وَ مَنْ يَتَّقِ اللهَ يَجْعَلْ لَهُ مَخْرَجاً وَ يَرْزُقْهُ مِنْ حَيْثُ لَا يَحْتَسِبُ

2 اِنَّ اَطْيَبَ مَا اَكَلَ الرَّجُلُ مِنْ كَسْبِهِ

3 مَنْ كَانَ فِى اَمْرِ دُنْيَاهُ كَسِلاً فَهُوَ فِى اَمْرِ آخِرَتِهِ اَكْسَلْ

4 لَيْسَ خَيْرُكُمْ مَنْ تَرَكَ دُنْيَاهُ لِآخِرَتِهِ وَلَا آخِرَتَهُ لِدُنْيَاهُ بَلْ مَنْ اَخَذَ مِنْ هَذِهِ وَهَذِهِ

5 وَ ابْتَغِ فِيمَا اٰتَاكَ اللهُ الدَّارَ الآخِرَةَ وَلَا تَنْسَ نَصِيبَكَ مِنَ الدُّنْيَا وَ اَحْسِنْ كَمَا اَحْسَنَ اللهُ اِلَيْكَ...

6 اِنَّمَا الْخَمْرُ وَ الْمَيْسِرُ وَ الْاَنْصَابُ وَ الْاَزْلَامُ رِجْسٌ مِنْ عَمَلِ الشَّيْطَانِ فَاجْتَنِبُوهُ لَعَلَّكُمْ تُفْلِحُونَ. اِنَّمَا يُرِيدُ الشَّيْطَانُ اَنْ يُوقِعَ بَيْنَكُمُ الْعَدَاوَةَ وَ الْبَغْضَاءَ فِى الْخَمْرِ وَ الْمَيْسِرِ فَهَلْ اَنْتُمْ مُنْتَهُونَ

7 اِنَّ اللهَ يَأْمُرُ بِالْعَدْلِ وَالْاِحْسَانِ وَ اِيتَاءِ ذِى الْقُرْبَى وَ يَنْهَى عَنِ الْفَحْشَاءِ وَ الْمُنْكَرِ وَ الْبَغْىِ يَعِظُكُمْ لَعَلَّكُمْ تَذَكَّرُونَ

8 اَحَبُّ النَّاسِ اِلَى اللهِ اَنْفَعُهُمْ لِلنَّاسِ.

9 اِصْطَنِعِ الْمَعْرُوفَ اِلَى مَنْ هُوَ اَهْلُهُ وَاِلَى مَنْ لَيْسَ مِنْ اَهْلِهِ فَاِنْ لَمْ يَكُنْ هُوَ مِنْ اَهْلِهِ فَكُنْ اَنْتَ مِنْ اَهْلِهِ

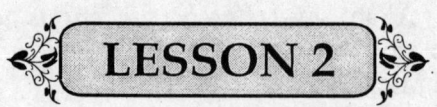

LESSON 2

1 طَلَبُ الْعِلْمِ فَرِيضَةٌ عَلَى كُلِّ مُسْلِمٍ

2 اُطْلُبُوا الْعِلْمَ مِنَ الْمَهْدِ اِلَى اللَّحْدِ

٣ اَلْحِكْمَةُ ضَالَّةُ الْمُؤْمِنِ اَيْنَمَا وَجَدَهَا اَحَذَهَا.

٤ اُطْلُبُوا الْعِلْمَ وَلَوْ بِالصِّينِ.

٥ يَرْفَعُ اللهُ الَّذِينَ اٰمَنُوا مِنْكُمْ وَالَّذِينَ اُوتُوا الْعِلْمَ دَرَجَاتٍ و خوانساه هَلْ يَسْتَوِي الَّذِينَ يَعْلَمُونَ وَالَّذِينَ لَا يَعْلَمُونَ

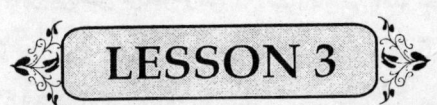

LESSON 3

١ اَلْجَنَّةُ تَحْتَ اَقْدَامِ الْاُمَّهَاتِ

٢ اَنِ اشْكُرْ لِي وَلِوَالِدَيْكَ

٣ لَنْ تَنَالُوا الْبِرَّ حَتَّى تُنْفِقُوا مِمَّا تُحِبُّونَ ۞

٤ وَمَا كُنْتَ تَدْرِي مَا الْكِتَابُ وَلَا الْاِيمَانُ وَلٰكِنْ جَعَلْنَاهُ نُورًا نَهْدِي بِهِ مَنْ نَشَاءُ .

LESSON 4

١ اِنَّ اللهَ يَأْمُرُ بِالْعَدْلِ وَالْاِحْسَانِ وَاِيتَاءِ ذِي الْقُرْبَى وَيَنْهَى عَنِ الْفَحْشَاءِ وَالْمُنْكَرِ وَالْبَغْيِ يَعِظُكُمْ لَعَلَّكُمْ تَذَكَّرُونَ.

٢ مَنْ جَاءَ بِالْحَسَنَةِ فَلَهُ عَشْرُ اَمْثَالِهَا وَمَنْ جَاءَ بِالسَّيِّئَةِ فَلَا يُجْزَى اِلَّا مِثْلَهَا.

٣ اِنْ اَحْسَنْتُمْ اَحْسَنْتُمْ لِاَنْفُسِكُمْ وَاِنْ اَسَأْتُمْ فَلَهَا.

٤ اِفْعَلُوا الْخَيْرَ وَلَا تَحْقِرُوا مِنْهُ شَيْئًا فَاِنَّ صَغِيرَهُ كَبِيرٌ وَقَلِيلَهُ كَثِيرٌ.

٥ لَا تَبْسُطْ يَدَكَ اِلَّا اِلَى الْخَيْرِ وَلَا تَقُلْ بِلِسَانِكَ اِلَّا الْمَعْرُوفَ.

٦ فَمَنْ اٰتَاهُ اللهُ مَالًا فَلْيَصِلْ بِهِ الْقَرَابَةَ وَلْيُحْسِنْ مِنْهُ الضِّيَافَةَ وَلْيَفُكَّ بِهِ الْاَسِيرَ وَالْعَا

تى وَلْيُعْطِ مِنْهُ الفَقِيرَ وَالغَارِمَ وَلْيَصْبِرْ نَفْسَهُ عَلَى الحُقُوقِ وَالنَوَائِبِ اِبْتِغَاءَ الثَوَابِ فَإِنْ فَازَ بِهَذِهِ الخِصَالِ شَرَفَ مَكَارِمَ الدُنْيَا وَدَرَكَ فَضَائِلِ الآخِرَةِ.

7. صَنَائِعُ المَعْرُوفِ صَدَقَةٌ تَقِي مَصَارِعَ السُوءِ وَكُلُّ مَعْرُوفٍ صَدَقَةٌ وَ أَهْلُ المَعْرُوفِ فِي الدُنْيَا أَهْلُ المَعْرُوفِ فِي الآخِرَةِ...

8. اِصْطَنِعِ الخَيْرَ إِلَى مَنْ هُوَ أَهْلُهُ وَإِلَى مَنْ لَيْسَ هُوَ مِنْ أَهْلِهِ فَإِنْ لَمْ تُصِبْ مَنْ هُوَ أَهْلُهُ فَأَنْتَ أَهْلُهُ.

9. رَأْسُ العَقْلِ بَعْدَ الدِينِ التَوَدُّدُ إِلَى النَاسِ وَاصْطِنَاعُ الخَيْرِ إِلَى كُلِّ أَحَدٍ بَرًّا أَوْ فَاجِرًا.

10. أَلَا أُخْبِرُكُمْ بِخَيْرِ خَلَائِقِ الدُنْيَا وَالآخِرَةِ، العَفْوُ عَمَّنْ ظَلَمَكَ وَتَصِلُ مَنْ قَطَعَكَ وَالإِحْسَانُ إِلَى مَنْ أَسَاءَ إِلَيْكَ وَاعْطَاءُ مَنْ حَرَمَكَ.

11. وَلَا تَقْرَبُوا مَالَ اليَتِيمِ الأَبَالَتِي هِيَ أَحْسَنُ حَتَّى يَبْلُغَ أَشُدَّهُ.

12. إِنَّ الَذِينَ يَأْكُلُونَ أَمْوَالَ اليَتَامَى ظُلْمًا إِنَّمَا يَأْكُلُونَ فِي بُطُونِهِمْ نَارًا وَسَيَصْلَوْنَ سَعِيرًا.

13. مَنْ أَرَادَ أَنْ يُدْخِلَهُ اللهُ عَزَّ وَجَلَّ فِي رَحْمَتِهِ وَيُسْكِنَهُ جَنَّتَهُ، فَلْيُحْسِنْ خُلُقَهُ، وَلْيُعْطِ النَصَفَةَ مِنْ نَفْسِهِ، وَلْيَرْحَمِ اليَتِيمَ وَلْيُعِنِ الضَعِيفَ وَلْيَتَوَاضَعْ لِلهِ الذِي خَلَقَهُ.

14. مَنْ كَفَلَ يَتِيمًا وَ كَفَلَ نَفَقَتَهُ كُنْتُ أَنَا وَ هُوَ فِي الجَنَّةِ كَهَاتَيْنِ وَقَرَنَ بَيْنَ إِصْبَعَيْهِ المُسَبِّحَةِ وَالوُسْطَى.

15. اللهَ اللهَ فِي الأَيْتَامِ فَلَا يُغِبُّوا أَفْوَاهَهُمْ وَلَا يُضَيَّعُوا بِحَضْرَتِكُمْ.

LESSON 5

1. مَنْ زَوَّجَ كَرِيمَتَهُ مِنْ شَارِبِ خَمْرٍ فَقَدْ قَطَعَ رَحِمَهَا.

2. مَنْ شَرِبَ الخَمْرَ بَعْدَ مَا حَرَّمَهَا اللهُ عَلَى لِسَانِي فَلَيْسَ بِأَهْلٍ أَنْ يُزَوَّجَ إِذَا خَطَبَ وَلَا يُشْفَعَ

356

اِذا شُفِعَ وَلا يُصَدَّقُ اِذا حَدَّثَ وَلا يُؤْتَمَنُ عَلَى اَمانَةٍ فَمَنِ ائْتَمَنَهُ بَعْدَ عِلْمِهِ عَلَيْهِ فَلَيْسَ لِلَّذى ائْتَمَنَهُ عَلَى اللهِ ضَمانٌ وَلَيْسَ لَهُ اَجْرٌ وَلاخَلَفٌ

3 اَيُّما امْرَأَةٍ اَطاعَتْ زَوْجَها وَهُوَ شارِبُ الْخَمْرِ كانَ لَها مِنَ الْخَطايا بِعَدَدِ نُجُومِ السَّماءِ وَكُلُّ مَوْلُودٍ يَلِدُهُ مِنْهُ فَهُوَ نَجِسٌ وَلا يَقْبَلُ اللهُ مِنْها صَرْفاً وَلا عَدْلاً حَتّى يَمُوتَ زَوْجُها اَوْ خَلَعَ عَنْهُ نَفْسَها.

4 يَسْئَلُونَكَ عَنِ الْخَمْرِ.

5 اِنَّ اللهَ حَرَّمَ الْخَمْرَ لِما فيها مِنَ الْفَسادِ وَبُطْلانِ الْعُقُولِ فِى الْحَقائِقِ وَذَهابِ الْحَياءِ مِنَ الْوَجْهِ

6 وَالذُّنُوبُ الَّتى تَهْتِكُ الْعِصَمَ شُرْبُ الْخَمْرِ وَاللَّعِبُ بِالْقِمارِ.

7 قالَ رَسُولُ اللهِ مَلْعُونٌ مَنْ جَلَسَ عَلى مائِدَةٍ يُشْرَبُ عَلَيْها الْخَمْرُ.

8 مُدْمِنُ الْخَمْرِ يَلْقَى اللهَ كَعابِدِ وَثَنٍ

9 حُرِّمَتِ الْجَنَّةُ عَلى ثَلاثَةٍ، مُدْمِنِ الْخَمْرِ..

10 لا يَنالُ شَفاعَتى مَنِ اسْتَخَفَّ بِصَلوتِهِ وَلا يَرِدُ عَلَىَّ الْحَوْضَ، لاوَاللهِ لا يَنالُ شَفاعَتى مَنْ شَرِبَ الْمُسْكِرَ وَلا يَرِدُ عَلَى الْحَوْضِ لاوَاللهِ.

LESSON 6

1 يَسْئَلُونَكَ عَنِ الْخَمْرِ وَالْمَيْسِرِ قُلْ فيهِما اِثْمٌ كَبيرٌ وَمَنافِعُ لِلنّاسِ وَاِثْمُهُما اَكْبَرُ مِنْ نَفْعِهِما.

2 اِنَّما يُريدُ الشَّيْطانُ اَنْ يُوقِعَ بَيْنَكُمُ الْعَداوَةَ وَالْبَغْضاءَ فِى الْخَمْرِ وَالْمَيْسِرِ

3 كانَتْ قُرَيْشٌ تُقَمِّرُ الرَّجُلَ بِاَهْلِهِ وَمالِهِ فَنَهاهُمُ اللهُ مِنْ ذلِكَ

4 اِنَّ اللهَ تَبارَكَ وَتَعالى نَهى عَنْ جَميعِ الْقِمارِ وَاَمَرَ الْعِبادَ بِالاجْتِنابِ مِنْها

وَسَمَّاهَا رِجْساً فقالَ رِجْسٌ مِنْ عَمَلِ الشَّيْطانِ فَاجْتَنِبُوهُ مِثْلَ اللَّعِبِ بِالشِّطْرَنْجِ وَالنَّرْدِ وَغَيْرِهِمَا مِنَ الْقِمَارِ وَالنَّرْدُ أَشَدُّ مِنَ الشِّطْرَنْجِ

5 إِنَّمَا الْخَمْرُ وَالْمَيْسِرُ وَالأَنْصَابُ وَالأَزْلاَمُ رِجْسٌ مِنْ عَمَلِ الشَّيْطانِ فَاجْتَنِبُوهُ

6 يَدْخُلُ فِي الْمَيْسِرِ اللَّعِبُ بِالشِّطْرَنْجِ وَالنَّرْدِ وَغَيْرُ ذَلِكَ مِنْ أَنْوَاعِ الْقِمَارِ

7 إِنَّمَا يُرِيدُ الشَّيْطانُ أَنْ يُوقِعَ بَيْنَكُمُ الْعَدَاوَةَ وَالْبَغْضَاءَ فِي الْخَمْرِ وَالْمَيْسِرِ

8 اتَّقِ اللَّعِبَ بِالْخَوَاتِيمِ وَالأَرْبَعَةَ عَشَرَ وَكُلَّ قِمَارٍ حَتَّى لَعِبُ الصِّبْيَانِ بِالْجَوْزِ وَاللَّوْزِ وَالْكِعَابِ.

9 وَقَدْ بَلَغَ الأِمَامَ أَبُو الْحَسَنِ مُوسَى بْنَ جَعْفَرٍ (ع) فِي النَّهْيِ عَنِ اللَّعِبِ بِالشِّطْرَنْجِ حَتَّى قَالَ لِرَجُلٍ مِنَ الْبَصْرِيِّينَ وَقَدْ سَأَلَهُ قَائِلاً إِنِّي مَعَ قَوْمٍ يَلْعَبُونَ بِالشِّطْرَنْجِ وَلَسْتُ أَلْعَبُ بِهَاوَ لَكِنْ أَنْظُرُ، فَقَالَ مَالَكَ وَالْمَجْلِسَ لأَيَنْظُرُ اللَّهُ إلى أَهْلِهِ.

LESSON 7

1 إِنَّمَا يَفْتَرِي الْكَذِبَ الَّذِينَ لاَ يُؤْمِنُونَ

2 لأَسْوَأَسْوَءُ مِنَ الْكَذِبِ

3 إِنَّ الْكَذِبَ هُوَ خَرَابُ الاِيْمَانِ

4 لاَيَجِدُ عَبْدٌ حَقِيقَةَ الاِيمَانِ حَتَّى يَدَعَ الْكَذِبَ جِدَّهُ وَهَزْلَهُ

5 سُئِلَ رَسُولُ اللَّهِ (ص): يَكُونُ الْمُؤْمِنُ جَبَاناً؟ قَالَ: نَعَمْ، قِيلَ: وَيَكُونُ بَخِيلاً؟ قَالَ: نَعَمْ، قِيلَ: وَيَكُونُ كَذَّاباً؟ قَالَ: لاَ

6 شَرُّ الرِّوَايَةِ رِوَايَةُ الْكَذِبِ.

7 اِعْتِيَادُ الكِذبِ يُورِثُ الفَقْرَ.

8 أَلَا أُخْبِرُكُم بِأَكْبَرِ الكَبَائِرِ، الإشراكُ بِاللهِ وَعُقُوقُ الوَالِدَينِ وَقَوْلُ الزَورِ، أي الكِذبُ.

9 حُطَّتِ الخَبَائِثُ في بَيتٍ وَجُعِلَ مِفتَاحُهُ الكِذبُ.

10 يا بُنَيّ إِيَّاكَ وَ مُصَادَقَةَ الأحمَقِ فَإِنَّهُ يُريدُ أَنْ يَنْفَعَكَ فَيَضُرَّكَ وَإِيَّاكَ وَ مُصَادَقَةَ البَخيلِ فَإِنَّهُ يَقْعُدُ عَنكَ أَحْوَجَ ما تَكُونُ إِلَيهِ وَإِيَّاكَ وَ مُصَادَقَةَ الفَاجِرِ فَإِنَّهُ يَبيعُكَ بالتَّافِهِ، وَإِيَّاكَ وَ مُصَادَقَةَ الكَذَّابِ فَإِنَّهُ كَالسَّرَابِ يُقَرِّبُ عَلَيكَ البَعِيدَ وَيُبعِدُ عَلَيكَ القَريبَ.

11 لا يَكْذِبُ الكَاذِبُ الآ مِنْ مَهَانَةِ نَفْسِهِ.

12 أَقَلُّ النَّاسِ مُرُوَّةً مَنْ كَانَ كَاذِباً.

13 لَو تَمَيَّزَتِ الأشياءُ لَكَانَ الصِّدقُ مَعَ الشَّجاعَةِ وَكَانَ الجُبْنُ مَعَ الكِذبِ.

14 رَحِمَ اللهُ مَنْ أَعَانَ وَلَدَهُ عَلَى بِرِّهِ قَالَ قُلْتُ كَيفَ يُعِينُهُ عَلَى بِرِّهِ؟ قَالَ يَقْبَلُ مَيْسُورَهُ وَيَتَجَاوَزُ عَنْ مَعسُورِهِ وَلَا يُرْهِقُهُ وَلَا يَخْرُقُ بِهِ.

15 الأفَاضِلُ قَوْا فَإِنَّ مَعَ اللهِ مَعَ الصَّادِقِينَ وَجَانِبُوا الكِذبَ فَإِنَّ الكِذبَ مُجَانِبُ الأيمَانِ، آلَا وَإِنَّ الصَّادِقَ عَلَى شَفَا نَجَاةٍ وَكَرَامَةٍ، آلَا وَإِنَّ الكَاذِبَ عَلَى شَفَا مَخْزَاةٍ وَهَلَكَةٍ.

16 إِيَّاكَ وَالكِذبَ فَإِنَّهُ يُسَوِّدُ الوَجْهَ.

17 أَيُّمَا مُسلِمٍ سُئِلَ عَنْ مُسلِمٍ فَصَدَقَ وَأُدْخِلَ عَلَى ذَلِكَ المُسلِمِ مَضَرَّةٌ كُتِبَ مِنَ الكَاذِبينَ وَمَنْ سُئِلَ عَنْ مُسلِمٍ فَكَذَبَ وَأُدْخِلَ عَلَى ذَلِكَ المُسلِمِ مَنْفَعَةٌ كُتِبَ عِنْدَاللهِ مِنَ الصَّادِقِينَ.

18 وَالكَاظِمِينَ الغَيْظَ وَالعَافِينَ عَنِ النَّاسِ.

19 لَا يُكْذَبُ عَلَى مُصْلِحٍ.

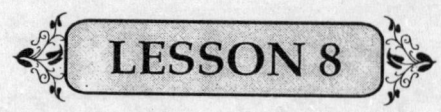

LESSON 8

1. اَوْلَى النَّاسِ بِاللهِ وَبِرَسُولِهِ مَنْ بَدَءَ بِالسَّلَامِ

2. اِنَّ اللهَ عَزَّوَجَلَّ يُحِبُّ اِفْشَاءَ السَّلَامِ

3. لَا تَغْضِبُوا وَلَا تُغْضِبُوا اَفْشُوا السَّلَامَ وَاَطِيبُوا الْكَلَامَ وَصَلُّوا بِاللَّيْلِ وَالنَّاسُ نِيَامٌ، تَدْخُلُوا الْجَنَّةَ بِسَلَامٍ

4. وَالَّذِي نَفْسِي بِيَدِهِ لَا تَدْخُلُونَ الْجَنَّةَ حَتَّى تُؤْمِنُوا وَلَا تُؤْمِنُونَ حَتَّى تَحَابُّوا، اَفَلَا اَدُلُّكُمْ عَلَى عَمَلٍ اِذَا عَمِلْتُمُوهُ تَحَابَبْتُمْ؟ قَالُوا بَلَى يَا رَسُولَ اللهِ قَالَ: اَفْشُوا السَّلَامَ بَيْنَكُمْ

5. مَنْ بَدَءَ بِالْكَلَامِ قَبْلَ السَّلَامِ فَلَا تُجِيبُوهُ

6. اَبْخَلُ النَّاسِ مَنْ بَخِلَ بِالسَّلَامِ

7. تَبَسُّمُ الرَّجُلِ فِي وَجْهِ اَخِيهِ حَسَنَةٌ

8. مَنْ تَبَسَّمَ فِي وَجْهِ اَخِيهِ الْمُؤْمِنِ كَتَبَ اللهُ لَهُ حَسَنَةً

9. اِذَا لَقِيَ اَحَدُكُمْ اَخَاهُ فَلْيُسَلِّمْ وَلْيُصَافِحْهُ

10. تَمَامُ تَحِيَّاتِكُمْ بَيْنَكُمُ الْمُصَافَحَةُ

11. عَنْ اَبِي الْحَسَنِ مُوسَى (ع) قَالَ: اِنَّ اَهْلَ الْاَرْضِ لَمَرْحُومُونَ مَا تَحَابُّوا وَاَدُّوا الْاَمَانَةَ وَعَمِلُوا الْحَقَّ.

12. قَالَ عَلِيٌّ (ع): اَبْلَغُ مَا تَسْتَدِرُّ بِهِ الرَّحْمَةَ اَنْ تُضْمِرَ لِجَمِيعِ النَّاسِ الرَّحْمَةَ

13. وَعَنْهُ عَلَيْهِ السَّلَامُ: اِنَّ اللهَ سُبْحَانَهُ يُحِبُّ اَنْ يَكُونَ نِيَّةُ الْاِنْسَانِ لِلنَّاسِ جَمِيلَةً

14. وَاعْتَصِمُوا بِحَبْلِ اللهِ جَمِيعاً وَلَا تَفَرَّقُوا وَاذْكُرُوا نِعْمَتَ اللهِ عَلَيْكُمْ اِذْ كُنْتُمْ اَعْدَاءً فَاَلَّفَ بَيْنَ قُلُوبِكُمْ فَاَصْبَحْتُمْ بِنِعْمَتِهِ اِخْوَاناً وَكُنْتُمْ عَلَى شَفَا حُفْرَةٍ مِنَ النَّارِ فَاَنْقَذَكُمْ مِنْهَا

15. مَثَلُ الْمُؤْمِنِينَ فِي تَوَادِّهِمْ وَتَرَاحُمِهِمْ وَتَعَاطُفِهِمْ مَثَلُ الْجَسَدِ الْوَاحِدِ اِذَا اشْتَكَى مِنْهُ عُضْوٌ

واحِدٌ تَداعَى لَهُ سايرُ الجَسَدِ بِالسَّهَرِ وَالحُمَّى.

16. إِنَّمَا المُؤمِنُونَ إِخْوَةٌ فَأَصْلِحُوا بَيْنَ أَخَوَيْكُمْ

17. عَنْ أَبِي عَبْدِاللهِ أَنَّ رَسُولَ اللهِ صَلَّى اللهُ عَلَيْهِ وَآلِهِ كَانَ يَقُولُ: إِنَّ لِلَّهِ خَلْقاً عَنْ يَمِينِ العَرْشِ بَيْنَ يَدَيِ اللهِ وَعَنْ يَمِينِ اللهِ وُجُوهُهُمْ أَبْيَضُ مِنَ الثَّلْجِ وَأَضْوَءُ مِنَ الشَّمْسِ الضَّاحِيَةِ. يَسْئَلُ السَّائِلُ مَا هَؤُلَاءِ؟ فَيُقَالُ: هَؤُلَاءِ الَّذِينَ تَحَابُّوا فِي جَلَالِ اللهِ

18. قَالَ رَسُولُ اللهِ (ص): مَنْ سَرَّ مُؤْمِناً فَقَدْ سَرَّنِي

19. قَالَ رَسُولُ اللهِ (ص) إِنَّ أَحَبَّ الأَعْمَالِ إِلَى اللهِ عَزَّوَجَلَّ إِدْخَالُ السُّرُورِ عَلَى المُؤْمِنِينَ

20. قَالَ رَسُولُ اللهِ (ص) مَنْ قَضَى لِأَخِيهِ المُؤْمِنِ حَاجَةً فَكَأَنَّمَا عَبَدَ اللهَ دَهْرَهُ

21. قَالَ أَبُو الحَسَنِ (ع) إِنَّ لِلَّهِ عِبَاداً فِي الأَرْضِ يَسْعَوْنَ فِي حَوَائِجِ النَّاسِ، هُمُ الآمِنُونَ يَوْمَ القِيَامَةِ

22. وَلَا يَغْتَبْ بَعْضُكُمْ بَعْضاً

23. وَقَالَ رَسُولُ اللهِ (ص) يَا مَعْشَرَ مَنْ آمَنَ بِلِسَانِهِ وَلَمْ يُؤْمِنْ بِقَلْبِهِ لَا تَغْتَابُوا المُسْلِمِينَ وَلَا تَتَّبِعُوا عَوْرَاتِهِمْ فَإِنَّ مَنْ تَتَبَّعَ عَوْرَةَ أَخِيهِ يَتَتَبَّعُ اللهُ عَوْرَتَهُ حَتَّى يَفْضَحَهُ فِي جَوْفِ بَيْتِهِ

24. وَقَالَ رَسُولُ اللهِ (ص): مَا عُمِرَ مَجْلِسٌ بِالغِيبَةِ إِلَّا خَرِبَ بِالدِّينِ فَنَزِّهُوا أَسْمَاعَكُمْ مِنِ اسْتِمَاعِ الغِيبَةِ فَإِنَّ القَائِلَ وَالمُسْتَمِعَ شَرِيكَانِ فِي الإِثْمِ

25. المُسْلِمُ مَنْ سَلِمَ المُسْلِمُونَ مِنْ يَدِهِ وَلِسَانِهِ

26. لَا يَحِلُّ لِلْمُسْلِمِ أَنْ يَنْظُرَ إِلَى أَخِيهِ بِنَظْرَةٍ تُؤْذِيهِ

27. مَنْ حَقَرَ مُؤْمِناً مِسْكِيناً أَوْ غَيْرَ مِسْكِينٍ لَمْ يَزَلِ اللهُ عَزَّوَجَلَّ خَاقِراً لَهُ مَاقِتاً، حَتَّى يَرْجِعَ عَنْ مَحْقَرَتِهِ إِيَّاهُ

28. كَفَى بِالمَرْءِ عَيْباً أَنْ يُبْصِرَ مِنَ النَّاسِ مَا يَعْمَى عَنْهُ مِنْ نَفْسِهِ أَوْ يُعَيِّرَ النَّاسَ بِمَا لَا يَسْتَطِيعُ تَرْكَهُ أَوْ يُؤْذِيَ خَلِيلَهُ بِمَا لَا يَعْنِيهِ

29 مَنْ بَحَثَ عَنْ عُيُوبِ النَّاسِ فَلْيَبْدَأْ بِنَفْسِهِ .

30 إِيَّاكَ وَمُعَاشَرَةَ مُبْتَغِي عُيُوبِ النَّاسِ فَإِنَّهُمْ لَمْ يَسْلَمْ مُصَاحِبُهُمْ مِنْهُمْ .

31 يَا أَيُّهَا الَّذِينَ آمَنُوا لَا يَسْخَرْ قَوْمٌ مِنْ قَوْمٍ عَسَى أَنْ يَكُونُوا خَيْراً مِنْهُمْ .

32 باور بكونيد إنّ لله يَوْماً يَخْسَرُ فِيهِ الْمُبْطِلُونَ . يعنى

33 وَأَنْتُمُ الأَعْلَوْنَ إِنْ كُنْتُمْ مُؤْمِنِينَ .

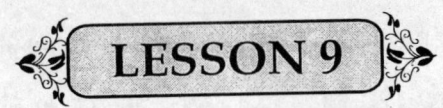

LESSON 9

1 يَا أَيُّهَا النَّاسُ إِنَّا خَلَقْنَاكُمْ مِنْ ذَكَرٍ وَأُنْثَى وَجَعَلْنَاكُمْ شُعُوباً وَقَبَائِلَ لِتَعَارَفُوا إِنَّ أَكْرَمَكُمْ عِنْدَاللهِ أَتْقَاكُمْ .

2 يَرْفَعِ اللهُ الَّذِينَ آمَنُوا مِنْكُمْ وَالَّذِينَ أُوتُوا الْعِلْمَ دَرَجَاتٍ .

3 لَا فَخْرَ لِعَرَبِيٍّ عَلَى عَجَمِيٍّ إِلَّا بِالتَّقْوَى .

4 كَانَ (ص) يُكْرِمُ مَنْ يَدْخُلُ عَلَيْهِ حَتَّى رُبَّمَا بَسَطَ ثَوْبَهُ وَيُؤْثِرُ الدَّاخِلَ بِالْوِسَادَةِ الَّتِي تَحْتَهُ .

5 بُعِثْتُ لِأُتَمِّمَ مَكَارِمَ الْأَخْلَاقِ .

6 قُلْ لِعِبَادِي يَقُولُوا الَّتِي هِيَ أَحْسَنُ .

7 عَظِّمُوا أَصْحَابَكُمْ وَوَقِّرُوهُمْ وَلَا يَتَهَجَّمْ بَعْضُكُمْ عَلَى بَعْضٍ .

8 لَا تُحَقِّرَنَّ أَحَداً مِنَ الْمُسْلِمِينَ فَإِنَّ صَغِيرَهُمْ عِنْدَاللهِ كَبِيرٌ .

9 لَا تُضَيِّعَنَّ حَقَّ أَخِيكَ اتِّكَالاً عَلَى مَا بَيْنَكَ وَبَيْنَهُ فَإِنَّهُ لَيْسَ لَكَ بِأَخٍ مَنْ ضَيَّعْتَ حَقَّهُ .

10 فَبِمَا رَحْمَةٍ مِنَ اللهِ لِنْتَ لَهُمْ وَلَوْ كُنْتَ فَظّاً غَلِيظَ الْقَلْبِ لَانْفَضُّوا مِنْ حَوْلِكَ .

11 سُئِلَ أَبُو عَبْدِاللهِ (ع) مَا حَدُّ حُسْنِ الْخُلُقِ ؟ قَالَ تُلَيِّنُ جَنَاحَكَ وَتُطَيِّبُ كَلَامَكَ وَتَلْقَى أَخَاكَ بِبِشْرٍ حَسَنٍ .

12 اِجْعَلْ نَفْسَكَ مِنْ أَخِيكَ عِنْدَ صَرْمِهِ عَلَى الصِّلَةِ وَعِنْدَ صُدُودِهِ عَلَى اللُّطْفِ وَالْمُقَارَبَةِ وَعِنْدَ جُمُودِهِ عَلَى الْبَذْلِ وَعِنْدَ تَبَاعُدِهِ عَلَى الدُّنُوِّ وَعِنْدَ شِدَّتِهِ عَلَى اللِّينِ وَعِنْدَ جُرْمِهِ عَلَى الْعُذْرِ .

13 قُولَا لَهُ قَوْلاً لَيِّناً لَعَلَّهُ يَتَذَكَّرُ أَوْ يَخْشَى

14 وَالْكَاظِمِينَ الْغَيْظَ وَالْعَافِينَ عَنِ النَّاسِ وَاللهُ يُحِبُّ الْمُحْسِنِينَ

15 وَعِبَادُ الرَّحْمَنِ الَّذِينَ يَمْشُونَ عَلَى الْأَرْضِ هَوْناً وَإِذَا خَاطَبَهُمُ الْجَاهِلُونَ قَالُوا سَلَاماً .

16 أَلَيْسَ فِي جَهَنَّمَ مَثْوًى لِلْمُتَكَبِّرِينَ .

17 وَلَا تُصَعِّرْ خَدَّكَ لِلنَّاسِ وَلَا تَمْشِ فِي الْأَرْضِ مَرَحاً إِنَّ اللهَ لَا يُحِبُّ كُلَّ مُخْتَالٍ فَخُورٍ .

18 مَا مِنْ أَحَدٍ يَتِيهُ الَّا مِنْ ذِلَّةٍ يَجِدُهَا فِي نَفْسِهِ .

19 قَدْ أَفْلَحَ الْمُؤْمِنُونَ. الَّذِينَ هُمْ فِي صَلَاتِهِمْ خَاشِعُونَ. وَالَّذِينَ هُمْ عَنِ اللَّغْوِ مُعْرِضُونَ..... الَّذِينَهُمْ لِأَمَانَاتِهِمْ وَعَهْدِهِمْ رَاعُونَ .

20 وَالْمُوفُونَ بِعَهْدِهِمْ إِذَا عَاهَدُوا .

21 مَنْ عَامَلَ النَّاسَ فَلَمْ يَظْلِمْهُمْ وَحَدَّثَهُمْ فَلَمْ يَكْذِبْهُمْ وَوَعَدَهُمْ فَلَمْ يُخْلِفْهُمْ فَهُوَ مِمَّنْ كَمُلَتْ مُرُوَّتُهُ وَظَهَرَتْ عَدَالَتُهُ وَوَجَبَتْ أُخُوَّتُهُ .

22 ثَلَاثٌ لَمْ يَجْعَلِ اللهُ عَزَّ وَجَلَّ لِأَحَدٍ فِيهِنَّ رُخْصَةً أَدَاءُ الْأَمَانَةِ إِلَى الْبِرِّ وَالْفَاجِرِ وَالْوَفَاءُ بِالْعَهْدِ لِلْبِرِّ وَالْفَاجِرِ وَ بِرُّ الْوَالِدَيْنِ بَرَّيْنِ كَانَا أَوْ فَاجِرَيْنِ .

LESSON 10

1 إِنَّمَا الْمُؤْمِنُونَ إِخْوَةٌ فَأَصْلِحُوا بَيْنَ أَخَوَيْكُمْ وَاتَّقُوا اللهَ لَعَلَّكُمْ تُرْحَمُونَ

2 وَاعْتَصِمُوا بِحَبْلِ اللهِ جَمِيعاً وَلَا تَفَرَّقُوا وَاذْكُرُوا نِعْمَتَ اللهِ عَلَيْكُمْ إِذْ كُنْتُمْ أَعْدَاءً فَأَلَّفَ

بَيْنَ قُلُوبِكُمْ فَأَصْبَحْتُمْ بِنِعْمَتِهِ إِخْوَاناً وَكُنْتُمْ عَلَى شَفَا حُفْرَةٍ مِنَ النَّارِ فَأَنْقَذَكُمْ مِنْها..

3 - وَأَمَّا حَقُّ مَلِيكٍ عَامَّةٍ فَإِضْمَارُ السَّلامَةِ وَنَشْرُ جَنَاحِ الرَّحْمَةِ وَالرِّفْقِ بِمُسِيئِهِمْ وَتَأْلِيفِهِمْ وَاسْتِصْلاحِهِمْ وَشُكْرُ مُحْسِنِيهِمْ..... فَعُمَّهُمْ جَمِيعاً بِدَعْوَتِكَ وَانْصُرْهُمْ جَمِيعاً بِنُصْرَتِكَ وَأَنْزِلْهُمْ جَمِيعاً مِنْكَ مَنَازِلَهُمْ كَبِيرُهُمْ بِمَنْزِلَةِ الْوَالِدِ وَصَغِيرُهُمْ بِمَنْزِلَةِ الْوَلَدِ وَأَوْسَطُهُمْ بِمَنْزِلَةِ الأخ، فَمَنْ أتَاكَ تَعَاهَدْتَهُ بِلُطْفٍ وَرَحْمَةٍ وَصِلْ أخَاكَ بِمَا يَجِبُ لِلأخِ عَلَى أخِيهِ

4 - الْمُسْلِمُ أخُو الْمُسْلِمِ وَهُوَ عَيْنُهُ وَمَرْآتُهُ وَدَلِيلُهُ، لاَيَخُونُهُ وَلاَيَظْلِمُهُ وَلاَيَخْدَعُهُ وَلاَيَكْذِبُهُ وَلاَيَغْتَابُهُ .

5 - .... يَغْفِرُ زَلَّتَهُ وَيَرْحَمُ عَبْرَتَهُ وَيَسْتُرُ عَوْرَتَهُ وَيُقِيلُ عَثْرَتَهُ وَيَقْبَلُ مَعْذِرَتَهُ وَيَرُدُّ غِيبَتَهُ وَيُدِيمُ نَصِيحَتَهُ وَيَحْفَظُ خُلَّتَهُ.......

6 - أحِبَّ لأخِيكَ الْمُسْلِمِ مَاتُحِبُّهُ لِنَفْسِكَ وَإِذَا احْتَجْتَ فَسَلْهُ إِنْ سَأَلَكَ فَأَعْطِهِ لاَتَمَلَّهُ خَيْراً وَلاَيَمَلَّهُ لَكَ، كُنْ لَهُ ظَهْراً، فَإِنَّهُ لَكَ ظَهْرٌ إِذَا غَابَ فَأَحْفَظْهُ فِي غَيْبَتِهِ فَإِذَا شَهِدَ فَزُرْهُ وَأجِلَّهُ وَأَكْرِمْهُ فَإِنَّهُ مِنْكَ وَأَنْتَ مِنْهُ....

7 - تَقَرَّبُوا إِلَى اللهِ تَعَالَى بِمُوَاسَاةِ إِخْوَانِكُمْ.

8 - سَيِّدُ الأعْمَالِ ثَلاثُ خِصَالٍ: إِنْصَافُكَ النَّاسَ مِنْ نَفْسِكَ وَمُوَاسَاةُ الأخِ فِي اللهِ عَزَّ وَجَلَّ، وَذِكْرُكَ اللهَ تَعَالَى عَلَى كُلِّ حَالٍ.

9 - مُوَاسَاةُ الأخِ فِي اللهِ عَزَّ وَجَلَّ تَزِيدُ فِي الرِّزْقِ

10 - مَنْ أَصْبَحَ لاَيَهْتَمُّ بِأُمُورِ الْمُسْلِمِينَ فَلَيْسَ بِمُسْلِمٍ

11 - خِيَارُكُمْ سُمَحَاؤُكُمْ وَشِرَارُكُمْ بُخَلاؤُكُمْ وَمِنْ صَالِحِ الأعْمَالِ الْبِرُّ بِالأخْوَانِ وَالسَّعْيُ فِي حَوَائِجِهِمْ، وَفِي ذَلِكَ مَرْغَمَةٌ لِلشَّيْطَانِ وَتَزَحْزُحٌ عَنِ النِّيرَانِ وَدُخُولُ الْجِنَانِ

12 - وَيُؤْثِرُونَ عَلَى أَنْفُسِهِمْ وَلَوْ كَانَ بِهِمْ خَصَاصَةٌ

13 - آمُرُكَ أنْ تُوَاسِيَ إِخْوَانَكَ الْمُطَابِقِينَ لَكَ عَلَى تَصْدِيقِ مُحَمَّدٍ (ص) وَتَصْدِيقِي

14 اِنَّ مِنْ حَقِّ الْمُؤْمِنِ عَلَى الْمُؤْمِنِ الْمَوَدَّةُ لَهُ فِى صَدْرِهِ وَ الْمُوَاسَاةُ لَهُ فِى مَالِهِ وَالنُّصْرَةُ لَهُ عَلَى مَنْ ظَلَمَهُ.... وَلَا يَظْلِمُهُ وَلَا يَغُشُّهُ وَلَا يَخُونُهُ وَلَا يَخْذُلُهُ وَلَا يَغْتَابُهُ وَلَا يُكَذِّبُهُ...

15 مَا قَضَى مُسْلِمٌ لِمُسْلِمٍ حَاجَةً اِلَّا نَادَاهُ اللهُ تَبَارَكَ وَتَعَالَى عَلَىَّ ثَوَابُكَ وَلَا أَرْضَى لَكَ بِدُونِ الْجَنَّةِ

LESSON 11

1 عَلَيْكُمْ بِالْإِخْوَانِ، فَاِنَّهُمْ عُدَّةٌ فِى الدُّنْيَا وَالْآخِرَةِ

2 مَنْ فَقَدَ أَخًا فِى اللهِ فَكَاَنَّمَا فَقَدَ اَشْرَفَ أَعْضَائِهِ

3 اَلْمَرْءُ عَلَى دِينِ خَلِيلِهِ وَ قَرِينِهِ.

4 لَا تَحْكُمُوا عَلَى رَجُلٍ بِشَىْءٍ، حَتَّى تَنْظُرُوا اِلَى مَنْ يُصَاحِبُ فَاِنَّمَا يُعْرَفُ الرَّجُلُ بِاَشْكَالِهِ وَ أَقْرَانِهِ وَيُنْسَبُ اِلَى أَصْحَابِهِ وَاَخْدَانِهِ.

5 جُمِعَ خَيْرُ الدُّنْيَا وَالْآخِرَةِ فِى كِتْمَانِ السِّرِّ وَمُصَادَقَةِ الْأَخْيَارِ وَجُمِعَ الشَّرُّ فِى الْإِذَاعَةِ وَمُوَاخَاةِ الْأَشْرَارِ

6 اَسْعَدُ النَّاسِ مَنْ خَالَطَ كِرَامَ النَّاسِ

7 يَا بُنَىَّ مَنْ يَصْحَبْ صَاحِبَ السُّوءِ لَا يَسْلَمْ وَمَنْ يَدْخُلْ مَدَاخِلَ السُّوءِ يُتَّهَمْ وَمَنْ لَا يَمْلِكْ لِسَانَهُ يَنْدَمْ.

8 اُنْظُرْ خَمْسَةً فَلَا تُصَاحِبْهُمْ وَلَا تُحَادِّهُمْ وَلَا تُرَافِقْهُمْ فِى طَرِيقٍ. اِيَّاكَ وَمُصَاحَبَةَ الْكَذَّابِ... وَاِيَّاكَ وَمُصَاحَبَةَ الْفَاسِقِ.... وَاِيَّاكَ وَمُصَاحَبَةَ الْبَخِيلِ..... وَاِيَّاكَ وَمُصَاحَبَةَ الْأَحْمَقِ..... وَاِيَّاكَ وَمُصَاحَبَةَ الْقَاطِعِ لِرَحِمِهِ....

9 اِيَّاكَ وَمَوَاطِنَ التُّهْمَةِ وَالْمَجْلِسَ الْمَظْنُونَ بِهِ السُّوءَ فَاِنَّ قَرِينَ السُّوءِ يُغَيِّرُ جَلِيسَهُ

10 اَلإِخْوانُ ثَلثَةٌ فَواحِدٌ كَالغَذاءِ الَّذي يُحْتاجُ إِلَيْهِ كُلَّ وَقْتٍ فَهُوَ العاقِلُ، والثاني في مَعْنى الدّاءِ وَهُوَ الأَحْمَقُ، والثّالِثُ في مَعْنى الدَّواءِ فَهُوَ اللَّبيبُ

11
وَلا خَيْرَ في وُدِّ امْرِئٍ مُتَلَوِّنٍ
إِذا الرِّيحُ مالَتْ، مالَ حَيْثُ تَميلُ
جَوادٍ إِذا اسْتَغْنَيْتَ عَنْ أَخْذِ مالِهِ
وَعِنْدَ احْتِمالِ الفَقْرِ عَنْكَ بَخيلُ
فَما أَكْثَرَ الإِخْوانَ حينَ تَعُدُّهُمْ
وَلكِنَّهُمْ في النّائِباتِ قَليلُ

12 اِحْذَرْ مِنَ النّاسِ ثَلاثَةَ الخائِنِ والظَّلومِ والنَّمّامِ لِأَنَّ مَنْ خانَ لَكَ خانَكَ وَمَنْ ظَلَمَ لَكَ سَيَظْلِمُكَ وَمَنْ نَمَّ إِلَيْكَ سَيَنِمُّ عَلَيْكَ

13 مَنِ اتَّخَذَ أَخاً بَعْدَ حُسْنِ الإِخْتِبارِ دامَتْ صُحْبَتُهُ وَتَأَكَّدَتْ مَوَدَّتُهُ.

14 فَلْيَكُنْ جُلَساؤُكَ الأَبْرارَ وَإِخْوانُكَ الأَتْقِياءَ والزُّهّادَ لِأَنَّ اللهَ تَعالى قالَ في كِتابِهِ الأَخِلّاءُ يَوْمَئِذٍ بَعْضُهُمْ لِبَعْضٍ عَدُوٌّ إِلّا المُتَّقينَ.

اَلصِّداقَةُ مَحْدودَةٌ وَمَنْ لَمْ تَكُنْ فيهِ تِلْكَ الحُدودُ فَلا تَنْسِبْهُ إِلى كَمالِ الصِّداقَةِ...... أَوَّلُها

15 أَنْ تَكُونَ سَريرَتُهُ وَعَلانِيَتُهُ لَكَ واحِدَةً والثّانِيَةُ أَنْ يَرى زَيْنَكَ زَيْنَهُ وَشَيْنَكَ شَيْنَهُ، والثّالِثَةُ لا يُغَيِّرُهُ عَلَيْكَ مالٌ وَلا وِلايَةٌ، والرّابِعَةُ أَنْ لا يَمْنَعَكَ شَيْئاً مِمّا تَصِلُ إِلَيْهِ مَقْدِرَتُهُ، والخامِسَةُ أَنْ لا يُسَلِّمَكَ عِنْدَ النَّكَباتِ

16 مَنْ غَضِبَ عَلَيْكَ مِنْ إِخْوانِكَ ثَلاثَ مَرّاتٍ فَلَمْ يَقُلْ فيكَ شَرّاً فاتَّخِذْهُ لِنَفْسِكَ صَديقاً

17 لا يَكُونُ الصَّديقُ صَديقاً حَتّى يَحْفَظَ أَخاهُ في ثَلاثٍ في نَكْبَتِهِ وَغَيْبَتِهِ وَوَفاتِهِ.

18 أَحِبَّ حَبيبَكَ هَوْناً ما، عَسى أَنْ يَكُونَ بَغيضَكَ يَوْماً ما وَأَبْغِضْ بَغيضَكَ هَوْناً ما عَسى أَنْ يَكُونَ حَبيبَكَ يَوْماً ما

19 اِبْذِلْ لِصَديقِكَ كُلَّ المَوَدَّةِ وَلا تَبْذِلْ لَهُ كُلَّ الطُّمَأْنينَةِ وَأَعْطِهِ كُلَّ المُواساةِ وَلا تُفِضْ

اِلَيْهِ بِكُلِّ الأَسْرارِ

20 أَعْجَزُ النّاسِ مَنْ عَجَزَ عَنِ اكْتِسابِ الإِخْوانِ وَأَعْجَزُ مِنْهُ مَنْ ضَيَّعَ مَنْ ظَفَرَ بِهِ مِنْهُمْ.

21 مَنْ أَطاعَ الواشِيَ، ضَيَّعَ الصَّديقَ

22 اِقْبَلْ عُذْرَ أَخيكَ وَاِنْ لَمْ يَكُنْ لَهُ عُذْرٌ فَالْتَمِسْ لَهُ عُذْراً

LESSON 12

1 اَلنَّظافَةُ مِنَ الإيمانِ   اِنَّ اللهَ يُحِبُّ التَّوّابينَ وَيُحِبُّ الْمُتَطَهِّرينَ

2 نِعْمَ الْبَيْتُ الْحَمّامُ يُذَكِّرُ فيهِ النّارَ وَيَذْهَبُ بِالدَّرَنِ

3 كانَ رَسولُ اللهِ (ص) يَحُثُّ أُمَّتَهُ عَلَى النَّظافَةِ وَيَأْمُرُهُمْ بِها

4 اَلنَّظافَةُ مِنَ الإيمانِ وَالإيمانُ فِى الْجَنَّةِ .

5 اَلطُّهْرُ نِصْفُ الإيمانِ

6 مَنِ اتَّخَذَ ثَوْباً فَلْيُنَظِّفْهُ

7 لَيْسَ مِنْ لِباسِكُمْ شَيْئٌ أَحْسَنُ مِنَ الْبَياضِ فَالْبِسوهُ

8 نِقاءُ الثَّوْبِ يَكْبِتُ الْعَدُوَّ وَغَسْلُ الثِّيابِ يُذْهِبُ الْهَمَّ وَالْحُزْنَ

9 اِكْنِسوا أَفْنِيَتَكُمْ وَلاَ تَشَبَّهوا بِالْيَهودِ

10 تَرْكُ نَسْجِ الْعَنْكَبوتِ فِى الْبَيْتِ يورِثُ الْفَقْرَ .... وَتَرْكُ الْقُمامَةِ فِى الْبَيْتِ يورِثُ الْفَقْرَ...

11 عِشْرونَ خَصْلَةً تورِثُ الْفَقْرَ... وَ وَضْعُ الْقِصاعِ وَالأَوانى غَيْرَ مَغْسولَةٍ وَ تَرْكُ بُيوتِ الْعَنْكَبوتِ وَ وَضْعُ أَوانى الْماءِ غَيْرَ مُغَطّاةِ الرُّؤوسِ...

12 لاَتُبيتُوا الْقُمامَةَ فى بُيوتِكُمْ فَإِنَّها مَقْعَدُ الشَّيْطانِ

13 اِنْ اسْتَتَرَ وَ اَخْفى مايُسَلَّطُ الشَّيْطانُ مِنِ ابْنِ آدَمَ أَنْ صارَ يَسْكُنُ تَحْتَ الأَظافيرِ

14 لايَطولَنَّ أَحَدُكُمْ شَعْرَ إِبْطَيْهِ فَإِنَّ الشَّيْطانَ يَتَّخِذُهُ مَخْبَأً يَسْتَتِرُ بِهِ

15 لاَتُؤْوُوا مِنْديلَ الْغَمْرِ فِى الْبَيْتِ فَإِنَّهُ مَرْبَضُ الشَّيْطانِ

16 لَايُكَلِّمُ الرَّجُلَ مَجذُوماً اِلَّا اَنْ تَكُونَ بَيْنَهُما قَدْرُ رُمْحٍ

17 قالَ اَمِيرُالمُومِنِينَ (ع): لَاتَضُرَّ بَوْلَ الْماءَ مِنْ ثُلْمَةِ الْاِناءِ وَلَا مِنْ عُرْوَتِهِ فَاِنَّ الشَّيْطانَ يَقْعُدُ عَلَى الْعُرْوَةِ وَالثُّلْمَةِ

18 مَنْ غَسَلَ يَدَهُ قَبْلَ الطَّعامِ وَبَعْدَهُ عاشَ فِى سَعَةٍ وَ عُوفِىَ مِنْ بَلْوىً فِى جَسَدِهِ

19 عَنْ مَزارِمٍ قالَ رَاَيْتُ اَبَالْحَسَنِ (ع) اِذا تَوَضَّاَ

20 قَبْلَ الطَّعامِ لَمْ يَمَسِّ الْمِنْدِيلَ وَاِذا تَوَضَّاَ بَعْدَ الطَّعامِ مَسَّ الْمِنْدِيلَ

21 تَخَلَّلُوا عَلَى اَثَرِ الطَّعامِ فَاِنَّهُ مُصِحَّةٌ لِلْفَمِ وَالنَّواجِذِ

22 لَايَزْدَرِدَنَّ اَحَدُكُمْ ما يَتَخَلَّلُ بِهِ فَاِنَّ مِنْهُ يَكُونُ الدُّبَيْلَةُ

23 مَنْ اَكَلَ فَما تَخَلَّلَ فَلا يَاْكُلْ

24 اَلسِّواكُ مِنْ سُنَنِ الْمُرْسَلِينَ

25 لَوْلا اَنْ اَشُقَّ عَلَى اُمَّتِى لَاَمَرْتُهُمْ بِالسِّواكِ مَعَ كُلِّ صَلوةٍ

26 اِسْنا كُوا عَرْضاً وَلاتَسْتَنُّوا طُولاً

27 عَلَى كُلِّ مِنْخَرٍ مِنَ الدَّوابِّ شَيْطانٌ

28 لِيُبالِغْ اَحَدُكُمْ فِى الْمَضْمَضَةِ وَالْاِسْتِنْشاقِ فَاِنَّهُ غُفْرانٌ لِما تَكَلَّمَ بِهِ الْعَبْدُ وَمُنَفِّرَةٌ لِلشَّيْطانِ

29 اَلْمَضْمَضَةُ وَالْاِسْتِنْشاقُ سُنَّةٌ وَطَهُورٌ لِلْفَمِ وَالْاَنْفِ

30 اِنَّ اللهَ يُحِبُّ التَّوَّابِينَ وَيُحِبُّ الْمُتَطَهِّرِينَ

31 اِنَّ اللهَ يحبّ التوّابين و يحبّ المتطهرين

LESSON 13

1 اَلْعادَةُ طَبْعٌ ثانٍ

2 لَعَنَ اللهُ الآمِرينَ بِالْمَعْرُوفِ، التارِكينَ لَهُ وَ الناهينَ عَنِ الْمُنْكَرِ، الْعامِلينَ بِهِ

3 كُونُوا دُعاةَ النّاسِ إِلَى اللهِ بِغَيْرِ أَلْسِنَتِكُمْ

4 لَقَدْ مَنَّ اللهُ عَلَى الْمُؤْمِنينَ إِذْ بَعَثَ فيهِمْ رَسُولاً مِنْ أَنْفُسِهِمْ يَتْلُوا عَلَيْهِمْ آياتِهِ وَيُزَكّيهِمْ وَيُعَلِّمُهُمُ الْكِتابَ وَ الْحِكْمَةَ.........

5 يا أَيُّهَا الَّذينَ آمَنُوا اسْتَجيبُوا لِلّهِ وَلِلرَّسُولِ إِذا دَعاكُمْ لِما يُحْييكُمْ

6 أَدِّبُوا أَوْلادَكُمْ بِغَيْرِ آدابِكُمْ فَإِنَّهُمْ خُلِقُوا لِغَيْرِ زَمانِكُمْ

LESSON 14

1 اَلشَّقِيُّ مَنْ شَقِيَ فِي بَطْنِ أُمِّهِ وَالسَّعيدُ مَنْ سَعِدَ فِي بَطْنِ أُمِّهِ.

2 اِخْتارُوا لِنُطَفِكُمْ.

3 إِيّاكُمْ وَخَضْراءَ الدِّمَنِ، قيلَ يا رَسُولَ اللهِ وَما خَضْراءُ الدِّمَنِ؟ قالَ: اَلْمَرْأَةُ الْحَسْناءُ في مَنْبِتِ السَّوْءِ.

4 نِساؤُكُمْ حَرْثٌ لَكُمْ

5 إِيّاكُمْ وَتَزْويجَ الْحَمْقاءِ فَإِنَّ صُحْبَتَها بَلاءٌ وَ وَلَدَها ضَياعٌ.

6 تَوَقَّوْا عَلَى أَوْلادِكُمْ مِنْ لَبَنِ الْبَغِيَّةِ وَالْمَجْنُونَةِ فَإِنَّ اللَّبَنَ يُعْدي.

7 وَإِنَّما قَلْبُ الْحَدَثِ كَالْأَرْضِ الْخالِيَةِ ما أُلْقِيَ فيها مِنْ شَيْءٍ قَبِلَتْهُ فَبادَرْتُكَ بِالْأَدَبِ قَبْلَ أَنْ يَقْسُوَ قَلْبُكَ وَيَشْتَغِلَ لُبُّكَ.

8 أَلا وَإِنَّ الدَّعِيَّ ابْنَ الدَّعِيِّ قَدْ رَكَزَ بَيْنَ اثْنَتَيْنِ بَيْنَ السِّلَّةِ وَالذِّلَّةِ وَهَيْهاتَ مِنَّا الذِّلَّةُ يَأْبَى اللهُ ذَلِكَ لَنا وَرَسُولُهُ وَالْمُؤْمِنُونَ وَحُجُورٌ طابَتْ وَطَهُرَتْ وَأُنُوفٌ حَمِيَّةٌ وَنُفُوسٌ أَبِيَّةٌ مِنْ أَنْ نُؤْثِرَ طاعَةَ اللِّئامِ عَلَى مَصارِعِ الْكِرامِ.

9 وَقَدْ عَلِمْتُمْ مَوْضِعي مِنْ رَسُولِ اللهِ بِالْقَرابَةِ الْقَريبَةِ وَالْمَنْزِلَةِ الْخَصيصَةِ، رَضَعَني

في حِجرِه وَأَنَا وَليدٌ يُضمّني اِلى صَدرِه ويُكنِفُني في فِراشِه ويُمِسّني جَسَدَه ويُشِمّني عَرفَه.

10 وَأَمّا حَقّ وَلَدِكَ فَأَن تَعلَمَ أَنّهُ مِنكَ ومُضافٌ اِلَيكَ في عاجِلِ الدُّنيا بِخَيرِه وَشَرِّه وَأَنَّكَ مَسؤولٌ عَمّا وُلّيتَهُ بِه مِن حُسنِ الأَدَبِ والدَّلالَةِ عَلى رَبِّه عَزَّ وَجَلَّ والمَعونَةِ لَهُ عَلى طاعَتِه فَاعمَل في أَمرِه عَمَلَ مَن يَعلَمُ أَنَّهُ مُثابٌ عَلَى الاِحسانِ اِلَيه مُعاقَبٌ عَلَى الاِسائَةِ

11 أَحِبّوا الصِّبيانَ وَارحَموهُم وَاِذا وَعَدتُموهُم فَفوا لَهُم فَاِنَّهُم لا يَرَونَ اِلاّ اَنَّكُم اَلبَيَّ تَرزُقونَهُم.

12 لا يَصلُحُ الكِذبُ جِدٌّ وَلا هَزلٌ وَلا اَن يَعِدَ اَحَدُكُم صَبيَّهُ ثُمَّ لا يَفِيَ لَهُ.

13 لا تَضرِبهُ واهجُرهُ وَلا تُطِل.

14 اِنَّكُم صِغارُ قَومٍ ويوشِكُ اَن تَكونوا كِبارَ قَومٍ آخَرينَ، فَتَعَلَّموا العِلمَ فَمَن لَم يَستَطِع اَن يَحفَظَهُ فَليَكتُبهُ وَليَضَعهُ في بَيتِه.

15 اَكرِموا اَولادَكُم واَحسِنوا آدابَكُم.

16 اَخَذَ مِنّي رَسولُ اللهِ حُسَيناً اَيّامَ رِضاعِه فَحَمَلَه فَاَراقَ ماءً عَلى ثَوبِه فَاَخَذتُهُ بِعُنفٍ حَتّى بَكى فَقالَ صَلَّى اللهُ عَلَيهِ وَآلِه: مَهلاً يا اُمَّ الفَضلِ اِنَّ هذِهِ الاِراقَةَ الماءُ يُطَهِّرُها فَاَيُّ شَيءٍ يُزيلُ هذا الغُبارَ عَن قَلبِ الحُسَينِ؟.

17 اَلتَّلَطُّفُ بِالصِّبيانِ مِن عادَةِ الرَّسولِ.

18 وَكانَ صَلَّى اللهُ عَلَيهِ وَآلِه يَقدُمُ مِنَ السَّفَرِ فَيَتَلَقّاهُ الصِّبيانُ فَيَقِفُ لَهُم ثُمَّ يَأمُرُ بِهِم فَيُرفَعونَ اِلَيه فَيَرفَعُ مِنهُم بَينَ يَدَيهِ وَمِن خَلفِه وَيَأمُرُ اَصحابَهُ اَن يَحمِلوا بَعضَهُم فَرُبَّما يَتَفاخَرُ الصِّبيانُ بَعدَ ذلِك.

19 شَرُّ الآباءِ مَن دَعاهُ البِرُّ اِلَى الاِفراطِ وَشَرُّ الاَبناءِ مَن دَعاهُ التَّقصيرُ اِلَى العُقوقِ.

20 وَيْلٌ لِاَوْلَادِ آخِرِ الزَّمَانِ مِنْ آبَائِهِمْ، فَقِيلَ يَا رَسُولَ اللهِ مِنْ آبَائِهِمُ الْمُشْرِكِينَ؟ فَقَالَ: لَا، مِنْ آبَائِهِمُ الْمُؤْمِنِينَ لَا يُعَلِّمُونَهُمْ شَيْئاً مِنَ الْفَرَائِضِ وَاِذَا تَعَلَّمُوا اَوْلَادُهُمْ مَنَعُوهُمْ وَرَضُوا عَنْهُمْ بِعَرَضٍ يَسِيرٍ مِنَ الدُّنْيَا فَاَنَا مِنْهُمْ بَرِىءٌ وَهُمْ مِنِّى بُرَآءُ.

21 اَيْنَ يَقَعُ مَا قَدَّمْتُهُ مِمَّا قَدْ اَعْطَى؟

22 بَادِرُوا اَوْلَادَكُمْ بِالْحَدِيثِ قَبْلَ اَنْ يَسْبِقَكُمْ اِلَيْهِمُ الْمُرْجِئَةُ.

23 فَيَقُولَانِ رَبَّنَا اَنَّى لَنَا هَذِهِ وَلَمْ تَبْلُغْهَا اَعْمَالُنَا؟.

24 فَيُقَالُ هَذِهِ بِتَعْلِيمِكُمَا وَلَدَكُمَا الْقُرْآنَ وَتَبْصِيرِكُمَا اِيَّاهُ بِدِينِ الْاِسْلَامِ وَبِرِيَاضَتِكُمَا اِيَّاهُ عَلَى حُبِّ مُحَمَّدٍ رَسُولِ اللهِ وَعَلِىٍّ وَلِىِّ اللهِ صَلَوَاتُ اللهِ عَلَيْهِمَا وَتَفَقُّهِكُمَا اِيَّاهُ بِفِقْهِهِمَا.

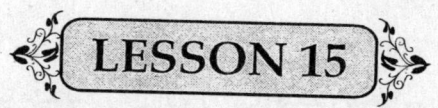

LESSON 15

1 عَنِ الصَّادِقِ عَلَيْهِ السَّلَامُ: قَالَ: مَا قَضَى مُسْلِمٌ لِمُسْلِمٍ حَاجَةً اِلَّا نَادَاهُ اللهُ عَزَّ وَجَلَّ عَلَى ثَوَابِكَ وَلَا اَرْضَى لَكَ بِدُونِ الْجَنَّةِ.

2 وَقَالَ رَسُولُ اللهِ صَلَّى اللهُ عَلَيْهِ وَآلِهِ: مَنْ اَجْرَى اللهُ عَلَى يَدِهِ فَرَجاً لِمُسْلِمٍ فَرَّجَ اللهُ عَنْهُ كُرَبَ الدُّنْيَا وَالْآخِرَةِ.

3 وَقَالَ اَبُو جَعْفَرٍ عَلَيْهِ السَّلَامُ: مَنْ اَقْرَضَ قَرْضاً اِلَى مَيْسَرَةٍ كَانَ مَالُهُ فِى زَكَوةٍ وَكَانَ هُوَ فِى صَلَوةٍ مِنَ الْمَلَائِكَةِ عَلَيْهِ حَتَّى يَقْضِيَهُ.

4 لَا خَيْرَ فِى كَثِيرٍ مِنْ نَجْوَيْهِمْ اِلَّا مَنْ اَمَرَ بِصَدَقَةٍ اَوْ مَعْرُوفٍ اَوْ اِصْلَاحٍ بَيْنَ النَّاسِ.

5 قَالَ الصَّادِقُ عَلَيْهِ السَّلَامُ: مَنْ اَقْرَضَ قَرْضاً وَضَرَبَ لَهُ اَجَلاً فَلَمْ يُؤْتَ بِهِ عِنْدَ ذَلِكَ الْاَجَلِ كَانَ لَهُ مِنَ الثَّوَابِ فِى كُلِّ يَوْمٍ يَتَاَخَّرُ عَنْ ذَلِكَ الْاَجَلِ بِمِثْلِ صَدَقَةِ دِينَارٍ وَاحِدٍ فِى كُلِّ يَوْمٍ.

6 - وَقَالَ النَّبِيُّ (ص) أَلْفُ دِرْهَمٍ أُقْرِضُهَا مَرَّتَيْنِ أَحَبُّ إِلَيَّ مِنْ أَنْ أَتَصَدَّقَ بِهَا مَرَّةً

7 - اَلَّذِينَ يَأْكُلُونَ الرِّبَا لَا يَقُومُونَ إِلَّا كَمَا يَقُومُ الَّذِى يَتَخَبَّطُهُ الشَّيْطَانُ مِنَ الْمَسِّ

8 - يَا أَيُّهَا الَّذِينَ آمَنُوا اتَّقُوا اللهَ وَذَرُوا مَا بَقِيَ مِنَ الرِّبَا إِنْ كُنْتُمْ مُؤْمِنِينَ فَإِنْ لَمْ تَفْعَلُوا فَأْذَنُوا بِحَرْبٍ مِنَ اللهِ وَرَسُولِهِ وَإِنْ تُبْتُمْ فَلَكُمْ رُؤُوسُ أَمْوَالِكُمْ لَا تَظْلِمُونَ وَلَا تُظْلَمُونَ وَإِنْ كَانَ ذُو عُسْرَةٍ فَنَظِرَةٌ إِلَى مَيْسَرَةٍ وَأَنْ تَصَدَّقُوا خَيْرٌ لَكُمْ إِنْ كُنْتُمْ تَعْلَمُونَ

9 - يَا أَيُّهَا الَّذِينَ آمَنُوا لَا تَأْكُلُوا أَمْوَالَكُمْ بَيْنَكُمْ بِالْبَاطِلِ إِلَّا أَنْ تَكُونَ تِجَارَةً عَنْ تَرَاضٍ مِنْكُمْ...

10 - فَبِظُلْمٍ مِنَ الَّذِينَ هَادُوا حَرَّمْنَا عَلَيْهِمْ طَيِّبَاتٍ أُحِلَّتْ لَهُمْ وَبِصَدِّهِمْ عَنْ سَبِيلِ اللهِ كَثِيرًا وَأَخْذِهِمُ الرِّبَا وَقَدْ نُهُوا عَنْهُ وَأَكْلِهِمْ أَمْوَالَ النَّاسِ بِالْبَاطِلِ وَأَعْتَدْنَا لِلْكَافِرِينَ مِنْهُمْ عَذَابًا أَلِيمًا

11 - عَنْ أَبِى عَبْدِاللهِ عَلَيْهِ السَّلَامُ الرِّبَا رِبَاآنِ، أَحَدُهُمَا رِبًا حَلَالٌ وَالْآخَرُ حَرَامٌ......

12 - عَنْ أَبِى جَعْفَرٍ عَلَيْهِ السَّلَامُ أَنَّهُ سُئِلَ عَنِ الرَّجُلِ يَكُونُ لَهُ عَلَى الرَّجُلِ الدَّرَاهِمُ أَوِ الْمَالُ فَيُهْدَى إِلَيْهِ الْهَدِيَّةُ قَالَ لَا بَأْسَ بِهَا

13 - قَالَ رَسُولُ اللهِ (ص) مَنْ مَطَلَ عَلَى ذِى حَقٍّ حَقَّهُ وَهُوَ يَقْدِرُ عَلَى أَدَاءِ حَقِّهِ فَعَلَيْهِ كُلَّ يَوْمٍ خَطِيئَةُ عَشَّارٍ

14 - عَنْ أَبِى عَبْدِاللهِ عَلَيْهِ السَّلَامُ: مَنِ اسْتَدَانَ دَيْنًا فَلَمْ يَنْوِ قَضَاءَهُ كَانَ بِمَنْزِلَةِ السَّارِقِ

15 - عَنْ أَبِى عَبْدِاللهِ عَلَيْهِ السَّلَامُ: أَيُّمَا رَجُلٍ أَتَى رَجُلًا فَاسْتَقْرَضَ مِنْهُ مَالًا وَفِى نِيَّتِهِ أَنْ لَا يُؤَدِّيَهُ فَذَلِكَ اللِّصُّ الْعَادِى

16 - عَنْ أَبِى جَعْفَرٍ عَلَيْهِ السَّلَامُ قَالَ كُلُّ ذَنْبٍ يُكَفِّرُهُ الْقَتْلُ فِى سَبِيلِ اللهِ إِلَّا الدَّيْنَ لَا كَفَّارَةَ لَهُ إِلَّا أَدَاؤُهُ أَوْ يَقْضِى صَاحِبُهُ أَوْ يَعْفُوَ الَّذِى لَهُ الْحَقُّ

17 - عَنْ أَبِى جَعْفَرٍ عَلَيْهِ السَّلَامُ قَالَ أَوَّلُ قَطْرَةٍ مِنْ دَمِ الشَّهِيدِ كَفَّارَةٌ لِذُنُوبِهِ إِلَّا الدَّيْنَ فَإِنَّ كَفَّارَتَهُ

قَضاؤُهُ

18 عَنْ أَبِي ثُمامَةَ قالَ قُلْتُ لِأَبِي جَعْفَرٍ الثّاني عَلَيْهِ السَّلامُ إِنّي أُرِيدُ أَنْ أَلْزَمَ مَكَّةَ وَالمَدينَةَ وَعَلَيَّ دَيْنٌ فَقالَ ارْجِعْ إِلى مُؤَدّى دَيْنِكَ، وَانْظُرْ أَنْ تَلْقى اللهَ وَلَيْسَ عَلَيْكَ دَيْنٌ، فَإِنَّ المُؤْمِنَ لا يَخُونُ

19 عَنْ عَلِيٍّ عَلَيْهِ السَّلامُ قالَ سَمِعْتُ رَسُولَ اللهِ (ص) يَقُولُ مَطْلُ المُسْلِمِ المُوسِرِ ظُلْمٌ لِلمُسْلِمين

20 عَنْ أَبِي جَعْفَرٍ عَلَيْهِ السَّلامُ قالَ الظُّلْمُ ثَلاثَةٌ: ظُلْمٌ يَغْفِرُهُ اللهُ عَزَّ وَجَلَّ وَظُلْمٌ لا يَغْفِرُهُ اللهُ عَزَّ وَجَلَّ وَظُلْمٌ لا يَدَعُهُ، فَأَمَّا الظُّلْمُ الَّذي لا يَغْفِرُهُ اللهُ فَالشِّرْكُ بِاللهِ وَأَمَّا الظُّلْمُ الَّذي يَغْفِرُهُ اللهُ فَظُلْمُ الرَّجُلِ نَفْسَهُ فيما بَيْنَهُ وَبَيْنَ اللهِ وَأَمَّا الظُّلْمُ الَّذي لا يَدَعُهُ فَالمُداينَةُ بَيْنَ العِبادِ

21 قالَ رَسُولُ اللهِ (ص) أَوَّلُ شَيْءٍ يُبْدَءُ بِهِ مِنَ المالِ الكَفَنُ، ثُمَّ الدَّيْنُ، ثُمَّ الوَصِيَّةُ، ثُمَّ المِيراثُ

22 كَما لا يَحِلُّ لِغَريمِكَ أَنْ يَمْطُلَكَ وَهُوَ مُوسِرٌ فَكَذلِكَ لا يَحِلُّ لَكَ أَنْ تُعْسِرَهُ إِذا عَلِمْتَ أَنَّهُ مُعْسِرٌ

23 لا تُباعُ الدّارُ وَلا الجارِيَةُ فِي الدَّيْنِ وَ ذلِكَ أَنَّهُ لا بُدَّ لِلرَّجُلِ مِنْ ظِلٍّ يَسْكُنُهُ

24 لا يُخْرَجُ الرَّجُلُ مِنْ مَسْقَطِ رَأْسِهِ بِالدَّيْنِ.

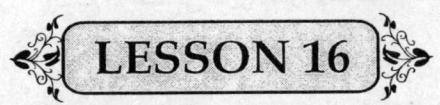

1 كَذَّبُوا بِآياتِ رَبِّهِمْ فَأَهْلَكْناهُمْ بِذُنُوبِهِمْ

2 ذلِكَ بِأَنَّ اللهَ لَمْ يَكُ مُغَيِّراً نِعْمَةً أَنْعَمَها عَلى قَوْمٍ حَتّى يُغَيِّرُوا ما بِأَنْفُسِهِمْ

3 إِنَّ اللهَ قَضى قَضاءً حَتْماً أَلّا يُنْعِمَ عَلَى العَبْدِ بِنِعْمَةٍ فَيَسْلُبَها إِيّاهُ حَتّى يُحْدِثَ العَبْدُ ذَنْباً

يَسْتَحِقُّ بِذلِكَ النِّقْمَةَ

4- عَنْ اَبِيعَبْدِاللهِ عَلَيْهِ السَّلامُ اِنَّ الذَّنْبَ يَحْرِمُ الْعَبْدَ الرِّزْقَ

5- كُلَّما اَحْدَثَ الْعِبادُ مِنَ الذُّنُوبِ مالَمْ يَكُونُوا يَعْمَلُونَ اَحْدَثَ اللهُ لَهُمْ مِنَ الْبَلاءِ مالَمْ يَكُونُوا يَعْرِفُونَ

6- وَ اَيْمُ اللهِ ما كانَ قَوْمٌ قَطُّ فى غَضِّ نِعْمَةٍ فى عَيْشٍ فَزالَ عَنْهُمْ اِلاّ بِذُنُوبٍ اجْتَرَحُوها لِاَنَّ اللهَ لَيْسَ بِظَلّامٍ لِلْعَبيدِ

7- قُلْ سيرُوا فِى الْاَرْضِ فَانْظُرُوا كَيْفَ كانَ عاقِبَةُ الْمُجْرِمينَ

8- اَوَلَمْ يَسيرُ وا فِى الْاَرْضِ فَيَنْظُرُ واكَيْفَ كانَ عاقِبَةُ الَّذينَ مِنْ قَبْلِهِمْ كانُوا اَشَدَّ مِنْهُمْ قُوَّةً وَ اَثارُوا فِى الْاَرْضِ فَاَخَذَهُمُ اللهُ بِذُنُوبِهِمْ وَ ماكانَ لَهُمْ مِنَ اللهِ مِنْ واقٍ

9- عَسى اَنْ تَكْرَهُوا شَيْئاً وَهُوَ خَيْرٌ لَكُمْ وَعَسى اَنْ تُحِبُّوا شَيْئاً وَهُوَ شَرٌّ لَكُمْ وَاللهُ يَعْلَمُ وَاَنْتُمْ لاتَعْلَمُونَ

10- اَلَمْ يَأْنِ لِلَّذينَ آمَنُوا اَنْ تَخْشَعَ قُلُوبُهُمْ لِذِكْرِ اللهِ

11- تَعاوَنُوا عَلَى الْبِرِّ وَالتَّقْوى وَلاتَعاوَنُوا عَلَى الْاِثْمِ وَالْعُدْوانِ

12- يا اَيُّهَا الَّذينَ آمَنُوا اجْتَنِبُوا كَثيراً مِنَ الظَّنِّ اِنَّ بَعْضَ الظَّنِّ اِثْمٌ وَلا تَجَسَّسُوا

13- اِنَّ الَّذينَ يُحِبُّونَ اَنْ تَشيعَ الْفاحِشَةُ فِى الَّذينَ آمَنُوا لَهُمْ عَذابٌ اَليمٌ فِى الدُّنْيا وَالْآخِرَةِ

14- وَ قالَ رَسُولُ اللهِ (ص) مَنْ اَذاعَ فاحِشَةً كانَ كَمُبْتَدِيها

15- وَ قالَ الصّادِقُ عَلَيْهِ السَّلامُ مَنِ اطَّلَعَ مِنْ مُؤْمِنٍ عَلى ذَنْبٍ اَوْ سَيِّئَةٍ فَاَفْشى ذلِكَ عَلَيْهِ وَلَمْ يَكْتُمْها وَلَمْ يَسْتَغْفِرِ اللهَ لَهُ كانَ عِنْدَاللهِ كَعامِلِها

16- كُنْتُمْ خَيْرَ اُمَّةٍ اُخْرِجَتْ لِلنّاسِ تَأْمُرُونَ بِالْمَعْرُوفِ وَ تَنْهَوْنَ عَنِ الْمُنْكَرِ...

17- يا بُنَىَّ اَقِمِ الصَّلوةَ وَاْمُرْ بِالْمَعْرُوفِ وَانْهَ عَنِ الْمُنْكَرِ وَاصْبِرْ عَلى ما اَصابَكَ اِنَّ ذلِكَ مِنْ عَزْمِ الْاُمُورِ

13 وَقَالَ رَسُولُ الله لَايَزَالُ النَّاسُ (أُمَّتِي) بِخَيْرٍ مَا أَمَرُوا بِالمَعْرُوفِ وَنَهَوْا عَنِ المُنْكَرِ وَتَعَاوَنُوا عَلَى البِرِّ فَإِذَا لَمْ يَفْعَلُوا ذَلِكَ نُزِعَتْ مِنْهُمُ البَرَكَاتُ وَسُلِّطَ بَعْضُهُمْ عَلَى بَعْضٍ وَلَمْ يَكُنْ نَاصِرٌ فِى الأَرْضِ وَلَا فِى السَّمَاءِ

19 لَاتَتْرُكُوا الأَمْرَ بِالمَعْرُوفِ وَ النَّهْىَ عَنِ المُنْكَرِ فَيُوَلَّى عَلَيْكُمْ شِرَارُكُمْ ثُمَّ تَدْعُونَ فَلَايُسْتَجَابُ لَكُمْ

20 وَلَوْ تَرَى إِذَا المُجْرِمُونَ نَاكِسُوا رُؤُسِهِمْ عِنْدَ رَبِّهِمْ رَبَّنَا أَبْصَرْنَا وَسَمِعْنَا فَارْجِعْنَا نَعْمَلْ صَالِحاً إِنَّا مُوقِنُونَ

21 يَوَدُّ المُجْرِمُ لَوْ يَفْتَدِى مِنْ عَذَابِ يَوْمَئِذٍ بِبَنِيهِ وَصَاحِبَتِهِ وَأَخِيهِ وَفَصِيلَتِهِ الَّتِى تُؤْوِيهِ وَمَنْ فِى الأَرْضِ جَمِيعاً ثُمَّ يُنْجِيهِ، كَلَّا إِنَّهَا لَظَى، نَزَّاعَةً لِلشَّوَى

LESSON 17
LESSON – 17

1 يَا أَيُّهَا النَّاسُ إِنَّا خَلَقْنَاكُمْ مِنْ ذَكَرٍ وَأُنْثَى وَجَعَلْنَاكُمْ شُعُوباً وَقَبَائِلَ لِتَعَارَفُوا إِنَّ أَكْرَمَكُمْ عِنْدَ اللهِ أَتْقَاكُمْ

2 اَلرِّجَالُ قَوَّامُونَ عَلَى النِّسَاءِ بِمَا فَضَّلَ اللهُ بَعْضَهُمْ عَلَى بَعْضٍ وَبِمَا أَنْفَقُوا مِنْ أَمْوَالِهِمْ

3 كُلُّ نَفْسٍ مِنْ بَنِى آدَمَ سَيِّدٌ فَالرَّجُلُ سَيِّدُ أَهْلِهِ وَالمَرْأَةُ سَيِّدَةُ بَيْتِهَا.

4 وَقَالَ النَّبِىُّ (ص) كُلُّكُمْ رَاعٍ وَكُلُّكُمْ مَسْؤُولٌ فَالإِمَامُ رَاعٍ وَهُوَ مَسْؤُولٌ وَالرَّجُلُ رَاعٍ عَلَى أَهْلِهِ وَهُوَ مَسْؤُولٌ وَالمَرْأَةُ رَاعِيَةٌ عَلَى بَيْتِ زَوْجِهَا وَعَلَى وَلَدِهِ فَكُلُّكُمْ مَسْؤُولٌ عَنْ رَعِيَّتِهِ

5 عَاشِرُوهُنَّ بِالمَعْرُوفِ.

6 وَقَالَ الصَّادِقُ عَلَيْهِ السَّلَامُ: رَحِمَ اللهُ عَبْداً أَحْسَنَ فِيمَا بَيْنَهُ وَبَيْنَ زَوْجَتِهِ

7 وَقَالَ رَسُولُ اللهِ (ص) خَيْرُكُمْ خَيْرُكُمْ لِأَهْلِهِ وَأَنَا خَيْرُكُمْ لِأَهْلِى

8 وَقَالَ رَسُولُ اللهِ (ص) مَلْعُونٌ مَلْعُونٌ مَنْ ضَيَّعَ مَنْ يَعُولُ

9 عَنْ أَبِي إِبْرَاهِيمَ عَلَيْهِ السَّلَامُ قَالَ : جِهَادُ الْمَرْأَةِ حُسْنُ التَّبَعُّلِ.

10 وَقَالَ رَسُولُ اللهِ (ص) فِي حَدِيثٍ: وَمَنِ اتَّخَذَ زَوْجَةً فَلْيُكْرِمْها.

11 لَا يَنْبَغِي لِلْمَرْأَةِ أَنْ تُعَطِّلَ نَفْسَها وَلَوْ أَنْ تُعَلِّقَ فِي عُنُقِها قِلَادَةً....

12 اَلْقَوْلُ الْحَسَنُ يُثْرِى الْمَالَ وَيُنْمِى الرِّزْقَ وَيُنْسِى فِى الْأَجَلِ وَيُحَبِّبُ إِلَى الْأَهْلِ وَيُدْخِلُ الْجَنَّةَ

LESSON 18

1 قَالَ عِيسَى بْنُ مَرْيَمَ يَا مَعْشَرَ الْحَوَارِيِّينَ لِي إِلَيْكُمْ حَاجَةٌ اقْضُوهَا لِي قَالُوا قُضِيَتْ حَاجَتُكَ يَا رُوحَ اللهِ فَقَامَ فَغَسَلَ أَقْدَامَهُمْ فَقَالُوا كُنَّا نَحْنُ أَحَقَّ بِهَذَا يَا رُوحَ اللهِ فَقَالَ إِنَّ أَحَقَّ النَّاسِ بِالْخِدْمَةِ الْعَالِمُ إِنَّمَا تَوَاضَعْتُ هَكَذَا لِكَيْمَا تَتَوَاضَعُوا بَعْدِى فِى النَّاسِ كَتَوَاضُعِى لَكُمْ

2 سَلُونِى قَبْلَ أَنْ تَفْقِدُونِى.

3 قَالَ عَلِيٌّ عَلَيْهِ السَّلَامُ: مَنْ نَصَبَ نَفْسَهُ لِلنَّاسِ إِمَامًا فَعَلَيْهِ أَنْ يَبْدَأَ بِتَعْلِيمِ نَفْسِهِ قَبْلَ تَعْلِيمِ غَيْرِهِ وَلْيَكُنْ تَأْدِيبُهُ بِسِيرَتِهِ قَبْلَ تَأْدِيبِهِ بِلِسَانِهِ وَمُعَلِّمُ نَفْسِهِ وَمُؤَدِّبُها أَحَقُّ بِالْإِجْلَالِ مِنْ مُعَلِّمِ النَّاسِ وَمُؤَدِّبِهِمْ

4 عَنْ عَلِيِّ بْنِ الْحُسَيْنِ عَلَيْهِ السَّلَامُ: وَحَقُّ سَائِسِكَ بِالْعِلْمِ التَّعْظِيمُ لَهُ وَالتَّوْقِيرُ لِمَجْلِسِهِ وَحُسْنُ الِاسْتِمَاعِ إِلَيْهِ وَالْإِقْبَالِ عَلَيْهِ وَأَنْ لَا تَرْفَعَ عَلَيْهِ صَوْتَكَ وَلَا تُجِيبَ أَحَدًا يَسْأَلُهُ عَنْ شَيْءٍ حَتَّى يَكُونَ هُوَ الَّذِى يُجِيبُ وَلَا تُحَدِّثْ فِى مَجْلِسِهِ أَحَدًا....

5 وَرُوِىَ عَنِ النَّبِيِّ (ص) أَنَّهُ قَالَ مَنْ عَلَّمَ مُسْلِمًا مَسْأَلَةً فَقَدْ مَلَكَ رَقَبَتَهُ. فَقِيلَ لَهُ يَا رَسُولَ

الله اَبَيبيعُهُ؟ قالَ لأوْلكِنْ يَأمُرُهُ وَيَنْهاهُ.

6 - عَنْ عَلَىٍّ عَلَيْهِ السَّلامُ قالَ: إِنَّ مِنْ حَقِّ المُعَلِّمِ عَلَى المُتَعَلِّمِ أَنْ لا يُكْثِرَ السُّؤالَ عَلَيْهِ وَلا يَسْبِقَهُ فى الجَوابِ وَلا يُلِحَّ عَلَيْهِ إذا أَعْرَضَ وَلا يَأْخُذَ بِثَوْبِهِ إذا كَسِلَ وَلا يُشيرَ إِلَيْهِ بِيَدِهِ وَلا يَغْمِزَهُ بِعَيْنِهِ......

7 - وَقالَ رَسُولُ اللهِ (ص): إِنَّ مُعَلِّمَ الخَيْرِ يَسْتَغْفِرُ لَهُ دَوابُّ الأَرْضِ وَحيتانُ البَحْرِ وَكُلُّ ذى رُوحٍ فى الهَواءِ وَجَميعُ أَهْلِ السَّماءِ وَالأَرْضِ

8 - وَقالَ عَلَىٌّ عَلَيْهِ السَّلامُ: ثَلاثٌ لا يَسْتَحْيى مِنْهُنَّ أَحَدٌ خِدْمَةُ الرَّجُلِ ضَيْفَهُ وَقِيامُهُ عَنْ مَجْلِسِهِ لأَبيهِ وَمُعَلِّمِهِ وَطَلَبُ الحَقِّ وَإِنْ قَلَّ

9 - وَقالَ الصّادِقُ عَلَيْهِ السَّلامُ: مَنْ عَلَّمَ خَيْراً فَلَهُ بِمِثْلِ أَجْرِ مَنْ عَمِلَ بِهِ قُلْتُ فَإِنْ عَلَّمَهُ غَيْرَهُ يَجْرى ذلِكَ لَهُ قالَ إِنْ عَلَّمَهُ النّاسَ كُلَّهُمْ جَرى لَهُ قُلْتُ فَإِنْ ماتَ؟ قالَ وَإِنْ ماتَ.

10 - بُعِثْتُ لاُتَمِّمَ مَكارِمَ الأَخْلاقِ.

11 - هُوَ الَّذى بَعَثَ فى الأُمِّيِّينَ رَسُولاً مِنْهُمْ يَتْلُوا عَلَيْهِمْ آياتِهِ وَيُزَكّيهِمْ وَيُعَلِّمُهُمُ الكِتابَ وَالحِكْمَةَ.....

12 - إِنَّ أَغْنى الغِنى العَقْلُ وَأَكْبَرُ الفَقْرِ الحُمْقُ وَأَوْحَشُ الوَحْشَةِ العُجْبُ وَأَكْرَمُ الحَسَبِ حُسْنُ الخُلْقِ.

13 - عَنِ النَّبىِّ (ص) قالَ أَرْبَعٌ تَلْزَمُ كُلَّ ذى حِجىً مِنْ أُمَّتى وَما هُنَّ قيلَ يا رَسُولَ اللهِ؟ قالَ اسْتِماعُ العِلْمِ وَحِفْظُهُ وَالعَمَلُ بِهِ وَنَشْرُهُ

14 - عَنِ النَّبىِّ (ص) ما تَصَدَّقَ النّاسُ بِصَدَقَةٍ مِثْلَ عِلْمٍ يُنْشَرُ

15 - وَقالَ صَلَّى اللهُ عَلَيْهِ وَآلِهِ: ما أَهْدى المَرْءُ المُسْلِمُ عَلى أَخيهِ هَدِيَّةً أَفْضَلَ مِنْ كَلِمَةِ حِكْمَةٍ يَزيدُهُ اللهُ بِها هُدىً وَيَرُدُّهُ عَنْ رَدىً

16 - وَقالَ أَميرُ المُؤْمِنينَ (ع) شُكْرُ العالِمِ عَلى عِلْمِهِ أَنْ يَبْذُلَهُ لِمَنْ يَسْتَحِقُّهُ

17 عَنْ أَبِيعَبْدِ اللهِ عَلَيْهِ السَّلَامُ: قَالَ اِذَا كَانَ يَوْمُ الْقِيَامَةِ بَعَثَ اللهُ عَزَّوَجَلَّ الْعَالِمَ وَالْعَابِدَ فَاِذَا وَقَفَا بَيْنَ يَدَي اللهِ عَزَّوَجَلَّ قِيلَ لِلْعَابِدِ اِنْطَلِقْ اِلَى الْجَنَّةِ وَقِيلَ لِلْعَالِمِ قِفْ تَشْفَعْ لِلنَّاسِ بِحُسْنِ تَأْدِيبِكَ لَهُمْ.

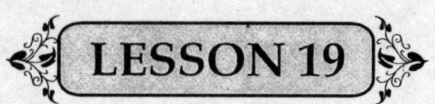

LESSON 19

1 اِنَّ اللهَ يَأْمُرُكُمْ أَنْ تُؤَدُّوا الْأَمَانَاتِ اِلَى أَهْلِهَا...

2 قَدْ أَفْلَحَ الْمُؤْمِنُونَ الَّذِينَ هُمْ فِي صَلَوَاتِهِمْ خَاشِعُونَ .... وَالَّذِينَ هُمْ لِأَمَانَاتِهِمْ وَعَهْدِهِمْ رَاعُونَ....

3 ...وَ أُوصِيكَ بِتَقْوَى اللهِ وَصِدْقِ الْحَدِيثِ وَ وَفَاءِ بِالْعَهْدِ وَ أَدَاءِ الْأَمَانَةِ وَ تَرْكِ الْخِيَانَةِ...

4 وَ قَالَ رَسُولُ اللهِ صَلَّى اللهُ عَلَيْهِ وَ آلِهِ: لَيْسَ مِنَّا مَنْ أَخْلَفَ الْأَمَانَةَ لَيْسَ مِنَّا مَنْ يُحْقِرُ الْأَمَانَةَ وَلَيْسَ مِنَّا مَنْ خَانَ مُسْلِماً فِي أَهْلِهِ وَ مَالِهِ

5 وَ قَالَ الْبَاقِرُ (ع): عَلَيْكُمْ بِالْوَرَعِ وَ الْاِجْتِهَادِ وَصِدْقِ الْحَدِيثِ وَأَدَاءِ الْأَمَانَةِ اِلَى مَنْ اِئْتَمَنَكُمْ عَلَيْهَا بَرّاً كَانَ أَوْفَاجِراً فَلَوْ أَنَّ قَاتِلَ عَلِيِّ بْنِ أَبِيطَالِبٍ (ع) اِئْتَمَنَنِي عَلَى أَمَانَةٍ لَأَدَّيْتُهَا اِلَيْهِ

6 أَلَا اُوصِيكَ؟ قُلْتُ بَلَى جُعِلْتُ فِدَاكَ. قَالَ عَلَيْكَ بِصِدْقِ الْحَدِيثِ وَ أَدَاءِ الْأَمَانَةِ تُشْرِكِ النَّاسَ فِي أَمْوَالِهِمْ...

7 وَ قَالَ رَسُولُ اللهِ (ص) مَنْ خَانَ أَمَانَةً فِي الدُّنْيَا وَ لَمْ يَرُدَّهَا اِلَى أَهْلِهَا ثُمَّ أَدْرَكَهُ الْمَوْتُ مَاتَ عَلَى غَيْرِ مِلَّتِي وَ يَلْقَى اللهَ وَ هُوَ عَلَيْهِ غَضْبَانٌ

8 وَ قَالَ النَّبِيُّ (ص): وَ مَنِ اشْتَرَى خِيَانَةً وَ هُوَ يَعْلَمُ أَنَّهَا خِيَانَةٌ فَهُوَ كَمَنْ خَانَهَا فِي عَارِهَا وَ اِثْمِهَا، وَ مَنِ اشْتَرَى سَرِقَةً وَ هُوَ يَعْلَمُ أَنَّهَا سَرِقَةٌ فَهُوَ كَمَنْ سَرَقَهَا فِي عَارِهَا وَ اِنَّهَا

9- أَرْبَعَةٌ لَا تَدْخُلُ وَاحِدَةٌ مِنْهُنَّ بَيْتاً إِلَّا خَرِبَ وَلَمْ يَعْمُرْ بِالْبَرَكَةِ: ٱلْخِيَانَةُ وَالسَّرِقَةُ وَشُرْبُ الْخَمْرِ وَالزِّنَا

10- وَقَالَ رَسُولُ اللهِ (ص): اَلْأَمَانَةُ تَجْلِبُ الْغِنَى وَالْخِيَانَةُ تَجْلِبُ الْفَقْرَ

11- عَنْ أَبِيعَبْدِاللهِ عَلَيْهِ السَّلَامُ قَالَ: ثَلَثَةٌ لَا بُدَّ مِنْ أَدَائِهِنَّ عَلَى كُلِّ حَالٍ، الْأَمَانَةُ إِلَى الْبَرِّ وَالْفَاجِرِ وَالْوَفَاءُ بِالْعَهْدِ إِلَى الْبَرِّ وَالْفَاجِرِ وَبِرُّالْوَالِدَيْنِ بَرَّيْنِ كَانَا أَوْ فَاجِرَيْنِ

12- يَا كُمَيْلُ اِعْلَمْ وَافْهَمْ إِنَّا لَا نُرَخِّصُ فِي تَرْكِ أَدَاءِ الْأَمَانَاتِ لِأَحَدٍ مِنَ الْخَلْقِ فَمَنْ رَوَى عَنِّي فِي ذَلِكَ رُخْصَةً فَقَدْ أَبْطَلَ وَأَئِمَ وَجَزَاؤُهُ النَّارُ بِمَا كَذِبَ، أَقْسَمْتُ لَقَدْ سَمِعْتُ رَسُولَ اللهِ (ص) يَقُولُ لِي قَبْلَ وَفَاتِهِ بِسَاعَةٍ مِرَاراً تَلَتاً يَا أَبَا الْحَسَنِ أَدِّ الْأَمَانَةَ إِلَى الْبَرِّ وَالْفَاجِرِ فِيمَا قَلَّ وَجَلَّ حَتَّى فِي الْخَيْطِ وَالْمَخِيطِ

13- أَدُّوا الْأَمَانَاتِ إِلَى أَهْلِهَا وَلَوْ كَانُوا مَجُوساً

14- سَأَلْتُ أَبَا الْحَسَنِ (ع) عَنْ رَجُلٍ اسْتَوْدَعَ رَجُلاً مِنْ مَوَالِيكَ مَالاً لَهُ قِيمَةٌ وَالرَّجُلُ الَّذِي عَلَيْهِ الْمَالُ رَجُلٌ مِنَ الْعَرَبِ...

15- وَقَالَ الصَّادِقُ (ع): اِتَّقُوا اللهَ وَعَلَيْكُمْ بِأَدَاءِ الْأَمَانَةِ فَلَوْ أَنَّ قَاتِلَ عَلِيٍّ (ع) اِئْتَمَنَنِي عَلَى الْأَمَانَةِ لَأَدَّيْتُهَا إِلَيْهِ

16- عَنْ مُوسَى بْنِ جَعْفَرٍ (ع): قَالَ رَسُولُ اللهِ (ص): لَا إِيمَانَ لِمَنْ لَا أَمَانَةَ لَهُ

17- وَقَالَ الصَّادِقُ (ع): ثَلَاثٌ مَنْ كُنَّ فِيهِ فَهُوَ مُنَافِقٌ وَإِنْ صَامَ وَصَلَّى: مَنْ إِذَا حَدَّثَ كَذِبَ وَإِذَا وَعَدَ أَخْلَفَ وَإِذَا ائْتُمِنَ خَانَ

18- وَقَالَ أَمِيرُ الْمُؤْمِنِينَ (ع): الْخِيَانَةُ رَأْسُ النِّفَاقِ. الْخِيَانَةُ دَلِيلٌ عَلَى قِلَّةِ الْوَرَعِ وَعَدَمِ الدِّيَانَةِ

19- وَقَالَ عَلِيٌّ (ع): إِيَّاكَ وَالْخِيَانَةَ فَإِنَّهَا شَرُّ مَعْصِيَةٍ وَإِنَّ الْخَائِنَ لَمُعَذَّبٌ بِالنَّارِ عَلَى خِيَانَتِهِ

20 مَنِ ائْتَمَنَكَ بِأَمانَةٍ فَأَدِّها اِلَيْهِ وَ مَنْ خانَكَ فَلاتَخُنْهُ

21 وَ قالَ رَسُولُ اللهِ (ص) لا تَخُنْ مَنْ خانَكَ فَتَكُونَ مِثْلَهُ

22 لا يَكُونُ الأَمينُ أميناً حَتّى يُؤْتَمَنَ عَلى ثَلاثَةٍ فَيُؤَدّيها: عَلَى الأَمْوالِ وَ الأَسْرارِ وَ الفُرُوج
وَاِنْ حَفِظَ اثْنَتَيْنِ وَضَيَّعَ واحِدَةً فَلَيْسَ بِأَمين

23 اَلْمَجالِسُ بِالأَمانَةِ

24 اَلمَجالِسُ بِالأَمانَةِ وَ لَيْسَ لِأَحَدٍ أَنْ يُحَدِّثَ بِحَديثٍ يَكْتُمُهُ صاحِبُهُ اِلّا بِاِذْنِهِ اِلّا أَنْ يَكُونَ
ثِقَةً اَوْذِكْراً لَهُ بِخَيْر

LESSON 20

1 لَوْ يَعْلَمُ العَبْدُ مالَهُ فى حُسْنِ الخُلْقِ لَعَلِمَ أَنَّهُ يَحْتاجُ أَنْ يَكُونَ لَهُ حُسْنُ الخُلْق

2 اِنَّ حَسَنَ الخُلْقِ ذَهَبَ بِخَيْرِ الدُّنْيا وَ الأخِرَة

3 لا عَيْشَ أَهْنَأُ مِنْ حُسْنِ الخُلْق

4 مَنْ ساءَ خُلْقُهُ عَذَّبَ نَفْسَهُ

5 وَقالَ عَلِىٌّ عليه السَّلام: حُسْنُ الخُلْقِ خَيْرُ رَفيق

6 اِنَّكَ لَعَلى خُلُقٍ عَظيم

7 فَبِما رَحْمَةٍ مِنَ اللهِ لِنْتَ لَهُمْ وَ لَوْ كُنْتَ فَظّاً غَليظَ القَلْبِ لاَنْفَضُّوا مِنْ حَوْلِكَ

8 بُعِثْتُ لِأُتَمِّمَ مَكارِمَ الأَخْلاق

9 لَقَدْ كانَ لَكُمْ فى رَسُولِ اللهِ أُسْوَةٌ حَسَنَة

10 قيلَ لِرَسُولِ اللهِ (ص): اِنَّ فُلانَةً تَصُومُ النَّهارَ وَ تَقُومُ اللَّيْلَ وَ هِىَ سَيِّئَةُ الخُلْقِ تُؤْذى
جيرانَها بِلِسانِها، فَقالَ: لاخَيْرَ فيها، هِىَ مِنْ أَهْلِ النّار

11 - و قال الصّادق (ع) لیس منّا من لم یملک نفسه عند الغضب و لم یحسن صحبة من صاحبه و مرافقة من رافقه

12 - و قال رسول الله (ص): علیکم بحسن الخلق فإنّ حسن الخلق فی الجنّة لا محالة و ایّاکم و سوء الخلق فإنّ سوء الخلق فی النّار لا محالة

13 - و قال الصّادق علیه السّلام: صنایع المعروف و حسن البشر یکسبان المحبّة و یدخلان الجنّة و البخل و عبوس الوجه یبعدان من الله و یدخلان النّار

14 - و قال رسول الله (ص): إنّ أحبّکم إلیّ و أقربکم منّی یوم القیامة مجلساً أحسنکم خلقاً و أشدّکم تواضعاً

15 - و قال رسول الله (ص): أکثر ما تلج به أمّتی الجنّة، تقوی الله و حسن الخلق

16 - فی سعة الأخلاق کنوز الأرزاق

17 - و قال علیّ علیه السّلام کفی بالقناعة ملکاً و بحسن الخلق نعیماً

18 - یا بنیّ إن عیمک ما تصل به قرابتک و تفضّل به علی إخوانک فلا یبعدمنّک حسن الخلق و بسط البشر فإنّ من أحسن خلقه أحبّه الأخیار و جانبه الکفّار

19 - و قال رسول الله (ص): إنّکم لن تسعوا النّاس بأموالکم فسعوهم بأخلاقکم

20 - قال رسول الله (ص): أفضل النّاس ایماناً أحسنهم خلقاً

21 - و قال الصّادق علیه السّلام: أربع من کنّ فیه کمل ایمانه و إن کان من قرنه إلی قدمیه ذنوب لم ینقصه ذلک، قال و هو الصّدق و أداء الأمانة و الحیاء و حسن الخلق

22 - و قال الصّادق علیه السّلام: إنّ حسن الخلق یبلغ بصاحبه درجة الصّائم القائم

23 - و قال رسول الله (ص): ما یوضع فی میزان امرء یوم القیامة أفضل من حسن الخلق

24 - ما من ذنب الاّ و له توبة و ما من تائب الاّ و قد تسلّم له توبته ما خلا سیّیء الخلق لا یکاد یتوب من ذنب الاّ وقع فی آخر منه

25 و قالَ النّبيُّ (ص): سوءُ الخُلُقِ يُفسِدُ العَمَلَ كَما يُفسِدُ الخَلُّ العَسَلَ

26 سُئِلَ أميرُ المؤمنينَ (ع) مَنْ أَكرَمُ النّاسِ غِنىً؟ قالَ أَحسَنُهُم خُلُقاً

27 أتى رَجُلٌ رَسولَ اللهِ (ص) فَقالَ يا رَسولَ اللهِ أوصِني، فَكانَ فيما أَوصَلَهُ أنْ قالَ:
القَ أخاكَ بِوَجهٍ مُنبَسِطٍ

28 و قالَ الصّادِقُ (ع) البِرُّ وَ حُسنُ الخُلُقِ يَعمُرانِ الدّيارَ وَ يَزيدانِ في الأَعمارِ فَقيلَ لَهُ ماحَدُّ
حُسنِ الخُلُقِ؟ قالَ تُلَيِّنُ جانِبَكَ وَ تُطيِّبُ كَلامَكَ وَ تَلقى أخاكَ بِبِشرٍ حَسَنٍ

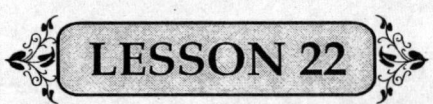

LESSON 22

1 قَدْ أَفْلَحَ المُؤْمِنونَ الّذينَ هُمْ في صَلوتِهِمْ خاشِعونَ... وَ الَّذينَهُمْ لِاماناتِهِمْ وَ عَهدِهِمْ راعُونَ

2 وَ أَوْفوا بِالعَهدِ إنَّ العَهدَ كانَ مَسْؤولاً

3 لا دينَ لِمَنْ لا عَهدَ لَهُ

4 وَ قالَ رَسولُ اللهِ (ص) مَنْ كانَ يُؤمِنُ بِاللهِ وَ اليَومِ الآخِرِ فَليَفِ إذا وَعَدَ

5 وَ قالَ رَسولُ اللهِ (ص) أقرَبُكُم مِنّي غَداً في المَوقِفِ أصدَقُكُم في الحَديثِ وَ أَدّاكُم
لِلأمانةِ وَ أَوفاكُم بِالعَهدِ وَ أَحسَنُكُم خُلُقاً وَ أَقرَبُكُم مِنَ النّاسِ

6 مَنْ عامَلَ النّاسَ فَلَم يَظلِمهُم وَ حَدَّثَهُم فَلَم يَكذِبهُم وَ وَعَدَهُم فَلَم يُخلِفهُم فَهُوَ مِمَّنْ كَمُلَتْ
مُرُوَّتُهُ وَ ظَهَرَت عَدالَتُهُ وَ وَجَبَت أُخُوَّتُهُ وَ حَرُمَت غيبَتُهُ

7 إذاً لا تَأخُذُ مالَكَ مِنّي، لَبِسَ مِثلى يُتَّحَفُ بِنِعْمَتِهِ

8 إنَّ اللهَ لا يُخلِفُ الميعادَ

9 قالَ الصّادِقُ (ع) ثَلاثٌ لَمْ يَجعَلِ اللهُ لِأَحَدٍ مِنَ النّاسِ فيهِنَّ رُخصَةً، بِرُّ الوالِدَينِ

كَانَا أَوْ فَاجِرَيْنِ وَ وَفَاهُ بِالْعَهْدِ بِالْبَرِّ وَالْفَاجِرِ وَ أَدَاءُ الْأَمَانَةِ إِلَى الْبَرِّ وَالْفَاجِرِ

10 إِنَّا أَهْلَ بَيْتٍ نَرَى مَا وَعَدْنَا عَلَيْنَا دَيْنَاً كَمَا صَنَعَ رَسُولُ اللهِ صَلَى اللهُ عَلَيْهِ وَآلِهِ

11 عِدَةُ الْمُؤْمِنِ نَذْرٌ لَا كَفَّارَةَ لَهُ

12 وَإِنْ عَقَدْتَ بَيْنَكَ وَبَيْنَ عَدُوِّكَ عُقْدَةً أَوْ أَلْبَسْتَهُ مِنْكَ ذِمَّةً فَحُطْ عَهْدَكَ بِالْوَفَاءِ ذِمَّتَكَ بِالْأَمَانَةِ.

13 قَالَهُ لَيْسَ مِنْ فَرَائِضِ اللهِ شَيْءٌ النَّاسُ أَشَدُّ عَلَيْهِ اجْتِمَاعًا مَعَ تَفَرُّقِ أَهْوَائِهِمْ، آرَائِهِمْ مِنْ تَعْظِيمِ الْوَفَاءِ بِالْعُهُودِ.

14 وَقَالَ أَمِيرُ الْمُؤْمِنِينَ عَلَيْهِ السَّلَامُ: لَا تَعِدْنَا تَعْجِزُ عَنِ الْوَفَاءِ بِهِ. لَأَنْ تَضْمَنَ مَالًا عَلَى الْوَفَاءِ بِهِ

15 لَا تَعِدَنَّ عِدَةً لَا تَثِقُ مِنْ نَفْسِكَ بِإِنْجَازِهَا.

16 قَالَ رَسُولُ اللهِ صَلَى اللهُ عَلَيْهِ وَآلِهِ. أَحِبُّوا الصِّبْيَانَ وَارْحَمُوهُمْ وَإِذَا وَعَدْتُمُوهُمْ فَإِنَّهُمْ لَا يَرَوْنَ إِلَّا أَنَّكُمْ تَرْزُقُونَهُمْ

17 عَنْ عَلِيٍّ عَلَيْهِ السَّلَامُ: لَا يَصْلُحُ الْكَذِبُ جِدٌّ وَلَا هَزْلٌ وَ لَا أَنْ يَعِدَ أَحَدُكُمْ صَبِيَّهُ ثُمَّ لَا لَهُ

18 وَقَالَ رَسُولُ اللهِ صَلَى اللهُ عَلَيْهِ وَآلِهِ: إِذَا وَعَدَ أَحَدُكُمْ صَبِيَّهُ فَلْيُنْجِزْ لَهُ

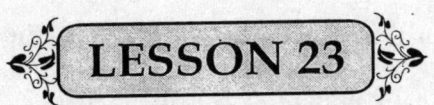

LESSON 23

1 وَكَذَلِكَ جَعَلْنَاكُمْ أُمَّةً وَسَطًا....

2 قَالَ تَعَالَى: وَإِنَّكَ لَعَلَى خُلُقٍ عَظِيمٍ. إِعْلَمْ وَفَّقَكَ اللَّهُ تَعَالَى أَنَّ الْأَخْلَاقَ الْحَ وَالْآدَابَ الشَّرِيفَةَ الَّتِي اتَّفَقَ جَمِيعُ الْعُقَلَاءِ عَلَى تَفْضِيلِ صَاحِبِهَا وَتَعْظِيمِ الْ

بالخُلُقِ الواحدِ منها فضلاً عنها قَدْ هِيَ المُسَمَّاةُ بِحُسْنِ الخُلُقِ، وَهُوَ الأَعْتِدَالُ فِى النَّفْسِ وَأوْصافِها وَالتَّوَسُّطِ فِيها دُونَ الْمَيْلِ إلَى مُنْحَرِفِ أَطْرَافِها...

3 قالَ عَلِىُّ عَلَيْهِ السَّلامُ: لَقَدْ عُلِّقَ بِنِياطِ هَذَا الإنْسَانِ بِضْعَةٌ هِىَ أَعْجَبُ ما فيهِ وَذَلِكَ الْقَلْبُ وَلَهُ مَوادٌ مِنَ الحِكْمَةِ وَأَضْدادٌ مِنْ خِلافِها فَإنْ سَنَحَ لَهُ الرَّجاءُ أَذَلَّهُ الطَّمَعُ وَأَنْ هَاجَ بِهِ الطَّمَعُ أَهْلَكَهُ الحِرْصُ...

4 قالَ عَلِىٌّ عَلَيْهِ السَّلامُ: لَوْ كُنَّا لا نَرْجُو جَنَّةً وَلا نَخْشَى نَاراً وَلا ثَوَاباً وَلا عِقاباً لَكَانَ يَنْبَغِى لَنا أنْ نُطَالِبَ بِمَكَارِمِ الأَخْلاقِ فَإنَّها مِمَّا تَدُلُّ عَلَى سَبِيلِ النَّجَاحِ

5 فَقَالَ (ص): يا عُثْمانُ لَمْ يُرْسِلْنِى اللهُ تَعالى بِالرَّهْبَانِيَّةِ وَلَكِنْ بَعَثَنِى بِالحَنِيفِيَّةِ السَّهْلَةِ السَّمْحَةِ أصُومُ وَأُصَلِّى وَألْمِسُ أهْلِى فَمَنْ أَحَبَّ فِطْرَتِى فَلْيَسْتَنَّ بِسُنَّتِى وَمِنْ سُنَّتِى النِّكاحُ

6 قَالَ رَسُولُ اللهِ (ص): إنَّ هَذَا الدِّينَ مَتِينٌ فَأَوْغِلُوا فِيهِ بِرِفْقٍ وَلا تُكَرِّهُوا عِبادَةَ اللهِ إلَى عِبادِ اللهِ فَتَكُونُوا كَالرَّاكِبِ الْمُنْبَتِّ الَّذِى لا سَفَراً قَطَعَ وَلا ظَهْراً أبْقَى

7 عَنْ أبِى عَبْدِ اللهِ عَلَيْهِ السَّلامُ: لا تُكَرِّهُوا إلَى أنْفُسِكُمُ الْعِبَادَةَ

8 فِى وَصِيَّةِ أَمِيرِ الْمُؤْمِنِينَ عِنْدَ وَفاتِهِ: واقْتَصِدْ يا بُنَىَّ فِى مَعِيشَتِكَ واقْتَصِدْ فِى عِبَادَتِكَ وَعَلَيْكَ فِيها بِالأَمْرِ الدَّائِمِ الَّذِى تُطِيقُهُ

9 وَقَالَ أبُو جَعْفَرٍ لِأبِى عَبْدِ اللهِ (ع): يا بُنَىَّ عَلَيْكَ بِالحَسَنَةِ بَيْنَ السَّيِّئَتَيْنِ...

10 قالَ أَمِيرُ الْمُؤْمِنِينَ عَلَيْهِ السَّلامُ: لا يُرَى الجاهِلُ إلاَّ مُفْرِطاً أوْ مُفَرِّطاً

11 عَنِ الْباقِرِ عَلَيْهِ السَّلامُ: أمَّا المُنْجِيَاتُ فَخَوْفُ اللهِ فِى السِّرِّ وَالعَلانِيَةِ، وَالْقَصْدُ فِى الغِنَى وَالفَقْرِ وَكَلِمَةُ العَدْلِ فِى الرِّضا والسُّخْطِ

12 قالَ عَلِىٌّ عَلَيْهِ السَّلامُ: مَنْ صَحِبَ الإقْتِصَادَ دامَتْ صُحْبَةُ الغِنَى لَهُ وَجَبَرَ الإقْتِصَادُ فَقْرَهُ وَخَلَلَهُ

13 وَقَالَ عَلِيٌّ عَلَيْهِ السَّلَامُ: مَنِ اقْتَصَدَ فِي الغِنَى وَالفَقْرِ فَقَدِ اسْتَعَدَّ لِنَوَائِبِ الدَّهْرِ

14 وَقَالَ عَلِيٌّ عَلَيْهِ السَّلَامُ: لَا هَلَاكَ مَعَ اقْتِصَادٍ

15 وَاعْلَمْ أَنَّ الجَسَدَ بِمَنْزِلَةِ الأَرْضِ الطَّيِّبَةِ مَتَى تُعُوهِدَتْ بِالعِمَارَةِ وَالسَّقْيِ مِنْ حَيْثُ لَا يَزْدَادُ فِي المَاءِ فَتَفْرَقَ وَلَا يَنْقُصُ مِنْهُ فَتَعْطِشَ دَامَتْ عِمَارَتُهَا وَكَثُرَ رَيْعُهَا وَبِالتَّدْبِيرِ فِي الأَغْذِيَةِ وَالأَشْرِبَةِ يَصْلُحُ وَيَصِحُّ وَتَرْكُوا العَافِيَةَ

16 المَعِدَةُ بَيْتُ كُلِّ دَاءٍ وَالحِمْيَةُ رَأْسُ كُلِّ دَوَاءٍ

17 قَالَ عَلِيٌّ عَلَيْهِ السَّلَامُ: لَا تَجْلِسْ عَلَى الطَّعَامِ الا وَأَنْتَ جَائِعٌ وَلَا تَقُمْ عَنْهُ الا وَأَنْتَ تَشْتَهِيهِ وَجَوِّدِ المَضْغَ وَإِذَا نِمْتَ فَأَعْرِضْ نَفْسَكَ عَلَى الخَلَاءِ

18 قَالَ عَلِيٌّ عَلَيْهِ السَّلَامُ: قَلَّ مَنْ أَكْثَرَ مِنَ الطَّعَامِ فَلَمْ يَسْقُمْ

19 وَقَالَ عَلِيٌّ عَلَيْهِ السَّلَامُ: إِدْمَانُ الشِّبَعِ يُورِثُ أَنْوَاعَ الوَجَعِ

20 وَقَالَ رَسُولُ اللهِ صَلَّى اللهُ عَلَيْهِ وَآلِهِ: لَا تُمِيتُوا القُلُوبَ بِكَثْرَةِ الطَّعَامِ وَالشَّرَابِ فَإِنَّ القَلْبَ كَالزَّرْعِ يَمُوتُ إِذَا كَثُرَ عَلَيْهِ المَاءُ

21 وَقَالَ لُقْمَانُ لِابْنِهِ: يَا بُنَيَّ إِذَا امْتَلَأَتِ المَعِدَةُ نَامَتِ الفِكْرَةُ وَخَرِسَتِ الحِكْمَةُ وَقَعَدَتِ الأَعْضَاءُ عَنِ العِبَادَةِ

22 أَحْبِبْ حَبِيبَكَ هَوْنًا مَا، عَسَى أَنْ يَكُونَ بَغِيظَكَ يَوْمًا مَا.

23 وَ أَبْغِضْ بَغِيضَكَ هَوْنًا مَا عَسَى أَنْ يَكُونَ حَبِيبَكَ يَوْمًا مَا

24 وَ اقْصِدْ فِي مَشْيِكَ وَاغْضُضْ مِنْ صَوْتِكَ

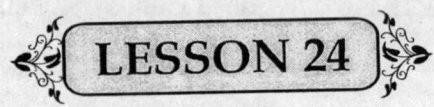

LESSON 24

1. وَقَالَ عَلَيْهِ السَّلَامُ لِجَابِرِ بْنِ عَبْدِ اللهِ الْأَنْصَارِي: يَاجَابِرُ قِوَامُ الدِّينِ وَالدُّنْيَا بِأَرْبَعَةٍ: عَالِمٍ مُسْتَعْمِلٍ عِلْمَهُ وَجَاهِلٍ لَا يَسْتَنْكِفُ أَنْ يَتَعَلَّمَ وَجَوَادٍ لَا يَبْخَلُ بِمَعْرُوفِهِ وَفَقِيرٍ لَا يَبِيعُ آخِرَتَهُ بِدُنْيَاهُ

2. فَقَالَ أَبُو عَبْدِ اللهِ (ع): اسْكُتْ فَإِنَّ الْغَنِيَّ إِذَا كَانَ وَصُولًا لِرَحِمِهِ بَارًّا بِإِخْوَانِهِ أَضْعَفَ اللهُ لَهُ الْأَجْرَ ضِعْفَيْنِ لِأَنَّ اللهَ تَعَالَى يَقُولُ: وَمَا أَمْوَالُكُمْ وَلَا أَوْلَادُكُمْ بِالَّتِي تُقَرِّبُكُمْ عِنْدَنَا زُلْفَى إِلَّا مَنْ آمَنَ وَعَمِلَ صَالِحًا فَأُولَئِكَ لَهُمْ جَزَاءُ الضِّعْفِ بِمَا عَمِلُوا وَهُمْ فِي الْغُرُفَاتِ آمِنُونَ

3. وَقَالَ عَلِيٌّ السَّلَامُ: إِنَّ لِلهِ عِبَاداً يَخْتَصُّهُمُ اللهُ بِالنِّعَمِ لِمَنَافِعِ الْعِبَادِ فَيُقِرُّهَا فِي أَيْدِيهِمْ مَا بَذَلُوهَا، فَإِذَا مَنَعُوهَا نَزَعَهَا مِنْهُمْ ثُمَّ حَوَّلَهَا إِلَى غَيْرِهِمْ

4. إِنَّ قَارُونَ كَانَ مِنْ قَوْمِ مُوسَى فَبَغَى عَلَيْهِمْ وَآتَيْنَاهُ مِنَ الْكُنُوزِ مَا إِنَّ مَفَاتِحَهُ لَتَنُوءُ بِالْعُصْبَةِ أُولِي الْقُوَّةِ إِذْ قَالَ لَهُ قَوْمُهُ لَا تَفْرَحْ إِنَّ اللهَ لَا يُحِبُّ الْفَرِحِينَ

5. وَلَا يَحْسَبَنَّ الَّذِينَ يَبْخَلُونَ بِمَا آتَاهُمُ اللهُ مِنْ فَضْلِهِ هُوَ خَيْرًا لَهُمْ، بَلْ هُوَ شَرٌّ لَهُمْ، سَيُطَوَّقُونَ مَا بَخِلُوا بِهِ يَوْمَ الْقِيَامَةِ وَللهِ مِيرَاثُ السَّمَوَاتِ وَالْأَرْضِ وَاللهُ بِمَا تَعْمَلُونَ خَبِيرٌ

6. لَنْ تَنَالُوا الْبِرَّ حَتَّى تُنْفِقُوا مِمَّا تُحِبُّونَ وَمَا تُنْفِقُوا مِنْ شَيْءٍ فَإِنَّ اللهَ بِهِ عَلِيمٌ

7. مَا كُنْتَ تَصْنَعُ بِسَعَةِ هَذِهِ الدَّارِ فِى الدُّنْيَا وَأَنْتَ إِلَيْهَا فِى الْآخِرَةِ أَحْوَجُ وَبَلَى إِنْ شِئْتَ بَلَغْتَ بِهَا الْآخِرَةَ تُقْرِي فِيهَا الضَّيْفَ وَتَصِلُ مِنْهَا الرَّحِمَ وَتُطْلِعُ مِنْهَا الْحُقُوقَ مَطَالِعَهَا فَإِذَا أَنْتَ بَلَغْتَ بِهَا الْآخِرَةَ

8. فَقَالَ لَهُ الْعَلَاءُ: يَا أَمِيرَ الْمُؤْمِنِينَ، أَشْكُو إِلَيْكَ أَخِي عَاصِمَ بْنَ زِيَادٍ، فَقَالَ وَمَا لَهُ؟

قالَ: لَيْسَ العَبَاءَةَ وتَخلّى مِنَ الدُّنيا......

9 وَأَمَّا حَقُّ مالِكَ فَأَنْ لا تَأخُذَهُ إلا مِنْ حِلِّهِ ولا تُنْفِقَهُ إلا في وَجْهِهِ

10 الفَقْرُ خَيْرٌ مِنَ الغِنى إلا مَنْ حَمَلَ في مَغْرَمٍ وأعطى في نائِبَةٍ

11 وَقالَ عَلِيٌّ عَلَيْهِ السَّلامُ: إنَّ اللهَ فَرَضَ في أموالِ الأغْنِياءِ أقواتَ الفُقَراءِ فَما جاعَ فَقيرٌ إلا بِما مَتَّعَ غَنِيٌّ، واللهُ تَعالى جَدُّهُ سائِلُهُمْ عَنْ ذلِكَ.

12 وَالَّذينَ يَكْنِزُونَ الذَّهَبَ وَالفِضَّةَ وَلا يُنْفِقُونَها في سَبيلِ اللهِ، فَبَشِّرْهُمْ بِعَذابٍ ألِيمٍ.

13 إنَّ اللهَ عَزَّ وَجَلَّ يُبْغِضُ الغَنِيَّ الظَّلومَ والشَّيْخَ الفاجِرَ والصِّعْلوكَ المُخْتالَ. ثُمَّ قالَ: أتَدْري مَا الصِّعلوكُ المُخْتالُ؟ قالَ فَقُلْنا القَليلُ المالِ. قالَ: لا هُوَ الَّذي لا يَتَقَرَّبُ إلى اللهِ بِشَيءٍ مِنْ مالِهِ.

14 وَلا يَأتَلِ أُولُوا الفَضْلِ مِنْكُمْ وَالسَّعَةِ أنْ يُؤْتوا أُولي القُرْبى وَالمَساكينَ وَالمُهاجِرينَ في سَبيلِ اللهِ وَلْيَعْفوا وَلْيَصْفَحوا أَلا تُحِبُّونَ أنْ يَغْفِرَ اللهُ لَكُمْ واللهُ غَفورٌ رَحيمٌ

15 وَقالَ عَلِيٌّ عَلَيْهِ السَّلامُ: فَمَنْ آتاهُ اللهُ مالاً فَلْيَصِلْ بِهِ القَرابَةَ وَلْيُحْسِنْ مِنْهُ الضِّيافَةَ وَلْيَفُكَّ بِهِ الأسيرَ وَالعاني وَلْيُعْطِ مِنْهُ الفَقيرَ وَالغارِمَ وَلْيَصْبِرْ نَفْسَهُ عَلى الحُقوقِ وَالنَّوائِبِ ابْتِغاءَ الثَّوابِ فإنَّ فَوْزاً بِهذِهِ الخِصالِ شَرَفُ مَكارِمِ الدُّنْيا وَدَرْكُ فَضائِلِ الآخِرَةِ إنْ شاءَ اللهُ.

16 وَقالَ أبو عَبْدِاللهِ عَلَيْهِ السَّلامُ: ما مِنْ عَبْدٍ يَسْألُ مِنْ غَيْرِ حاجَةٍ فَلا يَموتُ حَتى يُخْرِجَهُ اللهُ إلَيْها وَيُثْبِتَاللهُ لَهُ بِها النارَ.

17 قالَ أبو عَبْدِاللهِ عَلَيْهِ السَّلامُ: مَياسيرُ شيعَتِنا أمَناؤُنا عَلى مَحاويجِهِمْ فَاحْفَظوا فيهِمْ يَحْفَظْكُمُ اللهُ

18 وَقالَ رَسولُ اللهِ (ص) مَنْ واسى الفَقيرَ مِنْ مالِهِ والنَّصَفَ النَّاسَ مِنْ نَفْسِهِ فَذلِكَ

المُؤْمِنُ حَقًّا.

19 وَ قَالَ أَمِيرُ الْمُؤْمِنِينَ عَلَيْهِ السَّلَامُ .... وَمَنْ بَسَطَ يَدَهُ بِالْمَعْرُوفِ إِذَا وَجَدَهُ، يُخْلِفُ اللهُ لَهُ مَا أَنْفَقَ فِي دُنْيَاهُ وَ يُضَاعِفُ لَهُ فِي آخِرَتِهِ.

20 فَقَالَ عَلَيْهِ السَّلَامُ: اَلْمُسْلِمُ أَخُو الْمُسْلِمِ لَا يَظْلِمُهُ وَلَا يَخْذُلُهُ وَلَا يَحْرِمُهُ فَيَحِقُّ عَلَى الْمُسْلِمِينَ الْأِجْتِهَادُ فِيهِ وَالتَّوَاصُلُ وَالتَّعَاوُنُ عَلَيْهِ وَالْمُوَاسَاةُ لِأَهْلِ الْحَاجَةِ وَالْعَطْفُ مِنْكُمْ يَكُونُونَ عَلَى مَا أَمَرَ اللهُ فِيهِمْ. رُحَمَاءُ بَيْنَهُمْ، مُتَرَاحِمِينَ.

21 عَنْ أَبِي جَعْفَرٍ عَلَيْهِ السَّلَامُ .... لَأَنْ أَعُولَ أَهْلَ بَيْتٍ مِنَ الْمُسْلِمِينَ أُشْبِعَ جَوْعَتَهُمْ وَأَكْسُوَ عَوْرَتَهُمْ وَأَكُفَّ وُجُوهَهُمْ عَنِ النَّاسِ، أَحَبُّ إِلَيَّ مِنْ أَنْ أَحُجَّ حَجَّةً وَحَجَّةً وَ حَجَّةً...

22 مَنْ سَرَّهُ أَنْ يَدْفَعَ اللهُ عَنْهُ نَحْسَ يَوْمِهِ فَلْيَفْتَتِحْ يَوْمَهُ بِصَدَقَةٍ يَذْهَبُ اللهُ بِهَا عَنْهُ نَحْسَ يَوْمِهِ وَمَنْ أَحَبَّ أَنْ يَذْهَبَ اللهُ عَنْهُ نَحْسَ لَيْلَتِهِ فَلْيَفْتَتِحْ لَيْلَتَهُ بِصَدَقَةٍ يَدْفَعُ اللهُ عَنْهُ نَحْسَ لَيْلَتِهِ.

23 عَنْ أَبِي جَعْفَرٍ عَلَيْهِ السَّلَامُ قَالَ: اَلْبِرُّ وَالصَّدَقَةُ يَنْفِيَانِ الْفَقْرَ وَ يَزِيدَانِ فِي الْعُمْرِ وَيَدْفَعَانِ عَنْ سَبْعِينَ مِيتَةَ السُّوءِ.

24 اَللهَ اَللهَ فِي الْأَيْتَامِ فَلَا تُغِبُّوا أَفْوَاهَهُمْ وَلَا يَضِيعُوا بِحَضْرَتِكُمْ.

25 وَ قَالَ النَّبِيُّ (ص): مَنْ كَفَلَ يَتِيمًا وَكَفَلَ نَفَقَتَهُ كُنْتُ أَنَا وَهُوَ فِي الْجَنَّةِ كَهَاتَيْنِ وَقَرَنَ بَيْنَ إِصْبَعَيْهِ الْمُسَبِّحَةِ وَالْوُسْطَى.

26 قَالَ رَسُولُ اللهِ (ص): مَنْ أَكْرَمَ فَقِيرًا مُسْلِمًا لَقِيَ اللهَ يَوْمَ الْقِيَامَةِ وَ هُوَ عَنْهُ رَاضٍ.

27 وَ قَالَ رَسُولُ اللهِ (ص): أَلَا وَمَنِ اسْتَخَفَّ بِفَقِيرٍ مُسْلِمٍ فَقَدِ اسْتَخَفَّ بِحَقِّ اللهِ وَاللهُ يَسْتَخِفُّ بِهِ يَوْمَ الْقِيَامَةِ، إِلَّا أَنْ يَتُوبَ.

28 وَ قَالَ أَمِيرُ الْمُؤْمِنِينَ عَلَيْهِ السَّلَامُ: مَا أَحْسَنَ تَوَاضُعَ الْأَغْنِيَاءِ لِلْفُقَرَاءِ طَلَبًا لِمَا عِنْدَاللهِ

LESSON 25

1 قالَ عَلِيٌّ عَلَيْهِ السَّلامُ: إِنْ كُنْتُمْ لِلنَّجاةِ طالِبينَ فارْفُضُوا الغَفْلَةَ واللَّهوَ والزَمُوا الِاجْتِهادَ والجِدَّ.

2 وَقالَ عَلِيٌّ عَلَيْهِ السَّلامُ: عَلَيْكَ بِمَنْهَجِ الِاسْتِقامَةِ فَاِنَّهُ يَكْسِبُكَ الكَرامَةَ ويَكْفِيكَ المَلامَةَ.

3 قالَ عَلِيٌّ عَلَيْهِ السَّلامُ: مَنْ بَذَلَ جُهْدَ طاقَتِهِ بَلَغَ كُنْهَ إِرادَتِهِ.

4 وَقالَ عَلِيٌّ عَلَيْهِ السَّلامُ: مَنِ اسْتَنَدَ اِمْ قَرَعَ البابَ وَلَجَّ وَلَجَ.

5 إِنَّ الَّذينَ قالُوا رَبُّنَا اللهُ ثُمَّ اسْتَقامُوا فَلا خَوْفٌ عَلَيْهِمْ وَلا هُمْ يَحْزَنُونَ. أُولئِكَ أَصْحابُ الجَنَّةِ خالِدينَ فيها جَزاءً بِما كانُوا يَعْمَلُونَ.

6 وَقالَ: يا أَهْلَ مَكَّةَ هكَذا فافْعَلُوا بِسُفَهائِكُمْ كَما فَعَلْنا بِسُفَهائِنا.

7 عَنِ النَّبِيِّ (ص): مَثَلُ المُؤْمِنِ مَثَلُ السُّنْبُلَةِ يُحَرِّكُها الرِّيحُ فَتَقُومُ مَرَّةً وَتَقَعُ أُخْرى وَمَثَلُ الكافِرِ مَثَلُ الأَرْزَةِ لا تَزالُ قائِمَةً حَتّى تَنْقَعِرَ.

8 فَبِما رَحْمَةٍ مِنَ اللهِ لِنْتَ لَهُمْ وَلَوْ كُنْتَ فَظًّا غَليظَ القَلْبِ لَانْفَضُّوا مِنْ حَوْلِكَ فاعْفُ عَنْهُمْ واسْتَغْفِرْ لَهُمْ وَشاوِرْهُمْ فِي الأَمْرِ فَإِذا عَزَمْتَ فَتَوَكَّلْ عَلَى اللهِ إِنَّ اللهَ يُحِبُّ المُتَوَكِّلينَ.

9 قالَ عَلِيٌّ عَلَيْهِ السَّلامُ: لا تَتْرُكِ الِاجْتِهادَ في إِصْلاحِ نَفْسِكَ فَإِنَّهُ لا يُعينُكَ عَلَيْها إِلَّا الجِدُّ.

10 وَعَنْهُ عَلَيْهِ السَّلامُ: أَيُّها النّاسُ تَوَلَّوْا مِنْ أَنْفُسِكُمْ تَأْديبَها واعْدِلُوا بِها عَنْ ضَراوَةِ عاداتِها.

11 عَنْ أَبي عَبْدِاللهِ عَلَيْهِ السَّلامُ: اِقْصِرْ نَفْسَكَ عَمّا يَضُرُّها مِنْ قَبْلِ أَنْ تُفارِقَكَ واسْعَ في فِكا

كِها كَما تَسعَىٰ في طَلَبِ مَعيشَتِكَ فَإِنَّ نَفسَكَ رَهينَةٌ بِعَمَلِكَ.

12 ‎ اِستَعينوا بِالصَّبرِ وَالصَّلوةِ إِنَّ اللهَ مَعَ الصّابِرينَ.

13 ‎ قالَ عَليٌّ عَلَيهِ السَّلامُ: تَجَلبَبِ الصَّبرَ وَاليَقينَ فَإِنَّهُما نِعمَ العُدَّةُ فِى الرَّخاءِ وَالشِّدَّةِ.

14

هِيَ خِلالانِ، شِدَّةٌ وَرَخاءُ وَسِجالانِ، نِعمَةٌ وَبَلاءُ
وَالفَتى الحاذِقُ الأَديبُ إِذا ما خانَهُ الدَّهرُ لَم يَخُنهُ عَزاءُ
إِن أَلَمَّت مُلِمَّةٌ بي فَإِنّي فِى المُلِمّاتِ صَخرَةٌ صَمّاءُ

15 ‎ لا فَتى إِلّا عَليٌّ لا سَيفَ إِلّا ذُو الفَقار

16 ‎ أما وَاللهِ لَقَد تَقَمَّصَها ابنُ أَبي قُحافَةَ وَإِنَّهُ لَيَعلَمُ أَنَّ مَحَلّي مِنها مَحَلُّ القُطبِ مِنَ الرَّحىٰ

قالَ عَليٌّ عَلَيهِ السَّلامُ: لَم يَعدِمِ النَّصرَ مَنِ انتَصَرَ بِالصَّبرِ.

يَنحَدِرُ عَنّى السَّيلُ وَلا يَرقىٰ إِلَيَّ الطَّيرُ فَسَدَلتُ دونَها ثَوباً وَطَوَيتُ عَنها كَشحاً.

***

For ISLAMIC SEMINARY PUBLICATIONS
please write to your nearest centre

* **The Islamic Seminary**
  137-11, 90 Avenue,
  Jamaica, New York-11435.
  U. S. A.

* **Imam Hussain Foundation**
  P.O. Box 16086
  Air-Port - Accra
  GHANA (West Africa)

* **Mihrab Publishers**
  17 Kevi Crescent
  Richmond Hill,
  Ont. L4B 3C8, CANADA

* **Mr. Abdul Rahim A. Aziz**
  Isiamic Public Library International,
  P.O.Box 635, Osogbo, Osun State,
  NIGERIA (West Africa)

* **Al-Khoei Foundation**
  Chevening Road
  London NW6 6TN.
  ENGLAND

* **Bilal Muslim Mission**
  P.O. Box 10396, Nairobi,
  KENYA (East Africa)

* **Alif International**
  37, Prince Avenue,
  Watford Hearts,
  WD1 7RR ENGLAND

* **Mr. Amir Ali Walji**
  P.O.Box 144, Dar-es-Salaam,
  TANZANIA (East Africa)

* **Al-Zahra Muslim Association**
  1-5, Woolongong Road,
  Arncliffe NSW 2205,
  AUSTRALIA

* **The Islamic Seminary**
  150, Sheriff Devji Street,
  Bombay 400 003,
  INDIA

* **Islamic Social Institution**
  B.P. 1214, Dakar,
  SENEGAL (West Africa)

* **Madresah Darul Ilm Imam Khoei**
  1/2, Kudichraonpaa,
  Issaraphab Road, Bangkok-Yai,
  Bangkok-10600 - THAILAND

* **The Islamic Seminary**
  27, Rowden Street, Freetown,
  SIERRA LEONE (West Africa)

* **Mr. Abbas Ahmed al-Bostani**
  B.P. 73, 75662 Paris
  Cedex-14 - FRANCE
  (French Books only)

* **Mr. Ali Khan B. Masarang**
  Ja'fari Islamic Library,
  P.O.Box 5393,Iligan City,
  THE PHILIPPINES

* **Mr. M. Asad Shahab**
  Jl. Kencana 30,
  D' Jakarta 12970,
  INDONESIA

For enquiries: City P.O. Box 5425, Karachi-74000 - Pakistan.
E-mail: isp@fascom.com